Women's Liberation and Literature

D0061631

Women's Liberation and Literature

edited by Elaine Showalter
Douglass College

HBJ

Harcourt Brace Jovanovich, Inc.
New York / Chicago / San Francisco / Atlanta

COVER: feminist symbol by Lucinda Cisler

© 1971 by Harcourt Brace Jovanovich, Inc.

ISBN: 0-15-596195-0

Library of Congress Catalog Card Number: 79-153750

Printed in the United States of America

Preface

Women's Liberation and Literature provides students an opportunity to consider for themselves the essential issues raised by past and present movements to liberate women and encourages them to contemplate whether or not there is a feminine consciousness in literature. The subject of women figures significantly in many fields—psychology, sociology, and history, for example, in addition to literature—and the selections in this book, chosen to provide variations on feminist themes, suggest the range. The book brings together examples of fiction, poetry, and drama dealing with the feminine experience, and historical, psychological, and sociological statements about women. Part 1 presents the views of two early crusaders for women's rights, Mary Wollstonecraft and John Stuart Mill. Part 2 contains literary works about sexuality and marriage—Henrik Ibsen's play *A Doll's House*, which gave the women's movement one of its most famous heroines, a short story by Dorothy Parker and one by Mary McCarthy, and poems by Elizabeth Barrett Browning, Anne Sexton, and Sylvia Plath. Women writers and female literary characters are discussed in the critical articles in Part 3. The selections in Part 4 illustrate divergent theories of the psychology of women. Part 5 contains the second chapter of Kate Millett's *Sexual Politics*, the chapter in which she presents her theory of female oppression, and two reviews of her book by men.

Each selection is followed by questions for class discussion. At the end of the book are a list of topics for research and writing and a brief bibliography of works on feminism. Most of the readings listed in the bibliography are nonfiction. There are, of course, numerous well-known fictional works that take on new meaning in the light of feminism—the novels *Jane Eyre, The Mill on the Floss,* and *The Scarlet Letter* are outstanding examples—and they too might be studied in conjunction with this book.

For their initial encouragement I want to express my thanks to Wendy Martin of Queens College and to Kate Millett. David Levin of Stanford University has offered criticisms and suggestions as I prepared the manuscript, and I am grateful as well to my husband, English Showalter, Jr., of Princeton University for his advice and help. I owe a special debt to the women who contributed at every stage of the production of this book: to Gail Parker of Harvard University for her useful comments on the manuscript, to Ruth Gilbert and Jennifer Jewett, my student assistants, and finally to Louise Hockett, copy editor, and Geri Davis, designer, of Harcourt Brace Jovanovich.

Elaine Showalter

Contents

Women's Liberation and Literature

Introduction

"Women's liberation," the movement that began drawing attention in the late 1960's, is the latest and most powerful manifestation of a centuries-old struggle. Ever since antiquity, there have been women fighting to free their half of the population from oppression by the other. Feminism is not merely the latest fad of a society undergoing radical changes in its sexual ethic, nor is it the logical extension of the civil rights movement. The inequities against which the feminists protest—legal, economic, and social restrictions on the basic rights of women—have existed throughout history and in all civilizations, so it is not surprising that the principles of feminism were articulated long ago. Women's liberation seems new only because it follows a lull in feminist activism. When the suffragists won the vote for American women in 1920, many of them thought they had won the ultimate victory; but in the years that followed, social pressures continued to restrict women's freedom as effectively as the barrier in the Constitution had. A feminine mystique evolved, which sanctified the very elements of women's experience that were most oppressive. Not until the 1960's was there a reawakening of feminist feelings.

Yet this revival has its own character and has already made its unique contribution to history. In former periods of women's rights activism, the opportunity for education held a central place, and it continues to do so today. Universities in England did not admit women until 1878; in the United States, although Oberlin College first graduated a woman in 1841, Princeton University and Yale College barred women until 1969, and quotas in the medical, law, and graduate schools, still deny women equal admission to professional training. But educational goals have changed drastically since 1791, when Mary Wollstonecraft sat down to write her *Vindication of the Rights of Woman* in response to a program in France during the Revolution that denied girls schooling after the age of eight. Today women demand the right to study the same subjects in the same schools as men, and, in addition, they demand that feminine experience become part of the academic curriculum. Whereas the women's movement has previously been no more than a footnote or, worse, a cartoon in history books, it is now an important area for research. Similarly, the perspective of the woman artist, and the female

1

psyche itself, are increasingly the subjects of serious and exhilarating re-examination.

Although the specific targets of feminist protest—laws, prohibitions, social institutions—have varied from country to country and from generation to generation, the resistance to women's demands has had three sources in America and England. First, there has been a brutal and unabashed misogyny, which has appeared sporadically in the outbursts of individual men like Jonathan Swift in the eighteenth century and Norman Mailer in our own. The flagrant emotionalism of this attitude, however, has kept it from having a wide acceptance; it has evoked shock more than agreement.

A second and much more influential source has been the recurrent glorification of the wifely and maternal role that Betty Friedan named "the feminine mystique" and that flourished in the eighteenth and nineteenth centuries as the "feminine ideal." "Ideal" and "mystique" both derive their authority from beliefs that woman's "nature," either divinely ordained or biologically determined, requires her to find her total fulfillment in submissive domesticity. With such a rationalization, men and governments have been able to argue that they denied a woman freedom with her best interests at heart; and women who were frustrated and unsatisfied with the limits set for them were treated as subversive or neurotic.

A third source of resistance, weightier than the other two because of its apparent objectivity, has been the scientific confirmation of a negative feminine stereotype. Scientists, however, are as much influenced by cultural biases as anyone else, and even an accurate finding may give rise to conflicting interpretations, especially in the social sciences. For example, nineteenth-century doctors, prevented by Victorian prudery from careful study of the human reproductive system, believed that menstruation rendered women temporarily insane and made them lifelong invalids. At the same time, anthropologists thought they detected a particular kinship between women and animals, and in general believed women could be classified physically and intellectually somewhere between children and men. Later research has disproved these scientific "facts," but in their day they served to shore up the arguments of the antifeminists, especially the paternalistic notion that women were innately unfit to assume responsibility and required masculine guidance and protection.

Misogyny, mystique, and science have combined to provide a rationale for opposition to women's rights, and feminist authors have responded to all of them. It is a cruel fallacy to assume that all women are "ladies" under masculine protection and to deny them education and the opportunity to earn a reasonable living on these grounds. Many women never marry, and married or not, many must work from economic necessity. Further, cultural ethics, like the feminine ideal, insist that women's problems are merely personal and private and ignore the overwhelming evidence that we live in a patriarchal society that maintains its stronghold by keeping women down. John Stuart Mill was one of the first and most eloquent spokesmen for the theory that the subjection of women is akin to other oppressive political systems, such as slavery and feudalism, and that marriage is a legal bondage that a woman is forced to seek because her society has systematically deprived her of any attractive and dignified alternative. Marxist theoreticians (chiefly Engels and Lenin) saw the family as the first product of totalitarian and capitalistic impulses in men, with women held as property, and maintained that the myths of domesticity must be shattered in order for all people to enjoy equality and freedom. In 1963, Betty Friedan showed how the feminine mystique had been exploited in a consumer society for the economic benefit of male-dominated industries. Even more recently, scholarly activists of the women's liberation movement, such as Kate Millett, have found Western culture saturated by a male supremacy that affects all aspects of our lives from war to literature. And finally, the suppositions of social science and the theories of literary critics are being challenged by a new generation of academic women who find them inaccurate and insulting.

Because the literary professions were the first to be opened to women, the status of the woman writer has long served as an index of a society's views on female abilities and rights. Although writing has never been regarded as an unfeminine accomplishment, women writers have always encountered more critical resistance than men. This is so primarily because literary creativity has seemed to rival biological creativity in the most direct way. Normal female creativity, in other words, was expected to find its outlet in childbirth and maternity; the creativity that gave birth to a poem or a painting was regarded as unnatural in a woman. From this thesis, Victorian critics deduced ingenious arguments to undermine women's serious efforts and to consign them to an inferior sphere in art. They said that an unmarried or childless woman could never produce a major work because her very nature was incomplete; she was immature at best, warped and barren at worst. Elizabeth Barrett Browning's poet-heroine, Aurora Leigh, finally capitulated to this doctrine and married:

> Passioned to exalt
> The artist's instinct in me at the cost
> Of putting down the woman's—I forgot
> No perfect artist is developed here
> From any imperfect woman.

On the other hand, maternity conferred such immense and exhausting obligations, they maintained, that no mother could have the time, let alone the creative energy, to compete with male writers whose lives could be devoted to their profession. As a Victorian critic, Gerald Massey, put it,

> The nature of woman demands *that* to perfect it in life which must half lame it for art. . . . Thus a woman-Shakespeare would really have to be doubly as great as the man Shakespeare, for he had not to bear a family with all its precious burdens. . . . Women, who are happy in all home-ties, and who amply fill the sphere of their love and life, must in the very nature of things, very seldom become writers.

Massey's emphatic use of the term "nature" is typical of the confident and intimidating rhetoric with which critics approached the question of women's artistic potential. Nonetheless, Massey himself had to leave a loophole in the final phrase, for there have always been women in the ranks of literary genius, and not even the most vindictive misogynist nor the most abject matron has been able to indict them all as frustrated spinsters.

One might suppose that the nineteenth-century woman writer would have supported the feminists, since both were struggling against the same destructive stereotypes and discriminatory policies. The masculine pseudonym, for example, was usually the desperate ruse of a woman seeking an unbiased reading by reviewers and the public; the retractions of enthusiastic praise that followed the discovery that George Eliot was in reality Miss Mary Ann Evans were only one instance of many that showed how necessary the precaution was.

Yet the relationship between women writers and the feminist movement has generally been strained. Women writers have had enough to contend with fighting for their own artistic autonomy without taking a public stand in behalf of feminism. Often they have sought to defend themselves against imputations of unwomanliness by repudiating their more radical and demanding sisters. This phenomenon was sadly observed in 1851 by Harriet Taylor, the wife of John Stuart Mill, who wrote that "the literary class of women, especially in England, are ostentatious in disdaining the desire for equality or citizenship, and proclaiming their complete satisfaction with the place which society assigns to them." Mill himself thought that most of what women wrote about each other was mere sycophancy to men and that the literature of women existed so totally under the shadow of masculine influence as to be almost purely imitative.

The vision of a feminine consciousness in literature, as distinguished from a feminist bias, has nevertheless fascinated women writers. George Eliot, for example, predicted that women would eventually produce novels with "a precious speciality, lying quite apart from masculine aptitudes and experience." Whether women in fact have an artistic speciality unique to their sex and dependent upon it, whether there is anything that warrants treating them in a separate category, is a much-vexed question. Today many liberal scholars and critics resent the implications of lumping women together and discussing them as a class. They deny that the term "woman writer" has any validity and maintain that genius has no sex. Their arguments apply very tellingly to the sort of Victorian theorizing represented by George Henry Lewes' review "The Lady Novelists" and to the patronizing attitudes Mary Ellmann mocks in "Phallic Criticism."

Students should decide for themselves whether there is any value in considering the sex of an author. In my opinion, although genius may be sexless, an artist's potential cannot be realized without the freedom to explore individual perceptions of truth. All women have been forced to interpret their experience in men's terms and have even been intimidated into describing sensations that do not exist. How much they and we have lost as a result cannot yet be determined, but a new feminist criticism assumes that a woman writer's point of view will reflect authentic feminine experience to the degree that her society has allowed her to define it. If such critical attention can encourage feminine self-awareness, perhaps a future generation of women writers will produce an independent and confident literature unlike any we have ever seen.

part 1

MAJOR TEXTS OF FEMINISM

Mary Wollstonecraft

Mary Wollstonecraft (1759–1797) *serves as an extreme ironic example of the treatment posterity accords a feminist writer. Her own achievements as one of the earliest crusaders for the emancipation of women have been overlooked, and she is remembered by literary historians as the wife of the philosopher William Godwin and the mother-in-law of the poet Shelley. Yet her whole life and her works were one long protest against the institutions that forced women to find their identity through men.*

She knew through bitter experience the hardships women were exposed to simply by virtue of their sex. During her youth she had witnessed the domestic tyranny of her alcoholic father, had helped her sister escape from a brutal husband, and had seen her dearest friend die in childbirth—knowing all the while that legal recourse against these injustices was unavailable to her because she was a woman. She labored at a series of jobs typical of those open to "ladies": seamstress, companion, teacher, and governess, but at twenty-eight, determined to become a writer, she left her post as a governess in Dublin and moved to London. Through her publisher she met a group of radical writers, artists, and philosophers, including William Godwin and Thomas Paine, author of The Rights of Man, *and she was soon caught up in the revolutionary fervor of the time.*

A Vindication of the Rights of Woman (1792), *from which Chapter IV is reprinted below, was written in great haste—her husband said in six weeks —and aroused a wide and violent response upon its publication. Horace Walpole resolved never to read it, and attacked the author as a "hyena in petticoats." Other writers burlesqued and attacked it, and some readers then and later objected to the "contamination" of the book by revolutionary principles. Yet the general response was mostly favorable until her death, after which her husband unwisely chose to include the story of her life and loves in his memoirs. Unfortunately, the shock produced by his account of her love affairs, illegitimate child, and attempted suicide turned potential readers against her book. Thus* A Vindication of the Rights of Woman, *which anticipated virtually all the demands of the woman's movement— education, legal representation, the right to vote, the right to property, and admission to professions—was read by very few women in the nineteenth*

*century. It is a sad paradox that feminists have always had to conform to
the respectable feminine image before they could successfully attack it.*

*Mary Wollstonecraft, deserted and betrayed by her lovers, vilified by her
contemporaries and by posterity for her stand on feminism, and dead in
childbirth at thirty-eight, was, as the American feminist Margaret Fuller
wrote, "a woman whose existence better proved the need of some new interpretation of Woman's Rights than anything she wrote."*

Observations on the State
of Degradation to Which Woman
Is Reduced by Various Causes

That woman is naturally weak, or degraded by a concurrence
of circumstances is, I think, clear. But this position I shall simply contrast with a conclusion, which I have frequently heard fall from sensible
men in favour of an aristocracy: that the mass of mankind cannot be
any thing, or the obsequious slaves, who patiently allow themselves to be
penned up, would feel their own consequence, and spurn their chains.
Men, they further observe, submit every where to oppression, when they
have only to lift up their heads to throw off the yoke; yet, instead of as-
serting their birthright, they quietly lick the dust, and say, let us eat and
drink, for to-morrow we die. Women, I argue from analogy, are degraded
by the same propensity to enjoy the present moment; and, at last, despise
the freedom which they have not sufficient virtue to struggle to attain.
But I must be more explicit.

With respect to the culture of the heart, it is unanimously allowed
that sex is out of the question; but the line of subordination in the mental powers is never to be passed over. Only "absolute in loveliness," the
portion of rationality granted to woman is, indeed, very scanty; for,
denying her genius and judgment, it is scarcely possible to divine what
remains to characterize intellect.

The stamina of immortality, if I may be allowed the phrase, is the
perfectibility of human reason; for, was man created perfect, or did a
flood of knowledge break in upon him, when he arrived at maturity,
that precluded error, I should doubt whether his existence would be
continued after the dissolution of the body. But in the present state of

things, every difficulty in morals, that escapes from human discussion, and equally baffles the investigation of profound thinking, and the lightning glance of genius, is an argument on which I build my belief of the immortality of the soul. Reason is, consequently, the simple power of improvement; or, more properly speaking, of discerning truth. Every individual is in this respect a world in itself. More or less may be conspicuous in one being than other; but the nature of reason must be the same in all, if it be an emanation of divinity, the tie that connects the creature with the Creator; for, can that soul be stamped with the heavenly image, that is not perfected by the exercise of its own reason? Yet outwardly ornamented with elaborate care, and so adorned to delight man, "that with honour he may love," the soul of woman is not allowed to have this distinction, and man, ever placed between her and reason, she is always represented as only created to see through a gross medium, and to take things on trust. But, dismissing these fanciful theories, and considering woman as a whole, let it be what it will, instead of a part of man, the inquiry is, whether she has reason or not. If she has, which, for a moment, I will take for granted, she was not created merely to be the solace of man, and the sexual should not destroy the human character.

Into this error men have, probably, been led by viewing education in a false light; not considering it as the first step to form a being advancing gradually toward perfection; but only as a preparation for life. On this sensual error, for I must call it so, has the false system of female manners been reared, which robs the whole sex of its dignity, and classes the brown and fair with the smiling flowers that only adorn the land. This has ever been the language of men, and the fear of departing from a supposed sexual character, has made even women of superior sense adopt the same sentiments. Thus understanding, strictly speaking, has been denied to woman; and instinct, sublimated into wit and cunning, for the purposes of life, has been substituted in its stead.

The power of generalizing ideas, of drawing comprehensive conclusions from individual observations, is the only acquirement for an immortal being, that really deserves the name of knowledge. Merely to observe, without endeavouring to account for any thing, may, (in a very incomplete manner) serve as the common sense of life; but where is the store laid up that is to clothe the soul when it leaves the body?

This power has not only been denied to women; but writers have insisted that it is inconsistent, with a few exceptions, with their sexual character. Let men prove this, and I shall grant that woman only exists for man. I must, however, previously remark, that the power of generalizing ideas, to any great extent, is not very common amongst men or women. But this exercise is the true cultivation of the understanding; and every thing conspires to render the cultivation of the understanding more difficult in the female than the male world.

I am naturally led by this assertion to the main subject of the present

chapter, and shall now attempt to point out some of the causes that degrade the sex, and prevent women from generalizing their observations.

I shall not go back to the remote annals of antiquity to trace the history of woman; it is sufficient to allow, that she has always been either
a slave or a despot, and to remark, that each of these situations equally
retards the progress of reason. The grand source of female folly and vice
has ever appeared to me to arise from narrowness of mind; and the very
constitution of civil governments has put almost insuperable obstacles
in the way to prevent the cultivation of the female understanding: yet
virtue can be built on no other foundation! The same obstacles are
thrown in the way of the rich, and the same consequences ensue.

Necessity has been proverbially termed the mother of invention; the
aphorism may be extended to virtue. It is an acquirement, and an acquirement to which pleasure must be sacrificed, and who sacrifices
pleasure when it is within the grasp, whose mind has not been opened
and strengthened by adversity, or the pursuit of knowledge goaded on
by necessity? Happy is it when people have the cares of life to struggle
with; for these struggles prevent their becoming a prey to enervating
vices, merely from idleness! But, if from their birth men and women are
placed in a torrid zone, with the meridian sun of pleasure darting directly upon them, how can they sufficiently brace their minds to discharge the duties of life, or even to relish the affections that carry them
out of themselves?

Pleasure is the business of a woman's life, according to the present
modification of society, and while it continues to be so, little can be expected from such weak beings. Inheriting, in a lineal descent from the
first fair defect in nature, the sovereignty of beauty, they have, to maintain their power, resigned their natural rights, which the exercise of reason, might have procured them, and chosen rather to be short-lived
queens than labour to attain the sober pleasures that arise from equality.
Exalted by their inferiority (this sounds like a contradiction) they constantly demand homage as women, though experience should teach
them that the men who pride themselves upon paying this arbitrary in-
solent respect to the sex, with the most scrupulous exactness, are most
inclined to tyrannize over, and despise the very weakness they cherish.
Often do they repeat Mr. Hume's sentiments; when comparing the
French and Athenian character, he alludes to women.

> But what is more singular in this whimsical nation, say I to the
> Athenians, is, that a frolic of yours during the Saturnalia, when the
> slaves are served by their masters, is seriously continued by them
> through the whole year, and through the whole course of their
> lives; accompanied too with some circumstances, which still further
> augment the absurdity and ridicule. Your sport only elevates for a
> few days, those whom fortune has thrown down, and whom she too,
> in sport, may really elevate for ever above you. But this nation

gravely exalts those, whom nature has subjected to them, and whose inferiority and infirmities are absolutely incurable. The women, though without virtue, are their masters and sovereigns.

Ah! why do women, I write with affectionate solicitude, condescend to receive a degree of attention and respect from strangers, different from that reciprocation of civility which the dictates of humanity, and the politeness of civilization authorise between man and man? And why do they not discover, when "in the noon of beauty's power" that they are treated like queens only to be deluded by hollow respect, till they are led to resign, or not assume, their natural prerogatives? Confined then in cages, like the feathered race, they have nothing to do but to plume themselves, and stalk with mock-majesty from perch to perch. It is true, they are provided with food and raiment, for which they neither toil nor spin; but health, liberty, and virtue are given in exchange. But, where, amongst mankind has been found sufficient strength of mind to enable a being to resign these adventitious prerogatives; one who rising with the calm dignity of reason above opinion, dared to be proud of the privileges inherent in man? and it is vain to expect it whilst hereditary power chokes the affections, and nips reason in the bud.

The passions of men have thus placed women on thrones; and, till mankind become more reasonable, it is to be feared that women will avail themselves of the power which they attain with the least exertion, and which is the most indisputable. They will smile, yes, they will smile, though told that—

> In beauty's empire is no mean,
> And woman either slave or queen,
> Is quickly scorn'd when not ador'd.

But the adoration comes first, and the scorn is not anticipated.

Lewis the XIVth, in particular, spread factitious manners, and caught in a specious way, the whole nation in his toils; for establishing an artful chain of despotism, he made it the interest of the people at large, individually to respect his station, and support his power. And women, whom he flattered by a puerile attention to the whole sex, obtained in his reign that prince-like distinction so fatal to reason and virtue.

A king is always a king, and a woman always a woman: his authority and her sex, ever stand between them and rational converse. With a lover, I grant she should be so, and her sensibility will naturally lead her to endeavour to excite emotion, not to gratify her vanity but her heart. This I do not allow to be coquetry, it is the artless impulse of nature, I only exclaim against the sexual desire of conquest, when the heart is out of the question.

This desire is not confined to women; "I have endeavoured," says Lord Chesterfield, "to gain the hearts of twenty women, whose persons

I would not have given a fig for." The libertine who in a gust of passion, takes advantage of unsuspecting tenderness, is a saint when compared with this cold-hearted rascal; for I like to use significant words. Yet only taught to please, women are always on the watch to please, and with true heroic ardour endeavour to gain hearts merely to resign, or spurn them, when the victory is decided, and conspicuous.

I must descend to the minutiæ of the subject.

I lament that women are systematically degraded by receiving the trivial attentions, which men think it manly to pay to the sex, when, in fact, they are insultingly supporting their own superiority. It is not condescension to bow to an inferior. So ludicrous, in fact, do these ceremonies appear to me, that I scarcely am able to govern my muscles, when I see a man start with eager, and serious solicitude to lift a handkerchief, or shut a door, when the *lady* could have done it herself, had she only moved a pace or two.

A wild wish has just flown from my heart to my head, and I will not stifle it though it may excite a horse laugh. I do earnestly wish to see the distinction of sex confounded in society, unless where love animates the behaviour. For this distinction is, I am firmly persuaded, the foundation of the weakness of character ascribed to woman; is the cause why the understanding is neglected, whilst accomplishments are acquired with sedulous care: and the same cause accounts for their preferring the graceful before the heroic virtues.

Mankind, including every description, wish to be loved and respected for *something*; and the common herd will always take the nearest road to the completion of their wishes. The respect paid to wealth and beauty is the most certain and unequivocal; and of course, will always attract the vulgar eye of common minds. Abilities and virtues are absolutely necessary to raise men from the middle rank of life into notice; and the natural consequence is notorious, the middle rank contains most virtue and abilities. Men have thus, in one station, at least, an opportunity of exerting themselves with dignity, and of rising by the exertions which really improve a rational creature; but the whole female sex are, till their character is formed, in the same condition as the rich: for they are born, I now speak of a state of civilization, with certain sexual privileges, and whilst they are gratuitously granted them, few will ever think of works of supererogation, to obtain the esteem of a small number of superior people.

When do we hear of women, who starting out of obscurity, boldly claim respect on account of their great abilities or daring virtues? Where are they to be found? "To be observed, to be attended to, to be taken notice of with sympathy, complacency, and approbation, are all the advantages which they seek." True! my male readers will probably exclaim; but let them, before they draw any conclusion, recollect, that this was not written originally as descriptive of women, but of the rich. In Dr. Smith's Theory of Moral Sentiments, I have found a general character of people of rank and fortune, that in my opinion, might with the greatest propriety be applied to the female sex. I refer the sagacious reader to the whole comparison; but must be allowed to quote a passage to enforce an argument that I mean to insist on, as the one most conclusive against a sexual character. For if, excepting warriors, no great men of any denomination, have ever appeared amongst the nobility, may it not be fairly inferred, that their local situation swallowed up the man, and produced a character similar to that of women, who are *localized,* if I may be allowed the word, by the rank they are placed in, by *courtesy?* Women commonly called Ladies, are not to be contradicted in company, are not allowed to exert any manual strength; and from them the negative virtues only are expected, when any virtues are expected, patience, docility, good-humour, and flexibility; virtues incompatible with any vigorous exertion of intellect. Besides by living more with each other, and to being seldom absolutely alone, they are more under the influence of sentiments than passions. Solitude and reflection are necessary to give to wishes the force of passions, and enable the imagination to enlarge the object and make it the most desirable. The same may be said of the rich; they do not sufficiently deal in general ideas, collected by impassionate thinking, or calm investigation, to acquire that strength of character, on which great resolves are built. But hear what an acute observer says of the great.

Do the great seem insensible of the easy price at which they may acquire the public admiration? or do they seem to imagine, that to them, as to other men, it must be the purchase either of sweat or of blood? By what important accomplishments is the young nobleman instructed to support the dignity of his rank, and to render himself worthy of that superiority over his fellow citizens, to which the virtue of his ancestors had raised them? Is it by knowledge, by industry, by patience, by self-denial, or by virtue of any kind? As all his words, as all his motions are attended to, he learns an habitual regard for every circumstance of ordinary behaviour, and studies to perform all those small duties with the most exact propriety. As he is conscious how much he is observed, and how much mankind are disposed to favour all his inclinations, he acts, upon the most indifferent occasions, with that freedom and elevation which the thought of this naturally inspires. His air, his manner, his deportment all mark that elegant and graceful sense of his own superiority, which those who are born to an inferior station can hardly ever arrive at. These are the arts by which he proposes to make mankind more easily submit to his authority, and to govern their inclinations according to his own pleasure: and in this he is seldom disappointed. These arts, supported by rank and pre-eminence, are, upon ordinary occasions, sufficient to govern the world. Lewis XIV, during the greater part of his reign, was regarded, not only in France, but over all Europe, as the most perfect model of a great prince. But what were the talents and virtues, by which he acquired this great reputa-

tion? Was it by the scrupulous and inflexible justice of all his undertakings, by the immense dangers and difficulties with which they
were attended, or by the unwearied and unrelenting application
with which he pursued them? Was it by his extensive knowledge,
by his exquisite judgment, or by his heroic valour? It was by none
of these qualities. But he was, first of all, the most powerful prince
in Europe, and consequently held the highest rank among kings;
and then, says his historian, 'he surpassed all his courtiers in the
gracefulness of his shape, and the majestic beauty of his features.
The sound of his voice noble and affecting, gained those hearts
which his presence intimidated. He had a step and a deportment,
which could suit only him and his rank, and which would have been
ridiculous in any other person. The embarrassment which he oc-
casioned to those who spoke to him, flattered that secret satisfaction with which he felt his own superiority.' These frivolous accomplishments, supported by his rank, and, no doubt, too, by a degree
of other talents and virtues, which seems, however, not to have been
much above mediocrity, established this prince in the esteem of his
own age, and have drawn even from posterity, a good deal of respect
for his memory. Compared with these, in his own times, and in his
own presence, no other virtue, it seems appeared to have any merit.
Knowledge, industry, valour, and beneficence, trembling, were
abashed, and lost all dignity before them.

Woman, also, thus "in herself complete," by possessing all these
frivolous accomplishments, so changes the nature of things,

> That what she wills to do or say
> Seems wisest, virtuousest, discreetest, best:
> All higher knowledge in *her presence* falls
> Degraded. Wisdom in discourse with her
> Loses discountenanc'd, and like folly shows;
> Authority and reason on her wait.

And all this is built on her loveliness!
In the middle rank of life, to continue the comparison, men, in their
youth, are prepared for professions, and marriage is not considered as
the grand feature in their lives; whilst women, on the contrary, have no
other scheme to sharpen their faculties. It is not business, extensive
plans, or any of the excursive flights of ambition, that engross their attention; no, their thoughts are not employed in rearing such noble structures. To rise in the world, and have the liberty of running from pleasure
to pleasure, they must marry advantageously, and to this object their
time is sacrificed, and their persons often legally prostituted. A man,
when he enters any profession, has his eye steadily fixed on some future
advantage (and the mind gains great strength by having all its efforts
directed to one point) and, full of his business, pleasure is considered as
mere relaxation; whilst women seek for pleasure as the main purpose of

existence. In fact, from the education which they receive from society, the love of pleasure may be said to govern them all; but does this prove that there is a sex in souls? It would be just as rational to declare, that the courtiers in France, when a destructive system of despotism had formed their character, were not men, because liberty, virtue, and humanity, were sacrificed to pleasure and vanity. Fatal passions, which have ever domineered over the *whole* race!

The same love of pleasure, fostered by the whole tendency of their education, gives a trifling turn to the conduct of women in most circumstances: for instance, they are ever anxious about secondary things; and on the watch for adventures, instead of being occupied by duties.

A man, when he undertakes a journey, has, in general the end in view; a woman thinks more of the incidental occurrences, the strange things that may possibly occur on the road; the impression that she may make on her fellow travellers; and, above all, she is anxiously intent on the care of the finery that she carries with her, which is more than ever a part of herself, when going to figure on a new scene; when, to use an apt French turn of expression, she is going to produce a sensation. Can dignity of mind exist with such trivial cares?

In short, women, in general, as well as the rich of both sexes, have acquired all the follies and vices of civilization, and missed the useful fruit. It is not necessary for me always to premise, that I speak of the condition of the whole sex, leaving exceptions out of the question. Their senses are inflamed, and their understandings neglected; consequently they become the prey of their senses, delicately termed sensibility, and are blown about by every momentary gust of feeling. They are, therefore, in a much worse condition than they would be in, were they in a state nearer to nature. Ever restless and anxious, their over exercised sensibility not only renders them uncomfortable themselves, but troublesome, to use a soft phrase, to others. All their thoughts turn on things calculated to excite emotion; and, feeling, when they should reason, their conduct is unstable, and their opinions are wavering, not the wavering produced by deliberation or progressive views, but by contradictory emotions. By fits and starts they are warm in many pursuits; yet this warmth, never concentrated into perseverance, soon exhausts itself; exhaled by its own heat, or meeting with some other fleeting passion, to which reason has never given any specific gravity, neutrality ensues. Miserable, indeed, must be that being whose cultivation of mind has only tended to inflame its passions! A distinction should be made between inflaming and strengthening them. The passions thus pampered, whilst the judgment is left unformed, what can be expected to ensue? Undoubtedly, a mixture of madness and folly!

This observation should not be confined to the *fair* sex; however, at present, I only mean to apply it to them.

Novels, music, poetry and gallantry, all tend to make women the creatures of sensation, and their character is thus formed during the time they are acquiring accomplishments, the only improvement they are excited, by their station in society, to acquire. This overstretched sensibility naturally relaxes the other powers of the mind, and prevents intellect from attaining that sovereignty which it ought to attain, to render a rational creature useful to others, and content with its own station; for the exercise of the understanding, as life advances, is the only method pointed out by nature to calm the passions.

Satiety has a very different effect, and I have often been forcibly struck by an emphatical description of damnation, when the spirit is represented as continually hovering with abortive eagerness round the defiled body, unable to enjoy any thing without the organs of sense. Yet, to their senses, are women made slaves, because it is by their sensibility that they obtain present power.

And will moralists pretend to assert, that this is the condition in which one half of the human race should be encouraged to remain with listless inactivity and stupid acquiescence? Kind instructors! what were we created for? To remain, it may be said, innocent; they mean in a state of childhood. We might as well never have been born, unless it were necessary that we should be created to enable man to acquire the noble privilege of reason, the power of discerning good from evil, whilst we lie down in the dust from whence we were taken, never to rise again.

It would be an endless task to trace the variety of meannesses, cares, and sorrows, into which women are plunged by the prevailing opinion, that they were created rather to feel than reason, and that all the power they obtain, must be obtained by their charms and weakness; "Fine by defect, and amiably weak!" And, made by this amiable weakness entirely dependent, excepting what they gain by illicit sway, on man, not only for protection, but advice, it is surprising that, neglecting the duties that reason alone points out, and shrinking from trials calculated to strengthen their minds, they only exert themselves to give their defects a graceful covering, which may serve to heighten their charms in the eye of the voluptuary, though it sink them below the scale of moral excellence?

Fragile in every sense of the word, they are obliged to look up to man for every comfort. In the most trifling dangers they cling to their support, with parasitical tenacity, piteously demanding succour; and their *natural* protector extends his arm, or lifts up his voice, to guard the lovely trembler—from what? Perhaps the frown of an old cow, or the jump of a mouse; a rat, would be a serious danger. In the name of reason, and even common sense, what can save such beings from contempt, even though they be soft and fair?

These fears, when not affected, may be very pretty; but they show a degree of imbecility, that degrades a rational creature in a way women are not aware of—for love and esteem are very distinct things.

I am fully persuaded, that we should hear of none of these infantine airs, if girls were allowed to take sufficient exercise and not confined in close rooms till their muscles are relaxed and their powers of digestion destroyed. To carry the remark still further, if fear in girls, instead of being cherished, perhaps, created, was treated in the same manner as cowardice in boys, we should quickly see women with more dignified aspects. It is true, they could not then with equal propriety be termed the sweet flowers that smile in the walk of man; but they would be more respectable members of society, and discharge the important duties of life by the light of their own reason. "Educate women like men," says Rousseau, "and the more they resemble our sex the less power will they have over us." This is the very point I aim at. I do not wish them to have power over men; but over themselves.

In the same strain have I heard men argue against instructing the poor; for many are the forms that aristocracy assumes. "Teach them to read and write," say they "and you take them out of the station assigned them by nature." An eloquent Frenchman, has answered them; I will borrow his sentiments. But they know not, when they make man a brute, that they may expect every instant to see him transformed into a ferocious beast. Without knowledge there can be no morality!

Ignorance is a frail base for virtue! Yet, that it is the condition for which woman was organized, has been insisted upon by the writers who have most vehemently argued in favour of the superiority of man; a superiority not in degree, but essence; though, to soften the argument, they have laboured to prove, with chivalrous generosity, that the sexes ought not to be compared; man was made to reason, woman to feel: and that together, flesh and spirit, they make the most perfect whole, by blending happily reason and sensibility into one character.

And what is sensibility? "Quickness of sensation; quickness of perception; delicacy." Thus it is defined by Dr. Johnson; and the definition gives me no other idea than of the most exquisitely polished instinct. I discern not a trace of the image of God in either sensation or matter. Refined seventy times seven, they are still material; intellect dwells not there; nor will fire ever make lead gold!

I come round to my old argument; if woman be allowed to have an immortal soul, she must have as the employment of life, an understanding to improve. And when, to render the present state more complete, though every thing proves it to be but a fraction of a mighty sum, she is incited by present gratification to forget her grand destination. Nature is counteracted, or she was born only to procreate and rot. Or, granting brutes, of every description, a soul, though not a reasonable one, the exercise of instinct and sensibility may be the step, which they are to take, in this life, towards the attainment of reason in the next; so that through all eternity they will lag behind man, who, why we cannot tell, had the power given him of attaining reason in his first mode of existence.

When I treat of the peculiar duties of women, as I should treat of the peculiar duties of a citizen or father, it will be found that I do not mean to insinuate, that they should be taken out of their families, speaking of the majority. "He that hath wife and children," says Lord Bacon, "hath given hostages to fortune; for they are impediments to great enterprises, either of virtue or mischief. Certainly the best works, and of greatest merit for the public, have proceeded from the unmarried or childless men." I say the same of women. But, the welfare of society is not built on extraordinary exertions; and were it more reasonably organized, there would be still less need of great abilities, or heroic virtues.

In the regulation of a family, in the education of children, understanding, in an unsophisticated sense, is particularly required: strength both of body and mind; yet the men who, by their writings, have most earnestly laboured to domesticate women, have endeavoured by arguments dictated by a gross appetite, that satiety had rendered fastidious, to weaken their bodies and cramp their minds. But, if even by these sinister methods they really *persuaded* women, by working on their feelings, to stay at home, and fulfil the duties of a mother and mistress of a family, I should cautiously oppose opinions that led women to right conduct, by prevailing on them to make the discharge of a duty the business of life, though reason were insulted. Yet, and I appeal to experience, if by neglecting the understanding they are as much, nay, more attached from these domestic duties, than they could be by the most serious intellectual pursuit, though it may be observed, that the mass of mankind will never vigorously pursue an intellectual object, I may be allowed to infer, that reason is absolutely necessary to enable a woman to perform any duty properly, and I must again repeat, that sensibility is not reason.

The comparison with the rich still occurs to me; for, when men neglect the duties of humanity, women will do the same; a common stream hurries them both along with thoughtless celerity. Riches and honours prevent a man from enlarging his understanding, and enervate all his powers, by reversing the order of nature, which has ever made true pleasure the reward of labour. Pleasure—enervating pleasure is, likewise, within woman's reach without earning it. But, till hereditary possessions are spread abroad, how can we expect men to be proud of virtue? And, till they are, women will govern them by the most direct means, neglecting their dull domestic duties, to catch the pleasure that is on the wing of time.

"The power of women," says some author, "is her sensibility;" and men not aware of the consequence, do all they can to make this power swallow up every other. Those who constantly employ their sensibility will have most: for example; poets, painters, and composers. Yet, when the sensibility is thus increased at the expense of reason, and even the imagination, why do philosophical men complain of their fickleness? The sexual attention of man particularly acts on female sensibility, and this sympathy has been exercised from their youth up. A husband cannot long pay those attentions with the passion necessary to excite lively emotions, and the heart, accustomed to lively emotions, turns to a new lover, or pines in secret, the prey of virtue or prudence.

I mean when the heart has really been rendered susceptible, and the taste formed; for I am apt to conclude, from what I have seen in fashionable life, that vanity is oftener fostered than sensibility by the mode of education, and the intercourse between the sexes, which I have reprobated; and that coquetry more frequently proceeds from vanity than from that inconstancy, which overstrained sensibility naturally produces.

Another argument that has had a great weight with me, must, I think, have some force with every considerate benevolent heart. Girls, who have been thus weakly educated, are often cruelly left by their parents without any provision; and, of course, are dependent on, not only the reason, but the bounty of their brothers. These brothers are, to view the fairest side of the question, good sort of men, and give as a favour, what children of the same parents had an equal right to. In this equivocal humiliating situation, a docile female may remain some time, with a tolerable degree of comfort. But, when the brother marries, a probable circumstance, from being considered as the mistress of the family, she is viewed with averted looks as an intruder, an unnecessary burden on the benevolence of the master of the house, and his new partner.

Who can recount the misery, which many unfortunate beings, whose minds and bodies are equally weak, suffer in such situations—unable to work and ashamed to beg? The wife, a cold-hearted, narrow-minded woman, and this is not an unfair supposition; for the present mode of education does not tend to enlarge the heart any more than the understanding, is jealous of the little kindness which her husband shows to his relations; and her sensibility not rising to humanity, she is displeased at seeing the property of *her* children lavished on an helpless sister.

These are matters of fact, which have come under my eye again and again. The consequence is obvious, the wife has recourse to cunning to undermine the habitual affection, which she is afraid openly to oppose; and neither tears nor caresses are spared till the spy is worked out of her home, and thrown on the world, unprepared for its difficulties; or sent, as a great effort of generosity, or from some regard to propriety, with a small stipend, and an uncultivated mind into joyless solitude.

These two women may be much upon a par, with respect to reason and humanity; and changing situations, might have acted just the same selfish part; but had they been differently educated, the case would also have been very different. The wife would not have had that sensibility, of which self is the centre, and reason might have taught her not to expect, and not even to be flattered by the affection of her husband, if it led him to violate prior duties. She would wish not to love him, merely because he loved her, but on account of his virtues; and the sister might have been able to struggle for herself, instead of eating the bitter bread of dependence.

I am, indeed, persuaded that the heart, as well as the understanding, is opened by cultivation; and by, which may not appear so clear, strengthening the organs; I am not now talking of momentary flashes of sensibility, but of affections. And, perhaps, in the education of both sexes, the most difficult task is so to adjust instruction as not to narrow the understanding, whilst the heart is warmed by the generous juices of spring, just raised by the electric fermentation of the season; nor to dry up the feelings by employing the mind in investigations remote from life.

With respect to women, when they receive a careful education, they are either made fine ladies, brimful of sensibility, and teeming with capricious fancies; or mere notable women. The latter are often friendly, honest creatures, and have a shrewd kind of good sense joined with worldly prudence, that often render them more useful members of society than the fine sentimental lady, though they possess neither greatness of mind nor taste. The intellectual world is shut against them; take them out of their family or neighbourhood, and they stand still; the mind finding no employment, for literature affords a fund of amusement, which they have never sought to relish, but frequently to despise. The sentiments and taste of more cultivated minds appear ridiculous, even in those whom chance and family connexions have led them to love, but in mere acquaintance they think it all affectation.

A man of sense can only love such a woman on account of her sex, and respect her, because she is a trusty servant. He lets her, to preserve his own peace, scold the servants, and go to church in clothes made of the very best materials. A man of her own size of understanding would, probably, not agree so well with her; for he might wish to encroach on her prerogative, and manage some domestic concerns himself. Yet women, whose minds are not enlarged by cultivation, or the natural selfishness of sensibility expanded by reflection, are very unfit to manage a family; for by an undue stretch of power, they are always tyrannizing to support a superiority that only rests on the arbitrary distinction of fortune. The evil is sometimes more serious, and domestics are deprived of innocent indulgences, and made to work beyond their strength, in order to enable the notable woman to keep a better table, and outshine her neighbours in finery and parade. If she attend to her children, it is, in general, to dress them in a costly manner—and, whether, this attention arises from vanity or fondness, it is equally pernicious.

Besides, how many women of this description pass their days, or, at least their evenings, discontentedly. Their husbands acknowledge that they are good managers, and chaste wives; but leave home to seek for more agreeable, may I be allowed to use a significant French word, *piquant* society; and the patient drudge, who fulfils her task, like a blind horse in a mill, is defrauded of her just reward; for the wages due to her are the caresses of her husband; and women who have so few resources in themselves, do not very patiently bear this privation of a natural right.

A fine lady, on the contrary, has been taught to look down with contempt on the vulgar employments of life; though she has only been incited to acquire accomplishments that rise a degree above sense; for even corporeal accomplishments cannot be acquired with any degree of precision, unless the understanding has been strengthened by exercise. Without a foundation of principles taste is superficial; and grace must arise from something deeper than imitation. The imagination, however, is heated, and the feelings rendered fastidious, if not sophisticated; or, a counterpoise of judgment is not acquired, when the heart still remains artless, though it becomes too tender.

These women are often amiable; and their hearts are really more sensible to general benevolence, more alive to the sentiments that civilize life, than the square elbowed family drudge; but, wanting a due proportion of reflection and selfgovernment, they only inspire love; and are the mistresses of their husbands, whilst they have any hold on their affections; and the platonic friends of his male acquaintance. These are the fair defects in nature; the women who appear to be created not to enjoy the fellowship of man, but to save him from sinking into absolute brutality, by rubbing off the rough angles of his character, and by playful dalliance to give some dignity to the appetite that draws him to them. Gracious Creator of the whole human race! hast thou created such a being as woman, who can trace thy wisdom in thy works, and feel that thou alone art by thy nature, exalted above her—for no better purpose? Can she believe that she was only made to submit to man her equal; a being, who, like her, was sent into the world to acquire virtue? Can she consent to be occupied merely to please him; merely to adorn the earth, when her soul is capable of rising to thee? And can she rest supinely dependent on man for reason, when she ought to mount with him the arduous steeps of knowledge?

Yet, if love be the supreme good, let women be only educated to inspire it, and let every charm be polished to intoxicate the senses; but, if they are moral beings, let them have a chance to become intelligent; and let love to man be only a part of that glowing flame of universal love, which, after encircling humanity, mounts in grateful incense to God.

To fulfil domestic duties much resolution is necessary, and a serious kind of perseverance that requires a more firm support than emotions, however lively and true to nature. To give an example of order, the soul of virtue, some austerity of behaviour must be adopted, scarcely to be expected from a being who, from its infancy, has been made the weathercock of its own sensations. Whoever rationally means to be useful, must have a plan of conduct; and, in the discharge of the simplest duty, we are often obliged to act contrary to the present impulse of tenderness or compassion. Severity is frequently the most certain, as well as the most sublime proof of affection; and the want of this power over the feelings, and of that lofty, dignified affection, which makes a person prefer the future good of the beloved object to a present gratification, is the reason why so many fond mothers spoil their children, and has made it questionable, whether negligence or indulgence is more hurtful: but I am inclined to think, that the latter has done most harm.

Mankind seem to agree, that children should be left under the management of women during their childhood. Now, from all the observation that I have been able to make, women of sensibility are the most unfit for this task, because they will infallibly, carried away by their feelings, spoil a child's temper. The management of the temper, the first and most important branch of education, requires the sober steady eye of reason; a plan of conduct equally distant from tyranny and indulgence; yet these are the extremes that people of sensibility alternately fall into; always shooting beyond the mark. I have followed this train of reasoning much further, till I have concluded, that a person of genius is the most improper person to be employed in education, public or private. Minds of this rare species see things too much in masses, and seldom, if ever, have a good temper. That habitual cheerfulness, termed good humour, is, perhaps, as seldom united with great mental powers, as with strong feelings. And those people who follow, with interest and admiration, the flights of genius; or, with cooler approbation suck in the instruction, which has been elaborately prepared for them by the profound thinker, ought not to be disgusted, if they find the former choleric, and the latter morose; because liveliness of fancy, and a tenacious comprehension of mind, are scarcely compatible with that pliant urbanity which leads a man, at least to bend to the opinions and prejudices of others, instead of roughly confronting them.

But, treating of education or manners, minds of a superior class are not to be considered, they may be left to chance; it is the multitude, with moderate abilities, who call for instruction, and catch the colour of the atmosphere they breathe. This respectable concourse, I contend, men and women, should not have their sensations heightened in the hot-bed of luxurious indolence, at the expense of their understanding; for, unless there be a ballast of understanding, they will never become either virtuous or free: an aristocracy, founded on property, or sterling talents, will ever sweep before it, the alternately timid and ferocious slaves of feeling.

Numberless are the arguments, to take another view of the subject, brought forward with a show of reason; because supposed to be deduced from nature, that men have used morally and physically to degrade the sex. I must notice a few.

The female understanding has often been spoken of with contempt, as arriving sooner at maturity than the male. I shall not answer this argument by alluding to the early proofs of reason, as well as genius, in Cowley, Milton, and Pope, but only appeal to experience to decide whether young men, who are early introduced into company (and examples now abound) do not acquire the same precocity. So notorious is this fact, that the bare mentioning of it must bring before people, who at all mix in the world, the idea of a number of swaggering apes of men whose understandings are narrowed by being brought into the society of men when they ought to have been spinning a top or twirling a hoop.

It has also been asserted, by some naturalists, that men do not attain their full growth and strength till thirty; but that women arrive at maturity by twenty. I apprehend that they reason on false ground, led astray by the male prejudice, which deems beauty the perfection of woman—mere beauty of features and complexion, the vulgar accepta- tion of the world, whilst male beauty is allowed to have some con- nexion with the mind. Strength of body, and that character of counte- nance, which the French term a *physionomie,* women do not acquire before thirty, any more than men. The little artless tricks of children, it is true, are particularly pleasing and attractive; yet, when the pretty freshness of youth is worn off, these artless graces become studied airs, and disgust every person of taste. In the countenance of girls we only look for vivacity and bashful modesty; but the springtide of life over, we look for soberer sense in the face, and for traces of passion, instead of the dimples of animal spirits; expecting to see individuality of char- acter, the only fastener of the affections. We then wish to converse, not to fondle; to give scope to our imaginations, as well as to the sensations of our hearts.

At twenty the beauty of both sexes is equal; but the libertinism of man leads him to make the distinction, and superannuated coquettes are commonly of the same opinion; for when they can no longer in- spire love, they pay for the vigour and vivacity of youth. The French who admit more of mind into their notions of beauty, give the prefer- ence to women of thirty. I mean to say, that they allow women to be in their most perfect state, when vivacity gives place to reason, and to that majestic seriousness of character, which marks maturity; or, the resting point. In youth, till twenty the body shoots out; till thirty the solids are attaining a degree of density; and the flexible muscles, grow- ing daily more rigid, give character to the countenance; that is, they trace the operations of the mind with the iron pen of fate, and tell us not only what powers are within, but how they have been employed.

It is proper to observe, that animals who arrive slowly at maturity, are the longest lived, and of the noblest species. Men cannot, however, claim any natural superiority from the grandeur of longevity; for in this respect nature has not distinguished the male.

Polygamy is another physical degradation; and a plausible argument for a custom, that blasts every domestic virtue, is drawn from the well-attested fact, that in the countries where it is established, more females are born than males. This appears to be an indication of nature, and to nature apparently reasonable speculations must yield. A further conclusion obviously presents itself; if polygamy be necessary, woman must be inferior to man, and made for him.

With respect to the formation of the fœtus in the womb, we are very ignorant; but it appears to me probable, that an accidental physical cause may account for this phenomenon, and prove it not to be a law of nature. I have met with some pertinent observations on the subject in Forster's Account of the Isles of the South Sea, that will explain my meaning. After observing that of the two sexes amongst animals, the most vigorous and hottest constitution always prevails, and produces its kind; he adds,—

> If this be applied to the inhabitants of Africa, it is evident that the men there, accustomed to polygamy, are enervated by the use of so many women, and therefore less vigorous; the women on the contrary, are of a hotter constitution, not only on account of their more irritable nerves, more sensitive organization, and more lively fancy; but likewise because they are deprived in their matrimony of that share of physical love which in a monogamous condition, would all be theirs; and thus for the above reasons, the generality of children are born females.
>
> In the greater part of Europe it has been proved by the most accurate lists of mortality, that the proportion of men to women is nearly equal, or, if any difference takes place, the males born are more numerous, in the proportion of 105 to 100.

The necessity of polygamy, therefore, does not appear; yet when a man seduces a woman, it should I think, be termed a *left-handed* marriage, and the man should be *legally* obliged to maintain the woman and her children, unless adultery, a natural divorcement, abrogated the law. And this law should remain in force as long as the weakness of women caused the word seduction to be used as an excuse for their frailty and want of principle; nay, while they depend on man for a subsistence, instead of earning it by the exercise of their own hands or heads. But these women should not in the full meaning of the relationship, be termed wives, or the very purpose of marriage would be subverted, and all those endearing charities that flow from personal fidelity, and give a sanctity to the tie, when neither love nor friendship unites the hearts, would melt into selfishness. The woman who is faithful to the father of her children demands respect, and should not be treated like a prostitute; though I readily grant, that if it be necessary for a man and woman to live together in order to bring up their offspring, nature never intended that a man should have more than one wife.

Still, highly as I respect marriage, as the foundation of almost every social virtue, I cannot avoid feeling the most lively compassion for those unfortunate females who are broken off from society, and by one error torn from all those affections and relationships that improve the heart and mind. It does not frequently even deserve the name of error; for many innocent girls become the dupes of a sincere affectionate heart, and still more are, as it may be emphatically termed, *ruined* before they know the difference between virtue and vice: and thus prepared by their education for infamy, they become infamous. Asylums and Magdalens are not the proper remedies for these abuses. It is justice, not charity, that is wanting in the world!

A woman who has lost her honour, imagines that she cannot fall lower, and as for recovering her former station, it is impossible; no exertion can wash this stain away. Losing thus every spur, and having no other means of support, prostitution becomes her only refuge, and the character is quickly depraved by circumstances over which the poor wretch has little power, unless she possesses an uncommon portion of sense and loftiness of spirit. Necessity never makes prostitution the business of men's lives; though numberless are the women who are thus rendered systematically vicious. This, however, arises, in a great degree, from the state of idleness in which women are educated, who are always taught to look up to man for maintenance, and to consider their persons as the proper return for his exertions to support them. Meretricious airs, and the whole science of wantonness, has then a more powerful stimulus than either appetite or vanity; and this remark gives force to the prevailing opinion, that with chastity all is lost that is respectable in woman. Her character depends on the observance of one virtue, though the only passion fostered in her heart—is love. Nay the honour of a woman is not made even to depend on her will.

When Richardson makes Clarissa tell Lovelace that he had robbed her of her honour, he must have had strange notions of honour and virtue. For, miserable beyond all names of misery is the condition of a being, who could be degraded without its own consent! This excess of strictness I have heard vindicated as a salutary error. I shall answer in the words of Leibnitz—"Errors are often useful; but it is commonly to remedy other errors."

Most of the evils of life arise from a desire of present enjoyment that outruns itself. The obedience required of women in the marriage state, comes under this description; the mind, naturally weakened by depending on authority, never exerts its own powers, and the obedient wife is thus rendered a weak indolent mother. Or, supposing that this is not always the consequence, a future state of existence is scarcely taken into the reckoning when only negative virtues are cultivated. For in treating of morals, particularly when women are alluded to, writers have too often considered virtue in a very limited sense, and made the foundation of it *solely* worldly utility; nay, a still more fragile base has been given to this stupendous fabric, and the wayward fluctuating feelings of men have been made the standard of virtue. Yes, virtue as well as religion, has been subjected to the decisions of taste.

It would almost provoke a smile of contempt, if the vain absurdities of man did not strike us on all sides, to observe, how eager men are to degrade the sex from whom they pretend to receive the chief pleasure of life; and I have frequently, with full conviction, retorted Pope's sarcasm on them; or, to speak explicitly, it has appeared to me applicable to the whole human race. A love of pleasure or sway seems to divide mankind, and the husband who lords it in his little harem, thinks only of his pleasure or his convenience. To such lengths, indeed, does an intemperate love of pleasure carry some prudent men, or worn out libertines, who marry to have a safe companion, that they seduce their own wives. Hymen banishes modesty, and chaste love takes its flight.

Love, considered as an animal appetite, cannot long feed on itself without expiring. And this extinction, in its own flame, may be termed the violent death of love. But the wife who has thus been rendered licentious, will probably endeavour to fill the void left by the loss of her husband's attentions; for she cannot contentedly become merely an upper servant after having been treated like a goddess. She is still handsome, and, instead of transferring her fondness to her children, she only dreams of enjoying the sunshine of life. Besides, there are many husbands so devoid of sense and parental affection, that during the first effervescence of voluptuous fondness, they refuse to let their wives suckle their children. They are only to dress and live to please them: and love, even innocent love, soon sinks into lasciviousness when the exercise of a duty is sacrificed to its indulgence.

Personal attachment is a very happy foundation for friendship; yet, when even two virtuous young people marry, it would, perhaps, be happy if some circumstance checked their passion; if the recollection of some prior attachment, or disappointed affection, made it on one side, at least, rather a match founded on esteem. In that case they would look beyond the present moment, and try to render the whole of life respectable, by forming a plan to regulate a friendship which only death ought to dissolve.

Friendship is a serious affection; the most sublime of all affections, because it is founded on principle, and cemented by time. The very reverse may be said of love. In a great degree, love and friendship cannot subsist in the same bosom; even when inspired by different objects they weaken or destroy each other, and for the same object can only be felt in succession. The vain fears and fond jealousies, the winds which fan the flame of love, when judiciously or artfully tempered, are both incompatible with the tender confidence and sincere respect of friendship.

Love, such as the glowing pen of genius has traced, exists not on earth, or only resides in those exalted, fervid imaginations that have sketched such dangerous pictures. Dangerous, because they not only afford a plausible excuse to the voluptuary, who disguises sheer sensuality under a sentimental veil; but as they spread affectation, and take from the dignity of virtue. Virtue, as the very word imports, should have an appearance of seriousness, if not austerity; and to endeavour to trick her out in the garb of pleasure, because the epithet has been used as another name for beauty, is to exalt her on a quicksand; a most insiduous attempt to hasten her fall by apparent respect. Virtue, and pleasure are not, in fact, so nearly allied in this life as some eloquent writers have laboured to prove. Pleasure prepares the fading wreath, and mixes the intoxicating cup; but the fruit which virtue gives, is the recompence of toil: and, gradually seen as it ripens, only affords calm satisfaction; nay, appearing to be the result of the natural tendency of things, it is scarcely observed. Bread, the common food of life, seldom thought of as a blessing, supports the constitution, and preserves health; still feasts delight the heart of man, though disease and even death lurk in the cup or dainty that elevates the spirits or tickles the palate. The lively heated imagination, in the same style, draws the picture of love, as it draws every other picture, with those glowing colours, which the daring hand will steal from the rainbow that is directed by a mind, condemned, in a world like this, to prove its noble origin, by panting after unattainable perfection; ever pursuing what it acknowledges to be a fleeting dream. An imagination of this vigorous cast can give existence to insubstantial forms, and stability to the shadowy reveries which the mind naturally falls into when realities are found vapid. It can then depict love with celestial charms, and dote on the grand ideal object; it can imagine a degree of mutual affection that shall refine the soul, and not expire when it has served as a "scale to heavenly;" and, like devotion, make it absorb every meaner affection and desire. In each other's arms, as in a temple, with its summit lost in the clouds, the world is to be shut out, and every thought and wish, that do not nurture pure affection and permanent virtue. Permanent virtue! alas! Rousseau, respectable visionary! thy paradise would soon be violated by the entrance of some unexpected guest. Like Milton's, it would only contain angels, or men sunk below the dignity of rational creatures. Happiness is not material, it cannot be seen or felt! Yet the eager pursuit of the good which every one shapes to his own fancy, proclaims man the lord of this lower world, and to be an intelligential creature, who is not to receive, but acquire happiness. They, therefore, who complain of the delusions of passion, do not recollect that they are exclaiming against a strong proof of the immortality of the soul.

But, leaving superior minds to correct themselves, and pay dearly for their experience, it is necessary to observe, that it is not against strong, persevering passions, but romantic, wavering feelings, that I wish to guard the female heart by exercising the understanding; for these paradisiacal reveries are oftener the effect of idleness than of a lively fancy.

Women have seldom sufficient serious employment to silence their feelings; a round of little cares, or vain pursuits, frittering away all strength of mind and organs, they become naturally only objects of sense. In short, the whole tenor of female education (the education of society) tends to render the best disposed, romantic and inconstant; and the remainder vain and mean. In the present state of society, this evil can scarcely be remedied, I am afraid, in the slightest degree; should a more laudable ambition ever gain ground, they may be brought nearer to nature and reason; and become more virtuous and useful as they grow more respectable.

But I will venture to assert, that their reason will never acquire sufficient strength to enable it to regulate their conduct, whilst the making an appearance in the world is the first wish of the majority of mankind. To this weak wish the natural affections and the most useful virtues are sacrificed. Girls marry merely to *better themselves,* to borrow a significant vulgar phrase, and have such perfect power over their hearts as not to permit themselves to *fall in love* till a man with a superior fortune offers. On this subject I mean to enlarge in a future chapter; it is only necessary to drop a hint at present, because women are so often degraded by suffering the selfish prudence of age to chill the ardour of youth.

From the same source flows an opinion that young girls ought to dedicate great part of their time to needle work; yet, this employment contracts their faculties more than any other that could have been chosen for them, by confining their thoughts to their persons. Men order their clothes to be made, and have done with the subject; women make their own clothes, necessary or ornamental, and are continually talking about them; and their thoughts follow their hands. It is not indeed the making of necessaries that weakens the mind; but the frippery of dress. For when a woman in the lower rank of life makes her husband's and children's clothes, she does her duty, this is part of her business; but when women work only to dress better than they could otherwise afford, it is worse than sheer loss of time. To render the poor virtuous, they must be employed, and women in the middle rank of life did they not ape the fashions of the nobility, without catching their ease, might employ them, whilst they themselves managed their families, instructed their children, and exercised their own minds. Gardening, experimental philosophy, and literature, would afford them subjects to think of, and matter for conversation, that in some degree would exercise their understandings. The conversation of French women, who are not so rigidly nailed to their chairs, to twist lappets, and knot ribbands, is frequently superficial; but, I contend, that it is not half so insipid as that of those English women, whose time is spent in making caps, bonnets, and the whole mischief of trimmings, not to mention shopping, bargain-hunting, &c. &c.: and it is the decent, prudent women, who are most degraded by these practices; for their motive is simply vanity. The wanton, who exercises her taste to render her person alluring, has something more in view.

These observations all branch out of a general one, which I have before made, and which cannot be too often insisted upon, for, speaking of men, women, or professions, it will be found, that the employment of the thoughts shapes the character both generally and individually. The thoughts of women ever hover around their persons, and is it surprising that their persons are reckoned most valuable? Yet some degree of liberty of mind is necessary even to form the person; and this may be one reason why some gentle wives have so few attractions beside that of sex. Add to this, sedentary employments render the majority of women sickly, and false notions of female excellence make them proud of this delicacy, though it be another fetter, that by calling the attention continually to the body, cramps the activity of the mind.

Women of quality seldom do any of the manual part of their dress, consequently only their taste is exercised, and they acquire, by thinking less of the finery, when the business of their toilet is over, that ease, which seldom appears in the deportment of women, who dress merely for the sake of dressing. In fact, the observation with respect to the middle rank, the one in which talents thrive best, extends not to women; for those of the superior class, by catching, at least a smattering of literature, and conversing more with men, on general topics, acquire more knowledge than the women who ape their fashions and faults without sharing their advantages. With respect to virtue, to use the word in a comprehensive sense, I have seen most in low life. Many poor women maintain their children by the sweat of their brow, and keep together families that the vices of the fathers would have scattered abroad; but gentlewomen are too indolent to be actively virtuous, and are softened rather than refined by civilization. Indeed the good sense which I have met with among the poor women who have had few advantages of education, and yet have acted heroically, strongly confirmed me in the opinion, that trifling employments have rendered women a trifler. Men, taking her body, the mind is left to rust; so that while physical love enervates man, as being his favourite recreation, he will endeavour to enslave woman: and who can tell how many generations may be necessary to give vigour to the virtue and talents of the freed posterity of abject slaves?

In tracing the causes that in my opinion, have degraded woman, I have confined my observations to such as universally act upon the morals and manners of the whole sex, and to me it appears clear, that they all spring from want of understanding. Whether this arises from a physical or accidental weakness of faculties, time alone can determine; for I shall not lay any great stress upon the example of a few women, who, from having received a masculine education, have acquired courage and resolution; I only contend that the men who have been placed in similar situations have acquired a similar character, I speak of bodies of men, and that men of genius and talents have started out of a class, in which women have never yet been placed.

QUESTIONS

1. How does Mary Wollstonecraft make the apparent castigation of women a defense of their human rights?

2. How convincing is the extended comparison of women to the wealthy nobility? Which of the author's arguments are strongest and which are weakest?

3. Explain what Mary Wollstonecraft means by "ignorance" and "innocence." How does she think the terms have been confused in their application to women?

4. According to the author, what is "sensibility"? What has its cultivation led to concerning women and how has its cultivation led to this?

5. What does Mary Wollstonecraft consider the most serious causes of feminine degradation and how does she propose to remedy them?

6. Which of the proposals in this chapter seem the most radical and why?

7. What is Mary Wollstonecraft's attitude toward prostitution? From her comments, what can you infer about the treatment of prostitutes in the eighteenth century?

8. What evidence does this selection show of Mary Wollstonecraft's sympathy with the French Revolution? How is the cause of women related to revolutionary principles?

John Stuart Mill

The English philosopher John Stuart Mill (1806–1873) was one of the most extraordinary men of his century. As the son of the utilitarian philosopher James Mill, the younger Mill was a precocious genius forced into intellectual flowering by his domineering father. Mill matured to become a political economist and social reformer, an author of numerous philosophical works, and a supporter of liberal causes ranging from universal education to population control to Negro emancipation. Of all his works, however, The Subjection of Women (1869) was the most controversial and aroused the most antagonism, even among his friends. In Chapter III, reprinted below, Mill concentrates on the abilities of women and their right to enter the trades, the professions, and the arts.

Mill's sympathetic attitude toward feminism was one aspect of his belief that the liberty of the individual is necessary to the development of society. He wrote The Subjection of Women to show

> . . . that the principle which regulates the existing social relations between the two sexes—the legal subordination of one sex to the other—is wrong in itself, and now one of the chief hindrances to human improvement; and that it ought to be replaced by a principle of perfect equality, admitting no power or privilege on the one side, nor disability on the other.

The argument in The Subjection of Women is presented with Mill's customary lucid and compelling intelligence. The statement of his case—that women's position is not natural but the result of political oppression by men—is one of the more brilliant of its kind, and his analysis of the effects this use of power has had on both men and women is exceptionally persuasive. Yet the crux of the book, and the reason for the hostility it provoked, is its radical criticism of the family. Like most Victorians, Mill believed that the family was the model and the source of all social behavior, and he maintained that the masculine domination of the family was a corrupting influence, making boys selfish and girls abject.

Mill worked for women's rights as well as defending them. When elected to Parliament, he introduced a motion to include women's suffrage in the

*second Reform Bill of 1867, and although the motion was ridiculed and de-
feated, it won increasing support in subsequent years because of his influence.
With his stepdaughter, Helen Taylor, he formed the Women's Suffrage
Society in England and persuaded many prominent women to join, to contribute money, and, most important, to appear publicly in the organization's
behalf. At his death he left over half his fortune to women's education.*

*Yet even a man of Mill's stature had to obey the dictates of nineteenth-
century propriety and avoid causes in which he had too personal an interest.
Because he had fallen in love with a married woman, Harriet Taylor, who
later became his wife, and had carried on a platonic but nonetheless scandalous romance with her until her husband died, he dared not advocate
divorce in his book.*

from

The Subjection of Women

On the other point which is involved in the just equality of
women, their admissibility to all the functions and occupations hitherto
retained as the monopoly of the stronger sex, I should anticipate no
difficulty in convincing any one who has gone with me on the subject
of the equality of women in the family. I believe that their disabilities
elsewhere are only clung to in order to maintain their subordination in
domestic life; because the generality of the male sex cannot yet tolerate
the idea of living with an equal. Were it not for that, I think that
almost every one, in the existing state of opinion in politics and political
economy, would admit the injustice of excluding half the human race
from the greater number of lucrative occupations, and from almost all
high social functions; ordaining from their birth either that they are
not, and cannot by any possibility become, fit for employments which
are legally open to the stupidest and basest of the other sex, or else that
however fit they may be, those employments shall be interdicted to
them, in order to be preserved for the exclusive benefit of males. In
the last two centuries, when (which was seldom the case) any reason
beyond the mere existence of the fact was thought to be required to
justify the disabilities of women, people seldom assigned as a reason
their inferior mental capacity; which, in times when there was a real
trial of personal faculties (from which all women were not excluded)

in the struggles of public life, no one really believed in. The reason given in those days was not women's unfitness, but the interest of society, by which was meant the interest of men: just as the *raison d'état*, meaning the convenience of the government, and the support of existing authority, was deemed a sufficient explanation and excuse for the most flagitious crimes. In the present day, power holds a smoother language, and whomsoever it oppresses, always pretends to do so for their own good: accordingly, when anything is forbidden to women, it is thought necessary to say, and desirable to believe, that they are incapable of doing it, and that they depart from their real path of success and happiness when they aspire to it. But to make this reason plausible (I do not say valid), those by whom it is urged must be prepared to carry it to a much greater length than any one ventures to do in the face of present experience. It is not sufficient to maintain that women on the average are less gifted than men on the average, with certain of the higher mental faculties, or that a smaller number of women than of men are fit for occupations and functions of the highest intellectual character. It is necessary to maintain that no women at all are fit for them, and that the most eminent women are inferior in mental faculties to the most mediocre of the men on whom those functions at present devolve. For if the performance of the function is decided either by competition, or by any mode of choice which secures regard to the public interest, there needs be no apprehension that any important employments will fall into the hands of women inferior to average men, or to the average of their male competitors. The only result would be that there would be fewer women than men in such employments; a result certain to happen in any case, if only from the preference always likely to be felt by the majority of women for the one vocation in which there is nobody to compete with them. Now, the most determined depreciator of women will not venture to deny, that when we add the experience of recent times to that of ages past, women, and not a few merely, but many women, have proved themselves capable of everything, perhaps without a single exception, which is done by men, and of doing it successfully and creditably. The utmost that can be said is, that there are many things which none of them have succeeded in doing as well as they have been done by some men—many in which they have not reached the very highest rank. But there are extremely few, dependent only on mental faculties, in which they have not attained the rank next to the highest. Is not this enough, and much more than enough, to make it a tyranny to them, and a detriment to society, that they should not be allowed to compete with men for the exercise of these functions? Is it not a mere truism to say, that such functions are often filled by men far less fit for them than numbers of women, and who would be beaten by women in any fair field of competition? What difference does it make that there may be men somewhere, fully employed about other things, who may be still better qualified for the things in question than these women? Does not this take place in all competitions? Is there so great a superfluity of men fit for high duties, that society can afford to reject the service of any competent person? Are we so certain of always finding a man made to our hands for any duty or function of social importance which falls vacant, that we lose nothing by putting a ban upon one-half of mankind, and refusing beforehand to make their faculties available, however distinguished they may be? And even if we could do without them, would it be consistent with justice to refuse to them their fair share of honour and distinction, or to deny to them the equal moral right of all human beings to choose their occupation (short of injury to others) according to their own preferences, at their own risk? Nor is the injustice confined to them: it is shared by those who are in a position to benefit by their services. To ordain that any kind of persons shall not be physicians, or shall not be advocates, or shall not be members of parliament, is to injure not them only, but all who employ physicians or advocates, or elect members of parliament, and who are deprived of the stimulating effect of greater competition on the exertions of the competitors, as well as restricted to a narrower range of individual choice.

It will perhaps be sufficient if I confine myself, in the details of my argument, to functions of a public nature: since, if I am successful as to those, it probably will be readily granted that women should be admissible to all other occupations to which it is at all material whether they are admitted or not. And here let me begin by marking out one function, broadly distinguished from all others, their right to which is entirely independent of any question which can be raised concerning their faculties. I mean the suffrage, both parliamentary and municipal. The right to share in the choice of those who are to exercise a public trust, is altogether a distinct thing from that of competing for the trust itself. If no one could vote for a member of parliament who was not fit to be a candidate, the government would be a narrow oligarchy indeed. To have a voice in choosing those by whom one is to be governed, is a means of self-protection due to every one, though he were to remain for ever excluded from the function of governing: and that women are considered fit to have such a choice, may be presumed from the fact, that the law already gives it to women in the most important of all cases to themselves: for the choice of the man who is to govern a woman to the end of life, is always supposed to be voluntarily made by herself. In the case of election to public trusts, it is the business of constitutional law to surround the right of suffrage with all needful securities and limitations; but whatever securities are sufficient in the case of the male sex, no others need be required in the case of women. Under whatever conditions, and within whatever limits, men are admitted to the suffrage, there is not a shadow of justification for not admitting women under the same. The majority of the women of any class are not likely to differ in political opinion from the majority of the men of the same class, unless the question be one in which the interests of women, as such, are in some way involved; and if they are so, women require the suffrage, as their guarantee of just and equal consideration. This ought to be obvious even to those who coincide in no other of the doctrines for which I contend. Even if every woman were a wife, and if every wife ought to be a slave, all the more would these slaves stand in need of legal protection: and we know what legal protection the slaves have, where the laws are made by their masters.

With regard to the fitness of women, not only to participate in elections, but themselves to hold offices or practice professions involving important public responsibilities; I have already observed that this consideration is not essential to the practical question in dispute: since any woman, who succeeds in an open profession, proves by that very fact that she is qualified for it. And in the case of public offices, if the political system of the country is such as to exclude unfit men, it will equally exclude unfit women: while if it is not, there is no additional evil in the fact that the unfit persons whom it admits may be either women or men. As long therefore as it is acknowledged that even a few women may be fit for these duties, the laws which shut the door on those exceptions cannot be justified by any opinion which can be held respecting the capacities of women in general. But, though this last consideration is not essential, it is far from being irrelevant. An unprejudiced view of it gives additional strength to the arguments against the disabilities of women, and reinforces them by high considerations of practical utility.

Let us at first make entire abstraction of all psychological considerations tending to show, that any of the mental differences supposed to exist between women and men are but the natural effect of the differences in their education and circumstances, and indicate no radical difference, far less radical inferiority, of nature. Let us consider women only as they already are, or as they are known to have been; and the capacities which they have already practically shown. What they have done, that at least, if nothing else, it is proved that they can do. When we consider how sedulously they are all trained away from, instead of being trained towards, any of the occupations or objects reserved for men, it is evident that I am taking a very humble ground for them, when I rest their case on what they have actually achieved. For, in this case, negative evidence is worth little, while any positive evidence is conclusive. It cannot be inferred to be impossible that a woman should be a Homer, or an Aristotle, or a Michael Angelo, or a Beethoven, because no woman has yet actually produced works comparable to theirs in any of those lines of excellence. This negative fact at most leaves the question uncertain, and open to psychological discussion. But it is quite certain that a woman can be a Queen Elizabeth, or a Deborah, or a Joan of Arc, since this is not inference, but fact. Now it is a curious consideration, that the only things which the existing law excludes women from doing, are the things which they have proved that they are able to do. There is no law to prevent a woman from having written all the plays of Shakspeare, or composed all the operas of Mozart. But Queen Elizabeth or Queen Victoria, had they not inherited the throne, could not have been intrusted with the smallest of the political duties, of which the former showed herself equal to the greatest.

If anything conclusive could be inferred from experience, without psychological analysis, it would be that the things which women are not allowed to do are the very ones for which they are peculiarly qualified; since their vocation for government has made its way, and become conspicuous, through the very few opportunities which have been given; while in the lines of distinction which apparently were freely open to them, they have by no means so eminently distinguished themselves. We know how small a number of reigning queens history presents, in comparison with that of kings. Of this smaller number a far larger proportion have shown talents for rule; though many of them have occupied the throne in difficult periods. It is remarkable, too, that they have, in a great number of instances, been distinguished by merits the most opposite to the imaginary and conventional character of women: they have been as much remarked for the firmness and vigour of their rule, as for its intelligence. When, to queens and empresses, we add regents, and viceroys of provinces, the list of women who have been eminent rulers of mankind swells to a great length.[1] This fact is so undeniable, that someone, long ago, tried to retort the argument, and turned the admitted truth into an additional insult, by saying that queens are better than kings, because under kings women govern, but under queens, men.

It may seem a waste of reasoning to argue against a bad joke; but such things do affect people's minds; and I have heard men quote this

---

[1] Especially is this true if we take into consideration Asia as well as Europe. If a Hindu principality is strongly, vigilantly, and economically governed; if order is preserved without oppression; if cultivation is extending, and the people prosperous, in three cases out of four that principality is under a woman's rule. This fact, to me an entirely unexpected one, I have collected from a long official knowledge of Hindu governments. There are many such instances: for though, by Hindu institutions, a woman cannot reign, she is the legal regent of a kingdom during the minority of the heir; and minorities are frequent, the lives of the male rulers being so often prematurely terminated through the effect of inactivity and sensual excesses. When we consider that these princesses have never been seen in public, have never conversed with any man not of their own family except from behind a curtain, that they do not read, and if they did, there is no book in their languages which can give them the smallest instruction on political affairs; the example they afford of the natural capacity of women for government is very striking.

saying, with an air as if they thought that there was something in it. At any rate, it will serve as well as anything else for a starting point in discussion. I say, then, that it is not true that under kings, women govern. Such cases are entirely exceptional: and weak kings have quite as often governed ill through the influence of male favourites, as of female. When a king is governed by a woman merely through his amatory propensities, good government is not probable, though even then there are exceptions. But French history counts two kings who have voluntarily given the direction of affairs during many years, the one to his mother, the other to his sister: one of them, Charles VIII, was a mere boy, but in doing so he followed the intentions of his father Louis XI, the ablest monarch of his age. The other, Saint Louis, was the best, and one of the most vigorous rulers, since the time of Charlemagne. Both these princesses ruled in a manner hardly equalled by any prince among their cotemporaries. The emperor Charles the Fifth, the most politic prince of his time, who had as great a number of able men in his service as a ruler ever had, and was one of the least likely of all sovereigns to sacrifice his interest to personal feelings, made two princesses of his family successively Governors of the Netherlands, and kept one or other of them in that post during his whole life, (they were afterwards succeeded by a third). Both ruled very successfully, and one of them, Margaret of Austria, was one of the ablest politicians of the age. So much for one side of the question. Now as to the other. When it is said that under queens men govern, is the same meaning to be understood as when kings are said to be governed by women? Is it meant that queens choose as their instruments of government, the associates of their personal pleasures? The case is rare even with those who are as unscrupulous on the latter point as Catherine II: and it is not in these cases that the good government, alleged to arise from male influence, is to be found. If it be true, then, that the administration is in the hands of better men under a queen than under an average king, it must be that queens have a superior capacity for choosing them; and women must be better qualified than men both for the position of sovereign, and for that of chief minister; for the principal business of a prime minister is not to govern in person, but to find the fittest persons to conduct every department of public affairs. The more rapid insight into character, which is one of the admitted points of superiority in women over men, must certainly make them, with anything like parity of qualifications in other respects, more apt than men in that choice of instruments, which is nearly the most important business of every one who has to do with governing mankind. Even the unprincipled Catherine de' Medici could feel the value of a Chancellor de l'Hôpital. But it is also true that most great queens have been great by their own talents for government, and have been well served precisely for that reason. They retained the supreme direction of affairs in their own hands: and if they listened to good advisers, they gave by that fact the strongest proof that their judgment fitted them for dealing with the great questions of government.

Is it reasonable to think that those who are fit for the greater functions of politics, are incapable of qualifying themselves for the less? Is there any reason in the nature of things, that the wives and sisters of princes should, whenever called on, be found as competent as the princes themselves to *their* business, but that the wives and sisters of statesmen, and administrators, and directors of companies, and managers of public institutions, should be unable to do what is done by their brothers and husbands? The real reason is plain enough; it is that princesses, being more raised above the generality of men by their rank than placed below them by their sex, have never been taught that it was improper for them to concern themselves with politics; but have been allowed to feel the liberal interest natural to any cultivated human being, in the great transactions which took place around them, and in which they might be called on to take a part. The ladies of reigning families are the only women who are allowed the same range of interests and freedom of development as men; and it is precisely in their case that there is not found to be any inferiority. Exactly where and in proportion as women's capacities for government have been tried, in that proportion have they been found adequate.

This fact is in accordance with the best general conclusions which the world's imperfect experience seems as yet to suggest, concerning the peculiar tendencies and aptitudes characteristic of women, as women have hitherto been. I do not say, as they will continue to be; for, as I have already said more than once, I consider it presumption in any one to pretend to decide what women are or are not, can or cannot be, by natural constitution. They have always hitherto been kept, as far as regards spontaneous development, in so unnatural a state, that their nature cannot but have been greatly distorted and disguised; and no one can safely pronounce that if women's nature were left to choose its direction as freely as men's, and if no artificial bent were attempted to be given to it except that required by the conditions of human society, and given to both sexes alike, there would be any material difference, or perhaps any difference at all, in the character and capacities which would unfold themselves. I shall presently show, that even the least contestable of the differences which now exist, are such as may very well have been produced merely by circumstances, without any difference of natural capacity. But, looking at women as they are known in experience, it may be said of them, with more truth than belongs to most other generalizations on the subject, that the general bent of their talents is towards the practical. This statement is conformable to all the public history of women, in the present and the past. It is no less borne out by common and daily experience. Let us consider the special nature of the mental capacities most characteristic of a woman of talent. They are all of a kind which fits them for practice, and makes them tend towards it. What is meant by a woman's capacity of intuitive perception? It means, a rapid and correct insight into present fact. It has nothing to do with general principles. Nobody ever perceived a scientific law of nature by intuition, nor arrived at a general rule of duty or prudence by it. These are results of slow and careful collection and comparison of experience; and neither the men nor the women of intuition usually shine in this department, unless, indeed, the experience necessary is such as they can acquire by themselves. For what is called their intuitive sagacity makes them peculiarly apt in gathering such general truths as can be collected from their individual means of observation. When, consequently, they chance to be as well provided as men are with the results of other people's experience, by reading and education, (I use the word chance advisedly, for, in respect to the knowledge that tends to fit them for the greater concerns of life, the only educated women are the self-educated) they are better furnished than men in general with the essential requisites of skillfull and successful practice. Men who have been much taught, are apt to be deficient in the sense of present fact; they do not see, in the facts which they are called upon to deal with, what is really there, but what they have been taught to expect. This is seldom the case with women of any ability. Their capacity of "intuition" preserves them from it. With equality of experience and of general faculties, a woman usually sees much more than a man of what is immediately before her. Now this sensibility to the present, is the main quality on which the capacity for practice, as distinguished from theory, depends. To discover general principles, belongs to the speculative faculty: to discern and discriminate the particular cases in which they are and are not applicable, constitutes practical talent: and for this, women as they now are have a peculiar aptitude. I admit that there can be no good practice without principles, and that the predominant place which quickness of observation holds among a woman's faculties, makes her particularly apt to build over-hasty generalizations upon her own observation; though at the same time no less ready in rectifying those generalizations, as her observation takes a wider range. But the corrective to this defect, is access to the experience of the human race; general knowledge—exactly the thing which education can best supply. A woman's mistakes are specifically those of a clever self-educated man, who often sees what men trained in routine do not see, but falls into errors for want of knowing things which have long been known. Of course he has acquired much of the pre-existing knowledge, or he could not have got on at all; but what he knows of it he has picked up in fragments and at random, as women do.

But this gravitation of women's minds to the present, to the real, to actual fact, while in its exclusiveness it is a source of errors, is also a most useful counteractive of the contrary error. The principal and most characteristic aberration of speculative minds as such, consists precisely in the deficiency of this lively perception and ever-present sense of objective fact. For want of this, they often not only overlook the contradiction which outward facts oppose to their theories, but lose sight of the legitimate purpose of speculation altogether, and let their speculative faculties go astray into regions not peopled with real beings, animate or inanimate, even idealized, but with personified shadows created by the illusions of metaphysics or by the mere entanglement of words, and think these shadows the proper objects of the highest, the most transcendent, philosophy. Hardly anything can be of greater value to a man of theory and speculation who employs himself not in collecting materials of knowledge by observation, but in working them up by processes of thought into comprehensive truths of science and laws of conduct, than to carry on his speculations in the companionship, and under the criticism, of a really superior woman. There is nothing comparable to it for keeping his thoughts within the limits of real things, and the actual facts of nature. A woman seldom runs wild after an abstraction. The habitual direction of her mind to dealing with things as individuals rather than in groups, and (what is closely connected with it) her more lively interest in the present feelings of persons, which makes her consider first of all, in anything which claims to be applied to practice, in what manner persons will be affected by it—these two things make her extremely unlikely to put faith in any speculation which loses sight of individuals, and deals with things as if they existed for the benefit of some imaginary entity, some mere creation of the mind, not resolvable into the feelings of living beings. Women's thoughts are thus as useful in giving reality to those of thinking men, as men's thoughts in giving width and largeness to those of women. In depth, as distinguished from breadth, I greatly doubt if even now, women, compared with men, are at any disadvantage.

If the existing mental characteristics of women are thus valuable even in aid of speculation, they are still more important, when speculation has done its work, for carrying out the results of speculation into practice. For the reasons already given, women are comparatively unlikely to fall into the common error of men, that of sticking to their rules in a case whose specialities either take it out of the class to which the rules are applicable, or require a special adaptation of them. Let us now consider another of the admitted superiorities of clever women, greater quickness of apprehension. Is not this pre-eminently a quality which fits a person for practice? In action, everything continually depends upon deciding promptly. In speculation, nothing does. A mere thinker can wait, can take time to consider, can collect additional evidence; he is not obliged to complete his philosophy at once, lest the opportunity should go by. The power of drawing the best conclusion possible from insufficient data is not indeed useless in philosophy; the construction of a provisional hypothesis consistent with all known facts is often the needful basis for further inquiry. But this faculty is rather serviceable in philosophy, than the main qualification for it: and, for the auxiliary as well as for the main operation, the philosopher can allow himself any time he pleases. He is in no need of the capacity of doing rapidly what he does; what he rather needs is patience, to work on slowly until imperfect lights have become perfect, and a conjecture has ripened into a theorem. For those, on the contrary, whose business is with the fugitive and perishable—with individual facts, not kinds of facts—rapidity of thought is a qualification next only in importance to the power of thought itself. He who has not his faculties under immediate command, in the contingencies of action, might as well not have them at all. He may be fit to criticize, but he is not fit to act. Now it is in this that women, and the men who are most like women, confessedly excel. The other sort of man, however pre-eminent may be his faculties, arrives slowly at complete command of them: rapidity of judgment and promptitude of judicious action, even in the things he knows best, are the gradual and late result of strenuous effort grown into habit.

It will be said, perhaps, that the greater nervous susceptibility of women is a disqualification for practice, in anything but domestic life, by rendering them mobile, changeable, too vehemently under the influence of the moment, incapable of dogged perseverance, unequal and uncertain in the power of using their faculties. I think that these phrases sum up the greater part of the objections commonly made to the fitness of women for the higher class of serious business. Much of all this is the mere overflow of nervous energy run to waste, and would cease when the energy was directed to a definite end. Much is also the result of conscious or unconscious cultivation; as we see by the almost total disappearance of "hysterics" and fainting fits, since they have gone out of fashion. Moreover, when people are brought up, like many women of the higher classes (though less so in our own country than in any other) a kind of hothouse plants, shielded from the wholesome vicissitudes of air and temperature, and untrained in any of the occupations and exercises which give stimulus and development to the circulatory and muscular system, while their nervous system, especially in its emotional department, is kept in unnaturally active play; it is no wonder if those of them who do not die of consumption, grow up with constitutions liable to derangement from slight causes, both internal and external, and without stamina to support any task, physical or mental, requiring continuity of effort. But women brought up to work for their livelihood show none of these morbid characteristics, unless indeed they are chained to an excess of sedentary work in confined and unhealthy rooms. Women who in their early years have shared in the healthful physical education and bodily freedom of their brothers, and who obtain a sufficiency of pure air and exercise in after-life, very rarely have any excessive susceptibility of nerves which can disqualify them for active pursuits. There is indeed a certain proportion of persons, in both sexes, in whom an unusual degree of nervous sensibility is constitutional, and of so marked a character as to be the feature of their organization which exercises the greatest influence over the whole character of the vital phenomena. This constitution, like other physical conformations, is hereditary, and is transmitted to sons as well as daughters; but it is possible, and probable, that the nervous temperament (as it is called) is inherited by a greater number of women than of men. We will assume this as a fact: and let me then ask, are men of nervous temperament found to be unfit for the duties and pursuits usually followed by men? If not, why should women of the same temperament be unfit for them? The peculiarities of the temperament are, no doubt, within certain limits, an obstacle to success in some employments, though an aid to it in others. But when the occupation is suitable to the temperament, and sometimes even when it is unsuitable, the most brilliant examples of success are continually given by the men of high nervous sensibility. They are distinguished in their practical manifestations chiefly by this, that being susceptible of a higher degree of excitement than those of another physical constitution, their powers when excited differ more than in the case of other people, from those shown in their ordinary state: they are raised, as it were, above themselves, and do things with ease which they are wholly incapable of at other times. But this lofty excitement is not, except in weak bodily constitutions, a mere flash, which passes away immediately, leaving no permanent traces, and incompatible with persistent and steady pursuit of an object. It is the character of the nervous temperament to be capable of *sustained* excitement, holding out through long continued efforts. It is what is meant by *spirit*. It is what makes the highbred racehorse run without slackening speed till he drops down dead. It is what has enabled so many delicate women to maintain the most sublime constancy not only at the stake, but through a long preliminary succession of mental and bodily tortures. It is evident that people of this temperament are particularly apt for what may be called the executive department of the leadership of mankind. They are the material of great orators, great preachers, impressive diffusers of moral influences. Their constitution might be deemed less favourable to the qualities required from a statesman in the cabinet, or from a judge. It would be so, if the consequence necessarily followed that because people are excitable they must always be in a state of excitement. But this is wholly a question of training. Strong feeling is the instrument and element of strong self-control: but it requires to be cultivated in that direction. When it is, it forms not the heroes of impulse only, but those also of self-conquest. History and experience prove that the most passionate characters are the most fanatically rigid in their feelings of duty, when their passion has been trained to act in that direction. The judge who gives a just decision in a case where his feelings are intensely interested on the other side, derives from that same strength

of feeling the determined sense of the obligation of justice, which enables him to achieve this victory over himself. The capability of that
lofty enthusiasm which takes the human being out of his every-day
character, reacts upon the daily character itself. His aspirations and
powers when he is in this exceptional state, become the type with
which he compares, and by which he estimates, his sentiments and
proceedings at other times: and his habitual purposes assume a character moulded by and assimilated to the moments of lofty excitement,
although those, from the physical nature of a human being, can only
be transient. Experience of races, as well as of individuals, does not
show those of excitable temperament to be less fit, on the average,
either for speculation or practice, than the more unexcitable. The
French, and the Italians, are undoubtedly by nature more nervously
excitable than the Teutonic races, and, compared at least with the
English, they have a much greater habitual and daily emotional life:
but have they been less great in science, in public business, in legal
and judicial eminence, or in war? There is abundant evidence that
the Greeks were of old, as their descendants and successors still are,
one of the most excitable of the races of mankind. It is superfluous to
ask, what among the achievements of men they did not excell in. The
Romans, probably, as an equally southern people, had the same original
temperament: but the stern character of their national discipline, like
that of the Spartans, made them an example of the opposite type of
national character; the greater strength of their natural feelings being
chiefly apparent in the intensity which the same original temperament
made it possible to give to the artificial. If these cases exemplify what a
naturally excitable people may be made, the Irish Celts afford one of
the aptest examples of what they are when left to themselves; (if
those can be said to be left to themselves who have been for centuries
under the indirect influence of bad government, and the direct training of a Catholic hierarchy and of a sincere belief in the Catholic
religion.) The Irish character must be considered, therefore, as an unfavourable case: yet, whenever the circumstances of the individual
have been at all favourable, what people have shown greater capacity
for the most varied and multifarious individual eminence? Like the
French compared with the English, the Irish with the Swiss, the Greeks
or Italians compared with the German races, so women compared with
men may be found, on the average, to do the same things with some
variety in the particular kind of excellence. But, that they would do
them fully as well on the whole, if their education and cultivation
were adapted to correcting instead of aggravating the infirmities incident to their temperament, I see not the smallest reason to doubt.

Supposing it, however, to be true that women's minds are by nature
more mobile than those of men, less capable of persisting long in the
same continuous effort, more fitted for dividing their faculties among
many things than for travelling in any one path to the highest point

which can be reached by it: this may be true of women as they now are (though not without great and numerous exceptions), and may account for their having remained behind the highest order of men in precisely the things in which this absorption of the whole mind in one set of ideas and occupations may seem to be most requisite. Still, this difference is one which can only affect the kind of excellence, not the excellence itself, or its practical worth: and it remains to be shown whether this exclusive working of a part of the mind, this absorption of the whole thinking faculty in a single subject, and concentration of it on a single work, is the normal and healthful condition of the human faculties, even for speculative uses. I believe that what is gained in special development by this concentration, is lost in the capacity of the mind for the other purposes of life; and even in abstract thought, it is my decided opinion that the mind does more by frequently returning to a difficult problem, than by sticking to it without interruption. For the purposes, at all events, of practice, from its highest to its humblest departments, the capacity of passing promptly from one subject of consideration to another, without letting the active spring of the intellect run down between the two, is a power far more valuable; and this power women pre-eminently possess, by virtue of the very mobility of which they are accused. They perhaps have it from nature, but they certainly have it by training and education; for nearly the whole of the occupations of women consist in the management of small but multitudinous details, on each of which the mind cannot dwell even for a minute, but must pass on to other things, and if anything requires longer thought, must steal time at odd moments for thinking of it. The capacity indeed which women show for doing their thinking in circumstances and at times which almost any man would make an excuse to himself for not attempting it, has often been noticed: and a woman's mind, though it may be occupied only with small things, can hardly ever permit itself to be vacant, as a man's so often is when not engaged in what he chooses to consider the business of his life. The business of a woman's ordinary life is things in general, and can as little cease to go on as the world to go round.

But (it is said) there is anatomical evidence of the superior mental capacity of men compared with women: they have a larger brain. I reply, that in the first place the fact itself is doubtful. It is by no means established that the brain of a woman is smaller than that of a man. If it is inferred merely because a woman's bodily frame generally is of less dimensions than a man's, this criterion would lead to strange consequences. A tall and large-boned man must on this showing be wonderfully superior in intelligence to a small man, and an elephant or a whale must prodigiously excel mankind. The size of the brain in human beings, anatomists say, varies much less than the size of the body, or even of the head, and the one cannot be at all inferred from the other. It is certain that some women have as large a brain as any man. It is within my knowledge that a man who had weighed many human brains, said that the heaviest he knew of, heavier even than Cuvier's (the heaviest previously recorded,) was that of a woman. Next, I must observe that the precise relation which exists between the brain and the intellectual powers is not yet well understood, but is a subject of great dispute. That there is a very close relation we cannot doubt. The brain is certainly the material organ of thought and feeling: and (making abstraction of the great unsettled controversy respecting the appropriation of different parts of the brain to different mental faculties) I admit that it would be an anomaly, and an exception to all we know of the general laws of life and organization, if the size of the organ were wholly indifferent to the function; if no accession of power were derived from the greater magnitude of the instrument. But the exception and the anomaly would be fully as great if the organ exercised influence by its magnitude *only*. In all the more delicate operations of nature—of which those of the animated creation are the most delicate, and those of the nervous system by far the most delicate of these—differences in the effect depend as much on differences of quality in the physical agents, as on their quantity: and if the quality of an instrument is to be tested by the nicety and delicacy of the work it can do, the indications point to a greater average fineness of quality in the brain and nervous system of women than of men. Dismissing abstract difference of quality, a thing difficult to verify, the efficiency of an organ is known to depend not solely on its size but on its activity: and of this we have an approximate measure in the energy with which the blood circulates through it, both the stimulus and the reparative force being mainly dependent on the circulation. It would not be surprising—it is indeed an hypothesis which accords well with the differences actually observed between the mental operations of the two sexes—if men on the average should have the advantage in the size of the brain, and women in activity of cerebral circulation. The results which conjecture, founded on analogy, would lead us to expect from this difference of organization, would correspond to some of those which we most commonly see. In the first place, the mental operations of men might be expected to be slower. They would neither be so prompt as women in thinking, nor so quick to feel. Large bodies take more time to get into full action. On the other hand, when once got thoroughly into play, men's brain would bear more work. It would be more persistent in the line first taken; it would have more difficulty in changing from one mode of action to another, but, in the one thing it was doing, it could go on longer without loss of power or sense of fatigue. And do we not find that the things in which men most excel women are those which require most plodding and long hammering at a single thought, while women do best what must be done rapidly? A woman's brain is sooner fatigued, sooner exhausted; but given the degree of exhaustion, we should expect to find that it would recover itself sooner. I repeat that this speculation is entirely hypothetical; it pretends to no more than to suggest a line of enquiry. I have before repudiated the notion of its being yet certainly known that there is any natural difference at all in the average strength or direction of the mental capacities of the two sexes, much less what that difference is. Nor is it possible that this should be known, so long as the psychological laws of the formation of character have been so little studied, even in a general way, and in the particular case never scientifically applied at all; so long as the most obvious external causes of difference of character are habitually disregarded—left unnoticed by the observer, and looked down upon with a kind of supercilious contempt by the prevalent schools both of natural history and of mental philosophy: who, whether they look for the source of what mainly distinguishes human beings from one another, in the world of matter or in that of spirit, agree in running down those who prefer to explain these differences by the different relations of human beings to society and life.

To so ridiculous an extent are the notions formed of the nature of women, mere empirical generalizations, framed, without philosophy or analysis, upon the first instances which present themselves, that the popular idea of it is different in different countries, according as the opinions and social circumstances of the country have given to the women living in it any speciality of development or non-development. An Oriental thinks that women are by nature peculiarly voluptuous; see the violent abuse of them on this ground in Hindu writings. An Englishman usually thinks that they are by nature cold. The sayings about women's fickleness are mostly of French origin; from the famous district of Francis the First, upward and downward. In England it is a common remark, how much more constant women are than men. Inconstancy has been longer reckoned discreditable to a woman, in England than in France; and Englishwomen are besides, in their inmost nature, much more subdued to opinion. It may be remarked by the way, that Englishmen are in peculiarly unfavourable circumstances for attempting to judge what is or is not natural, not merely to women, but to men, or to human beings altogether, at least if they have only English experience to go upon: because there is no place where human nature shows so little of its original lineaments. Both in a good and a bad sense, the English are farther from a state of nature than any other modern people. They are, more than any other people, a product of civilization and discipline. England is the country in which social discipline has most succeeded, not so much in conquering, as in suppressing, whatever is liable to conflict with it. The English, more than any other people, not only act but feel according to rule. In other countries, the taught opinion, or the requirement of society, may be the stronger power, but the promptings of the individual nature are always visible under it, and often resisting it: rule may be stronger than nature, but nature is still there. In England, rule has to a great degree substituted itself for nature.

The greater part of life is carried on, not by following inclination under the control of rule, but by having no inclination but that of following a rule. Now this has its good side doubtless, though it has also a wretchedly bad one; but it must render an Englishman peculiarly ill-qualified to pass a judgment on the original tendencies of human nature from his own experience. The errors to which observers elsewhere are liable on the subject, are of a different character. An Englishman is ignorant respecting human nature, a Frenchman is prejudiced. An Englishman's errors are negative, a Frenchman's positive. An Englishman fancies that things do not exist, because he never sees them; a Frenchman thinks they must always and necessarily exist, because he does see them. An Englishman does not know nature, because he has had no opportunity of observing it; a Frenchman generally knows a great deal of it, but often mistakes it, because he has only seen it sophisticated and distorted. For the artificial state superinduced by society disguises the natural tendencies of the thing which is the subject of observation, in two different ways: by extinguishing the nature, or by transforming it. In the one case there is but a starved residuum of nature remaining to be studied; in the other case there is much, but it may have expanded in any direction rather than that in which it would spontaneously grow.

I have said that it cannot now be known how much of the existing mental differences between men and women is natural, and how much artificial; whether there are any natural differences at all; or, supposing all artificial causes of difference to be withdrawn, what natural character would be revealed. I am not about to attempt what I have pronounced impossible: but doubt does not forbid conjecture, and where certainty is unattainable, there may yet be the means of arriving at some degree of probability. The first point, the origin of the differences actually observed, is the one most accessible to speculation; and I shall attempt to approach it, by the only path by which it can be reached; by tracing the mental consequences of external influences. We cannot isolate a human being from the circumstances of his condition, so as to ascertain experimentally what he would have been by nature; but we can consider what he is, and what his circumstances have been, and whether the one would have been capable of producing the other.

Let us take, then, the only marked case which observation affords, of apparent inferiority of women to men, if we except the merely physical one of bodily strength. No production in philosophy, science, or art, entitled to the first rank, has been the work of a woman. Is there any mode of accounting for this, without supposing that women are naturally incapable of producing them?

In the first place, we may fairly question whether experience has afforded sufficient grounds for an induction. It is scarcely three generations since women, saving very rare exceptions, have begun to try their capacity in philosophy, science, or art. It is only in the present generation that their attempts have been at all numerous; and they are even now extremely few, everywhere but in England and France. It is a relevant question, whether a mind possessing the requisites of first-rate eminence in speculation or creative art could have been expected, on the mere calculation of chances, to turn up during that lapse of time, among the women whose tastes and personal position admitted of their devoting themselves to these pursuits. In all things which there has yet been time for—in all but the very highest grades in the scale of excellence, especially in the department in which they have been longest engaged, literature (both prose and poetry)—women have done quite as much, have obtained fully as high prizes and as many of them, as could be expected from the length of time and the number of competitors. If we go back to the earlier period when very few women made the attempt, yet some of those few made it with distinguished success. The Greek always accounted Sappho among their great poets; and we may well suppose that Myrtis, said to have been the teacher of Pindar, and Corinna, who five times bore away from him the prize of poetry, must at least have had sufficient merit to admit of being compared with that great name. Aspasia did not leave any philosophical writings; but it is an admitted fact that Socrates resorted to her for instruction, and avowed himself to have obtained it.

If we consider the works of women in modern times, and contrast them with those of men, either in the literary or the artistic department, such inferiority as may be observed resolves itself essentially into one thing: but that is a most material one; deficiency of originality. Not total deficiency; for every production of mind which is of any substantive value, has an originality of its own—is a conception of the mind itself, not a copy of something else. Thoughts original, in the sense of being unborrowed—of being derived from the thinker's own observations or intellectual processes—are abundant in the writings of women. But they have not yet produced any of those great and luminous new ideas which form an era in thought, nor those fundamentally new conceptions in art, which open a vista of possible effects not before thought of, and found a new school. Their compositions are mostly grounded on the existing fund of thought, and their creations do not deviate widely from existing types. This is the sort of inferiority which their works manifest: for in point of execution, in the detailed application of thought, and the perfection of style, there is no inferiority. Our best novelists in point of composition, and of the management of detail, have mostly been women; and there is not in all modern literature a more eloquent vehicle of thought than the style of Madame de Stael, nor, as a specimen of purely artistic excellence, anything superior to the prose of Madame Sand, whose style acts upon the nervous system like a symphony of Haydn or Mozart. High originality of conception is, as I have said, what is chiefly wanting. And now to examine if there is any manner in which this deficiency can be accounted for.

Let us remember, then, so far as regards mere thought, that during all that period in the world's existence, and in the progress of cultivation, in which great and fruitful new truths could be arrived at by mere force of genius, with little previous study and accumulation of knowledge—during all that time women did not concern themselves with speculation at all. From the days of Hypatia to those of the Reformation, the illustrious Heloisa is almost the only woman to whom any such achievement might have been possible; and we know not how great a capacity of speculation in her may have been lost to mankind by the misfortunes of her life. Never since any considerable number of women have began to cultivate serious thought, has originality been possible on easy terms. Nearly all the thoughts which can be reached by mere strength of original faculties, have long since been arrived at; and originality, in any high sense of the word, is now scarcely ever attained but by minds which have undergone elaborate discipline, and are deeply versed in the results of previous thinking. It is Mr. Maurice, I think, who has remarked on the present age, that its most original thinkers are those who have known most thoroughly what had been thought by their predecessors: and this will always henceforth be the case. Every fresh stone in the edifice has now to be placed on the top of so many others, that a long process of climbing, and of carrying up materials, has to be gone through by whoever aspires to take a share in the present stage of the work. How many women are there who have gone through any such process? Mrs. Somerville, alone perhaps of women, knows as much of mathematics as is now needful for making any considerable mathematical discovery: is it any proof of inferiority in women, that she has not happened to be one of the two or three persons who in her lifetime have associated their names with some striking advancement of the science? Two women, since political economy has been made a science, have known enough of it to write usefully on the subject: of how many of the innumerable men who have written on it during the same time, is it possible with truth to say more? If no woman has hitherto been a great historian, what woman has had the necessary erudition? If no woman is a great philologist, what woman has studied Sanscrit and Slavonic, the Gothic of Ulphila and the Persic of the Zendavesta? Even in practical matters we all know what is the value of the originality of untaught geniuses. It means, inventing over again in its rudimentary form something already invented and improved upon by many successive inventors. When women have had the preparation which all men now require to be eminently original, it will be time enough to begin judging by experience of their capacity for originality.

It no doubt often happens that a person, who has not widely and accurately studied the thoughts of others on a subject, has by natural sagacity a happy intuition, which he can suggest, but cannot prove, which yet when matured may be an important addition to knowledge: but even then, no justice can be done to it until some other person, who does possess the previous acquirements, takes it in hand, tests it, gives it a scientific or practical form, and fits it into its place among the existing truths of philosophy or science. Is it supposed that such felicitous thoughts do not occur to women? They occur by hundreds to every woman of intellect. But they are mostly lost, for want of a husband or friend who has the other knowledge which can enable him to estimate them properly and bring them before the world: and even when they are brought before it, they generally appear as his ideas, not their real author's. Who can tell how many of the most original thoughts put forth by male writers, belong to a woman by suggestion, to themselves only by verifying and working out? If I may judge by my own case, a very large proportion indeed.

If we turn from pure speculation to literature in the narrow sense of the term, and the fine arts, there is a very obvious reason why women's literature is, in its general conception and in its main features, an imitation of men's. Why is the Roman literature, as critics proclaim to satiety, not original, but an imitation of the Greek? Simply because the Greeks came first. If women lived in a different country from men, and had never read any of their writings, they would have had a literature of their own. As it is, they have not created one, because they found a highly advanced literature already created. If there had been no suspension of the knowledge of antiquity, or if the Renaissance had occurred before the Gothic cathedrals were built, they never would have been built. We see that, in France and Italy, imitation of the ancient literature stopped the original development even after it had commenced. All women who write are pupils of the great male writers. A painter's early pictures, even if he be a Raffaelle, are undistinguishable in style from those of his master. Even a Mozart does not display his powerful originality in his earliest pieces. What years are to a gifted individual, generations are to a mass. If women's literature is destined to have a different collective character from that of men, depending on any difference of natural tendencies, much longer time is necessary than has yet elapsed, before it can emancipate itself from the influence of accepted models, and guide itself by its own impulses. But if, as I believe, there will not prove to be any natural tendencies common to women, and distinguishing their genius from that of men, yet every individual writer among them has her individual tendencies, which at present are still subdued by the influence of precedent and example: and it will require generations more, before their individuality is sufficiently developed to make head against that influence.

It is in the fine arts, properly so called, that the *primâ facie* evidence of inferior original powers in women at first sight appears the strongest: since opinion (it may be said) does not exclude them from these, but rather encourages them, and their education, instead of passing over this department, is in the affluent classes mainly composed of it. Yet in this line of exertion they have fallen still more short than in many others, of the highest eminence attained by men. This shortcoming, however, needs no other explanation than the familiar fact, more universally true in the fine arts than in anything else; the vast superiority of professional persons over amateurs. Women in the educated classes are almost universally taught more or less of some branch or other of the fine arts, but not that they may gain their living or their social consequence by it. Women artists are all amateurs. The exceptions are only of the kind which confirm the general truth. Women are taught music, but not for the purpose of composing, only of executing it: and accordingly it is only as composers, that men, in music, are superior to women. The only one of the fine arts which women do follow, to any extent, as a profession, and an occupation for life, is the histrionic; and in that they are confessedly equal, if not superior, to men. To make the comparison fair, it should be made between the productions of women in any branch of art, and those of men not following it as a profession. In musical composition, for example, women surely have produced fully as good things as have ever been produced by male amateurs. There are now a few women, a very few, who practice painting as a profession, and these are already beginning to show quite as much talent as could be expected. Even male painters (*pace* Mr. Ruskin) have not made any very remarkable figure these last centuries, and it will be long before they do so. The reason why the old painters were so greatly superior to the modern, is that a greatly superior class of men applied themselves to the art. In the fourteenth and fifteenth centuries the Italian painters were the most accomplished men of their age. The greatest of them were men of encyclopædical acquirements and powers, like the great men of Greece. But in their times fine art was, to men's feelings and conceptions, among the grandest things in which a human being could excel; and by it men were made, what only political or military distinction now makes them, the companions of sovereigns, and the equals of the highest nobility. In the present age, men of anything like similar calibre find something more important to do, for their own fame and the uses of the modern world, than painting: and it is only now and then that a Reynolds or a Turner (of whose relative rank among eminent men I do not pretend to an opinion) applies himself to that art. Music belongs to a different order of things; it does not require the same general powers of mind, but seems more dependant on a natural gift: and it may be thought surprising that no one of the great musical composers has been a woman. But even this natural gift, to be made available for great creations, requires study, and professional devotion to the pursuit. The only countries which have produced first-rate composers, even of the male sex, are Germany and Italy—countries in which, both in point of special and of general cultivation, women have remained far behind France and England, being generally (it may be said without exaggeration) very little educated, and having scarcely cultivated at all any of the higher faculties of mind. And in those countries the men who are acquainted with the principles of musical composition must be counted by hundreds, or more probably by thousands, the women barely by scores: so that here again, on the doctrine of averages, we cannot reasonably expect to see more than one eminent woman to fifty eminent men; and the last three centuries have not produced fifty eminent male composers either in Germany or in Italy.

There are other reasons, besides those which we have now given, that help to explain why women remain behind men, even in the pursuits which are open to both. For one thing, very few women have time for them. This may seem a paradox; it is an undoubted social fact. The time and thoughts of every woman have to satisfy great previous demands on them for things practical. There is, first, the superintendence of the family and the domestic expenditure, which occupies at least one woman in every family, generally the one of mature years and acquired experience; unless the family is so rich as to admit of delegating that task to hired agency, and submitting to all the waste and malversation inseparable from that mode of conducting it. The superintendence of a household, even when not in other respects laborious, is extremely onerous to the thoughts; it requires incessant vigilance, an eye which no detail escapes, and presents questions for consideration and solution, foreseen and unforeseen, at every hour of the day, from which the person responsible for them can hardly ever shake herself free. If a woman is of a rank and circumstances which relieve her in a measure from these cares, she has still devolving on her the management for the whole family of its intercourse with others—of what is called society, and the less the call made on her by the former duty, the greater is always the development of the latter: the dinner parties, concerts, evening parties, morning visits, letter writing, and all that goes with them. All this is over and above the engrossing duty which society imposes exclusively on women, of making themselves charming. A clever woman of the higher ranks finds nearly a sufficient employment of her talents in cultivating the graces of manner and the arts of conversation. To look only at the outward side of the subject: the great and continual exercise of thought which all women who attach any value to dressing well (I do not mean expensively, but with taste, and perception of natural and of artificial *convenance*) must bestow upon their own dress, perhaps also upon that of their daughters, would alone go a great way towards achieving respectable results in art, or science, or literature, and does actually exhaust much of the time and mental power they might have to spare for either.[2] If it were possible that all

---

[2] "It appears to be the same turn of mind which enables a man to acquire the *truth*, or the just idea of what is right, in the ornaments, as in the more stable principles of art. It has still the same centre of perfection, though it is the centre of a smaller circle.—To illustrate this by the fashion of dress, in which there is allowed

this number of little practical interests (which are made great to them) should leave them either much leisure, or much energy and freedom of mind, to be devoted to art or speculation, they must have a much greater original supply of active faculty than the vast majority of men. But this is not all. Independently of the regular offices of life which devolve upon a woman, she is expected to have her time and faculties always at the disposal of everybody. If a man has not a profession to exempt him from such demands, still, if he has a pursuit, he offends nobody by devoting his time to it; occupation is received as a valid excuse for his not answering to every casual demand which may be made on him. Are a woman's occupations, especially her chosen and voluntary ones, ever regarded as excusing her from any of what are termed the calls of society? Scarcely are her most necessary and recognised duties allowed as an exemption. It requires an illness in the family, or something else out of the common way, to entitle her to give her own business the precedence over other people's amusement. She must always be at the beck and call of somebody, generally of everybody. If she has a study or a pursuit, she must snatch any short interval which accidentally occurs to be employed in it. A celebrated woman, in a work which I hope will some day be published, remarks truly that everything a woman does is done at odd times. Is it wonderful, then, if she does not attain the highest eminence in things which require consecutive attention, and the concentration on them of the chief interest of life? Such is philosophy, and such, above all, is art, in which, besides the devotion of the thoughts and feelings, the hand also must be kept in constant exercise to attain high skill.

There is another consideration to be added to all these. In the various arts and intellectual occupations, there is a degree of proficiency sufficient for living by it, and there is a higher degree on which depend the great productions which immortalize a name. To the attainment of the former, there are adequate motives in the case of all who follow the pursuit professionally: the other is hardly ever attained where there is not, or where there has not been at some period of life, an ardent desire of celebrity. Nothing less is commonly a sufficient stimulus to undergo the long and patient drudgery, which, in the case even of the greatest natural gifts, is absolutely required for great eminence in pursuits in which we already possess so many splendid memorials of the highest

---

to be a good or bad taste. The component parts of dress are continually changing from great to little, from short to long; but the general form still remains: it is still the same general dress which is comparatively fixed, though on a very slender foundation; but it is on this which fashion must rest. He who invents with the most success, or dresses in the best taste, would probably, from the same sagacity employed to greater purposes, have discovered equal skill, or have formed the same correct taste, in the highest labours of art."—*Sir Joshua Reynolds' Discourses*, Disc. vii.

genius. Now, whether the cause be natural or artificial, women seldom have this eagerness for fame. Their ambition is generally confined within narrower bounds. The influence they seek is over those who immediately surround them. Their desire is to be liked, loved, or admired, by those whom they see with their eyes: and the proficiency in knowledge, arts, and accomplishments, which is sufficient for that, almost always contents them. This is a trait of character which cannot be left out of the account in judging of women as they are. I do not at all believe that it is inherent in women. It is only the natural result of their circumstances. The love of fame in men is encouraged by education and opinion: to "scorn delights and live laborious days" for its sake, is accounted the part of "noble minds," even if spoken of as their "last infirmity," and is stimulated by the access which fame gives to all objects of ambition, including even the favour of women; while to women themselves all these objects are closed, and the desire of fame itself considered daring and unfeminine. Besides, how could it be that a woman's interests should not be all concentrated upon the impressions made on those who come into her daily life, when society has ordained that all her duties should be to them, and has contrived that all her comforts should depend on them? The natural desire of consideration from our fellow creatures is as strong in a woman as in a man; but society has so ordered things that public consideration is, in all ordinary cases, only attainable by her through the consideration of her husband or of her male relations, while her private consideration is forfeited by making herself individually prominent, or appearing in any other character than that of an appendage to men. Whoever is in the least capable of estimating the influence on the mind of the entire domestic and social position and the whole habit of a life, must easily recognise in that influence a complete explanation of nearly all the apparent differences between women and men, including the whole of those which imply any inferiority.

As for moral differences, considered as distinguished from intellectual, the distinction commonly drawn is to the advantage of women. They are declared to be better than men; an empty compliment, which must provoke a bitter smile from every· woman of spirit, since there is no other situation in life in which it is the established order, and considered quite natural and suitable, that the better should obey the worse. If this piece of idle talk is good for anything, it is only as an admission by men, of the corrupting influence of power; for that is certainly the only truth which the fact, if it be a fact, either proves or illustrates. And it *is* true that servitude, except when it actually brutalizes, though corrupting to both, is less so to the slaves than to the slave-masters. It is wholesomer for the moral nature to be restrained, even by arbitrary power, than to be allowed to exercise arbitrary power without restraint. Women, it is said, seldomer fall under the penal law—contribute a much smaller number of offenders to the criminal calendar, than men. I doubt not that the same thing may be said, with the same truth, of Negro slaves. Those who are under the control of others cannot often commit crimes, unless at the command and for the purposes of their masters. I do not know a more signal instance of the blindness with which the world, including the herd of studious men, ignore and pass over all the influences of social circumstances, than their silly depreciation of the intellectual, and silly panegyrics on the moral, nature of women.

The complimentary dictum about women's superior moral goodness may be allowed to pair off with the disparaging one respecting their greater liability to moral bias. Women, we are told, are not capable of resisting their personal partialities: their judgment in grave affairs is warped by their sympathies and antipathies. Assuming it to be so, it is still to be proved that women are oftener misled by their personal feelings than men by their personal interests. The chief difference would seem in that case to be, that men are led from the course of duty and the public interest by their regard for themselves, women (not being allowed to have private interests of their own) by their regard for somebody else. It is also to be considered, that all the education which women receive from society inculcates on them the feeling that the individuals connected with them are the only ones to whom they owe any duty—the only ones whose interest they are called upon to care for; while, as far as education is concerned, they are left strangers even to the elementary ideas which are presupposed in any intelligent regard for larger interests or higher moral objects. The complaint against them resolves itself merely into this, that they fulfil only too faithfully the sole duty which they are taught, and almost the only one which they are permitted to practice.

The concessions of the privileged to the unprivileged are so seldom brought about by any better motive than the power of the unprivileged to extort them, that any arguments against the prerogative of sex are likely to be little attended to by the generality, as long as they are able to say to themselves that women do not complain of it. That fact certainly enables men to retain the unjust privilege some time longer; but does not render it less unjust. Exactly the same thing may be said of the women in the harem of an Oriental: they do not complain of not being allowed the freedom of European women. They think our women insufferably bold and unfeminine. How rarely it is that even men complain of the general order of society; and how much rarer still would such complaint be, if they did not know of any different order existing anywhere else. Women do not complain of the general lot of women; or rather they do, for plaintive elegies on it are very common in the writings of women, and were still more so as long as the lamentations could not be suspected of having any practical object. Their complaints are like the complaints which men make of the general unsatisfactoriness of human life; they are not meant to imply blame, or to plead for any change. But though women do not complain of the power of husbands, each complains of her own husband, or of the husbands of her friends. It is the same in all other cases of servitude, at least in the commencement of the emancipatory movement. The serfs did not at first complain of the power of their lords, but only of their tyranny. The Commons began by claiming a few municipal privileges; they next asked an exemption for themselves from being taxed without their own consent; but they would at that time have thought it a great presumption to claim any share in the king's sovereign authority. The case of women is now the only case in which to rebel against established rules is still looked upon with the same eyes as was formerly a subject's claim to the right of rebelling against his king. A woman who joins in any movement which her husband disapproves, makes herself a martyr, without even being able to be an apostle, for the husband can legally put a stop to her apostleship. Women cannot be expected to devote themselves to the emancipation of women, until men in considerable number are prepared to join with them in the undertaking.

QUESTIONS

1. On what grounds does John Stuart Mill base his arguments for women's suffrage?

2. Analyze the persuasive techniques Mill employs in this essay. Discuss how he uses the arguments of the antifeminists in his criticism of this group and how he supports the logic of his own viewpoints.

3. How does Mill explain the failure of women to equal masculine achievements in art, science, and philosophy?

4. Does Mill believe that any of the differences between men and women are innate?

5. Many of the reforms to which Mill refers, such as women's suffrage and the right of married women to own property, have long since been put into effect, and many of the scientific disputes he mentions have been resolved. Which aspects of Mill's defense still seem relevant? In the context of today's society, do any of his ideas seem radical?

part 2
LITERATURE BY AND ABOUT WOMEN

Henrik Ibsen

Henrik Ibsen (1828–1906) is thought of as the father of modern dramatic realism. In a series of revolutionary plays, which included A Doll's House *(1879), Ibsen explored the religious, social, and political controversies of his century, even dealing with the forbidden subjects of incest, venereal disease, and mercy killing.*

Although A Doll's House *may no longer seem scandalous, its final act—Nora's famous departure from her husband—created a sensation when it was first produced, and there were many actresses who refused to play the part of a woman who deserts her husband and children. Ibsen was as much protesting the corrupted ideal of marriage as the subjection of women, and he conceived of the play not simply as a dramatization of feminist ideology, but as "the modern tragedy." In his notes for* A Doll's House, *Ibsen wrote:*

> *There are two kinds of spiritual law, two kinds of conscience, one in man, and another, altogether different, in woman. They do not understand each other; but in practical life the woman is judged by man's law, as though she were not a woman but a man.*
>
> *The wife in the play ends by having no idea of what is right or wrong; natural feeling on the one hand and belief in authority on the other have altogether bewildered her.*
>
> *A woman cannot be herself in the society of the present day, which is an exclusively masculine society, with laws framed by men and with a judicial system that judges feminine conduct from a masculine point of view.*

There has been a great deal of critical debate over the extent of Ibsen's feminism, and some critics, in their efforts to exonerate him, have gone so far as to claim that the play was meant to expose female hypocrisy. Ibsen refused to commit himself politically on the question of women's rights, but during the twenty-seven years he spent in Europe, in voluntary exile from his native Norway, he had many contacts with the ideas and the leaders of the feminist movement. One tradition holds that Laura Kieler, an unhappily married girl with whom Ibsen sympathized, was the model for Nora.

However Ibsen felt about female emancipation, there is no question that Nora Helmer is the most famous feminist in literature.

A Doll's House

CHARACTERS

TORVALD HELMER
NORA, his wife
DOCTOR RANK
MRS. LINDEN
NILS KROGSTAD
THE HELMERS' THREE CHILDREN
ANNA, their nurse
ELLEN, a maid
A PORTER

The action passes in Helmer's flat in Christiania

ACT I

A room, comfortably and tastefully, but not expensively, furnished. In the rear, on the right, a door leads to the hall; on the left another door leads to HELMER's study. Between the two doors a piano. In the middle of the left wall a door, and nearer the front a window. Near the window a round table with armchairs and a small sofa. In the right wall, somewhat to the rear, a door, and against the same wall, farther forward, a porcelain stove; in front of it a couple of armchairs and a rocking-chair. Between the stove and the side-door a small table. Engravings on the walls. A whatnot with china and bric-à-brac. A small bookcase filled with handsomely bound books. Carpet. A fire in the stove. It is a winter day.

A bell rings in the hall outside. Presently the outer door of the flat is heard to open. Then NORA enters, humming gaily. She is in outdoor dress, and carries several parcels, which she lays on the right-hand table. She leaves the door into the hall open, and a PORTER is seen outside, carrying a Christmas-tree and a basket, which he gives to the MAID-SERVANT who has opened the door.

NORA   Hide the Christmas-tree carefully, Ellen; the children must on no account see it before this evening, when it's lighted up. (*To the* PORTER, *taking out her purse*) How much?

PORTER   Fifty öre.

NORA   There is a crown. No, keep the change.

[*The* PORTER *thanks her and goes.* NORA *shuts the door. She continues smiling in quiet glee as she takes off her outdoor things. Taking from her pocket a bag of macaroons, she eats one or two. Then she goes on tiptoe to her husband's door and listens.*]

NORA   Yes; he is at home.

[*She begins humming again, crossing to the table on the right.*]

HELMER   (*in his room*) Is that my lark twittering there?

NORA   (*busy opening some of her parcels*) Yes, it is.

HELMER   Is it the squirrel frisking around?

NORA   Yes!

HELMER   When did the squirrel get home?

NORA   Just this minute. (*Hides the bag of macaroons in her pocket and wipes her mouth.*) Come here, Torvald, and see what I've been buying.

HELMER   Don't interrupt me. (*A little later he opens the door and looks in, pen in hand.*) Buying, did you say? What! All that? Has my little spendthrift been making the money fly again?

NORA   Why, Torvald, surely we can afford to launch out a little now. It's the first Christmas we haven't had to pinch.

HELMER   Come, come; we can't afford to squander money.

NORA   Oh, yes, Torvald, do let us squander a little, now—just the least little bit! You know you'll soon be earning heaps of money.

HELMER   Yes, from New Year's Day. But there's a whole quarter before my first salary is due.

NORA   Never mind; we can borrow in the meantime.

HELMER   Nora! (*He goes up to her and takes her playfully by the ear.*) Still my little featherbrain! Supposing I borrowed a thousand crowns today, and you made ducks and drakes of them during Christmas week, and then on New Year's Eve a tile blew off the roof and knocked my brains out—

NORA   (*laying her hand on his mouth*) Hush! How can you talk so horridly?

HELMER   But supposing it were to happen—what then?

NORA   If anything so dreadful happened, it would be all the same to me whether I was in debt or not.

HELMER   But what about the creditors?

NORA   They! Who cares for them? They're only strangers.

HELMER   Nora, Nora! What a *woman* you are! But seriously, Nora, you know my principles on these points. No debts! No borrowing!

Home life ceases to be free and beautiful as soon as it is founded on borrowing and debt. We two have held out bravely till now, and we are not going to give in at the last.

NORA   (*going to the fireplace*) Very well—as you please, Torvald.

HELMER   (*following her*) Come, come; my little lark mustn't droop her wings like that. What? Is my squirrel in the sulks? (*Takes out his purse.*) Nora, what do you think I have here?

NORA   (*turning round quickly*) Money!

HELMER   There! (*Gives her some notes.*) Of course I know all sorts of things are wanted at Christmas.

NORA   (*counting*) Ten, twenty, thirty, forty. Oh, thank you, thank you, Torvald! This will go a long way.

HELMER   I should hope so.

NORA   Yes, indeed; a long way! But come here, and let me show you all I've been buying. And so cheap! Look, here's a new suit for Ivar, and a little sword. Here are a horse and a trumpet for Bob. And here are a doll and a cradle for Emmy. They're only common; but they're good enough for her to pull to pieces. And dress-stuffs and handkerchiefs for the servants. I ought to have got something better for old Anna.

HELMER   And what's in that other parcel?

NORA   (*crying out*) No, Torvald, you're not to see that until this evening!

HELMER   Oh! Ah! But now tell me, you little spendthrift, have you thought of anything for yourself?

NORA   For myself! Oh, I don't want anything.

HELMER   Nonsense! Just tell me something sensible you would like to have.

NORA   No, really I don't know of anything—Well, listen, Torvald—

HELMER   Well?

NORA   (*playing with his coat-buttons, without looking him in the face*) If you really want to give me something, you might, you know—you might—

HELMER   Well? Out with it!

NORA   (*quickly*) You might give me money, Torvald. Only just what you think you can spare; then I can buy something with it later on.

HELMER   But, Nora—

NORA   Oh, please do, dear Torvald, please do! I should hang the money in lovely gilt paper on the Christmas-tree. Wouldn't that be fun?

HELMER   What do they call the birds that are always making the money fly?

NORA   Yes, I know—spendthrifts, of course. But please do as I ask you, Torvald. Then I shall have time to think what I want most. Isn't that very sensible, now?

HELMER   (*smiling*) Certainly; that is to say, if you really kept the money I gave you, and really spent it on something for yourself. But it all goes in housekeeping, and for all manner of useless things, and then I have to pay up again.

NORA But, Torvald—

HELMER Can you deny it, Nora dear? (*He puts his arm round her.*) It's a sweet little lark, but it gets through a lot of money. No one would believe how much it costs a man to keep such a little bird as you.

NORA. For shame! How can you say so? Why, I save as much as ever I can.

HELMER (*laughing*) Very true—as much as you can—but that's precisely nothing.

NORA (*hums and smiles with covert glee*) H'm! If you only knew, Torvald, what expenses we larks and squirrels have.

HELMER You're a strange little being! Just like your father—always on the lookout for all the money you can lay your hands on; but the moment you have it, it seems to slip through your fingers, you never know what becomes of it. Well, one must take you as you are. It's in the blood. Yes, Nora, that sort of thing is hereditary.

NORA I wish I had inherited many of papa's qualities.

HELMER And I don't wish you anything but just what you are—my own, sweet little song-bird. But I say—it strikes me you look so—so —what shall I call it—so suspicious today—

NORA Do I?

HELMER You do, indeed. Look me full in the face.

NORA (*looking at him*) Well?

HELMER (*threatening with his finger*) Hasn't the little sweet-tooth been playing pranks today?

NORA No; how can you think such a thing!

HELMER Didn't she just look in at the confectioner's?

NORA No, Torvald; really—

HELMER Not to sip a little jelly?

NORA No; certainly not.

HELMER Hasn't she even nibbled a macaroon or two?

NORA No, Torvald, indeed, indeed!

HELMER Well, well, well; of course I'm only joking.

NORA (*goes to the table on the right*) I shouldn't think of doing what you disapprove of.

HELMER No, I'm sure of that; and, besides, you've given me your word —(*Going towards her.*) Well, keep your little Christmas secrets to yourself, Nora darling. The Christmas-tree will bring them all to light, I dare say.

NORA Have you remembered to invite Doctor Rank?

HELMER No. But it's not necessary; he'll come as a matter of course. Besides, I shall ask him when he looks in today. I've ordered some capital wine. Nora, you can't think how I look forward to this evening.

NORA   And I too. How the children will enjoy themselves, Torvald!

HELMER   Ah, it's glorious to feel that one has an assured position and ample means. Isn't it delightful to think of?

NORA   Oh, it's wonderful!

HELMER   Do you remember last Christmas? For three whole weeks beforehand you shut yourself up every evening till long past midnight to make flowers for the Christmas-tree, and all sorts of other marvels that were to have astonished us. I was never so bored in my life.

NORA   I didn't bore myself at all.

HELMER   (*smiling*) But it came to little enough in the end, Nora.

NORA   Oh, are you going to tease me about that again? How could I help the cat getting in and pulling it all to pieces?

HELMER   To be sure you couldn't, my poor little Nora. You did your best to give us all pleasure, and that's the main point. But, all the same, it's a good thing the hard times are over.

NORA   Oh, isn't it wonderful?

HELMER   Now I needn't sit here boring myself all alone; and you needn't tire your blessed eyes and your delicate little fingers—

NORA   (*clapping her hands*) No, I needn't, need I, Torvald? Oh, how wonderful it is to think of! (*Takes his arm.*) And now I'll tell you how I think we ought to manage, Torvald. As soon as Christmas is over—(*The hall doorbell rings.*) Oh, there's a ring! (*Arranging the room.*) That's somebody come to call. How tiresome!

HELMER   I'm "not at home" to callers; remember that.

ELLEN   (*in the doorway*) A lady to see you, ma'am.

NORA   Show her in.

ELLEN   (*to* HELMER) And the doctor has just come, sir.

HELMER   Has he gone into my study?

ELLEN   Yes, sir.

[HELMER *goes into his study.* ELLEN *ushers in* MRS. LINDEN, *in traveling costume, and goes out, closing the door.*]

MRS. LINDEN   (*embarrassed and hesitating*) How do you do, Nora?

NORA   (*doubtfully*) How do you do?

MRS. LINDEN   I see you don't recognize me.

NORA   No, I don't think—oh, yes!—I believe (*Suddenly brightening.*) What, Christina! Is it really you?

MRS. LINDEN   Yes; really I!

NORA   Christina! And to think I didn't know you! But how could I— (*More softly.*) How changed you are, Christina!

MRS. LINDEN   Yes, no doubt. In nine or ten years—

NORA   Is it really so long since we met? Yes, so it is. Oh, the last eight years have been a happy time, I can tell you. And now you have come to town? All that long journey in midwinter! How brave of you!

MRS. LINDEN   I arrived by this morning's steamer.

NORA   To have a merry Christmas, of course. Oh, how delightful! Yes, we *will* have a merry Christmas. Do take your things off. Aren't you frozen? (*Helping her.*) There; now we'll sit cozily by the fire. No, you take the armchair; I shall sit in this rocking-chair. (*Seizes her hands.*) Yes, now I can see the dear old face again. It was only at the first glance—But you're a little paler, Christina—and perhaps a little thinner.

MRS. LINDEN   And much, much older, Nora.

NORA   Yes, perhaps a little older—not much—ever so little. (*She suddenly checks herself; seriously.*) Oh, what a thoughtless wretch I am! Here I sit chattering on, and—Dear, dear Christina, can you forgive me!

MRS. LINDEN   What do you mean, Nora?

NORA   (*softly*) Poor Christina! I forgot: you are a widow.

MRS. LINDEN   Yes; my husband died three years ago.

NORA   I know, I know; I saw it in the papers. Oh, believe me, Christina, I did mean to write to you; but I kept putting it off, and something always came in the way.

MRS. LINDEN   I can quite understand that, Nora dear.

NORA   No, Christina; it was horrid of me. Oh, you poor darling! how much you must have gone through!—And he left you nothing?

MRS. LINDEN   Nothing.

NORA   And no children?

MRS. LINDEN   None.

NORA   Nothing, nothing at all?

MRS. LINDEN   Not even a sorrow or a longing to dwell upon.

NORA   (*looking at her incredulously*) My dear Christina, how is that possible?

MRS. LINDEN   (*smiling sadly and stroking her hair*) Oh, it happens so sometimes, Nora.

NORA   So utterly alone! How dreadful that must be! I have three of the loveliest children. I can't show them to you just now; they're out with their nurse. But now you must tell me everything.

MRS. LINDEN   No, no; I want you to tell me—

NORA   No, you must begin; I won't be egotistical today. Today I'll think only of you. Oh! but I must tell you one thing—perhaps you've heard of our great stroke of fortune?

MRS. LINDEN   No. What is it?

NORA   Only think! my husband has been made manager of the Joint Stock Bank.

MRS. LINDEN   Your husband! Oh, how fortunate!

NORA   Yes; isn't it? A lawyer's position is so uncertain, you see, especially when he won't touch any business that's the least bit—shady, as of course Torvald never would; and there I quite agree with him. Oh, you can imagine how glad we are! He is to enter on his new position at the New Year, and then he'll have a large salary and percentages. In future we shall be able to live quite differently—just as we please, in fact. Oh, Christina, I feel so lighthearted and happy! It's delightful to have lots of money, and no need to worry about things, isn't it?

MRS. LINDEN   Yes; at any rate it must be delightful to have what you need.

NORA   No, not only what you need, but heaps of money—*heaps!*

MRS. LINDEN   (*smiling*) Nora, Nora, haven't you learnt reason yet? In our school days you were a shocking little spendthrift.

NORA   (*quietly smiling*) Yes; that's what Torvald says I am still. (*Holding up her forefinger.*) But "Nora, Nora" is not so silly as you all think. Oh! I haven't had the chance to much of a spendthrift. We have both had to work.

MRS. LINDEN   You too?

NORA   Yes, light fancywork: crochet, and embroidery, and things of that sort; (*carelessly*) and other work too. You know, of course, that Torvald left the Government service when we were married. He had little chance of promotion, and of course he needed to make more money. But in the first year after our marriage he overworked himself terribly. He had to undertake all sorts of extra work, you know, and to slave early and late. He couldn't stand it and fell dangerously ill. Then the doctors declared he must go to the South.

MRS. LINDEN   You spent a whole year in Italy, didn't you?

NORA   Yes, we did. It wasn't easy to manage, I can tell you. It was just after Ivar's birth. But of course we had to go. Oh, it was a wonderful, delicious journey! And it saved Torvald's life. But it cost a frightful lot of money, Christina.

MRS. LINDEN   So I should think.

NORA   Twelve hundred dollars! Four thousand eight hundred crowns! Isn't that a lot of money?

MRS. LINDEN   How lucky you had the money to spend.

NORA   We got it from father, you must know.

MRS. LINDEN   Ah, I see. He died just about that time, didn't he?

NORA   Yes, Christina, just then. And only think! I couldn't go and nurse him! I was expecting little Ivar's birth daily; and then I had my poor sick Torvald to attend to. Dear, kind old father! I never saw him again, Christina. Oh! that's the hardest thing I have had to bear since my marriage.

MRS. LINDEN   I know how fond you were of him. But then you went to Italy?

NORA   Yes; you see, we had the money, and the doctors said we must lose no time. We started a month later.

MRS. LINDEN   And your husband came back completely cured.

NORA   Sound as a bell.

MRS. LINDEN   But—the doctor?

NORA   What do you mean?

MRS. LINDEN   I thought as I came in your servant announced the doctor—

NORA   Oh, yes; Doctor Rank. But he doesn't come professionally. He is our best friend and never lets a day pass without looking in. No, Torvald hasn't had an hour's illness since that time. And the children are so healthy and well, and so am I. (*Jumps up and claps her hands.*) Oh, Christina, Christina, what a wonderful thing it is to live and to be happy!—Oh, but it's really too horrid of me! Here am I talking about nothing but my own concerns. (*Seats herself upon a footstool close to* CHRISTINA, *and lays her arms on her friend's lap.*) Oh, don't be angry with me! Now tell me, is it really true that you didn't love your husband? What made you marry him, then?

MRS. LINDEN   My mother was still alive, you see, bedridden and helpless; and then I had my two younger brothers to think of. I didn't think it would be right for me to refuse him.

NORA   Perhaps it wouldn't have been. I suppose he was rich then?

MRS. LINDEN   Very well off, I believe. But his business was uncertain. It fell to pieces at his death, and there was nothing left.

NORA   And then—?

MRS. LINDEN   Then I had to fight my way by keeping a shop, a little school, anything I could turn my hand to. The last three years have been one long struggle for me. But now it is over, Nora. My poor mother no longer needs me; she is at rest. And the boys are in business and can look after themselves.

NORA   How free your life must feel!

MRS. LINDEN   No, Nora; only inexpressibly empty. No one to live for! (*Stands up restlessly.*) That's why I could not bear to stay any longer in that out-of-the-way corner. Here it must be easier to find something to take one up—to occupy one's thoughts. If I could only get some settled employment—some office work.

NORA   But, Christina, that's such drudgery, and you look worn out already. It would be ever so much better for you to go to some watering-place and rest.

MRS. LINDEN   (*going to the window*) I have no father to give me the money, Nora.

NORA   (*rising*) Oh, don't be vexed with me.

MRS. LINDEN   (*going to her*) My dear Nora, don't you be vexed with me. The worst of a position like mine is that it makes one so bitter. You have no one to work for, yet you have to be always on the strain. You must live; and so you become selfish. When I heard of the happy change in your fortunes—can you believe it?—I was glad for my own sake more than for yours.

NORA   How do you mean? Ah, I see! You think Torvald can perhaps do something for you.

MRS. LINDEN   Yes; I thought so.

NORA   And so he shall, Christina. Just you leave it all to me. I shall lead up to it beautifully!—I shall think of some delightful plan to put him in a good humor! Oh, I should so love to help you.

MRS. LINDEN   How good of you, Nora, to stand by me so warmly! Doubly good in you, who know so little of the troubles and burdens of life.

NORA   I? I know so little of—?

MRS. LINDEN   (*smiling*) Oh well—a little fancywork, and so forth.— You're a child, Nora.

NORA   (*tosses her head and paces the room*) Oh, come, you mustn't be so patronizing!

MRS. LINDEN   No?

NORA   You're like the rest. You all think I'm fit for nothing really serious—

MRS. LINDEN   Well, well—

NORA   You think I've had no troubles in this weary world.

MRS. LINDEN   My dear Nora, you've just told me all your troubles.

NORA   Pooh—those trifles! (*Softly.*) I haven't told you the great thing.

MRS. LINDEN   The great thing? What do you mean?

NORA   I know you look down upon me, Christina; but you have no right to. You are proud of having worked so hard and so long for your mother.

MRS. LINDEN   I am sure I don't look down upon anyone; but it's true I am both proud and glad when I remember that I was able to keep my mother's last days free from care.

NORA   And you're proud to think of what you have done for your brothers, too.

MRS. LINDEN   Have I not the right to be?

NORA   Yes, indeed. But now let me tell you, Christina—I, too, have something to be proud and glad of.

MRS. LINDEN   I don't doubt it. But what do you mean?

NORA   Hush! Not so loud. Only think, if Torvald were to hear! He mustn't—not for worlds! No one must know about it, Christina— no one but you.

MRS. LINDEN   Why, what can it be?

NORA   Come over here. (*Draws her down beside her on the sofa.*) Yes, Christina—I, too, have something to be proud and glad of. I saved Torvald's life.

MRS. LINDEN   Saved his life? How?

NORA   I told you about our going to Italy. Torvald would have died but for that.

MRS. LINDEN   Well—and your father gave you the money.

NORA   (*smiling*) Yes, so Torvald and everyone believes; but—

MRS. LINDEN   But—?

NORA   Papa didn't give us one penny. It was I that found the money.

MRS. LINDEN   You? All that money?

NORA   Twelve hundred dollars. Four thousand eight hundred crowns. What do you say to that?

MRS. LINDEN   My dear Nora, how did you manage it? Did you win it in the lottery?

NORA   (*contemptuously*) In the lottery? Pooh! Anyone could have done *that*!

MRS. LINDEN   Then wherever did you get it from?

NORA   (*hums and smiles mysteriously*) H'm; tra-la-la-la.

MRS. LINDEN   Of course you couldn't borrow it.

NORA   No? Why not?

MRS. LINDEN   Why, a wife can't borrow without her husband's consent.

NORA   (*tossing her head*) Oh! when the wife has some idea of business, and knows how to set about things—

MRS. LINDEN   But, Nora, I don't understand—

NORA   Well, you needn't. I never said I borrowed the money. There are many ways I may have got it. (*Throws herself back on the sofa.*) I may have got it from some admirer. When one is so—attractive as I am—

MRS. LINDEN   You're too silly, Nora.

NORA   Now I'm sure you're dying of curiosity, Christina—

MRS. LINDEN   Listen to me, Nora dear: haven't you been a little rash?

NORA   (*sitting upright again*) Is it rash to save one's husband's life?

MRS. LINDEN   I think it was rash of you, without his knowledge—

NORA   But it would have been fatal for him to know! Can't you understand that? He wasn't even to suspect how ill he was. The doctors came to me privately and told me his life was in danger—that nothing could save him but a winter in the South. Do you think I didn't try diplomacy first? I told him how I longed to have a trip abroad. like other young wives; I wept and prayed; I said he ought to think of my condition, and not to thwart me; and then I hinted that he could borrow the money. But then, Christina, he got almost angry. He said I was frivolous, and that it was his duty as a husband not to yield to my whims and fancies—so he called them. Very well, thought I, but saved you must be; and then I found the way to do it.

MRS. LINDEN   And did your husband never learn from your father that the money was not from him?

NORA   No; never. Papa died at that very time. I meant to have told him all about it, and begged him to say nothing. But he was so ill— unhappily, it wasn't necessary.

MRS. LINDEN   And you have never confessed to your husband?

NORA   Good heavens! What can you be thinking of? *Tell him*, when he has such a loathing of debt! And besides—how painful and humiliating it would be for Torvald, with his manly self-respect, to know that he owed anything to me! It would utterly upset the relation between us; our beautiful, happy home would never again be what it is.

MRS. LINDEN   Will you never tell him?

NORA   (*thoughtfully, half-smiling*) Yes, sometime perhaps—many, many years hence, when I'm—not so pretty. You mustn't laugh at me! Of course I mean when Torvald is not so much in love with me as he is now; when it doesn't amuse him any longer to see me dancing about, and dressing up and acting. Then it might be well to have something in reserve. (*Breaking off.*) Nonsense! nonsense! That time will never come. Now, what do you say to my grand secret, Christina? Am I fit for nothing now? You may believe it has cost me a lot of anxiety. It has been no joke to meet my engagements punctually. You must know, Christina, that in business there are things called installments, and quarterly interest, that are terribly hard to provide for. So I've had to pinch a little here and there, wherever I could. I couldn't save much out of the housekeeping, for of course Torvald had to live well. And I couldn't let the children go about badly dressed; all I got for them, I spent on them, the blessed darlings!

MRS. LINDEN　Poor Nora! So it had to come out of your own pocket-money.

NORA　Yes, of course. After all, the whole thing was my doing. When Torvald gave me money for clothes, and so on, I never spent more than half of it; I always bought the simplest and cheapest things. It's a mercy that everything suits me so well—Torvald never had any suspicions. But it was often very hard, Christina dear. For it's nice to be beautifully dressed—now, isn't it?

MRS. LINDEN　Indeed it is.

NORA　Well, and besides that, I made money in other ways. Last winter I was so lucky—I got a heap of copying to do. I shut myself up every evening and wrote far into the night. Oh, sometimes I was so tired, so tired. And yet it was splendid to work in that way and earn money. I almost felt as if I was a man.

MRS. LINDEN　Then how much have you been able to pay off?

NORA　Well, I can't precisely say. It's difficult to keep that sort of business clear. I only know that I've paid everything I could scrape together. Sometimes I really didn't know where to turn. (*Smiles.*) Then I used to sit here and pretend that a rich old gentleman was in love with me—

MRS. LINDEN　What! What gentleman?

NORA　Oh, nobody!—that he was dead now, and that when his will was opened, there stood in large letters: "Pay over at once everything of which I die possessed to that charming person, Mrs. Nora Helmer."

MRS. LINDEN　But, my dear Nora—what gentleman do you mean?

NORA　Oh, dear, can't you understand? There wasn't any old gentleman: it was only what I used to dream and dream when I was at my wits' end for money. But it doesn't matter now—the tiresome old creature may stay where he is for me. I care nothing for him or his will; for now my troubles are over. (*Springing up.*) Oh, Christina, how glorious it is to think of! Free from all anxiety! Free, quite free. To be able to play and romp about with the children; to have things tasteful and pretty in the house, exactly as Torvald likes it! And then the spring will soon be here, with the great blue sky. Perhaps then we shall have a little holiday. Perhaps I shall see the sea again. Oh, what a wonderful thing it is to live and to be happy!

[*The hall doorbell rings.*]

MRS. LINDEN (*rising*) There's a ring. Perhaps I had better go.

NORA No; do stay. No one will come here. It's sure to be someone for Torvald.

ELLEN (*in the doorway*) If you please, ma'am, there's a gentleman to speak to Mr. Helmer.

NORA Who is the gentleman?

KROGSTAD (*in the doorway*) It is I, Mrs. Helmer.

[MRS. LINDEN *starts and turns away to the window.*]

NORA (*goes a step towards him, anxiously, speaking low*) You? What is it? What do you want with my husband?

KROGSTAD Bank business—in a way. I hold a small post in the Joint Stock Bank, and your husband is to be our new chief, I hear.

NORA Then it is—?

KROGSTAD Only tiresome business, Mrs. Helmer; nothing more.

NORA Then will you please go to his study.

[KROGSTAD *goes. She bows indifferently while she closes the door into the hall. Then she goes to the stove and looks to the fire.*]

MRS. LINDEN Nora—who was that man?

NORA A Mr. Krogstad—a lawyer.

MRS. LINDEN Then it was really he?

NORA Do you know him?

MRS. LINDEN I used to know him—many years ago. He was in a lawyer's office in our town.

NORA Yes, so he was.

MRS. LINDEN How he has changed!

NORA I believe his marriage was unhappy.

MRS. LINDEN And he is a widower now?

NORA With a lot of children. There! Now it will burn up.

[*She closes the stove and pushes the rocking-chair a little aside.*]

MRS. LINDEN His business is not of the most creditable, they say?

NORA Isn't it? I dare say not. I don't know. But don't let us think of business—it's so tiresome.

[DR. RANK *comes out of* HELMER'S *room.*]

RANK (*still in the doorway*) No, no; I'm in your way. I shall go and have a chat with your wife. (*Shuts the door and sees* MRS. LINDEN.) Oh, I beg your pardon. I'm in the way here too.

NORA No, not in the least. (*Introduces them.*) Doctor Rank—Mrs. Linden.

RANK Oh, indeed; I've often heard Mrs. Linden's name; I think I passed you on the stairs as I came up.

MRS. LINDEN Yes; I go so very slowly. Stairs try me so much.

RANK Ah—you are not very strong?

MRS. LINDEN Only overworked.

RANK Nothing more? Then no doubt you've come to town to find rest in a round of dissipation?

MRS. LINDEN I have come to look for employment.

RANK Is that an approved remedy for overwork?

MRS. LINDEN One must live, Doctor Rank.

RANK Yes, that seems to be the general opinion.

NORA Come, Doctor Rank—you want to live yourself.

RANK To be sure I do. However wretched I may be, I want to drag on as long as possible. All my patients, too, have the same mania. And it's the same with people whose complaint is moral. At this very moment Helmer is talking to just such a moral incurable—

MRS. LINDEN (*softly*) Ah!

NORA Whom do you mean?

RANK Oh, a fellow named Krogstad, a man you know nothing about —corrupt to the very core of his character. But even he began by announcing, as a matter of vast importance, that he must live.

NORA Indeed? And what did he want with Torvald?

RANK I haven't an idea; I only gathered that it was some bank business.

NORA I didn't know that Krog—that this Mr. Krogstad had anything to do with the Bank?

RANK Yes. He has some sort of place there. (*To* MRS. LINDEN) I don't know whether, in your part of the country, you have people who go grubbing and sniffing around in search of moral rottenness—and then, when they have found a "case," don't rest till they have got their man into some good position where they can keep a watch upon him. Men with a clean bill of health they leave out in the cold.

MRS. LINDEN Well, I suppose the—delicate characters require most care.

RANK (*shrugs his shoulders*) There we have it! It's that notion that makes society a hospital.

[NORA, *deep in her own thoughts, breaks into half-stifled laughter and claps her hands.*]

RANK Why do you laugh at that? Have you any idea what "society" is?

NORA What do I care for your tiresome society? I was laughing at something else—something excessively amusing. Tell me, Doctor Rank, are all the employees at the Bank dependent on Torvald now?

RANK Is that what strikes you as excessively amusing?

NORA (*smiles and hums*) Never mind, never mind! (*Walks about the room.*) Yes, it is funny to think that we—that Torvald has such power over so many people. (*Takes the bag from her pocket.*) Doctor Rank, will you have a macaroon?

RANK What—macaroons! I thought they were contraband here.

NORA Yes; but Christina brought me these.

MRS. LINDEN What! I—?

NORA Oh, well! Don't be frightened. You couldn't possibly know that Torvald had forbidden them. The fact is, he's afraid of my spoiling my teeth. But, oh, bother, just for once!—That's for you, Doctor Rank! (*Puts a macaroon into his mouth.*) And you too, Christina. And I'll have one while we're about it—only a tiny one, or at most two. (*Walks about again.*) Oh, dear, I am happy! There's only one thing in the world I really want.

RANK Well; what's that?

NORA There's something I should so like to say—in Torvald's hearing.

RANK Then why don't you say it?

NORA Because I daren't, it's so ugly.

MRS. LINDEN Ugly?

RANK In that case you'd better not. But to us you might—What is it you would so like to say in Helmer's hearing?

NORA I should so love to say "Damn it all!"

RANK Are you out of your mind?

MRS. LINDEN Good gracious, Nora—!

RANK Say it—there he is!

NORA (*hides the macaroons*) Hush—sh—sh!

[HELMER *comes out of his room, hat in hand, with his overcoat on his arm.*]

NORA (*going to him*) Well, Torvald dear, have you got rid of him?

HELMER Yes; he has just gone.

NORA Let me introduce you—this is Christina, who has come to town—

HELMER Christina? Pardon me, I don't know—

NORA Mrs. Linden, Torvald dear—Christina Linden.

HELMER (*to* MRS. LINDEN) Indeed! A school-friend of my wife's, no doubt?

MRS. LINDEN Yes; we knew each other as girls.

NORA And only think! she has taken this long journey on purpose to speak to you.

HELMER To speak to me!

MRS. LINDEN Well, not quite—

NORA You see, Christina is tremendously clever at office-work, and she's so anxious to work under a first-rate man of business in order to learn still more—

HELMER (*to* MRS. LINDEN) Very sensible indeed.

NORA And when she heard you were appointed manager—it was telegraphed, you know—she started off at once, and—Torvald dear, for my sake, you must do something for Christina. Now can't you?

HELMER It's not impossible. I presume Mrs. Linden is a widow?

MRS. LINDEN Yes.

HELMER   And you have already had some experience of business?

MRS. LINDEN   A good deal.

HELMER   Well, then, it's very likely I may be able to find a place for you.

NORA   (*clapping her hands*) There now! There now!

HELMER   You have come at a fortunate moment, Mrs. Linden.

MRS. LINDEN   Oh, how can I thank you—?

HELMER   (*smiling*) There is no occasion. (*Puts on his overcoat.*) But for the present you must excuse me—

RANK   Wait; I am going with you.

[*Fetches his fur coat from the hall and warms it at the fire.*]

NORA   Don't be long, Torvald dear.

HELMER   Only an hour; not more.

NORA   Are you going too, Christina?

MRS. LINDEN   (*putting on her walking things*) Yes; I must set about looking for lodgings.

HELMER   Then perhaps we can go together?

NORA   (*helping her*) What a pity we haven't a spare room for you; but it's impossible—

MRS. LINDEN   I shouldn't think of troubling you. Good-by, dear Nora, and thank you for all your kindness.

NORA   Good-by for the present. Of course you'll come back this evening. And you, too, Doctor Rank. What! If you're well enough? Of course you'll be well enough. Only wrap up warmly. (*They go out, talking, into the hall. Outside on the stairs are heard children's voices.*) There they are! There they are! (*She runs to the outer door and opens it. The nurse, ANNA, enters the hall with the children.*) Come in! Come in! (*Stoops down and kisses the children.*) Oh, my sweet darlings! Do you see them, Christina? Aren't they lovely?

RANK   Don't let us stand here chattering in the draft.

HELMER   Come, Mrs. Linden; only mothers can stand such a temperature.

[DR. RANK, HELMER, *and* MRS. LINDEN *go down the stairs;* ANNA *enters the room with the children;* NORA *also, shutting the door.*]

NORA   How fresh and bright you look! And what red cheeks you've got! Like apples and roses. (*The children chatter to her during what follows.*) Have you had great fun? That's splendid! Oh, really! You've been giving Emmy and Bob a ride on your sled!—both at once, only think! Why, you're quite a man, Ivar. Oh, give her to me a little, Anna. My sweet little dolly! (*Takes the smallest from the nurse and dances with her.*) Yes, yes; mother will dance with Bob too. What! Did you have a game of snowballs? Oh, I wish I'd been there! No; leave them, Anna; I'll take their things off. Oh, yes, let me do it; it's such fun. Go to the nursery; you look frozen. You'll find some hot coffee on the stove.

[*The* NURSE *goes into the room on the left.* NORA *takes off the children's things and throws them down anywhere, while the children talk all together.*]
Really! A big dog ran after you? But he didn't bite you? No; dogs don't bite dear little dolly children. Don't peep into those parcels.

IVAR What is it? Wouldn't you like to know? Take care—it'll bite! What? Shall we have a game? What shall we play at? Hide-and-seek? Yes, let's play hide-and-seek. Bob shall hide first. Am I to? Yes, let me hide first.

[*She and the children play, with laughter and shouting, in the room and the adjacent one to the right. At last* NORA *hides under the table; the children come rushing in, look for her, but cannot find her, hear her half-choked laughter, rush to the table, lift up the cover and see her. Loud shouts. She creeps out, as though to frighten them. Fresh shouts. Meanwhile there has been a knock at the door leading into the hall. No one has heard it. Now the door is half opened and* KROGSTAD *appears. He waits a little; the game is renewed.*]

KROGSTAD I beg your pardon, Mrs. Helmer—

NORA (*with a suppressed cry, turns round and half jumps up*) Ah! What do you want?

KROGSTAD Excuse me; the outer door was ajar—somebody must have forgotten to shut it—

NORA (*standing up*) My husband is not at home, Mr. Krogstad.

KROGSTAD I know it.

NORA Then what do you want here?

KROGSTAD To say a few words to you.

NORA To me? (*To the children, softly.*) Go in to Anna. What? No, the strange man won't hurt mamma. When he's gone we'll go on playing. (*She leads the children into the left-hand room, and shuts the door behind them. Uneasy, in suspense.*) It is to me you wish to speak?

KROGSTAD Yes, to you.

NORA Today? But it's not the first yet—

KROGSTAD No, today is Christmas Eve. It will depend upon yourself whether you have a merry Christmas.

NORA What do you want? I'm not ready today—

KROGSTAD Never mind that just now. I have come about another matter. You have a minute to spare?

NORA Oh, yes, I suppose so; although—

KROGSTAD Good. I was sitting in the restaurant opposite, and I saw your husband go down the street—

NORA Well?

KROGSTAD —with a lady.

NORA What then?

KROGSTAD May I ask if the lady was a Mrs. Linden?

NORA   Yes.

KROGSTAD   Who has just come to town?

NORA   Yes. Today.

KROGSTAD   I believe she is an intimate friend of yours.

NORA   Certainly. But I don't understand—

KROGSTAD   I used to know her too.

NORA   I know you did.

KROGSTAD   Ah! You know all about it. I thought as much. Now, frankly, is Mrs. Linden to have a place in the Bank?

NORA   How dare you catechize me in this way, Mr. Krogstad—you, a subordinate of my husband's? But since you ask, you shall know. Yes, Mrs. Linden is to be employed. And it is I who recommended her, Mr. Krogstad. Now you know.

KROGSTAD   Then my guess was right.

NORA   (*walking up and down*) You see one has a wee bit of influence, after all. It doesn't follow because one's only a woman—When people are in a subordinate position, Mr. Krogstad, they ought really to be careful how they offend anybody who—h'm—

KROGSTAD   —who has influence?

NORA   Exactly.

KROGSTAD   (*taking another tone*) Mrs. Helmer, will you have the kindness to employ your influence on my behalf?

NORA   What? How do you mean?

KROGSTAD   Will you be so good as to see that I retain my subordinate position in the Bank?

NORA   What do you mean? Who wants to take it from you?

KROGSTAD   Oh, you needn't pretend ignorance. I can very well understand that it cannot be pleasant for your friend to meet me; and I can also understand now for whose sake I am to be hounded out.

NORA   But I assure you—

KROGSTAD   Come, come now, once for all: there is time yet, and I advise you to use your influence to prevent it.

NORA   But, Mr. Krogstad, I have no influence—absolutely none.

KROGSTAD   None? I thought you said a moment ago—

NORA   Of course not in that sense. I! How can you imagine that I should have any such influence over my husband?

KROGSTAD   Oh, I know your husband from our college days. I don't think he is any more inflexible than other husbands.

NORA   If you talk disrespectfully of my husband, I must request you to leave the house.

KROGSTAD   You are bold, madam.

NORA   I am afraid of you no longer. When New Year's Day is over, I shall soon be out of the whole business.

KROGSTAD   (*controlling himself*) Listen to me, Mrs. Helmer. If need be, I shall fight as though for my life to keep my little place in the Bank.

NORA   Yes, so it seems.

KROGSTAD   It's not only for the salary: that is what I care least about. It's something else—Well, I had better make a clean breast of it. Of course you know, like everyone else, that some years ago I—got into trouble.

NORA   I think I've heard something of the sort.

KROGSTAD   The matter never came into court; but from that moment all paths were barred to me. Then I took up the business you know about. I had to turn my hand to something; and I don't think I've been one of the worst. But now I must get clear of it all. My sons are growing up; for their sake I must try to recover my character as well as I can. This place in the Bank was the first step; and now your husband wants to kick me off the ladder, back into the mire.

NORA   But I assure you, Mr. Krogstad, I haven't the least power to help you.

KROGSTAD   That is because you have not the will; but I can compel you.

NORA   You won't tell my husband that I owe you money?

KROGSTAD   H'm; suppose I were to?

NORA   It would be shameful of you. (*With tears in her voice.*) The secret that is my joy and my pride—that he should learn it in such an ugly, coarse way—and from you. It would involve me in all sorts of unpleasantness—

KROGSTAD   Only unpleasantness?

NORA   (*hotly*) But just do it. It's you that will come off worst, for then my husband will see what a bad man you are, and then you certainly won't keep your place.

KROGSTAD   I asked whether it was only domestic unpleasantness you feared.

NORA   If my husband gets to know about it, he will of course pay you off at once, and then we shall have nothing more to do with you.

KROGSTAD   (*coming a pace nearer*) Listen, Mrs. Helmer: either your memory is defective, or you don't know much about business. I must make the position a little clearer to you.

NORA   How so?

KROGSTAD   When your husband was ill, you came to me to borrow twelve hundred dollars.

NORA   I knew of nobody else.

KROGSTAD   I promised to find you the money—

NORA   And you did find it.

KROGSTAD   I promised to find you the money, on certain conditions. You were so much taken up at the time about your husband's illness, and so eager to have the wherewithal for your journey, that you probably did not give much thought to the details. Allow me to remind you of them. I promised to find you the amount in exchange for a promissory note, which I drew up.

NORA   Yes, and I signed it.

KROGSTAD   Quite right. But then I added a few lines, making your father security for the debt. Your father was to sign this.

NORA   Was to—? He did sign it!

KROGSTAD   I had left the date blank. That is to say, your father was himself to date his signature. Do you recollect that?

NORA   Yes, I believe—

KROGSTAD   Then I gave you the paper to send to your father, by mail. Is not that so?

NORA   Yes.

KROGSTAD   And of course you did so at once; for within five or six days you brought me back the document with your father's signature; and I handed you the money.

NORA   Well? Have I not made my payments punctually?

KROGSTAD   Fairly—yes. But to return to the point: you were in great trouble at the time, Mrs. Helmer.

NORA   I was indeed!

KROGSTAD   Your father was very ill, I believe?

NORA   He was on his deathbed.

KROGSTAD   And died soon after?

NORA   Yes.

KROGSTAD   Tell me, Mrs. Helmer: do you happen to recollect the day of his death? The day of the month, I mean.

NORA   Father died on the twenty-ninth of September.

KROGSTAD   Quite correct. I have made inquiries. And here comes in the remarkable point—(*Produces a paper.*) which I cannot explain.

NORA   What remarkable point? I don't know—

KROGSTAD   The remarkable point, madam, that your father signed this paper three days after his death!

NORA   What! I don't understand—

KROGSTAD   Your father died on the twenty-ninth of September. But look here: he has dated his signature October 2nd! Is not that remarkable, Mrs. Helmer? (NORA *is silent.*) Can you explain it? (NORA *continues silent.*) It is noteworthy, too, that the words "October 2nd" and the year are not in your father's handwriting, but in one which I believe I know. Well, this may be explained; your father may have forgotten to date his signature, and somebody may have added the date at random, before the fact of your father's death was known. There is nothing wrong in that. Everything depends on the signature. Of course it is genuine, Mrs. Helmer? It was really your father himself who wrote his name here?

NORA   (*after a short silence, throws her head back and looks defiantly at him*) No, it was not. I wrote father's name.

KROGSTAD   Ah!—Are you aware, madam, that that is a dangerous admission?

NORA   How so? You will soon get your money.

KROGSTAD May I ask you one more question? Why did you not send the paper to your father?

NORA It was impossible. Father was ill. If I had asked him for his signature, I should have had to tell him why I wanted the money, but he was so ill I really could not tell him that my husband's life was in danger. It was impossible.

KROGSTAD Then it would have been better to have given up your tour.

NORA No, I couldn't do that; my husband's life depended on that journey. I couldn't give it up.

KROGSTAD And did it never occur to you that you were playing me false?

NORA That was nothing to me. I didn't care in the least about you. I couldn't endure you for all the cruel difficulties you made, although you knew how ill my husband was.

KROGSTAD Mrs. Helmer, you evidently do not realize what you have been guilty of. But I can assure you it was nothing more and nothing worse that made me an outcast from society.

NORA You! You want me to believe that you did a brave thing to save your wife's life?

KROGSTAD The law takes no account of motives.

NORA Then it must be a very bad law.

KROGSTAD Bad or not, if I produce this document in court, you will be condemned according to law.

NORA I don't believe that. Do you mean to tell me that a daughter has no right to spare her dying father trouble and anxiety?—that a wife has no right to save her husband's life? I don't know much about the law, but I'm sure you'll find, somewhere or another, that that is allowed. And you don't know that—you, a lawyer! You must be a bad one, Mr. Krogstad.

KROGSTAD Possibly. But business—such business as ours—I do understand. You believe that? Very well; now do as you please. But this I may tell you, that if I am flung into the gutter a second time, you shall keep me company.

[*Bows and goes out through hall.*]

NORA (*stands a while thinking, then tosses her head*) Oh, nonsense! He wants to frighten me. I'm not so foolish as that. (*Begins folding the children's clothes. Pauses.*) But—? No, it's impossible! Why, I did it for love!

CHILDREN (*at the door, left*) Mamma, the strange man has gone now.

NORA Yes, yes, I know. But don't tell anyone about the strange man. Do you hear? Not even papa!

CHILDREN No, mamma; and now will you play with us again?

NORA No, no; not now.

CHILDREN Oh, do, mamma; you know you promised.

NORA Yes, but I can't just now. Run to the nursery; I have so much to do. Run along, run along, and be good, my darlings! (*She pushes*

*them gently into the inner room, and closes the door behind them.
Sits on the sofa, embroiders a few stitches but soon pauses.)* No!
(*Throws down the work, rises, goes to the hall door and calls out.*)
Ellen, bring in the Christmas-tree! (*Goes to table, left, and opens the
drawer; again pauses.*) No, it's quite impossible!

ELLEN   (*with Christmas-tree*) Where shall I stand it, ma'am?

NORA   There, in the middle of the room.

ELLEN   Shall I bring in anything else?

NORA   No, thank you, I have all I want.

> [ELLEN, *having put down the tree, goes out.*]

NORA   (*busy dressing the tree*) There must be a candle here—and
flowers there.—That horrible man! Nonsense, nonsense! there's nothing to be afraid of. The Christmas-tree shall be beautiful. I'll do
everything to please you, Torvald; I'll sing and dance, and—

> [*Enter* HELMER *by the hall door, with a bundle of documents.*]

NORA   Oh! You're back already?

HELMER   Yes. Has anybody been here?

NORA   Here? No.

HELMER   That's odd. I saw Krogstad come out of the house.

NORA   Did you? Oh, yes, by-the-bye, he was here for a minute.

HELMER   Nora, I can see by your manner that he has been begging
you to put in a good word for him.

NORA   Yes.

HELMER   And you were to do it as if of your own accord? You were to
say nothing to me of his having been here. Didn't he suggest that
too?

NORA   Yes, Torvald; but—

HELMER   Nora, Nora! And you could condescend to that! To speak
to such a man, to make him a promise! And then to tell me an
untruth about it!

NORA   An untruth!

HELMER   Didn't you say that nobody had been here? (*Threatens with
his finger.*) My little bird must never do that again! A song-bird
must sing clear and true; no false notes. (*Puts his arm around her.*)
That's so, isn't it? Yes, I was sure of it. (*Lets her go.*) And now we'll
say no more about it. (*Sits down before the fire.*) Oh, how cozy and
quiet it is here! (*Glances into his documents.*)

NORA   (*busy with the tree, after a short silence*) Torvald!

HELMER   Yes.

NORA   I'm looking forward so much to the Stenborgs' fancy ball the
day after tomorrow.

HELMER   And I'm on tenterhooks to see what surprise you have in
store for me.

NORA   Oh, it's too tiresome!

HELMER   What is?

NORA   I can't think of anything good. Everything seems so foolish and meaningless.

HELMER   Has little Nora made that discovery?

NORA   (*behind his chair, with her arms on the back*) Are you very busy, Torvald?

HELMER   Well—

NORA   What papers are those?

HELMER   Bank business.

NORA   Already!

HELMER   I have got the retiring manager to let me make some necessary changes in the staff and the organization. I can do this during Christmas week. I want to have everything straight by the New Year.

NORA   Then that's why that poor Krogstad—

HELMER   H'm.

NORA   (*still leaning over the chair-back and slowly stroking his hair*) If you hadn't been so very busy, I should have asked you a great, great favor, Torvald.

HELMER   What can it be? Out with it.

NORA   Nobody has such perfect taste as you; and I should so love to look well at the fancy ball. Torvald dear, couldn't you take me in hand, and settle what I'm to be, and arrange my costume for me?

HELMER   Aha! So my willful little woman is at a loss and making signals of distress.

NORA   Yes, please, Torvald, I can't get on without your help.

HELMER   Well, well, I'll think it over, and we'll soon hit upon something.

NORA   Oh, how good that is of you! (*Goes to the tree again; pause.*) How well the red flowers show.—Tell me, was it anything so very dreadful this Krogstad got into trouble about?

HELMER   Forgery, that's all. Don't you know what that means?

NORA   Mayn't he have been driven to it by need?

HELMER   Yes; or, like so many others, he may have done it in pure heedlessness. I am not so hard-hearted as to condemn a man absolutely for a single fault.

NORA   No, surely not, Torvald!

HELMER   Many a man can retrieve his character, if he owns his crime and takes the punishment.

NORA   Punishment—?

HELMER   But Krogstad didn't do that. He evaded the law by means of tricks and subterfuges; and that is what has morally ruined him.

NORA   Do you think that—?

HELMER   Just think how a man with a thing of that sort on his conscience must be always lying and canting and shamming. Think of the mask he must wear even towards those who stand nearest him —towards his own wife and children. The effect on the children— that's the most terrible part of it, Nora.

NORA   Why?

HELMER   Because in such an atmosphere of lies home life is poisoned and contaminated in every fiber. Every breath the children draw contains some germ of evil.

NORA   (*closer behind him*) Are you sure of that?

HELMER   As a lawyer, my dear, I have seen it often enough. Nearly all cases of early corruption may be traced to lying mothers.

NORA   Why—mothers?

HELMER   It generally comes from the mother's side; but of course the father's influence may act in the same way. Every lawyer knows it too well. And here has this Krogstad been poisoning his own children for years past by a life of lies and hypocrisy—that is why I call him morally ruined. (*Holds out both hands to her.*) So my sweet little Nora must promise not to plead his cause. Shake hands upon it. Come, come, what's this? Give me your hand. That's right. Then it's a bargain. I assure you it would have been impossible for me to work with him. It gives me a positive sense of physical discomfort to come in contact with such people.

[NORA *draws her hand away and moves to the other side of the Christmas-tree.*]

NORA   How warm it is here. And I have so much to do.

HELMER   (*rises and gathers up his papers*) Yes, and I must try to get some of these papers looked through before dinner. And I shall think over your costume too. Perhaps I may even find something to hang in gilt paper on the Christmas-tree. (*Lays his hand on her head.*) My precious little song-bird!

[*He goes into his room and shuts the door.*]

NORA   (*softly, after a pause*) It can't be. It's impossible. It must be impossible!

ANNA   (*at the door, left*) The little ones are begging so prettily to come to mamma.

NORA   No, no, no; don't let them come to me! Keep them with you, Anna.

ANNA   Very well, ma'am.

[*Shuts the door.*]

NORA   (*pale with terror*) Corrupt my children!—Poison my home! (*Short pause. She throws back her head.*) It's not true! It can never, never be true!

[CURTAIN]

ACT II

The same room. In the corner, beside the piano, stands the Christmas-tree, stripped, and with the candles burnt out. NORA's *outdoor things lie on the sofa.*

NORA, *alone, is walking about restlessly. At last she stops by the sofa and takes up her cloak.*

NORA (*dropping the cloak*) There's somebody coming! (*Goes to the hall door and listens.*) Nobody; of course nobody will come today, Christmas-day; nor tomorrow either. But perhaps—(*Opens the door and looks out.*)—No, nothing in the letter-box; quite empty. (*Comes forward.*) Stuff and nonsense! Of course he won't really do anything. Such a thing couldn't happen. It's impossible! Why, I have three little children.

       [ANNA *enters from the left with a large cardboard box.*]
ANNA I've found the box with the fancy dress at last!
NORA Thanks; put it down on the table.
ANNA (*does so*) But I'm afraid it's very much out of order.
NORA Oh, I wish I could tear it into a hundred thousand pieces!
ANNA Oh, no. It can easily be put to rights—just a little patience.
NORA I shall go and get Mrs. Linden to help me.
ANNA Going out again? In such weather as this! You'll catch cold, ma'am, and be ill.
NORA Worse things might happen.—What are the children doing?
ANNA They're playing with their Christmas presents, poor little dears; but—
NORA Do they often ask for me?
ANNA You see they've been so used to having their mamma with them.
NORA Yes; but, Anna, I can't have them so much with me in future.
ANNA Well, little children get used to anything.
NORA Do you think they do? Do you believe they would forget their mother if she went quite away?
ANNA Gracious me! Quite away?
NORA Tell me, Anna—I've so often wondered about it—how could you bring yourself to give your child up to strangers?
ANNA I had to when I came to nurse my little Miss Nora.
NORA But how could you make up your mind to it?
ANNA When I had the chance of such a good place? A poor girl who's been in trouble must take what comes. That wicked man did nothing for me.
NORA But your daughter must have forgotten you.
ANNA Oh, no, ma'am, that she hasn't. She wrote to me both when she was confirmed and when she was married.

NORA (*embracing her*) Dear old Anna—you were a good mother to me when I was little.

ANNA My poor little Nora had no mother but me.

NORA And if my little ones had nobody else, I'm sure you would— Nonsense, nonsense! (*Opens the box.*) Go in to the children. Now I must—You'll see how lovely I shall be tomorrow.

ANNA I'm sure there will be no one at the ball so lovely as my Miss Nora.

[*She goes into the room on the left.*]

NORA (*takes the costume out of the box but soon throws it down again*) Oh, if I dared go out. If only nobody would come. If only nothing would happen here in the meantime. Rubbish; nobody is coming. Only not to think. What a delicious muff! Beautiful gloves, beautiful gloves! To forget—to forget! One, two, three, four, five, six —(*With a scream.*) Ah, there they come.

[*Goes towards the door, then stands irresolute.*]

[MRS. LINDEN *enters from the hall, where she has taken off her things.*]

NORA Oh, it's you, Christina. There's nobody else there? I'm so glad you have come.

MRS. LINDEN I hear you called at my lodgings.

NORA Yes, I was just passing. There's something you *must* help me with. Let us sit here on the sofa—so. Tomorrow evening there's to be a fancy ball at Consul Stenborg's overhead, and Torvald wants me to appear as a Neapolitan fisher-girl, and dance the tarantella; I learned it at Capri.

MRS. LINDEN I see—quite a performance.

NORA Yes, Torvald wishes it. Look, this is the costume; Torvald had it made for me in Italy. But now it's all so torn, I don't know—

MRS. LINDEN Oh, we shall soon set that to rights. It's only the trimming that has come loose here and there. Have you a needle and thread? Ah, here's the very thing.

NORA Oh, how kind of you!

MRS. LINDEN (*sewing*) So you're to be in costume tomorrow, Nora? I'll tell you what—I shall come in for a moment to see you in all your glory. But I've quite forgotten to thank you for the pleasant evening yesterday.

NORA (*rises and walks across the room*) Oh, yesterday, it didn't seem so pleasant as usual.—You should have come to town a little sooner, Christina.—Torvald has certainly the art of making home bright and beautiful.

MRS. LINDEN You too, I should think, or you wouldn't be your father's daughter. But tell me—is Doctor Rank always so depressed as he was last evening?

NORA No, yesterday it was particularly noticeable. You see, he suffers from a dreadful illness. He has spinal consumption, poor fellow. They say his father was a horrible man, who kept mistresses and all sorts of things—so the son has been sickly from his childhood, you understand.

MRS. LINDEN   (*lets her sewing fall into her lap*) Why, my darling Nora, how do you come to know such things?

NORA   (*moving about the room*) Oh, when one has three children, one sometimes has visits from women who are half—half doctors—and they talk of one thing and another.

MRS. LINDEN   (*goes on sewing; a short pause*) Does Doctor Rank come here every day?

NORA   Every day of his life. He has been Torvald's most intimate friend from boyhood, and he's a good friend of mine too. Doctor Rank is quite one of the family.

MRS. LINDEN   But tell me—is he quite sincere? I mean, isn't he rather given to flattering people?

NORA   No, quite the contrary. Why should you think so?

MRS. LINDEN   When you introduced us yesterday he said he had often heard my name; but I noticed afterwards that your husband had no notion who I was. How could Doctor Rank—?

NORA   He was quite right, Christina. You see, Torvald loves me so indescribably, he wants to have me all to himself, as he says. When we were first married he was almost jealous if I even mentioned any of my old friends at home; so naturally I gave up doing it. But I often talk of the old times to Doctor Rank, for he likes to hear about them.

MRS. LINDEN   Listen to me, Nora! You are still a child in many ways. I am older than you and have had more experience. I'll tell you something. You ought to get clear of all this with Dr. Rank.

NORA   Get clear of what?

MRS. LINDEN   The whole affair, I should say. You were talking yesterday of a rich admirer who was to find you money—

NORA   Yes, one who never existed, worse luck. What then?

MRS. LINDEN   Has Doctor Rank money?

NORA   Yes, he has.

MRS. LINDEN   And nobody to provide for?

NORA   Nobody. But—?

MRS. LINDEN   And he comes here every day?

NORA   Yes, I told you so.

MRS. LINDEN   I should have thought he would have had better taste.

NORA   I don't understand you a bit.

MRS. LINDEN   Don't pretend, Nora. Do you suppose I can't guess who lent you the twelve hundred dollars?

NORA   Are you out of your senses? How can you think such a thing? A friend who comes here every day! Why, the position would be unbearable!

MRS. LINDEN   Then it really is not he?

NORA No, I assure you. It never for a moment occurred to me—
Besides, at that time he had nothing to lend; he came into his
property afterwards.

MRS. LINDEN Well, I believe that was lucky for you, Nora dear.

NORA No, really, it would never have struck me to ask Dr. Rank—And
yet, I'm certain that if I did—

MRS. LINDEN But of course you never would.

NORA Of course not. It's inconceivable that it should ever be necessary.
But I'm quite sure that if I spoke to Doctor Rank—

MRS. LINDEN Behind your husband's back?

NORA I must get clear of the other thing; that's behind his back too.
I *must* get clear of that.

MRS. LINDEN Yes, yes, I told you so yesterday; but—

NORA (*walking up and down*) A man can manage these things much
better than a woman.

MRS. LINDEN One's own husband, yes.

NORA Nonsense. (*Stands still.*) When everything is paid, one gets back
the paper.

MRS. LINDEN Of course.

NORA And can tear it into a hundred thousand pieces, and *burn* it up,
the nasty, filthy thing!

MRS. LINDEN (*looks at her fixedly, lays down her work, and rises
slowly*) Nora, you are hiding something from me.

NORA Can you see it in my face?

MRS. LINDEN Something has happened since yesterday morning. Nora,
what is it?

NORA (*going towards her*) Christina—! (*Listens.*) Hush! There's Torvald coming home. Do you mind going into the nursery for the
present? Torvald can't bear to see dressmaking going on. Get Anna
to help you.

MRS. LINDEN (*gathers some of the things together*) Very well; but I
shan't go away until you have told me all about it.

[*She goes out to the left, as* HELMER *enters from the hall.*]

NORA (*runs to meet him*) Oh, how I've been longing for you to
come, Torvald dear!

HELMER Was that the dressmaker—?

NORA No, Christina. She's helping me with my costume. You'll see
how nice I shall look.

HELMER Yes, wasn't that a happy thought of mine?

NORA Splendid! But isn't it good of me, too, to have given in to you
about the tarantella?

HELMER (*takes her under the chin*) Good of you! To give in to your
own husband? Well, well, you little madcap, I know you don't mean
it. But I won't disturb you. I dare say you want to be "trying on."

NORA And you are going to work, I suppose?

HELMER Yes. (*Shows her a bundle of papers.*) Look here. I've just come from the Bank—

[*Goes towards his room.*]

NORA Torvald.

HELMER (*stopping*) Yes?

NORA If your little squirrel were to beg you for something so prettily—

HELMER Well?

NORA Would you do it?

HELMER I must know first what it is.

NORA The squirrel would skip about and play all sorts of tricks if you would only be nice and kind.

HELMER Come, then, out with it.

NORA Your lark would twitter from morning till night—

HELMER Oh, that she does in any case.

NORA I'll be an elf and dance in the moonlight for you, Torvald.

HELMER Nora—you can't mean what you were hinting at this morning?

NORA (*coming nearer*) Yes, Torvald, I beg and implore you!

HELMER. Have you really the courage to begin that again?

NORA Yes, yes; for my sake, you *must* let Krogstad keep his place in the Bank.

HELMER My dear Nora, it's his place I intend for Mrs. Linden.

NORA Yes, that's so good of you. But instead of Krogstad, you could dismiss some other clerk.

HELMER Why, this is incredible obstinacy! Because you have thoughtlessly promised to put in a word for him, I am to—!

NORA It's not that, Torvald. It's for your own sake. This man writes for the most scurrilous newspapers; you said so yourself. He can do you no end of harm. I'm so terribly afraid of him—

HELMER Ah, I understand; it's old recollections that are frightening you.

NORA What do you mean?

HELMER Of course you're thinking of your father.

NORA Yes—yes, of course. Only think of the shameful slanders wicked people used to write about father. I believe they would have got him dismissed if you hadn't been sent to look into the thing, and been kind to him, and helped him.

HELMER My little Nora, between your father and me there is all the difference in the world. Your father was not altogether impeccable. I am; and I hope to remain so.

NORA Oh, no one knows what wicked men may hit upon. We could live so quietly and happily now, in our cozy, peaceful home, you and I and the children, Torvald! That's why I beg and implore you—

HELMER And it is just by pleading his cause that you make it impossible for me to keep him. It's already known at the Bank that I intend to dismiss Krogstad. If it were now reported that the new manager let himself be turned round his wife's little finger—

NORA   What then?

HELMER   Oh, nothing, so long as a willful woman can have her way—! I am to make myself a laughing-stock to the whole staff and set people saying that I am open to all sorts of outside influence? Take my word for it, I should soon feel the consequences. And besides— there is one thing that makes Krogstad impossible for me to work with—

NORA   What thing?

HELMER   I could perhaps have overlooked his moral failings at a pinch—

NORA   Yes, couldn't you, Torvald?

HELMER   And I hear he is good at his work. But the fact is, he was a college chum of mine—there was one of those rash friendships be- tween us that one so often repents of later. I may as well confess it at once—he calls me by my Christian name; and he is tactless enough to do it even when others are present. He delights in putting on airs of familiarity—Torvald here, Torvald there! I assure you it's most painful to me. He would make my position at the Bank per- fectly unendurable.

NORA   Torvald, surely you're not serious?

HELMER   No? Why not?

NORA   That's such a petty reason.

HELMER   What! Petty! Do you consider me petty!

NORA   No, on the contrary, Torvald dear; and that's just why—

HELMER   Never mind; you call my motives petty; then I must be petty too. Petty! Very well!—Now we'll put an end to this, once for all. (*Goes to the door into the hall and calls.*) Ellen!

NORA   What do you want?

HELMER   (*searching among his papers*) To settle the thing.

[ELLEN *enters.*]

Here; take this letter; give it to a messenger. See that he takes it at once. The address is on it. Here's the money.

ELLEN   Very well, sir.

[*Goes with the letter.*]

HELMER   (*putting his papers together*) There, Madam Obstinacy.

NORA   (*breathless*) Torvald—what was in the letter?

HELMER   Krogstad's dismissal.

NORA   Call it back again, Torvald! There's still time. Oh, Torvald, call it back again! For my sake, for your own, for the children's sake! Do you hear, Torvald? Do it! You don't know what that letter may bring upon us all.

HELMER   Too late.

NORA   Yes, too late.

HELMER My dear Nora, I forgive your anxiety, though it's anything but flattering to me. Why should you suppose that I would be afraid of a wretched scribbler's spite? But I forgive you all the same, for it's a proof of your great love for me. (*Takes her in his arms.*) That's as it should be, my own dear Nora. Let what will happen— when it comes to the pinch, I shall have strength and courage enough. You shall see: my shoulders are broad enough to bear the whole burden.

NORA (*terror-struck*) What do you mean by that?

HELMER The whole burden, I say—

NORA (*with decision*) That you shall never, never do!

HELMER Very well; then we'll share it, Nora, as man and wife. That is how it should be. (*Petting her.*) Are you satisfied now? Come, come, come, don't look like a scared dove. It's all nothing—foolish fancies.—Now you ought to play the tarantella through and practice with the tambourine. I shall sit in my inner room and shut both doors, so that I shall hear nothing. You can make as much noise as you please. (*Turns round in doorway.*) And when Rank comes, just tell him where I'm to be found.

[*He nods to her, and goes with his papers into his room, closing the door.*]

NORA (*bewildered with terror, stands as though rooted to the ground, and whispers*) He would do it. Yes, he would do it. He would do it, in spite of all the world.—No, never that, never, never! Anything rather than that! Oh, for some way of escape! What shall I do—! (*Hall bell rings.*) Doctor Rank—!—Anything, anything, rather than—!

[NORA *draws her hands over her face, pulls herself together, goes to the door and opens it.* RANK *stands outside hanging up his fur coat. During what follows it begins to grow dark.*]

NORA Good-afternoon, Doctor Rank. I knew you by your ring. But you mustn't go to Torvald now. I believe he's busy.

RANK And you?

[*Enters and closes the door.*]

NORA Oh, you know very well, I have always time for *you.*

RANK Thank you. I shall avail myself of your kindness as long as I can.

NORA What do you mean? As long as you can?

RANK Yes. Does *that* frighten you?

NORA I think it's an odd expression. Do you expect anything to happen?

RANK Something I have long been prepared for; but I didn't think it would come so soon.

NORA (*catching at his arm*) What have you discovered? Doctor Rank, you must tell me!

RANK   (*sitting down by the stove*) I am running down hill. There's
no help for it.

NORA   (*draws a long breath of relief*) It's you—

RANK   Who else should it be?—Why lie to oneself? I am the most
wretched of all my patients, Mrs. Helmer. In these last days I have
been auditing my life-account—bankrupt! Perhaps before a month
is over, I shall lie rotting in the churchyard.

NORA   Oh! What an ugly way to talk.

RANK   The thing itself is so confoundedly ugly, you see. But the worst
of it is, so many other ugly things have to be gone through first.
There is only one last investigation to be made, and when that is over
I shall know pretty certainly when the break-up will begin. There's
one thing I want to say to you: Helmer's delicate nature shrinks so
from all that is horrible: I will not have him in my sickroom—

NORA   But, Doctor Rank—

RANK   I won't have him, I say—not on any account. I shall lock my
door against him.—As soon as I am quite certain of the worst, I shall
send you my visiting-card with a black cross on it; and then you will
know that the final horror has begun.

NORA   Why, you're perfectly unreasonable today; and I did so want you
to be in a really good humor.

RANK   With death staring me in the face?—And to suffer thus for
another's sin! Where's the justice of it? And in one way or another
you can trace in every family some such inexorable retribution—

NORA   (*stopping her ears*) Nonsense, nonsense! Now cheer up!

RANK   Well, after all, the whole thing's only worth laughing at. My
poor innocent spine must do penance for my father's wild oats.

NORA   (*at table, left*) I suppose he was too fond of asparagus and
Strasbourg pâté, wasn't he?

RANK   Yes; and truffles.

NORA   Yes, truffles, to be sure. And oysters, I believe?

RANK   Yes, oysters; oysters, of course.

NORA   And then all the port and champagne! It's sad that all these good
things should attack the spine.

RANK   Especially when the luckless spine attacked never had any good
of them.

NORA   Ah, yes, that's the worst of it.

RANK   (*looks at her searchingly*) H'm—

NORA   (*a moment later*) Why did you smile?

RANK   No; it was you that laughed.

NORA   No; it was you that smiled, Dr. Rank.

RANK   (*standing up*) I see you're deeper than I thought.

NORA   I'm in such a crazy mood today.

RANK   So it seems.

NORA   (*with her hands on his shoulders*) Dear, dear Doctor Rank,
death shall not take you away from Torvald and me.

RANK   Oh, you'll easily get over the loss. The absent are soon forgotten.

NORA   (*looks at him anxiously*) Do you think so?

RANK   People make fresh ties, and then—

NORA   Who make fresh ties?

RANK   You and Helmer will, when I am gone. You yourself are taking time by the forelock it seems to me. What was that Mrs. Linden doing here yesterday?

NORA   Oh!—you're surely not jealous of poor Christina?

RANK   Yes, I am. She will be my successor in this house. When I am out of the way, this woman will perhaps—

NORA   Hush! Not so loud! She's in there.

RANK   Today as well? You see!

NORA   Only to put my costume in order—dear me, how unreasonable you are! (*Sits on sofa.*) Now do be good, Doctor Rank! Tomorrow you shall see how beautifully I shall dance; and then you may fancy that I'm doing it all to please you—and of course Torvald as well. (*Takes various things out of box.*) Doctor Rank, sit down here, and I'll show you something.

RANK   (*sitting*) What is it?

NORA   Look here. Look!

RANK   Silk stockings.

NORA   Flesh-colored. Aren't they lovely? It's so dark here now; but tomorrow—No, no, no; you must only look at the feet. Oh, well, I suppose you may look at the rest too.

RANK   H'm—

NORA   What are you looking so critical about? Do you think they won't fit me?

RANK   I can't possibly give any competent opinion on that point.

NORA   (*looking at him a moment*) For shame! (*Hits him lightly on the ear with the stockings.*) Take that.

[*Rolls them up again.*]

RANK   And what other wonders am I to see?

NORA   You shan't see anything more; for you don't behave nicely.

[*She hums a little and searches among the things.*]

RANK   (*after a short silence*) When I sit here gossiping with you, I can't imagine—I simply cannot conceive—what would have become of me if I had never entered this house.

NORA   (*smiling*) Yes, I think you do feel at home with us.

RANK   (*more softly—looking straight before him*) And now to have to leave it all—

NORA   Nonsense. You shan't leave us.

RANK   (*in the same tone*) And not to be able to leave behind the slightest token of gratitude; scarcely even a passing regret—nothing but an empty place, that can be filled by the first comer.

NORA   And if I were to ask you for—? No—

RANK   For what?

NORA   For a great proof of your friendship.

RANK   Yes—yes?

NORA   I mean—for a very, very great service—

RANK   Would you really, for once, make me so happy?

NORA   Oh, you don't know what it is.

RANK   Then tell me.

NORA   No, I really can't, Doctor Rank. It's far, far too much—not only a service, but help and advice besides—

RANK   So much the better. I can't think what you can mean. But go on. Don't you trust me?

NORA   As I trust no one else. I know you are my best and truest friend. So I will tell you. Well then, Doctor Rank, there is something you must help me to prevent. You know how deeply, how wonderfully Torvald loves me; he wouldn't hesitate a moment to give his very life for my sake.

RANK   (*bending towards her*) Nora—do you think he is the only one who—?

NORA   (*with a slight start*) Who—?

RANK   Who would gladly give his life for you?

NORA   (*sadly*) Oh!

RANK   I have sworn that you shall know it before I—go. I shall never find a better opportunity.—Yes, Nora, now I have told you; and now you know that you can trust me as you can no one else.

NORA   (*standing up; simply and calmly*) Let me pass, please.

RANK   (*makes way for her, but remains sitting*) Nora—

NORA   (*in the doorway*) Ellen, bring the lamp. (*Crosses to the stove.*) Oh, dear Doctor Rank, that was too bad of you.

RANK   (*rising*) That I have loved you as deeply as—anyone else? Was that too bad of me?

NORA   No, but that you should have told me so. It was so unnecessary—

RANK   What do you mean? Did you know—?

[ELLEN *enters with the lamp; sets it on the table and goes out again.*]

RANK   Nora—Mrs. Helmer—I ask you, did you know?

NORA   Oh, how can I tell what I knew or didn't know? I really can't say—How could you be so clumsy, Doctor Rank? It was all so nice!

RANK   Well, at any rate, you know now that I am at your service, body and soul. And now, go on.

NORA   (*looking at him*) Go on—now?

RANK   I beg you to tell me what you want.

NORA   I can tell you nothing now.

RANK   Yes, yes! You mustn't punish me in that way. Let me do for you whatever a man can.

NORA   You can do nothing for me now.—Besides, I really want no

help. You shall see it was only my fancy. Yes, it must be so. Of
course! (*Sits in the rocking-chair, looks at him and smiles.*) You are
a nice person, Doctor Rank! Aren't you ashamed of yourself, now
that the lamp is on the table?

RANK   No; not exactly. But perhaps I ought to go—forever.

NORA   No, indeed you mustn't. Of course you must come and do as
you've always done. You know very well that Torvald can't do without you.

RANK   Yes, but you?

NORA   Oh, you know I always like to have you here.

RANK   That is just what led me astray. You are a riddle to me. It has
often seemed to me as if you liked being with me almost as much
as being with Helmer.

NORA   Yes; don't you see? There are people one loves, and others one
likes to talk to.

RANK   Yes—there's something in that.

NORA   When I was a girl, of course I loved papa best. But it always
delighted me to steal into the servants' room. In the first place they
never lectured me, and in the second it was such fun to hear them
talk.

RANK   Ah, I see; then it's *their* place I have taken?

NORA   (*jumps up and hurries towards him*) Oh, my dear Doctor Rank,
I don't mean that. But you understand, with Torvald it's the same
as with papa—

[ELLEN *enters from the hall.*]

ELLEN   Please, ma'am—

[*Whispers to* NORA, *and gives her a card.*]

NORA   (*glancing at card*) Ah! (*Puts it in her pocket.*)

RANK   Anything wrong?

NORA   No, no, not in the least. It's only—it's my new costume—

RANK   Your costume! Why, it's there.

NORA   Oh, that one, yes. But this is another that—I have ordered it—
Torvald mustn't know—

RANK   Aha! So that's the great secret.

NORA   Yes, of course. Please go to him; he's in the inner room. Do keep
him while I—

RANK   Don't be alarmed; he shan't escape.

[*Goes into* HELMER's *room.*]

NORA   (*to* ELLEN) Is he waiting in the kitchen?

ELLEN   Yes, he came up the back stair—

NORA   Didn't you tell him I was engaged?

ELLEN   Yes, but it was no use.

NORA   He won't go away?

ELLEN   No, ma'am, not until he has spoken to you.

NORA Then let him come in; but quietly. And, Ellen—say nothing about it; it's a surprise for my husband.

ELLEN Oh, yes, ma'am, I understand.

[*She goes out.*]

NORA It is coming! The dreadful thing is coming, after all. No, no, no, it can never be; it shall not!

[*She goes to* HELMER's *door and slips the bolt.* ELLEN *opens the hall door for* KROGSTAD, *and shuts it after him. He wears a traveling-coat, high boots, and a fur cap.*]

NORA (*goes towards him*) Speak softly; my husband is at home.

KROGSTAD All right. That's nothing to me.

NORA What do you want?

KROGSTAD A little information.

NORA Be quick, then. What is it?

KROGSTAD You know I have got my dismissal.

NORA I couldn't prevent it, Mr. Krogstad. I fought for you to the last, but it was of no use.

KROGSTAD Does your husband care for you so little? He knows what I can bring upon you, and yet he dares—

NORA How could you think I should tell him?

KROGSTAD Well, as a matter of fact, I didn't think it. It wasn't like my friend Torvald Helmer to show so much courage—

NORA Mr. Krogstad, be good enough to speak respectfully of my husband.

KROGSTAD Certainly, with all due respect. But since you are so anxious to keep the matter secret, I suppose you are a little clearer than yesterday as to what you have done.

NORA Clearer than you could ever make me.

KROGSTAD Yes, so bad a lawyer as I—

NORA What is it you want?

KROGSTAD Only to see how you are getting on, Mrs. Helmer. I've been thinking about you all day. Even a mere money-lender, a gutter-journalist, a—in short, a creature like me—has a little bit of what people call feeling.

NORA Then show it; think of my little children.

KROGSTAD Did you and your husband think of mine? But enough of that. I only wanted to tell you that you needn't take this matter too seriously. I shall not lodge any information, for the present.

NORA No, surely not. I knew you wouldn't.

KROGSTAD The whole thing can be settled quite amicably. Nobody need know. It can remain among us three.

NORA My husband must never know.

KROGSTAD How can you prevent it? Can you pay off the balance?

NORA No, not at once.

KROGSTAD Or have you any means of raising the money in the next few days?

NORA   None—that I will make use of.

KROGSTAD   And if you had, it would not help you now. If you offered me ever so much money down, you should not get back your I.O.U.

NORA   Tell me what you want to do with it.

KROGSTAD   I only want to keep it—to have it in my possession. No outsider shall hear anything of it. So, if you have any desperate scheme in your head—

NORA   What if I have?

KROGSTAD   If you should think of leaving your husband and children—

NORA   What if I do?

KROGSTAD   Or if you should think of—something worse—

NORA   How do you know that?

KROGSTAD   Put all that out of your head.

NORA   How did you know what I had in my mind?

KROGSTAD   Most of us think of *that* at first. I thought of it, too; but I hadn't the courage—

NORA   (*tonelessly*) Nor I.

KROGSTAD   (*relieved*) No, one hasn't. You haven't the courage either, have you?

NORA   I haven't, I haven't.

KROGSTAD   Besides, it would be very foolish.—Just one domestic storm, and it's all over. I have a letter in my pocket for your husband—

NORA   Telling him everything?

KROGSTAD   Sparing you as much as possible.

NORA   (*quickly*) He must never read that letter. Tear it up. I will manage to get the money somehow—

KROGSTAD   Pardon me, Mrs. Helmer, but I believe I told you—

NORA   Oh, I'm not talking about the money I owe you. Tell me how much you demand from my husband—I will get it.

KROGSTAD   I demand no money from your husband.

NORA   What *do* you demand then?

KROGSTAD   I will tell you. I want to regain my footing in the world. I want to rise; and your husband shall help me to do it. For the last eighteen months my record has been spotless; I have been in bitter need all the time; but I was content to fight my way up, step by step. Now, I've been thrust down again, and I will not be satisfied with merely being reinstated as a matter of grace. I want to rise, I tell you. I must get into the Bank again, in a higher position than before. Your husband shall create a place on purpose for me—

NORA   He will never do that!

KROGSTAD   He will do it; I know him—he won't dare to show fight! And when he and I are together there, you shall soon see! Before a year is out I shall be the manager's right hand. It won't be Torvald Helmer, but Nils Krogstad, that manages the Joint Stock Bank.

NORA   That shall never be.

KROGSTAD   Perhaps you will—?

NORA   *Now* I have the courage for it.

KROGSTAD   Oh, you don't frighten me! A sensitive, petted creature like you—

NORA   You shall see, you shall see!

KROGSTAD   Under the ice, perhaps? Down into the cold, black water? And next spring to come up again, ugly, hairless, unrecognizable—

NORA   You can't terrify me.

KROGSTAD   Nor you me. People don't do that sort of thing, Mrs. Helmer. And, after all, what would be the use of it? I have your husband in my pocket, all the same.

NORA   Afterwards? When I am no longer—?

KROGSTAD   You forget, your reputation remains in my hands! (*NORA stands speechless and looks at him.*) Well, now you are prepared. Do nothing foolish. As soon as Helmer has received my letter, I shall expect to hear from him. And remember that it is your husband himself who has forced me back again into such paths. That I will never forgive him. Good-by, Mrs. Helmer.

[*Goes out through the hall.* NORA *hurries to the door, opens it a little, and listens.*]

NORA   He's going. He's not putting the letter into the box. No, no, it would be impossible! (*Opens the door farther and farther.*) What's that? He's standing still; not going downstairs. Has he changed his mind? Is he—? (*A letter falls into the box.* KROGSTAD's *footsteps are heard gradually receding down the stair.* NORA *utters a suppressed shriek, and rushes forward towards the sofa-table; pause.*) In the letter-box! (*Slips shrinkingly up to the hall door.*) There it lies.—Torvald, Torvald—now we are lost!

[MRS. LINDEN *enters from the left with the costume.*]

MRS. LINDEN   There, I think it's all right now. Shall we just try it on?

NORA   (*hoarsely and softly*) Christina, come here.

MRS. LINDEN   (*throws down the dress on the sofa*) What's the matter? You look quite distracted.

NORA   Come here. Do you see that letter? *There,* see—through the glass of the letter-box.

MRS. LINDEN   Yes, yes, I see it.

NORA   That letter is from Krogstad—

MRS. LINDEN   Nora—it was Krogstad who lent you the money?

NORA   Yes; and now Torvald will know everything.

MRS. LINDEN   Believe me, Nora, it's the best thing for both of you.

NORA   You don't know all yet. I have forged a name—

MRS. LINDEN   Good heavens!

NORA   Now, listen to me, Christina; you shall bear me witness—

MRS. LINDEN   How "witness"? What am I to—?

NORA   If I should go out of my mind—it might easily happen—

MRS. LINDEN   Nora!

NORA   Or if anything else should happen to me—so that I couldn't be here—!

MRS. LINDEN   Nora, Nora, you're quite beside yourself!

NORA   In case anyone wanted to take it all upon himself—the whole blame—you understand—

MRS. LINDEN   Yes, yes; but how can you think—?

NORA   You shall bear witness that it's not true, Christina. I'm not out of my mind at all; I know quite well what I'm saying; and I tell you nobody else knew anything about it; I did the whole thing, I myself. Remember that.

MRS. LINDEN   I shall remember. But I don't understand what you mean—

NORA   Oh, how should you? It's the miracle coming to pass.

MRS. LINDEN   The miracle?

NORA   Yes, the miracle. But it's so terrible, Christina; it mustn't happen for all the world.

MRS. LINDEN   I shall go straight to Krogstad and talk to him.

NORA   Don't; he'll do you some harm.

MRS. LINDEN   Once he would have done anything for me.

NORA   He?

MRS. LINDEN   Where does he live?

NORA   Oh, how can I tell—? Yes—(*Feels in her pocket.*) Here's his card. But the letter, the letter—!

HELMER   (*knocking outside*) Nora!

NORA   (*shrieks in terror*) Oh, what is it? What do you want?

HELMER   Well, well, don't be frightened. We're not coming in; you've bolted the door. Are you trying on your dress?

NORA   Yes, yes, I'm trying it on. It suits me so well, Torvald.

MRS. LINDEN   (*who has read the card*) Why, he lives close by here.

NORA   Yes, but it's no use now. We are lost. The letter is there in the box.

MRS. LINDEN   And your husband has the key?

NORA   Always.

MRS. LINDEN   Krogstad must demand his letter back, unread. He must find some pretext—

NORA   But this is the very time when Torvald generally—

MRS. LINDEN   Prevent him. Keep him occupied. I shall come back as quickly as I can.

[*She goes out hastily by the hall door.*]

NORA   (*opens HELMER's door and peeps in*) Torvald!

HELMER   Well, may one come into one's own room again at last? Come, Rank, we'll have a look—(*In the doorway.*) But how's this?

NORA   What, Torvald dear?

HELMER   Rank led me to expect a grand transformation.

RANK   (*in the doorway*) So I understood. I suppose I was mistaken.

NORA   No, no one shall see me in my glory till tomorrow evening.

HELMER   Why, Nora dear, you look so tired. Have you been practicing too hard?

NORA   No, I haven't practiced at all yet.

HELMER   But you'll have to—

NORA   Oh, yes, I must, I must! But, Torvald, I can't get on at all without your help. I've forgotten everything.

HELMER   Oh, we shall soon freshen it up again.

NORA   Yes, do help me, Torvald. You must promise me—Oh, I'm so nervous about it. Before so many people—This evening you must give yourself up entirely to me. You mustn't do a stroke of work; you mustn't even touch a pen. Do promise, Torvald dear!

HELMER   I promise. All this evening I shall be your slave. Little helpless thing—! But, by-the-bye, I must just—

[*Going to hall door.*]

NORA   What do you want there?

HELMER   Only to see if there are any letters.

NORA   No, no, don't do that, Torvald.

HELMER   Why not?

NORA   Torvald, I beg you not to. There are none there.

HELMER   Let me just see.

[*Is going.* NORA, *at the piano, plays the first bars of the tarantella.*]

HELMER   (*at the door, stops*) Aha!

NORA   I can't dance tomorrow if I don't rehearse with you first.

HELMER   (*going to her*) Are you really so nervous, dear Nora?

NORA   Yes, dreadfully! Let me rehearse at once. We have time before dinner. Oh, do sit down and play for me, Torvald dear; direct me and put me right, as you used to do.

HELMER   With all the pleasure in life, since you wish it.

[*Sits at piano.* NORA *snatches the tambourine out of the box, and hurriedly drapes herself in a long parti-colored shawl; then, with a bound, stands in the middle of the floor.*]

NORA   Now play for me! Now I'll dance!

[HELMER *plays and* NORA *dances.* RANK *stands at the piano behind* HELMER *and looks on.*]

HELMER   (*playing*) Slower! Slower!

NORA   Can't do it slower.

HELMER   Not so violently, Nora.

NORA   I must! I must!

HELMER   (*stops*) No, no, Nora—that will never do.

NORA   (*laughs and swings her tambourine*) Didn't I tell you so!

RANK   Let me play for her.

HELMER   (*rising*) Yes, do—then I can direct her better.

[RANK *sits down at the piano and plays;* NORA *dances more and more wildly.* HELMER *stands by the stove and addresses frequent corrections to her; she seems not to hear. Her hair breaks loose and falls over her shoulders. She does not notice it, but goes on dancing.* MRS. LINDEN *enters and stands spellbound in the doorway.*]

MRS. LINDEN Ah—!

NORA (*dancing*) We're having such fun here, Christina!

HELMER Why, Nora dear, you're dancing as if it were a matter of life and death.

NORA So it is.

HELMER Rank, stop! This is the merest madness. Stop, I say!

[RANK *stops playing and* NORA *comes to a sudden standstill.*]

HELMER (*going towards her*) I couldn't have believed it. You've positively forgotten all I taught you.

NORA (*throws the tambourine away*) You see for yourself.

HELMER You really do want teaching.

NORA Yes, you see how much I need it. You must practice with me up to the last moment. Will you promise me, Torvald?

HELMER Certainly, certainly.

NORA Neither today nor tomorrow must you think of anything but me. You mustn't open a single letter—mustn't look at the letter-box.

HELMER Ah, you're still afraid of that man—

NORA Oh, yes, yes, I am.

HELMER Nora, I can see it in your face—there's a letter from him in the box.

NORA I don't know. I believe so. But you're not to read anything now; nothing ugly must come between us until all is over.

RANK (*softly, to* HELMER) You mustn't contradict her.

HELMER (*putting his arm around her*) The child shall have her own way. But tomorrow night, when the dance is over—

NORA Then you shall be free.

[ELLEN *appears in the doorway, right.*]

ELLEN Dinner is on the table, ma'am.

NORA We'll have some champagne, Ellen.

ELLEN Yes, ma'am.

[*Goes out.*]

HELMER Dear me! Quite a banquet.

NORA Yes, and we'll keep it up till morning. (*Calling out.*) And macaroons, Ellen—plenty—just this once.

HELMER (*seizing her hand*) Come, come, don't let us have this wild excitement! Be my own little lark again.

NORA Oh, yes, I will. But now go into the dining-room; and you too, Doctor Rank. Christina, you must help me to do up my hair.

RANK (*softly, as they go*) There's nothing in the wind? Nothing—I mean—?

HELMER Oh, no, nothing of the kind. It's merely this babyish anxiety I was telling you about.

[*They go out to the right.*]

NORA   Well?

MRS. LINDEN   He's gone out of town.

NORA   I saw it in your face.

MRS. LINDEN   He comes back tomorrow evening. I left a note for him.

NORA   You shouldn't have done that. Things must take their course. After all, there's something glorious in waiting for the miracle.

MRS. LINDEN   What is it you're waiting for?

NORA   Oh, you can't understand. Go to them in the dining-room; I shall come in a moment.

[MRS. LINDEN *goes into the dining-room.* NORA *stands for a moment as though collecting her thoughts; then looks at her watch.*]

NORA   Five. Seven hours till midnight. Then twenty-four hours till the next midnight. Then the tarantella will be over. Twenty-four and seven? Thirty-one hours to live.

[HELMER *appears at the door, right.*]

HELMER   What has become of my little lark?

NORA   (*runs to him with open arms*) Here she is!

[CURTAIN]

ACT III

The same room. The table, with the chairs around it, in the middle. A lighted lamp on the table. The door to the hall stands open. Dance music is heard from the floor above.

MRS. LINDEN *sits by the table and absently turns the pages of a book. She tries to read, but seems unable to fix her attention; she frequently listens and looks anxiously towards the hall door.*

MRS. LINDEN   (*looks at her watch*) Not here, yet; and the time is nearly up. If only he hasn't—(*Listens again.*) Ah, there he is. (*She goes into the hall and cautiously opens the outer door; soft footsteps are heard on the stairs; she whispers.*) Come in; there is no one here.

KROGSTAD   (*in the doorway*) I found a note from you at my house. What does it mean?

MRS. LINDEN   I *must* speak to you.

KROGSTAD   Indeed? And in this house?

MRS. LINDEN   I could not see you at my rooms. They have no separate entrance. Come in; we are quite alone. The servants are asleep, and the Helmers are at the ball upstairs.

KROGSTAD   (*coming into the room*) Ah! So the Helmers are dancing this evening? Really?

MRS. LINDEN   Yes. Why not?

KROGSTAD   Quite right. Why not?

MRS. LINDEN   And now let us talk a little.

KROGSTAD   Have we two anything to say to each other?

MRS. LINDEN   A great deal.

KROGSTAD   I should not have thought so.

MRS. LINDEN   Because you have never really understood me.

KROGSTAD   What was there to understand? The most natural thing in the world—a heartless woman throws a man over when a better match offers.

MRS. LINDEN   Do you really think me so heartless? Do you think I broke with you lightly?

KROGSTAD   Didn't you?

MRS. LINDEN   Do you really think so?

KROGSTAD   If not, why did you write me that letter?

MRS. LINDEN   Was it not best? Since I had to break with you, was it not right that I should try to put an end to all that you felt for me?

KROGSTAD   (*clenching his hands together*) So that was it? And all this —for the sake of money!

MRS. LINDEN   You ought not to forget that I had a helpless mother and two little brothers. We could not wait for you, Nils, as your prospects then stood.

KROGSTAD   Perhaps not; but you had no right to cast me off for the sake of others, whoever the others might be.

MRS. LINDEN   I don't know. I have often asked myself whether I had the right.

KROGSTAD   (*more softly*) When I had lost you, I seemed to have no firm ground left under my feet. Look at me now. I am a shipwrecked man clinging to a spar.

MRS. LINDEN   Rescue may be at hand.

KROGSTAD   It *was* at hand; but then you came and stood in the way.

MRS. LINDEN   Without my knowledge, Nils. I did not know till today that it was you I was to replace in the Bank.

KROGSTAD   Well, I take your word for it. But now that you do know, do you mean to give way?

MRS. LINDEN   No, for that would not help you in the least.

KROGSTAD   Oh, help, help—! I should do it whether or no.

MRS. LINDEN   I have learnt prudence. Life and bitter necessity have schooled me.

KROGSTAD   And life has taught me not to trust fine speeches.

MRS. LINDEN   Then life has taught you a very sensible thing. But deeds you *will* trust?

KROGSTAD   What do you mean?

MRS. LINDEN   You said you were a shipwrecked man, clinging to a spar.

KROGSTAD   I have good reason to say so.

MRS. LINDEN   I too am shipwrecked and clinging to a spar. I have no one to mourn for, no one to care for.

KROGSTAD   You made your own choice.

MRS. LINDEN   No choice was left me.

KROGSTAD   Well, what then?

MRS. LINDEN   Nils, how if we two shipwrecked people could join hands?

KROGSTAD   What!

MRS. LINDEN   Two on a raft have a better chance than if each clings to a separate spar.

KROGSTAD   Christina!

MRS. LINDEN   What do you think brought me to town?

KROGSTAD   Had you any thought of me?

MRS. LINDEN   I must have work or I can't bear to live. All my life, as long as I can remember, I have worked; work has been my one great joy. Now I stand quite alone in the world, aimless and forlorn. There is no happiness in working for oneself. Nils, give me somebody and something to work for.

KROGSTAD   I cannot believe in all this. It is simply a woman's romantic craving for self-sacrifice.

MRS. LINDEN   Have you ever found me romantic?

KROGSTAD   Would you really—? Tell me: do you know all my past?

MRS. LINDEN   Yes.

KROGSTAD   And do you know what people say of me?

MRS. LINDEN   Did you not say just now that with me you could have been another man?

KROGSTAD   I am sure of it.

MRS. LINDEN   Is it too late?

KROGSTAD   Christina, do you know what you are doing? Yes, you do; I see it in your face. Have you the courage then—?

MRS. LINDEN   I need someone to be a mother to, and your children need a mother. You need me, and I—I need you. Nils, I believe in your better self. With you I fear nothing.

KROGSTAD   (*seizing her hands*) Thank you—thank you, Christina. Now I shall make others see me as you do.—Ah, I forgot—

MRS. LINDEN   (*listening*) Hush! The tarantella! Go! go!

KROGSTAD   Why? What is it?

MRS. LINDEN   Don't you hear the dancing overhead? As soon as that is over they will be here.

KROGSTAD   Oh, yes, I shall go. Nothing will come of this, after all. Of course, you don't know the step I have taken against the Helmers.

MRS. LINDEN   Yes, Nils, I do know.

KROGSTAD   And yet you have the courage to—?

MRS. LINDEN   I know to what lengths despair can drive a man.

KROGSTAD   Oh, if I could only undo it!

MRS. LINDEN   You could. Your letter is still in the box.

KROGSTAD   Are you sure?

MRS. LINDEN   Yes; but—

KROGSTAD   (*looking at her searchingly*) Is that what it all means? You want to save your friend at any price. Say it out—is that your idea?

MRS. LINDEN   Nils, a woman who has once sold herself for the sake of others, does not do so again.

KROGSTAD   I shall demand my letter back again.

MRS. LINDEN   No, no.

KROGSTAD   Yes, of course. I shall wait till Helmer comes; I shall tell him to give it back to me—that it's only about my dismissal—that I don't want it read—

MRS. LINDEN   No, Nils, you must not recall the letter.

KROGSTAD   But tell me, wasn't that just why you got me to come here?

MRS. LINDEN   Yes, in my first alarm. But a day has passed since then, and in that day I have seen incredible things in this house. Helmer must know everything; there must be an end to this unhappy secret. These two must come to a full understanding. They must have done with all these shifts and subterfuges.

KROGSTAD   Very well, if you like to risk it. But *one* thing I can do, and at once—

MRS. LINDEN   (*listening*) Make haste! Go, go! The dance is over; we're not safe another moment.

KROGSTAD   I shall wait for you in the street.

MRS. LINDEN   Yes, do; you must see me home.

KROGSTAD   I never was so happy in all my life!

[KROGSTAD *goes out by the outer door. The door between the room and the hall remains open.*]

MRS. LINDEN   (*arranging the room and getting her outdoor things together*) What a change! What a change! To have someone to work for, to live for; a home to make happy! Well, it shall not be my fault if I fail.—I wish they would come.—(*Listens.*) Ah, here they are! I must get my things on.

[*Takes bonnet and cloak.* HELMER'S *and* NORA'S *voices are heard outside, a key is turned in the lock, and* HELMER *drags* NORA *almost by force into the hall. She wears the Italian costume with a large black shawl over it. He is in evening dress and wears a black domino, open.*]

NORA   (*struggling with him in the doorway*) No, no, no! I won't go in! I want to go upstairs again; I don't want to leave so early!

HELMER   But, my dearest girl—!

NORA Oh, please, please, Torvald, I beseech you—only one hour more!

HELMER Not one minute more, Nora dear; you know what we agreed. Come, come in; you're catching cold here.

[*He leads her gently into the room in spite of her resistance.*]

MRS. LINDEN Good-evening.

NORA Christina!

HELMER What, Mrs. Linden! You here so late?

MRS. LINDEN Yes, I ought to apologize. I did so want to see Nora in her costume.

NORA Have you been sitting here waiting for me?

MRS. LINDEN Yes; unfortunately I came too late. You had gone upstairs already, and I felt I couldn't go away without seeing you.

HELMER (*taking* NORA's *shawl off*) Well then, just look at her! I assure you she's worth it. Isn't she lovely, Mrs. Linden?

MRS. LINDEN Yes, I must say—

HELMER Isn't she exquisite? Everyone said so. But she's dreadfully obstinate, dear little creature. What's to be done with her? Just think, I had almost to force her away.

NORA Oh, Torvald, you'll be sorry some day that you didn't let me stay, if only for one half-hour more.

HELMER There! You hear her, Mrs. Linden? She dances her tarantella with wild applause, and well she deserved it, I must say—though there was, perhaps, a little too much nature in her rendering of the idea—more than was, strictly speaking, artistic. But never mind—the point is, she made a great success, a tremendous success. Was I to let her remain after that—to weaken the impression? Not if I know it. I took my sweet little Capri girl—my capricious little Capri girl, I might say—under my arm; a rapid turn round the room, a curtsy to all sides, and—as they say in novels—the lovely apparition vanished! An exit should always be effective, Mrs. Linden; but I can't get Nora to see it. By Jove! it's warm here. (*Throws his domino on a chair and opens the door to his room*). What! No light there? Oh, of course. Excuse me—

[*Goes in and lights candles.*]

NORA (*whispers breathlessly*) Well?

MRS. LINDEN (*softly*) I've spoken to him.

NORA And—?

MRS. LINDEN Nora—you must tell your husband everything—

NORA (*tonelessly*) I knew it!

MRS. LINDEN You have nothing to fear from Krogstad; but you must speak out.

NORA I shall not speak.

MRS. LINDEN Then the letter will.

NORA Thank you, Christina. Now I know what I have to do. Hush—!

HELMER (*coming back*) Well, Mrs. Linden, have you admired her?

MRS. LINDEN Yes; and now I must say good-night.

HELMER What, already? Does this knitting belong to you?

MRS. LINDEN (*takes it*) Yes, thanks; I was nearly forgetting it.

HELMER Then you do knit?

MRS. LINDEN Yes.

HELMER Do you know, you ought to embroider instead?

MRS. LINDEN Indeed! Why?

HELMER Because it's so much prettier. Look now! You hold the embroidery in the left hand, so, and then work the needle with the right
hand, in a long, graceful curve—don't you?

MRS. LINDEN Yes, I suppose so.

HELMER But knitting is always ugly. Just look—your arms close to your
sides, and the needles going up and down—there's something Chinese
about it.—They really gave us splendid champagne tonight.

MRS. LINDEN Well, good-night, Nora, and don't be obstinate any more.

HELMER Well said, Mrs. Linden!

MRS. LINDEN Good-night, Mr. Helmer.

HELMER (*accompanying her to the door*) Good-night, good-night; I
hope you'll get safely home. I should be glad to—but you have such a
short way to go. Good-night, good-night. (*She goes;* HELMER *shuts
the door after her and comes forward again.*) At last we've got rid of
her: she's a terrible bore.

NORA Aren't you very tired, Torvald?

HELMER No, not in the least.

NORA Nor sleepy?

HELMER Not a bit. I feel particularly lively. But you? You do look tired
and sleepy.

NORA Yes, very tired. I shall soon sleep now.

HELMER There, you see. I was right after all not to let you stay longer.

NORA Oh, everything you do is right.

HELMER (*kissing her forehead*) Now my lark is speaking like a reasonable being. Did you notice how jolly Rank was this evening?

NORA Indeed? Was he? I had no chance of speaking to him.

HELMER Nor I, much; but I haven't seen him in such good spirits for
a long time. (*Looks at* NORA *a little, then comes nearer her.*) It's
splendid to be back in our own home, to be quite alone together!—
Oh, you enchanting creature!

NORA Don't look at me in that way, Torvald.

HELMER I am not to look at my dearest treasure?—at all the loveliness
that is mine, mine only, wholly and entirely mine?

NORA (*goes to the other side of the table*) You mustn't say these
things to me this evening.

HELMER (*following*) I see you have the tarantella still in your blood
—and that makes you all the more enticing. Listen! the other people
are going now. (*More softly.*) Nora—soon the whole house will be still.

NORA Yes, I hope so.

HELMER   Yes, don't you, Nora darling? When we are among strangers, do you know why I speak so little to you, and keep so far away, and only steal a glance at you now and then—do you know why I do it? Because I am fancying that we love each other in secret, that I am secretly betrothed to you, and that no one dreams that there is anything between us.

NORA   Yes, yes, yes. I know all your thoughts are with me.

HELMER   And then, when the time comes to go, and I put the shawl about your smooth, soft shoulders, and this glorious neck of yours, I imagine you are my bride, that our marriage is just over, that I am bringing you for the first time to my home—that I am alone with you for the first time—quite alone with you, in your trembling loveliness! All this evening I have been longing for you, and you only. When I watched you swaying and whirling in the tarantella—my blood boiled—I could endure it no longer; and that's why I made you come home with me so early—

NORA   Go now, Torvald! Go away from me. I won't have all this.

HELMER   What do you mean? Ah, I see you're teasing me, little Nora! Won't—won't! Am I not your husband—?

[*A knock at the outer door.*]

NORA   (*starts*) Did you hear—?

HELMER   (*going towards the hall*) Who's there?

RANK   (*outside*) It is I; may I come in for a moment?

HELMER   (*in a low tone, annoyed*) Oh! what can he want just now? (*Aloud.*) Wait a moment. (*Opens door.*) Come, it's nice of you to look in.

RANK   I thought I heard your voice, and that put it into my head. (*Looks round.*) Ah, this dear old place! How cozy you two are here!

HELMER   You seemed to find it pleasant enough upstairs, too.

RANK   Exceedingly. Why not? Why shouldn't one take one's share of everything in this world? All one can, at least, and as long as one can. The wine was splendid—

HELMER   Especially the champagne.

RANK   Did you notice it? It's incredible the quantity I contrived to get down.

NORA   Torvald drank plenty of champagne, too.

RANK   Did he?

NORA   Yes, and it always puts him in such spirits.

RANK   Well, why shouldn't one have a jolly evening after a well-spent day?

HELMER   Well-spent! Well, I haven't much to boast of in that respect.

RANK   (*slapping him on the shoulder*) But I *have*, don't you see?

NORA   I suppose you have been engaged in a scientific investigation, Doctor Rank?

RANK   Quite right.

HELMER   Bless me! Little Nora talking about scientific investigations!
NORA   Am I to congratulate you on the result?
RANK   By all means.
NORA   It was good then?
RANK   The best possible, both for doctor and patient—certainty.
NORA   (*quickly and searchingly*) Certainty?
RANK   Absolute certainty. Wasn't I right to enjoy myself after that?
NORA   Yes, quite right, Doctor Rank.
HELMER   And so say I, provided you don't have to pay for it tomorrow.
RANK   Well, in this life nothing is to be had for nothing.
NORA   Doctor Rank—I'm sure you are very fond of masquerades.
RANK   Yes, when there are plenty of amusing disguises—
NORA   Tell me, what shall we two be at our next masquerade?
HELMER   Little featherbrain! Thinking of your next already!
RANK   We two? I'll tell you. You must go as a good fairy.
HELMER   Ah, but what costume would indicate *that*?
RANK   She has simply to wear her everyday dress.
HELMER   Capital! But don't you know what you will be yourself?
RANK   Yes, my dear friend, I am perfectly clear upon that point.
HELMER   Well?
RANK   At the next masquerade I shall be invisible.
HELMER   What a comical idea!
RANK   There's a big black hat—haven't you heard of the invisible hat?
    It comes down all over you, and then no one can see you.
HELMER   (*with a suppressed smile*) No, you're right there.
RANK   But I'm quite forgetting what I came for. Helmer, give me a
    cigar—one of the dark Havanas.
HELMER   With the greatest pleasure.

[*Hands cigar-case.*]

RANK   (*takes one and cuts the end off*) Thank you.
NORA   (*striking a wax match*) Let me give you a light.
RANK   A thousand thanks.

[*She holds the match. He lights his cigar at it.*]

RANK   And now, good-by!
HELMER   Good-by, good-by, my dear fellow.
NORA   Sleep well, Doctor Rank.
RANK   Thanks for the wish.
NORA   Wish me the same.
RANK   You? Very well, since you ask me—Sleep well. And thanks for
    the light.

[*He nods to them both and goes out.*]

HELMER   (*in an undertone*) He's been drinking a good deal.
NORA   (*absently*) I dare say. (HELMER *takes his bunch of keys from
    his pocket and goes into the hall.*) Torvald, what are you doing
    there?

HELMER   I must empty the letter-box; it's quite full; there will be no room for the newspapers tomorrow morning.

NORA   Are you going to work tonight?

HELMER   You know very well I am not.—Why, how is this? Someone has been at the lock.

NORA   The lock—?

HELMER   I'm sure of it. What does it mean? I can't think that the servants—? Here's a broken hairpin. Nora, it's one of yours.

NORA   (*quickly*) It must have been the children—

HELMER   Then you must break them of such tricks.—There! At last I've got it open. (*Takes contents out and calls into the kitchen.*) Ellen!—Ellen, just put the hall-door lamp out.

[*He returns with letters in his hand and shuts the inner door.*]

HELMER   Just see how they've accumulated. (*Turning them over.*) Why, what's this?

NORA   (*at the window*) The letter! Oh, no, no, Torvald!

HELMER   Two visiting-cards—from Rank.

NORA   From Doctor Rank?

HELMER   (*looking at them*) Doctor Rank. They were on the top. He must just have put them in.

NORA   Is there anything on them?

HELMER   There's a black cross over the name. Look at it. What an unpleasant idea! It looks just as if he were announcing his own death.

NORA   So he is.

HELMER   What! Do you know anything? Has he told you anything?

NORA   Yes. These cards mean that he has taken his last leave of us. He is going to shut himself up and die.

HELMER   Poor fellow! Of course I knew we couldn't hope to keep him long. But so soon—! And to go and creep into his lair like a wounded animal—

NORA   When we *must* go, it is best to go silently. Don't you think so, Torvald?

HELMER   (*walking up and down*) He had so grown into our lives, I can't realize that he is gone. He and his sufferings and his loneliness formed a sort of cloudy background to the sunshine of our happiness. —Well, perhaps it's best as it is—at any rate for him. (*Stands still.*) And perhaps for us too, Nora. Now we two are thrown entirely upon each other. (*Takes her in his arms.*) My darling wife! I feel as if I could never hold you close enough. Do you know, Nora, I often wish some danger might threaten you, that I might risk body and soul, and everything, everything, for your dear sake.

NORA   (*tears herself from him and says firmly*) Now you shall read your letters, Torvald.

HELMER   No, no; not tonight. I want to be with you, my sweet wife.

NORA   With the thought of your dying friend—?

HELMER   You are right. This has shaken us both. Unloveliness has come between us—thoughts of death and decay. We must seek to cast them off. Till then—we will remain apart.

NORA   (*her arms round his neck*) Torvald! Good-night! good-night!

HELMER   (*kissing her forehead*) Good-night, my little song-bird. Sleep well, Nora. Now I shall go and read my letters.

[*He goes with the letters in his hand into his room and shuts the door.*]

NORA   (*with wild eyes, gropes about her, seizes* HELMER'S *domino, throws it round her, and whispers quickly, hoarsely, and brokenly*) Never to see him again. Never, never, never. (*Throws her shawl over her head.*) Never to see the children again. Never, never.—Oh, that black, icy water! Oh, that bottomless—! If it were only over! Now he has it; he's reading it. Oh, no, no, no, not yet. Torvald, good-by—! Good-by, my little ones—!

[*She is rushing out by the hall; at the same moment* HELMER *flings his door open and stands there with an open letter in his hand.*]

HELMER   Nora!

NORA   (*shrieks*) Ah—!

HELMER   What is this? Do you know what is in this letter?

NORA   Yes, I know. Let me go! Let me pass!

HELMER   (*holds her back*) Where do you want to go?

NORA   (*tries to break away from him*) You shall not save me, Torvald.

HELMER   (*falling back*) True! Is what he writes true? No, no, it is impossible that this can be true.

NORA   It is true. I have loved you beyond all else in the world.

HELMER   Pshaw—no silly evasions!

NORA   (*a step nearer him*) Torvald—!

HELMER   Wretched woman—what have you done?

NORA   Let me go—you shall not save me! You shall not take my guilt upon yourself!

HELMER   I don't want any melodramatic airs. (*Locks the outer door.*) Here you shall stay and give an account of yourself. Do you understand what you have done? Answer! Do you understand it?

NORA   (*looks at him fixedly and says with a stiffening expression*) Yes; now I begin fully to understand it.

HELMER   (*walking up and down*) Oh! what an awful awakening! During all these eight years—she who was my pride and my joy—a hypocrite, a liar—worse, worse—a criminal. Oh, the unfathomable hideousness of it all! Ugh! Ugh! (NORA *says nothing and continues to look fixedly at him.*) I ought to have known how it would be. I ought to have foreseen it. All your father's want of principle—be silent!—all your father's want of principle you have inherited—no religion, no morality, no sense of duty. How I am punished for screening him! I did it for your sake; and you reward me like this.

NORA   Yes—like this.

HELMER   You have destroyed my whole happiness. You have ruined my future. Oh, it's frightful to think of! I am in the power of a scoundrel; he can do whatever he pleases with me, demand whatever he chooses; he can domineer over me as much as he likes, and I must submit. And all this disaster and ruin is brought upon me by an unprincipled woman!

NORA   When I am out of the world, you will be free.

HELMER   Oh, no fine phrases. Your father, too, was always ready with them. What good would it do me, if you were "out of the world," as you say? No good whatever! He can publish the story all the same; I might even be suspected of collusion. People will think I was at the bottom of it all and egged you on. And for all this I have you to thank—you whom I have done nothing but pet and spoil during our whole married life. Do you understand now what you have done to me?

NORA   (*with cold calmness*) Yes.

HELMER   The thing is so incredible, I can't grasp it. But we must come to an understanding. Take that shawl off. Take it off, I say! I must try to pacify him in one way or another—the matter must be hushed up, cost what it may.—As for you and me, we must make no outward change in our way of life—no *outward* change, you understand. Of course, you will continue to live here. But the children cannot be left in your care. I dare not trust them to you.—Oh, to have to say this to one I have loved so tenderly—whom I still—! But that must be a thing of the past. Henceforward there can be no question of happiness, but merely of saving the ruins, the shreds, the show—(*A ring;* HELMER *starts.*) What's that? So late! Can it be the worst? Can he—? Hide yourself, Nora; say you are ill.

        [NORA *stands motionless.* HELMER *goes to the door and opens it.*]

ELLEN   (*half dressed, in the hall*) Here is a letter for you, ma'am.

HELMER   Give it to me. (*Seizes the letter and shuts the door.*) Yes, from him. You shall not have it. I shall read it.

NORA   Read it!

HELMER   (*by the lamp*) I have hardly the courage to. We may both be lost, both you and I. Ah! I *must* know. (*Hastily tears the letter open; reads a few lines, looks at an enclosure; with a cry of joy.*) Nora! (NORA *looks inquiringly at him.*) Nora!—Oh! I must read it again.—Yes, yes, it is so. I am saved! Nora, I am saved!

NORA   And I?

HELMER   You too, of course; we are both saved, both of us. Look here —he sends you back your promissory note. He writes that he regrets and apologizes—that a happy turn in his life—Oh, what matter what he writes? We are saved, Nora! No one can harm you. Oh, Nora, Nora—; but first get rid of this hateful thing. I'll just see—(*Glances at the I.O.U.*) No, I will not look at it; the whole thing shall be nothing but a dream to me. (*Tears the I.O.U. and both letters in pieces. Throws them into the fire and watches them burn.*) There! it's gone!—He said that ever since Christmas Eve—Oh, Nora, they must have been three terrible days for you!

NORA   I have fought a hard fight for the last three days.

HELMER   And in your agony you saw no other outlet but—No; we won't think of that horror. We will only rejoice and repeat—it's over, all over! Don't you hear, Nora? You don't seem able to grasp it. Yes, it's over. What is this set look on your face? Oh, my poor Nora, I understand; you cannot believe that I have forgiven you. But I have, Nora; I swear it. I have forgiven everything. I know that what you did was all for love of me.

NORA   That is true.

HELMER   You loved me as a wife should love her husband. It was only the means that, in your inexperience, you misjudged. But do you think I love you the less because you cannot do without guidance? No, no. Only lean on me; I will counsel you and guide you. I should be no true man if this very womanly helplessness did not make you doubly dear in my eyes. You mustn't dwell upon the hard things I said in my first moment of terror, when the world seemed to be tumbling about my ears. I have forgiven you, Nora—I swear I have forgiven you.

NORA   I thank you for your forgiveness.

[*Goes out to the right.*]

HELMER   No, stay—! (*Looking through the doorway.*) What are you going to do?

NORA   (*inside*) To take off my masquerade dress.

HELMER   (*in the doorway*) Yes, do, dear. Try to calm down and recover your balance, my scared little song-bird. You may rest secure. I have broad wings to shield you. (*Walking up and down near the door.*) Oh, how lovely—how cozy our home is, Nora! Here you are safe; here I can shelter you like a hunted dove whom I have saved from the claws of the hawk. I shall soon bring your poor beating heart to rest; believe me, Nora, very soon. Tomorrow all this will seem quite different—everything will be as before. I shall not need to tell you again that I forgive you; you will feel for yourself that it is true. How could you think I could find it in my heart to drive you away, or even so much as to reproach you? Oh, you don't know a true man's heart, Nora. There is something indescribably sweet and soothing to a man in having forgiven his wife—honestly forgiven her, from the bottom of his heart. She becomes his property in a double sense. She is as though born again; she has become, so to speak, at once his wife and his child. That is what you shall henceforth be to me, my bewildered, helpless darling. Don't be troubled about anything, Nora; only open your heart to me, and I will be both will and conscience to you.

[NORA *enters in everyday dress.*]

Why, what's this? Not gone to bed? You have changed your dress?

NORA Yes, Torvald; now I have changed my dress.

HELMER But why now, so late—?

NORA I shall not sleep tonight.

HELMER But, Nora dear—

NORA (*looking at her watch*) It's not so late yet. Sit down, Torvald; you and I have much to say to each other.

[*She sits at one side of the table.*]

HELMER Nora—what does this mean? Your cold, set face—

NORA Sit down. It will take some time. I have much to talk over with you.

[HELMER *sits at the other side of the table.*]

HELMER You alarm me, Nora. I don't understand you.

NORA No, that is just it. You don't understand me; and I have never understood you—till tonight. No, don't interrupt. Only listen to what I say.—We must come to a final settlement, Torvald.

HELMER How do you mean?

NORA (*after a short silence*) Doesn't one thing strike you as we sit here?

HELMER What should strike me?

NORA We have been married eight years. Doesn't it strike you that this is the first time we two, you and I, man and wife, have talked together seriously?

HELMER Seriously! What do you call seriously?

NORA During eight whole years, and more—ever since the day we first met—we have never exchanged one serious word about serious things.

HELMER Was I always to trouble you with the cares you could not help me to bear?

NORA I am not talking of cares. I say that we have never yet set ourselves seriously to get to the bottom of anything.

HELMER Why, my dearest Nora, what have you to do with serious things?

NORA There we have it! You have never understood me.—I have had great injustice done me, Torvald; first by father, and then by you.

HELMER What! By your father and me?—By us, who have loved you more than all the world?

NORA (*shaking her head*) You have never loved me. You only thought it amusing to be in love with me.

HELMER Why, Nora, what a thing to say!

NORA Yes, it is so, Torvald. While I was at home with father, he used to tell me all his opinions, and I held the same opinions. If I had others I said nothing about them, because he wouldn't have liked it. He used to call me his doll-child and played with me as I played with my dolls. Then I came to live in your house—

HELMER What an expression to use about our marriage!

NORA (*undisturbed*) I mean I passed from father's hands into yours.

You arranged everything according to your taste; and I got the same tastes as you; or I pretended to—I don't know which—both ways, perhaps; sometimes one and sometimes the other. When I look back on it now, I seem to have been living here like a beggar, from hand to mouth. I lived by performing tricks for you, Torvald. But you would have it so. You and father have done me a great wrong. It is your fault that my life has come to nothing.

HELMER Why, Nora, how unreasonable and ungrateful you are! Have you not been happy here?

NORA No, never. I thought I was; but I never was.

HELMER Not—not happy!

NORA No; only merry. And you have always been so kind to me. But our house has been nothing but a play-room. Here I have been your doll-wife, just as at home I used to be papa's doll-child. And the children, in their turn, have been my dolls. I thought it fun when you played with me, just as the children did when I played with them. That has been our marriage, Torvald.

HELMER There is some truth in what you say, exaggerated and over-strained though it be. But henceforth it shall be different. Playtime is over; now comes the time for education.

NORA Whose education? Mine, or the children's?

HELMER Both, my dear Nora.

NORA Oh, Torvald, you are not the man to teach me to be a fit wife for you.

HELMER And you can say that?

NORA And I—how have I prepared myself to educate the children?

HELMER Nora!

NORA Did you not say yourself, a few minutes ago, you dared not trust them to me?

HELMER In the excitement of the moment! Why should you dwell upon that?

NORA No—you were perfectly right. That problem is beyond me. There is another to be solved first—I must try to educate myself. You are not the man to help me in that. I must set about it alone. And that is why I am leaving you.

HELMER (jumping up) What—do you mean to say—?

NORA I must stand quite alone if I am ever to know myself and my surroundings; so I cannot stay with you.

HELMER Nora! Nora!

NORA I am going at once. I dare say Christina will take me in for to-night—

HELMER You are mad! I shall not allow it! I forbid it!

NORA It is of no use your forbidding me anything now. I shall take with me what belongs to me. From you I will accept nothing, either now or afterwards.

HELMER   What madness this is!

NORA   Tomorrow I shall go home—I mean to what was my home. It will be easier for me to find some opening there.

HELMER   Oh, in your blind inexperience—

NORA   I must try to *gain* experience, Torvald.

HELMER   To forsake your home, your husband, and your children! And you don't consider what the world will say.

NORA   I can pay no heed to that. I only know that I must do it.

HELMER   This is monstrous! Can you forsake your holiest duties in this way?

NORA   What do you consider my holiest duties?

HELMER   Do I need to tell you that? Your duties to your husband and your children.

NORA   I have other duties equally sacred.

HELMER   Impossible! What duties do you mean?

NORA   My duties towards myself.

HELMER   Before all else you are a wife and a mother.

NORA   That I no longer believe. I believe that before all else I am a human being, just as much as you are—or at least that I should try to become one. I know that most people agree with you, Torvald, and that they say so in books. But henceforth I can't be satisfied with what most people say, and what is in books. I must think things out for myself and try to get clear about them.

HELMER   Are you not clear about your place in your own home? Have you not an infallible guide in questions like these? Have you no religion?

NORA   Oh, Torvald, I don't really know what religion is.

HELMER   What do you mean?

NORA   I know nothing but what Pastor Hansen told me when I was confirmed. He explained that religion was this and that. When I get away from all this and stand alone, I will look into that matter too. I will see whether what he taught me is right, or, at any rate, whether it is right for me.

HELMER   Oh, this is unheard of! and from so young a woman! But if religion cannot keep you right, let me appeal to your conscience—for I suppose you have some moral feeling? Or, answer me: perhaps you have none?

NORA   Well, Torvald, it's not easy to say. I really don't know—I am all at sea about these things. I only know that I think quite differently from you about them. I hear, too, that the laws are different from what I thought; but I can't believe that they can be right. It appears that a woman has no right to spare her dying father or to save her husband's life! I don't believe that.

HELMER   You talk like a child. You don't understand the society in which you live.

NORA   No, I do not. But now I shall try to learn. I must make up my mind which is right—society or I.

HELMER   Nora, you are ill; you are feverish; I almost think you are out of your senses.

NORA   I have never felt so much clearness and certainty as tonight.

HELMER   You are clear and certain enough to forsake husband and children?

NORA   Yes, I am.

HELMER   Then there is only one explanation possible.

NORA   What is that?

HELMER   You no longer love me.

NORA   No; that is just it.

HELMER   Nora! Can you say so!

NORA   Oh, I'm so sorry, Torvald; for you've always been so kind to me. But I can't help it. I do not love you any longer.

HELMER   (*mastering himself with difficulty*) Are you clear and certain on this point too?

NORA   Yes, quite. That is why I will not stay here any longer.

HELMER   And can you also make clear to me how I have forfeited your love?

NORA   Yes, I can. It was this evening, when the miracle did not happen; for then I saw you were not the man I had imagined.

HELMER   Explain yourself more clearly; I don't understand.

NORA   I have waited so patiently all these eight years; for of course I saw clearly enough that miracles don't happen every day. When this crushing blow threatened me, I said to myself so confidently, "Now comes the miracle!" When Krogstad's letter lay in the box, it never for a moment occurred to me that you would think of submitting to that man's conditions. I was convinced that you would say to him, "Make it known to all the world"; and that then—

HELMER   Well? When I had given my own wife's name up to disgrace and shame—?

NORA   Then I firmly believed that you would come forward, take everything upon yourself, and say, "I am the guilty one."

HELMER   Nora—!

NORA   You mean I would never have accepted such a sacrifice? No, certainly not. But what would my assertions have been worth in opposition to yours?—*That* was the miracle that I hoped for and dreaded. And it was to hinder *that* that I wanted to die.

HELMER   I would gladly work for you day and night, Nora—bear sorrow and want for your sake. But no man sacrifices his honor, even for one he loves.

NORA   Millions of women have done so.

HELMER   Oh, you think and talk like a silly child.

NORA   Very likely. But you neither think nor talk like the man I can share my life with. When your terror was over—not for what threatened me, but for yourself—when there was nothing more to fear—then it seemed to you as though nothing had happened. I was your lark again, your doll, just as. before—whom you would take twice as much care of in future, because she was so weak and fragile. (*Stands up.*) Torvald—in that moment it burst upon me that I had been living here these eight years with a strange man, and had borne him three children.—Oh, I can't bear to think of it! I could tear myself to pieces!

HELMER (*sadly*) I see it, I see it; an abyss has opened between us.—But, Nora, can it never be filled up?

NORA As I now am, I am no wife for you.

HELMER I have strength to become another man.

NORA Perhaps—when your doll is taken away from you.

HELMER To part—to part from you! No, Nora, no; I can't grasp the thought.

NORA (*going into room on the right*) The more reason for the thing to happen.

[*She comes back with outdoor things and a small traveling-bag, which she places on a chair.*]

HELMER Nora, Nora, not now! Wait till tomorrow.

NORA (*putting on cloak*) I can't spend the night in a strange man's house.

HELMER But can we not live here, as brother and sister—?

NORA (*fastening her hat*) You know very well that wouldn't last long. (*Puts on the shawl.*) Good-by, Torvald. No, I won't go to the children. I know they are in better hands than mine. As I now am, I can be nothing to them.

HELMER But sometime, Nora—sometime—?

NORA How can I tell? I have no idea what will become of me.

HELMER But you are my wife, now and always!

NORA Listen, Torvald—when a wife leaves her husband's house, as I am doing, I have heard that in the eyes of the law he is free from all duties towards her. At any rate, I release you from all duties. You must not feel yourself bound, any more than I shall. There must be perfect freedom on both sides. There, I give you back your ring. Give me mine.

HELMER That too?

NORA That too.

HELMER Here it is.

NORA Very well. Now it is all over. I lay the keys here. The servants know about everything in the house—better than I do. Tomorrow, when I have started, Christina will come to pack up the things I brought with me from home. I will have them sent after me.

HELMER All over! all over! Nora, will you never think of me again?

NORA   Oh, I shall often think of you, and the children, and this house.
HELMER   May I write to you, Nora?
NORA   No—never. You must not.
HELMER   But I must send you—
NORA   Nothing, nothing.
HELMER   I must help you if you need it.
NORA   No, I say. I take nothing from strangers.
HELMER   Nora—can I never be more than a stranger to you?
NORA   (*taking her traveling-bag*) Oh, Torvald, then the miracle of miracles would have to happen—
HELMER   What is the miracle of miracles?
NORA   Both of us would have to change so that—Oh, Torvald, I no longer believe in miracles.
HELMER   But *I* will believe. Tell me! We must so change that—?
NORA   That communion between us shall be a marriage. Good-by.
              [*She goes out by the hall door.*]
HELMER   (*sinks into a chair by the door with his face in his hands*) Nora! Nora! (*He looks round and rises.*) Empty. She is gone. (*A hope springs up in him.*) Ah! the miracle of miracles—?
      [*From below is heard the reverberation of a heavy door closing.*]

[CURTAIN]

QUESTIONS

1. It has been said that Ibsen thinks too much of woman's rights and too little of her duties. With this in mind, do you think Nora is justified in leaving her husband?

2. What is the significance of the subplot between Mrs. Linden and Krogstad?

3. What is Mrs. Linden's function in the play?

4. How does Nora's behavior up until the last scene show her acceptance of the feminine ideal and her efforts to live up to it?

5. Discuss the character of Torvald. What indications does Ibsen give of the traits that made Nora fall in love with him?

6. How does Ibsen's portrayal of sexuality reveal his attitudes? How would you classify him in regard to sexual morality?

7. What symbolic use does Ibsen make of costume?

8. Are Nora's problems personal only, or do they have a political and social basis?

Elizabeth Barrett Browning

Elizabeth Barrett Browning (1806–1861) wrote her verse-novel, Aurora Leigh *(1856), as a study of the intellectual, emotional, and creative development of a poet. It is one of the very few self-portraits produced by a woman writer in the nineteenth century and is important for its analysis of the ambivalence, the self-doubt, and the social pressures tormenting the woman with creative ambitions.* Aurora Leigh *shocked many critics with its heroine's insistence on her need to define her own life and to do her own work, rather than accept a man's vision of her, however affectionate. One of the finest sections of the poem is the Second Book, reprinted below, which contains Aurora's rejection of her cousin Romney's proposal.*

Though she is best known today as the wife of Robert Browning and the heroine of one of literature's most romantic love stories, Elizabeth Barrett Browning was in her own day, much more famous as a poet than her husband, and she continued to write throughout their marriage, despite illness, four miscarriages, and the birth of a son. Although she held many feminist views, she was not an activist. The theory of male supremacy, which Romney Leigh articulates so winningly in the poem, was difficult to overcome, and she had serious doubts about women's capacity for the responsibilities of legal equality.

from

Aurora Leigh

Times followed one another. Came a morn
I stood upon the brink of twenty years,

And looked before and after, as I stood
Woman and artist,—either incomplete,
Both credulous of completion. There I held
The whole creation in my little cup,
And smiled with thirsty lips before I drank,
'Good health to you and me, sweet neighbour mine,
And all these peoples.'
              I was glad, that day;
The June was in me, with its multitudes   10
Of nightingales all singing in the dark,
And rosebuds reddening where the calyx split.
I felt so young, so strong, so sure of God!
So glad, I could not choose be very wise!
And, old at twenty, was inclined to pull
My childhood backward in a childish jest
To see the face of't once more, and farewell!
In which fantastic mood I bounded forth
At early morning,—would not wait so long
As even to snatch my bonnet by the strings,   20
But, brushing a green trail across the lawn
With my gown in the dew, took will and way
Among the acacias of the shrubberies.
To fly my fancies in the open air
And keep my birthday, till my aunt awoke
To stop good dreams. Meanwhile I murmured on,
As honeyed bees keep humming to themselves;
'The worthiest poets have remained uncrowned
Till death has bleached their foreheads to the bone,
And so with me it must be, unless I prove   30
Unworthy of the grand adversity,—
And certainly I would not fail so much.
What, therefore, if I crown myself to-day
In sport, not pride, to learn the feel of it,
Before my brows be numb as Dante's own
To all the tender pricking of such leaves?
Such leaves! what leaves?'
              I pulled the branches down,
To choose from.
           'Not the bay! I choose no bay;
The fates deny us if we are overbold:
Nor myrtle—which means chiefly love; and love   40
Is something awful which one dare not touch

So early o' mornings. This verbena strains
The point of passionate fragrance; and hard by,
This guelder rose, at far too slight a beck
Of the wind, will toss about her flower-apples.
Ah—there's my choice,—that ivy on the wall,
That headlong ivy! not a leaf will grow
But thinking of a wreath. Large leaves, smooth leaves,
Serrated like my vines, and half as green.
I like such ivy; bold to leap a height   50
'Twas strong to climb! as good to grow on graves
As twist about a thyrsus; pretty too,
(And that's not ill) when twisted round a comb.'
Thus speaking to myself, half singing it,
Because some thoughts are fashioned like a bell
To ring with once being touched, I drew a wreath
Drenched, blinding me with dew, across my brow,
And fastening it behind so, . . turning faced
. . My public!—cousin Romney—with a mouth
Twice graver than his eyes.
               I stood there fixed—   60
My arms up, like the caryatid, sole
Of some abolished temple, helplessly
Persistent in a gesture which derides
A former purpose. Yet my blush was flame,
As if from flax, not stone.
               'Aurora Leigh,
The earliest of Aurora's!'
               Hand stretched out
I clasped, as shipwrecked men will clasp a hand,
Indifferent to the sort of palm. The tide
Had caught me at my pastime, writing down
My foolish name too near upon the sea   70
Which drowned me with a blush as foolish. 'You,
My cousin!'
         The smile died out in his eyes
And dropped upon his lips, a cold dead weight,
For just a moment . . 'Here's a book, I found!
No name writ on it—poems, by the form;
Some Greek upon the margin,—lady's Greek,
Without the accents. Read it? Not a word.
I saw at once the thing had witchcraft in't,
Whereof the reading calls up dangerous spirits;

I rather bring it to the witch.'
                   'My book!   80
You found it' . .
              'In the hollow by the stream,
That beach leans down into—of which you said,
The Oread in it has a Naiad's heart
And pines for waters.'
                'Thank you.'
                     'Rather *you*,
My cousin! that I have seen you not too much
A witch, a poet, scholar, and the rest,
To be a woman also.'
               With a glance
The smile rose in his eyes again, and touched
The ivy on my forehead, light as air.
I answered gravely, 'Poets needs must be   90
Or men or women—more's the pity.'
                       'Ah,
But men, and still less women, happily,
Scarce need be poets. Keep to the green wreath,
Since even dreaming of the stone and bronze
Brings headaches, pretty cousin, and defiles
The clean white morning dresses.'
                  'So you judge!
Because I love the beautiful, I must
Love pleasure chiefly, and be overcharged
For ease and whiteness! Well—you know the world,
And only miss your cousin; 'tis not much!—   100
But learn this: I would rather take my part
With God's Dead, who afford to walk in white
Yet spread His glory, than keep quiet here,
And gather up my feet from even a step,
For fear to soil my gown in so much dust.
I choose to walk at all risks.—Here, if heads
That hold a rhythmic thought, must ache perforce,
For my part, I choose headaches,—and to-day's
My birthday.'
             'Dear Aurora, choose instead
To cure such. You have balsams.'
                     'I perceive!—   110
The headache is too noble for my sex.
You think the heartache would sound decenter,

Since that's the woman's special, proper ache,
And altogether tolerable, except
To a woman.'
        Saying which, I loosed my wreath,
And, swinging it beside me as I walked,
Half petulant, half playful, as we walked,
I sent a sidelong look to find his thought,—
As falcon set on falconer's finger may,
With sidelong head, and startled, braving eye,   120
Which means, 'You'll see—you'll see! I'll soon take flight—
You shall not hinder.' He, as shaking out
His hand and answering 'Fly then,' did not speak,
Except by such a gesture. Silently
We paced, until, just coming into sight
Of the house-windows, he abruptly caught
At one end of the swinging wreath, and said
'Aurora!' There I stopped short, breath and all.

'Aurora, let's be serious, and throw by
This game of head and heart. Life means, be sure,   130
Both heart and head,—both active, both complete,
And both in earnest. Men and women make
The world, as head and heart make human life.
Work man, work woman, since there's work to do
In this beleaguered earth, for head and heart,
And thought can never do the work of love!
But work for ends, I mean for uses; not
For such sleek fringes (do you call them ends?
Still less God's glory) as we sew ourselves
Upon the velvet of those baldaquins   140
Held 'twixt us and the sun. That book of yours,
I have not read a page of; but I toss
A rose up—it falls calyx down, you see! . .
The chances are that, being a woman, young,
And pure, with such a pair of large, calm eyes, . .
You write as well . . and ill . . upon the whole,
As other women. If as well, what then?
If even a little better, . . still what then?
We want the Best in art now, or no art.
The time is done for facile settings up   150
Of minnow gods, nymphs here, and tritons there;
The polytheists have gone out in God,

That unity of Bests. No best, no God!—
And so with art, we say. Give art's divine,
Direct, indubitable, real as grief,—
Or leave us to the grief we grow ourselves
Divine by overcoming with mere hope
And most prosaic patience. You, you are young
As Eve with nature's daybreak on her face;
But this same world you are come to, dearest coz,   160
Has done with keeping birthdays, saves her wreaths
To hang upon her ruins,—and forgets
To rhyme the cry with which she still beats back
Those savage, hungry dogs that hunt her down
To the empty grave of Christ. The world's hard pressed;
The sweat of labour in the early curse
Has (turning acrid in six thousand years)
Become the sweat of torture. Who has time,
An hour's time . . think! . . to sit upon a bank
And hear the cymbal tinkle in white hands?   170
When Egypt's slain, I say, let Miriam sing!—
Before . . where's Moses?'
                              'Ah—exactly that
Where's Moses?—is a Moses₁ to be found?—
You'll seek him vainly in the bulrushes,
While I in vain touch cymbals. Yet, concede,
Such sounding brass has done some actual good,
(The application in a woman's hand,
If that were credible, being scarcely spoilt,)
In colonising beehives.'
                              'There it is!—
You play beside a death-bed like a child,   180
Yet measure to yourself a prophet's place
To teach the living. None of all these things,
Can women understand. You generalise
Oh, nothing!—not even grief! Your quick-breathed hearts,
So sympathetic to the personal pang,
Close on each separate knife-stroke, yielding up
A whole life at each wound; incapable
Of deepening, widening a large lap of life
To hold the world-full woe. The human race
To you means, such a child, or such a man,   190
You saw one morning waiting in the cold,
Beside that gate, perhaps. You gather up

A few such cases, and, when strong, sometimes
Will write of factories and of slaves, as if
Your father were a negro, and your son
A spinner in the mills. All's yours and you,—
All, coloured with your blood, or otherwise
Just nothing to you. Why, I call you hard
To general suffering. Here's the world half blind
With intellectual light, half brutalised   200
With civilisation, having caught the plague
In silks from Tarsus, shrieking east and west
Along a thousand railroads, mad with pain
And sin too! . . does one woman of you all,
(You who weep easily) grow pale to see
This tiger shake his cage?—does one of you
Stand still from dancing, stop from stringing pearls,
And pine and die, because of the great sum
Of universal anguish?—Show me a tear
Wet as Cordelia's, in eyes bright as yours,   210
Because the world is mad! You cannot count,
That you should weep for this account, not you!
You weep for what you know. A red-haired child
Sick in a fever, if you touch him once,
Though but so little as with a finger-tip,
Will set you weeping; but a million sick . .
You could as soon weep for the rule of three,
Or compound fractions. Therefore, this same world
Uncomprehended by you, must remain
Uninfluenced by you. Women as you are,   220
Mere women, personal and passionate,
You give us doating mothers, and chaste wives,
Sublime Madonnas, and enduring saints!
We get no Christ from you,—and verily
We shall not get a poet, in my mind.'

'With which conclusion you conclude' . .
                                        'But this—
That you, Aurora, with the large live brow
And steady eyelids, cannot condescend
To play at art, as children play at swords,
To show a pretty spirit, chiefly admired   230
Because true action is impossible.
You never can be satisfied with praise

Which men give women when they judge a book
Not as mere work, but as mere woman's work,
Expressing the comparative respect
Which means the absolute scorn. 'Oh, excellent!
What grace! what facile turns! what fluent sweeps!
What delicate discernment . . almost thought!
The book does honour to the sex, we hold.
Among our female authors we make room   240
For this fair writer, and congratulate
The country that produces in these times
Such women, competent to . . spell.'
                                    'Stop there!'
I answered—burning through his thread of talk
With a quick flame of emotion,—'You have read
My soul, if not my book, and argue well
I would not condescend . . we will not say
To such a kind of praise, (a worthless end
Is praise of all kinds) but to such a use
Of holy art and golden life. I am young,   250
And peradventure weak—you tell me so—
Through being a woman. And, for all the rest,
Take thanks for justice. I would rather dance
At fairs on tight-rope, till the babies dropped
Their gingerbread for joy,—than shift the types
For tolerable verse, intolerable
To men who act and suffer. Better far,
Pursue a frivolous trade by serious means,
Than a sublime art frivolously.'
                                    'You,
Choose nobler work than either, O moist eyes,   260
And hurrying lips, and heaving heart! We are young
Aurora, you and I. The world . . look round . .
The world, we're come to late, is swollen hard
With perished generations and their sins:
The civiliser's spade grinds horribly
On dead men's bones, and cannot turn up soil
That's otherwise than fetid. All success
Proves partial failure; all advance implies
What's left behind; all triumph, something crushed
At the chariot-wheels; all government, some wrong: 270
And rich men make the poor, who curse the rich,

Who agonise together, rich and poor,
Under and over, in the social spasm
And crisis of the ages. Here's an age,
That makes its own vocation! here, we have stepped
Across the bounds of time! here's nought to see,
But just the rich man and just Lazarus,
And both in torments; with a mediate gulph,
Though not a hint of Abraham's bosom. Who,
Being man and human, can stand calmly by   280
And view these things, and never tease his soul
For some great cure? No physic for this grief,
In all the earth and heavens too?'
                                  'You believe
In God, for your part?—ay? that He who makes,
Can make good things from ill things, best from worst,
As men plant tulips upon dunghills when
They wish them finest?'
                                  'True. A death-heat is
The same as life-heat, to be accurate;
And in all nature is no death at all,
As men account of death, as long as God   290
Stands witnessing for life perpetually
By being just God. That's abstract truth, I know,
Philosophy, or sympathy with God:
But I, I sympathise with man, not God,
I think I was a man for chiefly this;
And when I stand beside a dying bed,
It's death to me. Observe,—it had not much
Consoled the race of mastodons to know
Before they went to fossil, that anon
Their place should quicken with the elephant;   300
They were not elephants but mastodons:
And I, a man, as men are now, and not
As men may be hereafter, feel with men
In the agonising present.'
                                  'Is it so,'
I said, 'my cousin? is the world so bad,
While I hear nothing of it through the trees?
The world was always evil,—but so bad?'

'So bad, Aurora. Dear, my soul is grey

With poring over the long sum of ill;
So much for vice, so much for discontent,   310
So much for the necessities of power,
So much for the connivances of fear,—
Coherent in statistical despairs
With such a total of distracted life, . .
To see it down in figures on a page,
Plain, silent, clear . . as God sees through the earth
The sense of all the graves! . . that's terrible
For one who is not God, and cannot right
The wrong he looks on. May I choose indeed
But vow away my years, my means, my aims,   320
Among the helpers, if there's any help
In such a social strait? The common blood
That swings along my veins, is strong enough
To draw me to this duty.'
                         Then I spoke.
'I have not stood long on the strand of life,
And these salt waters have had scarcely time
To creep so high up as to wet my feet.
I cannot judge these tides—I shall, perhaps.
A woman's always younger than a man
At equal years, because she is disallowed   330
Maturing by the outdoor sun and air,
And kept in long-clothes past the age to walk.
Ah well, I know you men judge otherwise!
You think a woman ripens as a peach,—
In the cheeks, chiefly. Pass it to me now;
I'm young in age, and younger still, I think,
As a woman. But a child may say amen
To a bishop's prayer and see the way it goes;
And I, incapable to loose the knot
Of social questions, can approve, applaud   340
August compassion, christian thoughts that shoot
Beyond the vulgar white of personal aims.
Accept my reverence.'
                         There he glowed on me
With all his face and eyes. 'No other help?'
Said he—'no more than so?'
                         'What help?' I asked.
'You'd scorn my help,—as Nature's self, you say,
Has scorned to put her music in my mouth,

Because a woman's. Do you now turn round
And ask for what a woman cannot give?'

'For what she only can, I turn and ask,'   350
He answered, catching up my hands in his,
And dropping on me from his high-eaved brow
The full weight of his soul,—'I ask for love,
And that, she can; for life in fellowship
Through bitter duties—that, I know she can;
For wifehood . . will she?'
                              'Now,' I said, 'may God
Be witness 'twixt us two!' and with the word,
Meseemed I floated into a sudden light
Above his stature,—'am I proved too weak
To stand alone, yet strong enough to bear   360
Such leaners on my shoulder? poor to think,
Yet rich enough to sympathise with thought?
Incompetent to sing, as blackbirds can,
Yet competent to love, like Him?'
                                   I paused:
Perhaps I darkened, as the light house will
That turns upon the sea. 'It's always so!
Anything does for a wife.'
                            'Aurora, dear,
And dearly honoured' . . he pressed in at once
With eager utterance,—'you translate me ill.
I do not contradict my thought of you   370
Which is most reverent, with another thought
Found less so. If your sex is weak for art,
(And I who said so, did but honour you
By using truth in courtship) it is strong
For life and duty. Place your fecund heart
In mine, and let us blossom for the world
That wants love's colour in the grey of time.
With all my talk I can but set you where
You look down coldly on the arena-heaps
Of headless bodies, shapeless, indistinct!   380
The Judgment-Angel scarce would find his way
Through such a heap of generalised distress,
To the individual man with lips and eyes—
Much less Aurora. Ah, my sweet, come down,
And, hand in hand, we'll go where yours shall touch

These victims, one by one! till one by one,
The formless, nameless trunk of every man
Shall seem to wear a head, with hair you know,
And every woman catch your mother's face
To melt you into passion.'
               'I am a girl,'   390
I answered slowly; 'you do well to name
My mother's face. Though far too early, alas,
God's hand did interpose 'twixt it and me,
I know so much of love, as used to shine
In that face and another. Just so much;
No more indeed at all. I have not seen
So much love since, I pray you pardon me,
As answers even to make a marriage with,
In this cold land of England. What you love,
Is not a woman, Romney, but a cause: 400
You want a helpmate, not a mistress, sir,—
A wife to help your ends . . in her no end!
Your cause is noble, your ends excellent,
But I, being most unworthy of these and that,
Do otherwise conceive of love. Farewell.'

'Farewell, Aurora? you reject me thus?'
He said.
       'Why, sir, you are married long ago.
You have a wife already whom you love,
Your social theory. Bless you both, I say.
For my part, I am scarcely meek enough   410
To be the handmaid of a lawful spouse.
Do I look a Hagar, think you?'
               'So, you jest!'

'Nay so, I speak in earnest,' I replied.
'You treat of marriage too much like, at least,
A chief apostle; you would bear with you
A wife . . a sister . . shall we speak it out?
A sister of charity.'
         'Then, must it be
Indeed farewell? And was I so far wrong
In hope and in illusion, when I took
The woman to be nobler than the man,   420
Yourself the noblest woman,—in the use

And comprehension of what love is,—love,
That generates the likeness of itself
Through all heroic duties? so far wrong,
In saying bluntly, venturing truth on love,
'Come, human creature, love and work with me,'—
Instead of, 'Lady, thou art wondrous fair,
'And, where the Graces walk before, the Muse
'Will follow at the lighting of the eyes,
'And where the Muse walks, lovers need to creep: 430
'Turn round and love me, or I die of love."

With quiet indignation I broke in.
'You misconceive the question like a man,
Who sees a woman as the complement
Of his sex merely. You forget too much
That every creature, female as the male,
Stands single in responsible act and thought,
As also in birth and death. Whoever says
To a loyal woman, 'Love and work with me,'
Will get fair answers, if the work and love,   440
Being good themselves, are good for her—the best
She was born for. Women of a softer mood,
Surprised by men when scarcely awake to life,
Will sometimes only hear the first word, love,
And catch up with it any kind of work,
Indifferent, so that dear love go with it:
I do not blame such women, though, for love,
They pick much oakum; earth's fanatics make
Too frequently heaven's saints. But *me*, your work
Is not the best for,—nor your love the best,   450
Nor able to commend the kind of work
For love's sake merely. Ah, you force me, sir,
To be over-bold in speaking of myself,—
I, too, have my vocation,—work to do,
The heavens and earth have set me, since I changed
My father's face for theirs,—and, though your world
Were twice as wretched as you represent,
Most serious work, most necessary work,
As any of the economists'. Reform,
Make trade a Christian possibility,   460
And individual right no general wrong;
Wipe out earth's furrows of the Thine and Mine,

And leave one green, for men to play at bowls;
With innings for them all! . . what then, indeed,
If mortals were not greater by the head
Than any of their prosperities? what then,
Unless the artist keep up open roads
Betwixt the seen and unseen,—bursting through
The best of your conventions with his best,
The speakable, imaginable best   470
God bids him speak, to prove what lies beyond
Both speech and imagination? A starved man
Exceeds a fat beast: we'll not barter, sir,
The beautiful for barley.—And, even so,
I hold you will not compass your poor ends
Of barley-feeding and material ease,
Without a poet's individualism
To work your universal. It takes a soul,
To move a body: it takes a high-souled man,
To move the masses . . even to a cleaner stye: 480
It takes the ideal, to blow a hair's-breadth off
The dust of the actual.—Ah (your Fouriers failed,
Because not poets enough to understand
That life develops from within.—For me,
Perhaps I am not worthy, as you say,
Of work like this! . . perhaps a woman's soul
Aspires, and not creates! yet we aspire,
And yet I'll try out your perhapses, sir;
And if I fail . . why, burn me up my straw
Like other false works—I'll not ask for grace,   490
Your scorn is better, cousin Romney. I
Who love my art, would never wish it lower
To suit my stature. I may love my art.
You'll grant that even a woman may love art,
Seeing that to waste true love on anything,
Is womanly, past question.'
                              I retain
The very last word which I said, that day,
As you the creaking of the door, years past,
Which let upon you such disabling news
You ever after have been graver. He,   500
His eyes, the motions in his silent mouth,
Were fiery points on which my words were caught,
Transfixed for ever in my memory

For his sake, not their own. And yet I know
I did not love him . . nor he me . . that's sure . .
And what I said, is unrepented of,
As truth is always. Yet . . a princely man!—
If hard to me, heroic for himself!
He bears down on me through the slanting years,
The stronger for the distance. If he had loved,   510
Ay, loved me, with that retributive face, . .
I might have been a common woman now,
And happier, less known and less left alone;
Perhaps a better woman after all,—
With chubby children hanging on my neck
To keep me low and wise. Ah me, the vines
That bear such fruit, are proud to stoop with it.
The palm stands upright in a realm of sand.

And I, who spoke the truth then, stand upright,
Still worthy of having spoken out the truth,   520
By being content I spoke it, though it set
Him there, me here.—O woman's vile remorse,
To hanker after a mere name, a show,
A supposition, a potential love!
Does every man who names love in our lives,
Become a power for that? is love's true thing
So much best to us, that what personates love
Is next best? A potential love, forsooth!
We are not so vile. No, no—he cleaves, I think,
This man, this image, . . chiefly for the wrong   530
And shock he gave my life, in finding me
Precisely where the devil of my youth
Had set me, on those mountain-peaks of hope
All glittering with the dawn-dew, all erect
And famished for the morning,—saying, while
I looked for empire and much tribute, 'Come,
I have some worthy work for thee below.
Come, sweep my barns, and keep my hospitals,—
And I will pay thee with a current coin
Which men give women.'
                    As we spoke, the grass   540
Was trod in haste beside us, and my aunt,
With smile distorted by the sun,—face, voice,
As much at issue with the summer-day

As if you brought a candle out of doors,—
Broke in with, 'Romney, here!—My child, entreat
Your cousin to the house, and have your talk,
If girls must talk upon their birthdays. Come.

He answered for me calmly, with pale lips
That seemed to motion for a smile in vain.
'The talk is ended, madam, where we stand.   550
Your brother's daughter has dismissed me here;
And all my answer can be better said
Beneath the trees, than wrong by such a word
Your house's hospitalities. Farewell.'

QUESTIONS

1. What is the significance of Aurora's choice of ivy for her wreath?

2. Why is Aurora so insulted by the terms of Romney's proposal? Is her indignation justified?

3. Describe Romney's attitude toward women.

4. Does Aurora's narration of this episode show any ambivalence in her attitude toward Romney?

Anne Sexton

In explosive, self-lacerating verse, Anne Sexton (b. 1928) lays bare her anxieties, guilt, and suffering with a confessional frankness few women writers have ever been able to afford. Her poetry deals both with the suppressed aspects of feminine experience, such as adultery and abortion, and the normative ones, such as housekeeping and childbirth. Like Elizabeth Barrett Browning's heroine, she accepts no one's definition of woman, and her poetry is not at the service of any external ethic or system.

Anne Sexton studied with Robert Lowell at Boston University, where she met Sylvia Plath, and she was one of the first women to hold a fellowship at Radcliffe College's Institute for Independent Study. She has written a play, Mercy Street *(1969), and several books of poetry, including* To Bedlam and Part Way Back *(1960),* All My Pretty Ones *(1962),* Live or Die *(1966), and* Love Poems *(1969). She is married and the mother of two daughters.*

For My Lover,
Returning to His Wife

She is all there.
She was melted carefully down for you
and cast up from your childhood,
cast up from your one hundred favorite aggies.

FROM *Love Poems*. Copyright © 1967, 1968, 1969, by Anne Sexton. Reprinted by permission of the publisher, Houghton Mifflin Company.

She has always been there, my darling.
She is, in fact, exquisite.
Fireworks in the dull middle of February
and as real as a cast-iron pot.

Let's face it, I have been momentary.
A luxury. A bright red sloop in the harbor.   10
My hair rising like smoke from the car window.
Littleneck clams out of season.

She is more than that. She is your have to have,
has grown you your practical your tropical growth.
This is not an experiment. She is all harmony.
She sees to oars and oarlocks for the dinghy,

has placed wild flowers at the window at breakfast,
sat by the potter's wheel at midday,
set forth three children under the moon,
three cherubs drawn by Michelangelo,   20

done this with her legs spread out
in the terrible months in the chapel.
If you glance up, the children are there
like delicate balloons resting on the ceiling.

She has also carried each one down the hall
after supper, their heads privately bent,
two legs protesting, person to person,
her face flushed with a song and their little sleep.

I give you back your heart.
I give you permission—   30

for the fuse inside her, throbbing
angrily in the dirt, for the bitch in her
and the burying of her wound—
for the burying of her small red wound alive—

for the pale flickering flare under her ribs,
for the drunken sailor who waits in her left pulse,

for the mother's knee, for the stockings,
for the garter belt, for the call—

the curious call
when you will burrow in arms and breasts   40
and tug at the orange ribbon in her hair
and answer the call, the curious call.

She is so naked and singular.
She is the sum of yourself and your dream.
Climb her like a monument, step after step.
She is solid.

As for me, I am a watercolor.
I wash off.

The Abortion

Somebody who should have been born
is gone.

Just as the earth puckered its mouth,
each bud puffing out from its knot,
I changed my shoes, and then drove south.

Up past the Blue Mountains, where
Pennsylvania humps on endlessly,
wearing, like a crayoned cat, its green hair,

its roads sunken in like a gray washboard;
where, in truth, the ground cracks evilly,   10
a dark socket from which the coal has poured,

Somebody who should have been born
is gone.

The grass as bristly and stout as chives,
and me wondering when the ground would break,
and me wondering how anything fragile survives;

up in Pennsylvania, I met a little man,
not Rumpelstiltskin, at all, at all . . .
he took the fullness that love began.

Returning north, even the sky grew thin   20
like a high window looking nowhere.
The road was as flat as a sheet of tin.

Somebody who should have been born
is gone.

Yes, woman, such logic will lead
to loss without death. Or say what you meant,
you coward . . . this baby that I bleed.

Housewife

Some women marry houses.
It's another kind of skin; it has a heart,
a mouth, a liver and bowel movements.
The walls are permanent and pink.
See how she sits on her knees all day,
faithfully washing herself down.
Men enter by force, drawn back like Jonah
into their fleshy mothers.

A woman *is* her mother.
That's the main thing.

QUESTIONS

1. In "For My Lover, Returning to His Wife," Anne Sexton dramatizes two images of woman—the wife and the mistress. How are they different?

2. What is the meaning of the reference to Rumpelstiltskin in "The Abortion"?

3. Explain the image in "Housewife." What is the significance of the title?

Sylvia Plath

Sylvia Plath (1932–1963), *who committed suicide shortly after the birth of her second child, was a brilliant American poet and novelist. A graduate of Smith College, she won a fellowship to Newnham College, Cambridge, England, where she met and married the English poet Ted Hughes. Throughout her life, Sylvia Plath struggled with the agonizing and precarious selfhood of the woman who combines several identities. Haunted at one extreme by the specter of the frigid bluestocking, at the other by the image of the domestic drudge, she returned again and again in her work to the themes of female experience. In her autobiographical novel* The Bell Jar (1963), *and in her BBC radio play* Three Women, *set in a maternity ward, she explored the psyche of woman from adolescent sexual awakening to childbirth. Her first book of poems,* The Colossus (1960), *had only moderate success, but* Ariel, *which contains the poem reprinted below, was written in the tormented months preceding her suicide and was widely acclaimed for its fiery intensity and heroic self-discipline. Her husband wrote of her:*

> She had none of the usual guards and remote controls to protect herself from her own reality. She lived right in it, especially during the last two years of her life. Perhaps that is one of the privileges, or prices, of being a woman, and at the same time an initiate into the poetic order of events.

Lesbos

Viciousness in the kitchen!
The potatoes hiss.
It is all Hollywood, windowless,
The fluorescent light wincing off and on like a terrible migraine.
Coy paper strips for doors . . .
Stage curtains, a widow's frizz!
And I, love, am a pathological liar,
And my child—look at her, face down on the floor!
Little unstrung puppet, kicking to disappear!
Why she is a schizophrenic,   10
Her face red and white, a panic.
You have stuck her kittens outside your window
In a sort of cement well
Where they crap and puke and cry and she can't hear,
You say you can't stand her.
The bastard's a girl!
You who have blown your tubes like a bad radio
Clear of voices and history, the staticky
Noise of the new.
You say I should drown the kittens. Their smell!   20
You say I should drown my girl.
She'll cut her throat at ten if she's mad at two.
The baby smiles, fat snail,
From the polished lozenges of orange linoleum.
You could eat him. He's a boy.
You say your husband is just no good for you,
His Jew-mama guards his sweet sex like a pearl.
You have one baby, I have two.

I should sit on a rock off Cornwall and comb my hair.
I should wear tiger pants, I should have an affair.   30
We should meet in another life, we should meet in the air,
Me and you.

Meanwhile there's a stink of fat and baby crap.
I'm doped and thick from my last sleeping pill.
The smog of cooking, the smog of hell
Floats our heads, two venomous opposites,
Our bones, our hair.
I call you Orphan, orphan. You are ill.
The sun gives you ulcers, the wind gives you t.b.

Once you were beautiful.   40
In New York, Hollywood, the men said: 'Through?
Gee, baby, you are rare'.
You acted, acted, acted for the thrill.
Your impotent husband slumps out for a coffee.
I try to keep him in,
An old pole for the lightning,
The acid baths, the skyfulls off of you.
He lumps it down the plastic cobbled hill,
Flogged trolley. The spars are blue.
The blue sparks spill,   50
Splitting like quartz into a million bits.
O jewel! O valuable!
That night the moon
Dragged its blood bag, sick
animal
Up over the harbor lights.
And then grew normal,
Hard and apart and white.
The scale-sheen on the sand scared me to death.
We kept picking up handfuls, loving it,   60
Working it like dough, a mulatto body,
The silk grits.
A dog picked up your doggy husband. They went on.

Now I am silent, hate
Up to my neck,
Thick, thick!
I do not speak.
I am packing the hard potatoes like good clothes,
I am packing the babies,

I am packing the sick cats.   70
O vase of acid!

It is love you are full of. You know who you hate.
He is hugging his ball and chain down by the gate
That opens to the sea
Where it drives in, white and black,
Then spews it back.
Every day you fill him with soul-stuff, like a pitcher.

You are so exhausted!
Your voice my ear-ring,
Flapping and sucking, blood-loving bat.   80
That is that! That is that!
You peer from the door,
Sad hag. 'Every woman's a whore.
I can't communicate'.

I see your cute décor
Close on you like the fist of a baby
Or an anemone, that sea
Sweetheart, that kleptomaniac.
I am still raw.
I say I may be back.   90
You know what lies are for!

Even in your Zen heaven we shan't meet.

QUESTIONS

1. What is the meaning of the title, "Lesbos"?
2. The narrator of the poem has a son and a daughter; how do the attitudes toward them differ between the narrator and the other woman in the poem?
3. To what extent is the poem description and to what extent is it the projection of the narrator's emotion?
4. What is the significance of the reference to the moon in lines 53–58?
5. Compare the imagery Sylvia Plath uses for the housewife in her kitchen with the imagery in Anne Sexton's "Housewife."
6. Read Robert Lowell's comment on Sylvia Plath, quoted by Mary Ellmann on page 216. Discuss what he means by "female" and "feminine." Do you agree with him?

Dorothy Parker

Although she is best known for her light verse, the American humorist and critic Dorothy Parker also wrote short stories. Mr. Durant is a study of the bourgeois male supremacist. Dorothy Parker's feminism, in contrast to that of Mary McCarthy, often takes the form of hostility toward men and sentimentalized pity for their female victims. In this story, however, her witty and restrained evocation of Mr. Durant's complacent sensuality balances the conventionality of her condemnation of the base seducer.

Mr. Durant

Not for some ten days had Mr. Durant known any such ease of mind. He gave himself up to it, wrapped himself, warm and soft, as in a new and an expensive cloak. God, for Whom Mr. Durant entertained a good-humored affection, was in His heaven, and all was again well with Mr. Durant's world.

Curious how this renewed peace sharpened his enjoyment of the accustomed things about him. He looked back at the rubber works, which he had just left for the day, and nodded approvingly at the solid red pile, at the six neat stories rising impressively into the darkness. You would go far, he thought, before you would find a more up-and-coming outfit, and there welled in him a pleasing, proprietary sense of being a part of it.

He gazed amiably down Center Street, noting how restfully the lights glowed. Even the wet, dented pavement, spotted with thick puddles, fed his pleasure by reflecting the discreet radiance above it. And to complete his comfort, the car for which he was waiting, admirably on time, swung into view far down the track. He thought, with a sort of jovial tenderness, of what it would bear him to; of his dinner—it was fish-chowder night—of his children, of his wife, in the order named. Then he turned his kindly attention to the girl who stood near him, obviously awaiting the Center Street car, too. He was delighted to feel a sharp interest in her. He regarded it as being distinctly creditable to himself that he could take a healthy notice of such matters once more. Twenty years younger—that's what he felt.

Rather shabby, she was, in her rough coat with its shagginess rubbed off here and there. But there was a something in the way her cheaply smart turban was jammed over her eyes, in the way her thin young figure moved under the loose coat. Mr. Durant pointed his tongue, and moved it delicately along his cool, smooth upper lip.

The car approached, clanged to a stop before them. Mr. Durant stepped gallantly aside to let the girl get in first. He did not help her to enter, but the solicitous way in which he superintended the process gave all the effect of his having actually assisted her.

Her tight little skirt slipped up over her thin, pretty legs as she took the high step. There was a run in one of her flimsy silk stockings. She was doubtless unconscious of it; it was well back toward the seam, extending, probably from her garter, half-way down the calf. Mr. Durant had an odd desire to catch his thumb-nail in the present end of the run, and to draw it on down until the slim line of the dropped stitches reached to the top of her low shoe. An indulgent smile at his whimsy played about his mouth, broadening to a grin of affable evening greeting for the conductor, as he entered the car and paid his fare.

The girl sat down somewhere far up at the front. Mr. Durant found a desirable seat toward the rear, and craned his neck to see her. He could catch a glimpse of a fold of her turban and a bit of her brightly rouged cheek, but only at a cost of holding his head in a strained, and presently painful, position. So, warmed by the assurance that there would always be others, he let her go, and settled himself restfully. He had a ride of twenty minutes or so before him. He allowed his head to fall gently back, to let his eyelids droop, and gave himself to his thoughts. Now that the thing was comfortably over and done with, he could think of it easily, almost laughingly. Last week, now, and even part of the week before, he had had to try with all his strength to force it back every time it wrenched itself into his mind. It has positively affected his sleep. Even though he was shielded by his newly acquired amused attitude, Mr. Durant felt indignation flood within him when he recalled those restless nights.

He had met Rose for the first time about three months before. She had been sent up to his office to take some letters for him. Mr. Durant was assistant manager of the rubber company's credit department; his wife was wont to refer to him as one of the officers of the company, and, though she often spoke thus of him to people in his presence, he never troubled to go more fully into detail about his position. He rated a room, a desk, and a telephone to himself; but not a stenographer. When he wanted to give dictation or to have some letters typewritten, he telephoned around to the various other offices until he found a girl who was not busy with her own work. That was how Rose had come to him.

She was not a pretty girl. Distinctly, no. But there was a rather sweet fragility about her, and an almost desperate timidity that Mr. Durant had once found engaging, but that he now thought of with a prickling irritation. She was twenty, and the glamour of youth was around her. When she bent over her work, her back showing white through her sleazy blouse, her clean hair coiled smoothly on her thin neck, her straight, childish legs crossed at the knee to support her pad, she had an undeniable appeal.

But not pretty—no. Her hair wasn't the kind that went up well, her eyelashes and lips were too pale, she hadn't much knack about choosing and wearing her cheap clothes. Mr. Durant, in reviewing the thing, felt a surprise that she should ever have attracted him. But it was a tolerant surprise, not an impatient one. Already he looked back on himself as being just a big boy in the whole affair.

It did not occur to him to feel even a flicker of astonishment that Rose should have responded so eagerly to him, an immovably married man of forty-nine. He never thought of himself in that way. He used to tell Rose, laughingly, that he was old enough to be her father, but neither of them ever really believed it. He regarded her affection for him as the most natural thing in the world—there she was, coming from a much smaller town, never the sort of girl to have had admirers; naturally, she was dazzled at the attentions of a man who, as Mr. Durant put it, was approaching the prime. He had been charmed with the idea of there having been no other men in her life; but lately, far from feeling flattered at being the first and only one, he had come to regard it as her having taken a sly advantage of him, to put him in that position.

It had all been surprisingly easy. Mr. Durant knew it would be almost from the first time he saw her. That did not lessen its interest in his eyes. Obstacles discouraged him, rather than led him on. Elimination of bother was the main thing.

Rose was not a coquettish girl. She had that curious directness that some very timid people possess. There were her scruples, of course, but Mr. Durant readily reasoned them away. Not that he was a master of technique, either. He had had some experiences, probably a third as many as he habitually thought of himself as having been through, but none that taught him much of the delicate shadings of wooing. But then, Rose's simplicity asked exceedingly little.

She was never one to demand much of him, anyway. She never

thought of stirring up any trouble between him and his wife, never besought him to leave his family and go away with her, even for a day. Mr. Durant valued her for that. It did away with a lot of probable fussing.

It was amazing how free they were, how little lying there was to do. They stayed in the office after hours—Mr. Durant found many letters that must be dictated. No one thought anything of that. Rose was busy most of the day, and it was only considerate that Mr. Durant should not break in on her employer's time, only natural that he should want as good a stenographer as she was to attend to his correspondence.

Rose's only relative, a married sister, lived in another town. The girl roomed with an acquaintance named Ruby, also employed at the rubber works, and Ruby, who was much taken up with her own affairs of the emotions, never appeared to think it strange if Rose was late to dinner, or missed the meal entirely. Mr. Durant readily explained to his wife that he was detained by a rush of business. It only increased his importance, to her, and spurred her on to devising especially pleasing dishes, and solicitously keeping them hot for his return. Sometimes, important in their guilt, Rose and he put out the light in the little office and locked the door, to trick the other employees into thinking that they had long ago gone home. But no one ever so much as rattled the doorknob, seeking admission.

It was all so simple that Mr. Durant never thought of it as anything outside the usual order of things. His interest in Rose did not blunt his appreciation of chance attractive legs or provocative glances. It was an entanglement of the most restful, comfortable nature. It even held a sort of homelike quality, for him.

And then everything had to go and get spoiled. "Wouldn't you know?" Mr. Durant asked himself, with deep bitterness.

Ten days before, Rose had come weeping to his office. She had the sense to wait till after hours, for a wonder, but anybody might have walked in and seen her blubbering there; Mr. Durant felt it to be due only to the efficient management of his personal God that no one had. She wept, as he sweepingly put it, all over the place. The color left her cheeks and collected damply in her nose, and rims of vivid pink grew around her pale eyelashes. Even her hair became affected; it came away from the pins, and stray ends of it wandered limply over her neck. Mr. Durant hated to look at her, could not bring himself to touch her.

All his energies were expended in urging her for God's sake to keep quiet; he did not ask her what was the matter. But it came out, between bursts of unpleasant-sounding sobs. She was "in trouble." Neither then nor in the succeeding days did she and Mr. Durant ever use any less delicate phrase to describe her condition. Even in their thoughts, they referred to it that way.

She had suspected it, she said, for some time, but she hadn't wanted to bother him about it until she was absolutely sure. "Didn't want to bother me!" thought Mr. Durant.

Naturally, he was furious. Innocence is a desirable thing, a dainty thing, an appealing thing, in its place; but carried too far, it is merely ridiculous. Mr. Durant wished to God that he had never seen Rose. He explained this desire to her.

But that was no way to get things done. As he had often jovially remarked to his friends, he knew "a thing or two." Cases like this could be what people of the world called "fixed up"—New York society women, he understood, thought virtually nothing of it. This case could be fixed up, too. He got Rose to go home, telling her not to worry, he would see that everything was all right. The main thing was to get her out of sight, with that nose and those eyes.

But knowing a thing or two and putting the knowledge into practice turned out to be vastly different things. Mr. Durant did not know whom to seek for information. He pictured himself inquiring of his intimates if they could tell him of "someone that this girl he had heard about could go to." He could hear his voice uttering the words, could hear the nervous laugh that would accompany them, the terrible flatness of them as they left his lips. To confide in one person would be confiding in at least one too many. It was a progressing town, but still small enough for gossip to travel like a typhoon. Not that he thought for a moment that his wife would believe any such thing, if it reached her; but where would be the sense in troubling her?

Mr. Durant grew pale and jumpy over the thing as the days went by. His wife worried herself into one of her sick spells over his petulant refusals of second helpings. There daily arose in him an increasing anger that he should be drawn into conniving to find a way to break the law of his country—probably the law of every country in the world. Certainly of every decent, Christian place.

It was Ruby, finally, who got them out of it. When Rose confessed to him that she had broken down and told Ruby, his rage leaped higher than any words. Ruby was secretary to the vice-president of the rubber company. It would be pretty, wouldn't it, if she let it out? He had lain wide-eyed beside his wife all that night through. He shuddered at the thought of chance meetings with Ruby in the hall.

But Ruby had made it delightfully simple, when they did meet. There were no reproachful looks, no cold turnings away of the head. She had given him her usual smiling "good-morning," and added a little upward glance, mischievous, understanding, with just the least hint of admiration in it. There was a sense of intimacy, of a shared secret binding them cozily together. A fine girl, that Ruby!

Ruby had managed it all without any fuss. Mr. Durant was not directly concerned in the planning. He heard of it only through Rose, on the infrequent occasions when he had had to see her. Ruby knew, through some indistinct friends of hers, of "a woman." It would be twenty-five dollars. Mr. Durant had gallantly insisted upon giving Rose the money. She had started to sniffle about taking it, but he had finally prevailed. Not that he couldn't have used the twenty-five very nicely himself, just then, with Junior's teeth, and all!

Well, it was all over now. The invaluable Ruby had gone with Rose to "the woman"; had that very afternoon taken her to the station and put her on a train for her sister's. She had even thought of wiring the sister beforehand that Rose had had influenza and must have a rest.

Mr. Durant had urged Rose to look on it as just a little vacation. He promised, moreover, to put in a good word for her whenever she wanted her job back. But Rose had gone pink about the nose again at the thought. She had sobbed her rasping sobs, then had raised her face from her stringy handkerchief and said, with an entirely foreign firmness, that she never wanted to see the rubber works or Ruby or Mr. Durant again. He had laughed indulgently, had made himself pat her thin back. In his relief at the outcome of things, he could be generous to the pettish.

He chuckled inaudibly, as he reviewed that last scene. "I suppose she thought she'd make me sore, saying she was never coming back," he told himself. "I suppose I was supposed to get down on my knees and coax her."

It was fine to dwell on the surety that it was all done with. Mr. Durant had somewhere picked up a phrase that seemed ideally suited to the occasion. It was to him an admirably dashing expression. There was something stylish about it; it was the sort of thing you would expect to hear used by men who wore spats and swung canes without self-consciousness. He employed it now, with satisfaction.

"Well, that's that," he said to himself. He was not sure that he didn't say it aloud.

The car slowed, and the girl in the rough coat came down toward the door. She was jolted against Mr. Durant—he would have sworn she did it purposely—uttered a word of laughing apology, gave him what he interpreted as an inviting glance. He half rose to follow her, then sank back again. After all, it was a wet night, and his corner was five blocks farther on. Again there came over him the cozy assurance that there would always be others.

In high humor, he left the car at his street, and walked in the direction of his house. It was a mean night, but the insinuating cold and the black rain only made more graphic his picture of the warm, bright house, the great dish of steaming fish chowder, the well-behaved children and wife that awaited him. He walked rather slowly to make them seem all the better for the wait, humming a little on his way down the neat sidewalk, past the solid, reputably shabby houses.

Two girls ran past him, holding their hands over their heads to protect their hats from the wet. He enjoyed the click of their heels on the pavement, their little bursts of breathless laughter, their arms upraised in a position that brought out all the neat lines of their bodies. He knew who they were—they lived three doors down from him, in the house with the lamp-post in front of it. He had often lingeringly noticed their fresh prettiness. He hurried, so that he might see them run up the steps, their narrow skirts sliding up over their legs. His mind went back to the girl with the run in her stocking, and amusing thoughts filled him as he entered his own house.

His children rushed, clamoring, to meet him, as he unlocked the door. There was something exciting going on, for Junior and Charlotte were usually too careful-mannered to cause people discomfort by rushing and babbling. They were nice, sensible children, good at their lessons, and punctilious about brushing their teeth, speaking the truth, and avoiding playmates who used bad words. Junior would be the very picture of his father, when they got the bands off his teeth, and little Charlotte strongly resembled her mother. Friends often commented on what a nice arrangement it was.

Mr. Durant smiled good-naturedly through their racket, carefully hanging up his coat and hat. There was even pleasure for him in the arrangement of his apparel on the cool, shiny knob of the hatrack. Everything was pleasant, tonight. Even the children's noise couldn't irritate him.

Eventually he discovered the cause of the commotion. It was a little stray dog that had come to the back door. They were out in the kitchen helping Freda, and Charlotte thought she heard something scratching, and Freda said nonsense, but Charlotte went to the door, anyway, and there was this little dog, trying to get in out of the wet. Mother helped them give it a bath, and Freda fed it, and now it was in the living-room. Oh, Father, couldn't they keep it, please, couldn't they, couldn't they, please, Father, couldn't they? It didn't have any collar on it—so you see it didn't belong to anybody. Mother said all right, if he said so, and Freda liked it fine.

Mr. Durant still smiled his gentle smile. "We'll see," he said.

The children looked disappointed, but not despondent. They would have liked more enthusiasm, but "we'll see," they knew by experience, meant a leaning in the right direction.

Mr. Durant proceeded to the living-room, to inspect the visitor. It was not a beauty. All too obviously, it was the living souvenir of a mother who had never been able to say no. It was a rather stocky little beast with shaggy white hair and occasional, rakishly placed patches of black. There was a suggestion of Sealyham terrier about it, but that was almost blotted out by hosts of reminiscences of other breeds. It looked, on the whole, like a composite photograph of Popular Dogs. But you could tell at a glance that it had a way with it. Scepters have been tossed aside for that.

It lay, now, by the fire, waving its tragically long tail wistfully, its eyes pleading with Mr. Durant to give it a fair trial. The children had told it to lie down there, and so it did not move. That was something it could do toward repaying them.

Mr. Durant warmed to it. He did not dislike dogs, and he somewhat fancied the picture of himself as a softhearted fellow who extended shelter to friendless animals. He bent, and held out a hand to it.

"Well, sir," he said, genially. "Come here, good fellow."

The dog ran to him, wriggling ecstatically. It covered his cold hand with joyous, though respectful kisses, then laid its warm, heavy head on his palm. "You are beyond a doubt the greatest man in America," it told him with its eyes.

Mr. Durant enjoyed appreciation and gratitude. He patted the dog graciously.

"Well, sir, how'd you like to board with us?" he said. "I guess you can plan to settle down." Charlotte squeezed Junior's arm wildly. Neither of them, though, thought it best to crowd their good fortune by making any immediate comment on it.

Mrs. Durant entered from the kitchen, flushed with her final attentions to the chowder. There was a worried line between her eyes. Part of the worry was due to the dinner, and part to the disturbing entrance of the little dog into the family life. Anything not previously included in her day's schedule threw Mrs. Durant into a state resembling that of one convalescing from shell-shock. Her hands jerked nervously, beginning gestures that they never finished.

Relief smoothed her face when she saw her husband patting the dog. The children, always at ease with her, broke their silence and jumped about her, shrieking that Father said it might stay.

"There, now—didn't I tell you what a dear, good father you had?" she said in the tone parents employ when they have happened to guess right. "That's fine, Father. With that big yard and all, I think we'll make out all right. She really seems to be an awfully good little—"

Mr. Durant's hand stopped sharply in its patting motions, as if the dog's neck had become red-hot to his touch. He rose, and looked at his wife as at a stranger who had suddenly begun to behave wildly.

"She?" he said. He maintained the look and repeated the word. "She?"

Mrs. Durant's hands jerked.

"Well—" she began, as if about to plunge into a recital of extenuating circumstances. "Well—yes," she concluded.

The children and the dog looked nervously at Mr. Durant, feeling something was gone wrong. Charlotte whimpered wordlessly.

"Quiet!" said her father, turning suddenly upon her. "I said it could stay, didn't I? Did you ever know Father to break a promise?"

Charlotte politely murmured, "No, Father," but conviction was not hers. She was a philosophical child, though, and she decided to leave the whole issue to God, occasionally jogging Him up a bit with prayer.

Mr. Durant frowned at his wife, and jerked his head backward. This indicated that he wished to have a few words with her, for adults only, in the privacy of the little room across the hall, known as "Father's den."

He had directed the decoration of his den, had seen that it had been made a truly masculine room. Red paper covered its walls, up to the wooden rack on which were displayed ornamental steins, of domestic manufacture. Empty pipe-racks—Mr. Durant smoked cigars—were nailed against the red paper at frequent intervals. On one wall was an indifferent reproduction of a drawing of a young woman with wings like a vampire bat, and on another, a water-colored photograph of "September Morn," the tints running a bit beyond the edges of the figure as if the artist's emotions had rendered his hand unsteady. Over the table was carefully flung a tanned and fringed hide with the profile of an unknown Indian maiden painted on it, and the rocking-chair held a leather pillow bearing the picture, done by pyrography, of a girl in a fencing costume which set off her distressingly dated figure.

Mr. Durant's books were lined up behind the glass of the bookcase. They were all tall, thick books, brightly bound, and they justified his pride in their showing. They were mostly accounts of favorites of the French court, with a few volumes on odd personal habits of various monarchs, and the adventures of former Russian monks. Mrs. Durant, who never had time to get around to reading, regarded them with awe, and thought of her husband as one of the country's leading bibliophiles. There were books, too, in the living-room, but those she had inherited or been given. She had arranged a few on the living-room table; they looked as if they had been placed there by the Gideons.

Mr. Durant thought of himself as an indefatigable collector and an insatiable reader. But he was always disappointed in his books, after he had sent for them. They were never so good as the advertisements had led him to believe.

Into his den Mr. Durant preceded his wife, and faced her, still frowning. His calm was not shattered, but it was punctured. Something annoying always had to go and come up. Wouldn't you know?

"Now you know perfectly well, Fan, we can't have that dog around," he told her. He used the low voice reserved for underwear and bathroom articles and kindred shady topics. There was all the kindness in his tones that one has for a backward child, but a Gibraltar-like firmness was behind it. "You must be crazy to even think we could for a minute. Why, I wouldn't give a she-dog house-room, not for any amount of money. It's disgusting, that's what it is."

"Well, but, Father—" began Mrs. Durant, her hands again going off into their convulsions.

"Disgusting," he repeated. "You have a female around, and you know what happens. All the males in the neighborhood will be running after her. First thing you know, she'd be having puppies—and the way they look after they've had them, and all! That would be nice for the children to see, wouldn't it? I should think you'd think of the children, Fan. No, sir, there'll be nothing like that around here, not while I know it. Disgusting!"

"But the children," she said. "They'll be just simply—"

"Now you just leave all that to me," he reassured her. "I told them the dog could stay, and I've never broken a promise yet, have I? Here's what I'll do—I'll wait till they're asleep, and then I'll just take this little dog and put it out. Then, in the morning, you can tell them it ran away during the night, see?"

She nodded. Her husband patted her shoulder, in its crepy-smelling black silk. His peace with the world was once more intact, restored by this simple solution of the little difficulty. Again his mind wrapped itself in the knowledge that everything was all fixed, all ready for a nice, fresh start. His arm was still about his wife's shoulder as they went on in to dinner.

QUESTIONS

1. What does Mr. Durant's den reveal about his character?

2. How would you relate Mr. Durant's attitude toward God to an aspect of his personality?

3. What point of view does Dorothy Parker adopt in describing Mr. Durant? What is the author's feeling about her character? Which details and phrases indicate her attitude toward him?

4. What is the significance of the device by which Mr. Durant rids himself of the dog?

Mary McCarthy

Mary McCarthy (b. 1912) is one of America's most versatile serious writers. In addition to her fiction, for which she is best known, she has also written travel books, literary and dramatic criticism, and, most recently, a book on Vietnam. The memorable epithets that have been applied to her, including "lady with a switchblade" and "Dark Lady of American Letters," suggest the persistence of her reputation for intellectual bloodthirstiness. Most of her fiction has been satirical; her targets include progressive education (The Groves of Academe, 1952), socialist utopias (The Oasis, 1949), and, most recently, the myth of feminine progress (The Group, 1963). Her most frequent satiric victim, however, has been herself. Although no fictional work can be literally interpreted as autobiography, Mary McCarthy tends to use recognizable material of her own life as the basis for her books.

In the Preface to The Company She Keeps (1942), Mary McCarthy explains that she wrote the book in an attempt to define the self. The heroine of the stories, like Mary McCarthy, herself, is a woman of beauty, charm, intelligence, and wit, who appears to enjoy every advantage. But this apparent control of her life is an illusion; she is in fact continually exploited by men, for she is the prisoner of her obsessive self-doubt. In "Cruel and Barbarous Treatment," one of the stories in this book, the author exposes her heroine's desperate need for social approval. Despite her freedom to have a love affair or a divorce, this heroine is not liberated; she substitutes for the oppression of law a pettier oppression of etiquette and convention. According to Mary McCarthy, custom makes slaves of us all, but particularly of women.

Cruel and Barbarous Treatment

She could not bear to hurt her husband. She impressed this on the Young Man, on her confidantes, and finally on her husband himself. The thought of Telling Him actually made her heart turn over in a sudden and sickening way, she said. This was true, and yet she knew that being a potential divorcee was deeply pleasurable in somewhat the same way that being an engaged girl had been. In both cases, there was at first a subterranean courtship, whose significance it was necessary to conceal from outside observers. The concealment of the original, premarital courtship had, however, been a mere superstitious gesture, briefly sustained. It had also been, on the whole, a private secretiveness, not a partnership of silence. One put one's family and one's friends off the track because one was still afraid that the affair might not come out right, might not lead in a clean, direct line to the altar. To confess one's aspirations might be, in the end, to publicize one's failure. Once a solid understanding had been reached, there followed a short intermission of ritual bashfulness, in which both parties awkwardly participated, and then came the Announcement.

But with the extramarital courtship, the deception was prolonged where it had been ephemeral, necessary where it had been frivolous, conspiratorial where it had been lonely. It was, in short, serious where it had been dilettantish. That it was accompanied by feelings of guilt, by sharp and genuine revulsions, only complicated and deepened its delight, by abrading the sensibilities, and by imposing a sense of outlawry and consequent mutual dependence upon the lovers. But what this interlude of deception gave her, above all, she recognized, was an opportunity, unparalleled in her experience, for exercising feelings of superiority over others. For her husband she had, she believed, only sympathy and compunction. She got no fun, she told the Young Man, out of putting horns on her darling's head, and never for a moment, she said, did he appear to her as the comic figure of the cuckolded

---

FROM *The Company She Keeps*, Harcourt Brace Jovanovich, Inc. Copyright, 1939, by Mary McCarthy. Reprinted by permission of Brandt & Brandt.

husband that one saw on the stage. (The Young Man assured her that his own sentiments were equally delicate, that for the wronged man he felt the most profound respect, tinged with consideration.) It was as if by the mere act of betraying her husband, she had adequately bested him; it was supererogatory for her to gloat, and, if she gloated at all, it was over her fine restraint in not-gloating, over the integrity of her moral sense, which allowed her to preserve even while engaged in sinfulness the acute realization of sin and shame. Her overt superiority feelings she reserved for her friends. Lunches and teas, which had been time-killers, matters of routine, now became perilous and dramatic adventures. The Young Man's name was a bright, highly explosive ball which she bounced casually back and forth in these feminine *tête-à-têtes*. She would discuss him in his status of friend of the family, speculate on what girls he might have, attack him or defend him, anatomize him, keeping her eyes clear and impersonal, her voice empty of special emphasis, her manner humorously detached. *While all the time. . . !*

Three times a week or oftener, at lunch or tea, she would let herself tremble thus on the exquisite edge of self-betrayal, involving her companions in a momentous game whose rules and whose risks only she herself knew. The Public Appearances were even more satisfactory. To meet at a friend's house by design and to register surprise, to strike just the right note of young-matronly affection at cocktail parties, to treat him formally as "my escort" at the theater during intermissions—these were triumphs of stage management, more difficult of execution, more nerve-racking than the lunches and teas, because *two* actors were involved. His over-ardent glance must be hastily deflected; his too-self-conscious reading of his lines must be entered in the debit side of her ledger of love, in anticipation of an indulgent accounting in private.

The imperfections of his performance were, indeed, pleasing to her. Not, she thought, because his impetuosities, his gaucheries, demonstrated the sincerity of his passion for her, nor because they proved him a new hand at this game of intrigue, but rather because the high finish of her own acting showed off well in comparison. "I should have gone on the stage," she could tell him gaily, "or been a diplomat's wife or an international spy," while he would admiringly agree. Actually, she doubted whether she could ever have been an actress, acknowledging that she found it more amusing and more gratifying to play herself than to interpret any character conceived by a dramatist. In these private theatricals it was her own many-faceted nature that she put on exhibit, and the audience, in this case unfortunately limited to two, could applaud both her skill of projection and her intrinsic variety. Furthermore, this was a play in which the *donnée* was real, and the penalty for a missed cue or an inopportune entrance was, at first anyway, unthinkable.

She loved him, she knew, for being a bad actor, for his docility in accepting her tender, mock-impatient instruction. Those superiority feelings were fattening not only on the gullibility of her friends, but also on the comic flaws of her lover's character, and on the vulnerability of her lover's position. In this particular hive she was undoubtedly queen bee.

The Public Appearances were not exclusively duets. They sometimes took the form of a trio. On these occasions the studied and benevolent carefulness which she always showed for her husband's feelings served a double purpose. She would affect a conspicuous domesticity, an affectionate conjugal demonstrativeness, would sprinkle her conversation with "Darlings," and punctuate it with pats and squeezes till her husband would visibly expand and her lover plainly and painfully shrink. For the Young Man no retaliation was possible. These endearments of hers were sanctioned by law, usage, and habit; they belonged to her role of wife and could not be condemned or paralleled by a young man who was himself unmarried. They were clear provocations, but they could not be called so, and the Young Man preferred not to speak of them. *But she knew.* . . . Though she was aware of the sadistic intention of these displays, she was not ashamed of them, as she was sometimes twistingly ashamed of the hurt she was preparing to inflict on her husband. Partly she felt that they were punishments which the Young Man richly deserved for the wrong he was doing her husband, and that she herself in contriving them was acting, quite fittingly, both as judge and accused. Partly, too, she believed herself justified in playing the fond wife, whatever the damage to her lover's ego, because, in a sense, she actually was a fond wife. She *did* have these feelings, she insisted, whether she was exploiting them or not.

Eventually, however, her reluctance to wound her husband and her solicitude for his pride were overcome by an inner conviction that her love affair must move on to its next preordained stage. The possibilities of the subterranean courtship had been exhausted; it was time for the Announcement. She and the Young Man began to tell each other in a rather breathless and literary style that The Situation Was Impossible, and Things Couldn't Go On This Way Any Longer. The ostensible meaning of these flurried laments was that, under present conditions, they were not seeing enough of each other, that their hours together were too short and their periods of separation too dismal, that the whole business of deception had become morally distasteful to them. Perhaps the Young Man really believed these things; she did not. For the first time, she saw that the virtue of marriage as an institution lay in its public character. Private cohabitation, long continued, was, she concluded, a bore. Whatever the coziness of isolation, the warm delights of having a secret, a love affair finally reach the point where it needed the glare of publicity to revive the interest of its protagonists. Hence, she thought, the engagement parties, the showers, the big church weddings, the presents, the receptions. These were simply socially approved devices by which the lovers got themselves talked about. The gossip value of a divorce and remarriage was obviously far greater than the gossip value of a mere engagement, and she was now ready, indeed hungry, to hear What People Would Say.

The lunches, the teas, the Public Appearances were getting a little flat. It was not, in the end, enough to be a Woman With A Secret, if to one's friends one appeared to be a woman without a secret. The bliss of having a secret required, in short, the consummation of telling it, and she looked forward to the My-dear-I-had-no-idea's, the I-thought-you-and-Tom-were-so-happy-together's, the How-did-you-keep-it-so-dark's with which her intimates would greet her announcement. The audience of two no longer sufficed her; she required a larger stage. She tried it first, a little nervously, on two or three of her closest friends, swearing them to secrecy. "Tom must hear it first from me," she declared. "It would be too terrible for his pride if he found out afterwards that the whole town knew it before he did. So you mustn't tell, even later on, that I told you about this today. I felt I had to talk to someone." After these lunches she would hurry to a phone booth to give the Young Man the gist of the conversation. "She certainly was surprised," she could always say with a little gush of triumph. "But she thinks it's fine." *But did they actually?* She could not be sure. Was it possible that she sensed in these luncheon companions, her dearest friends, a certain reserve, a certain unexpressed judgment?

It was a pity, she reflected, that she was so sensitive to public opinion. "I couldn't really love a man," she murmured to herself once, "if everybody didn't think he was wonderful." Everyone seemed to like the Young Man, of course. *But still . . .* She was getting panicky, she thought. Surely it was only common sense that nobody is admired by everybody. And even if a man were universally despised, would there not be a kind of defiant nobility in loving him in the teeth of the whole world? There would, certainly, but it was a type of heroism that she would scarcely be called upon to practice, for the Young Man was popular, he was invited everywhere, he danced well, his manners were ingratiating, he kept up intellectually. But was he not perhaps *too* amiable, *too* accommodating? Was it for this that her friends seemed silently to criticize him?

At this time a touch of acridity entered into her relations with the Young Man. Her indulgent scoldings had an edge to them now, and it grew increasingly difficult for her to keep her make-believe impatience from becoming real. She would look for dark spots in his character and drill away at them as relentlessly as a dentist at a cavity. A compulsive didacticism possessed her: no truism of his, no cliché, no ineffectual joke could pass the rigidity of her censorship. And, hard as she tried to maintain the character of charming schoolmistress, the Young Man, she saw, was taking alarm. She suspected that, frightened and puzzled, he contemplated flight. She found herself watching him with impersonal interest, speculating as to what course he would take, and she was relieved but faintly disappointed when it became clear that he ascribed her sharpness to the tension of the situation and had decided to stick it out.

The moment had come for her to tell her husband. By this single, cathartic act, she would, she believed, rid herself of the doubts and anxieties that beset her. If her husband were to impugn the Young Man's character, she could answer his accusations and at the same time discount them as arising from jealousy. From her husband, at least, she might expect the favor of an open attack, to which she could respond with the prepared defense that she carried, unspoken, about with her. Further, she had an intense, childlike curiosity as to How Her Husband Would Take It, a curiosity which she disguised for decency's sake as justifiable apprehension. The confidences already imparted to her friends seemed like pale dress rehearsals of the supreme confidence she was about to make. Perhaps it was toward this moment that the whole affair had been tending, for this moment that the whole affair had been designed. This would be the ultimate testing of her husband's love, its final, rounded, quintessential expression. Never, she thought, when you live with a man do you feel the full force of his love. It is gradually rationed out to you in an impure state, compounded with all the other elements of daily existence, so that you are hardly sensible of receiving it. There is no single point at which it is concentrated; it spreads out into the past and the future until it appears as a nearly imperceptible film over the surface of your life. Only face to face with its own annihilation could it show itself wholly, and, once shown, drop into the category of completed experiences.

She was not disappointed. She told him at breakfast in a fashionable restaurant, because, she said, he would be better able to control his feelings in public. When he called at once for the check, she had a spasm of alarm lest in an access of brutality or grief he leave her there alone, conspicuous, and, as it were, unfulfilled. But they walked out of the restaurant together and through the streets, hand in hand, tears streaming "unchecked," she whispered to herself, down their faces. Later they were in the Park, by an artificial lake, watching the ducks swim. The sun was very bright, and she felt a kind of superb pathos in the careful and irrelevant attention they gave to the pastoral scene. This was, she knew, the most profound, the most subtle, the most idyllic experience of her life. All the strings of her nature were, at last, vibrant. She was both doer and sufferer: she inflicted pain and participated in it. And she was, at the same time, physician, for, as she was the weapon that dealt the wound, she was also the balm that could assuage it. Only she could know the hurt that engrossed him, and it was to her that he turned for the sympathy she had ready for him. Finally, though she offered him his discharge slip with one hand, with the other she beckoned him to approach. She was wooing him all over again, but wooing him to a deeper attachment than he had previously experienced, to an unconditional surrender. She was demanding his total understanding of her, his compassion, and his forgiveness. When at last he answered her repeated and agonized I-love-you's by grasping her hand more tightly and saying gently, "I know," she saw that she had won him over. She had drawn him into a truly mystical union. Their marriage was complete.

Afterwards everything was more prosaic. The Young Man had to be telephoned and summoned to a conference à trois, a conference, she said, of civilized, intelligent people. The Young Man was a little awkward, even dropped a tear or two, which embarrassed everyone else, but what, after all, she thought, could you expect? He was in a difficult position; his was a thankless part. With her husband behaving so well, indeed, so gallantly, the Young Man could not fail to look a trifle inadequate. The Young Man would have preferred it, of course, if her husband had made a scene, had bullied or threatened her, so that he himself might have acted the chivalrous protector. She, however, did not hold her husband's heroic courtesy against him: in some way, it reflected credit on herself. The Young Man, apparently, was expecting to Carry Her Off, but this she would not allow. "It would be too heartless," she whispered when they were alone for a moment. "We must all go somewhere together."

So the three went out for a drink, and she watched with a sort of desperation her husband's growing abstraction, the more and more perfunctory attention he accorded the conversation she was so bravely sustaining. "He is bored," she thought. "He is going to leave." The prospect of being left alone with the Young Man seemed suddenly unendurable. If her husband were to go now, he would take with him the third dimension that had given the affair depth, and abandon her to a flat and vulgar love scene. Terrified, she wondered whether she had not already prolonged the drama beyond its natural limits, whether the confession in the restaurant and the absolution in the Park had not rounded off the artistic whole, whether the sequel of divorce and remarriage would not, in fact, constitute an anticlimax. Already she sensed that behind her husband's good manners an ironical attitude toward herself had sprung up. Was it possible that he had believed that they would return from the Park and all would continue as before? It was conceivable that her protestations of love had been misleading, and that his enormous tenderness toward her had been based, not on the idea that he was giving her up, but rather on the idea that he was taking her back—with no questions asked. If that were the case, the telephone call, the conference, and the excursion had in his eyes been a monstrous *gaffe*, a breach of sensibility and good taste, for which he would never forgive her. She blushed violently. Looking at him again, she thought he was watching her with an expression which declared: I have found you out: now I know what you are like. For the first time, she felt him utterly alienated.

When he left them she experienced the let-down she had feared but also a kind of relief. She told herself that it was as well that he had cut himself off from her: it made her decision simpler. There was now nothing for her to do but to push the love affair to its conclusion, whatever that might be, and this was probably what she most deeply desired. Had the poignant intimacy of the Park persisted, she might have been tempted to drop the adventure she had begun and return to her routine. But that was, looked at coldly, unthinkable. For if the adventure would seem a little flat after the scene in the Park, the resumption of her marriage would seem even flatter. If the drama of the triangle had been amputated by her confession, the curtain had been brought down with a smack on the drama of wedlock.

And, as it turned out, the drama of the triangle was not quite ended by the superficial rupture of her marriage. Though she had left her husband's apartment and been offered shelter by a confidante, it was still necessary for her to see him every day. There were clothes to be packed, and possessions to be divided, love letters to be reread and mementoes to be wept over in common. There were occasional passionate, unconsummated embraces; there were endearments and promises. And though her husband's irony remained, it was frequently vulnerable. It was not, as she had at first thought, an armor against her, but merely a sword, out of *Tristan and Isolde,* which lay permanently between them and enforced discretion.

. They met often, also, at the houses of friends, for, as she said, "What can I do? I know it's not tactful, but we all know the same people. You can't expect me to give up my friends." These Public Appearances were heightened in interest by the fact that these audiences, unlike the earlier ones, had, as it were, purchased librettos, and were in full possession of the intricacies of the plot. She preferred, she decided, the evening parties to the cocktail parties, for there she could dance alternately with her lover and her husband to the accompaniment of subdued gasps on the part of the bystanders.

This interlude was at the same time festive and heart-rending: her only dull moments were the evenings she spent alone with the Young Man. Unfortunately, the Post-Announcement period was only too plainly an interlude and its very nature demanded that it be followed by something else. She could not preserve her anomalous status indefinitely. It was not decent, and, besides, people would be bored. From the point of view of one's friends, it was all very well to entertain a Triangle as a novelty; to cope with it as a permanent problem was a different matter. Once they had all three got drunk, and there was a scene, and, though everyone talked about it afterwards, her friends were, she thought, a little colder, a little more critical. People began to ask her when she was going to Reno. Furthermore, she noticed that her husband was getting a slight edge in popularity over the Young Man. It was natural, of course, that everyone should feel sorry for him, and be especially nice. *But yet . . .*

When she learned from her husband that he was receiving attentions from members of her own circle, invitations in which she and the Young Man were unaccountably not included, she went at once to the station and bought her ticket. Her good-bye to her husband, which she had privately allocated to her last hours in town, took place prematurely, two days before she was to leave. He was rushing off to what she inwardly feared was a Gay Week End in the country; he had only a few minutes; he wished her a pleasant trip; and he would write, of course. His highball was drained while her glass still stood half full; he sat forward nervously on his chair; and she knew herself to be acting the Ancient Mariner, but her dignity would not allow her to hurry. She hoped that he would miss his train for her, but he did not. He left her sitting in the bar, and that night the Young Man could not, as he put it, do a thing with her. There was nowhere, absolutely nowhere, she said passionately, that she wanted to go, nobody she wanted to see, nothing she wanted to do. "You need a drink," he said with the air of a diagnostician. "A drink," she answered bitterly. "I'm sick of the drinks we've been having. Gin, whisky, rum, what else is there?" He took her into a bar, and she cried, but he bought her a fancy mixed drink, something called a Ramos gin fizz, and she was a little appeased because she had never had one before. Then some friends came in, and they all had another drink together, and she felt better. "There," said the Young Man, on the way home, "don't I know what's good for you? Don't I know how to handle you?" "Yes," she answered in her most humble and feminine tones, but she knew that they had suddenly dropped into a new pattern, that they were no longer the cynosure of a social group, but merely another young couple with an evening to pass, another young couple looking desperately for entertainment, wondering whether to call on a married couple or to drop in somewhere for a drink. This time the Young Man's prescription had worked, but it was pure luck that they had chanced to meet someone they knew. A second or a third time they would scan the faces of the other drinkers in vain, would order a second drink and surreptitiously watch the door, and finally go out alone, with a quite detectable air of being unwanted.

When, a day and a half later, the Young Man came late to take her to the train, and they had to run down the platform to catch it, she found him all at once detestable. He would ride to 125th Street with her, he declared in a burst of gallantry, but she was angry all the way because she was afraid there would be trouble with the conductor. At 125th Street, he stood on the platform blowing kisses to her and shouting something that she could not hear through the glass. She made a gesture of repugnance, but, seeing him flinch, seeing him weak and charming and incompetent, she brought her hand reluctantly to her lips and blew a kiss back. The other passengers were watching, she was aware, and though their looks were doting and not derisive, she felt herself to be humiliated and somehow vulgarized. When the train began to move, and the Young Man began to run down the platform after it, still blowing kisses and shouting alternately, she got up, turned sharply away from the window and walked back to the club car. There she sat down and ordered a whisky and soda.

There were a number of men in the car, who looked up in unison as she gave her order, but, observing that they were all the middle-aged, small-businessmen who "belonged" as inevitably to the club car as the white-coated porter and the leather-bound *Saturday Evening Post*, she paid them no heed. She was now suddenly overcome by a sense of depression and loss that was unprecedented for being in no way dramatic or pleasurable. In the last half-hour she had seen clearly that she would never marry the Young Man, and she found herself looking into an insubstantial future with no signpost to guide her. Almost all women, she thought, when they are girls never believe that they will get married. The terror of spinsterhood hangs over them from adolescence on. Even if they are popular they think that no one really interesting will want them enough to marry them. Even if they get engaged they are afraid that something will go wrong, something will intervene. When they do get married it seems to them a sort of miracle, and, after they have been married for a time, though in retrospect the whole process looks perfectly natural and inevitable, they retain a certain unarticulated pride in the wonder they have performed. Finally, however, the terror of spinsterhood has been so thoroughly exorcised that they forget ever having been haunted by it, and it is at this stage that they contemplate divorce. "How could I have forgotten?" she said to herself and began to wonder what she would do.

She could take an apartment by herself in the Village. She would meet new people. She would entertain. But, she thought, if I have people in for cocktails, there will always come the moment when they have to leave, and I shall be alone and have to pretend to have another engagement in order to save embarrassment. If I have them to dinner, it will be the same thing, but at least I shan't have to pretend to have an engagement. I will give dinners. Then, she thought, there will be the cocktail parties, and, if I go alone, I shall always stay a little too late, hoping that a young man or even a party of people will ask me to dinner. And if I fail, if no one asks me, I shall have the ignominy of walking out alone, trying to look as if I had somewhere to go. Then there will be the evenings at home with a good book when there will be no reason at all for going to bed, and I shall perhaps sit up all night. And the mornings when there will be no point in getting up, and I shall perhaps stay in bed till dinnertime. There will be the dinners in tearooms with other unmarried women, tearooms because women alone look conspicuous and forlorn in good restaurants. And then, she thought, I shall get older.

She would never, she reflected angrily, have taken this step, had she felt that she was burning her bridges behind her. She would never have left one man unless she had had another to take his place. But the Young Man, she now saw, was merely a sort of mirage which she had allowed herself to mistake for an oasis. "If the Man," she muttered, "did not exist, the Moment would create him." This was what had happened to her. She had made herself the victim of an imposture. But, she argued, with an access of cheerfulness, if this were true, if out of the need of a second, a new, husband she had conjured up the figure of one, she had possibly been impelled by unconscious forces to behave more intelligently than appearances would indicate. She was perhaps acting out in a sort of hypnotic trance a ritual whose meaning had not yet been revealed to her, a ritual which required that, first of all, the Husband be eliminated from the cast of characters. Conceivably, she was designed for the role of *femme fatale*, and for such a personage considerations of safety, provisions against loneliness and old age, were not only philistine but irrelevant. She might marry a second, a third, a fourth time, or she might never marry again. But, in any case, for the thrifty bourgeois love insurance, with its daily payments of patience, forbearance, and resignation, she was no longer eligible. She would be, she told herself delightedly, a bad risk.

She was, or soon would be, a Young Divorcee, and the term still carried glamour. Her divorce decree would be a passport conferring on her the status of citizeness of the world. She felt gratitude toward the Young Man for having unwittingly effected her transit into a new life. She looked about her at the other passengers. Later she would talk to them. They would ask, of course, where she was bound; that was the regulation opening move of train conversations. But it was a delicate question what her reply should be. To say "Reno" straight out would be vulgar; it would smack of confidences too cheaply given. Yet to lie, to say "San Francisco," for instance, would be to cheat herself, to minimize her importance, to mislead her interlocutor into believing her an ordinary traveler with a commonplace destination. There must be some middle course which would give information without appearing to do so, which would hint at a *vie galante* yet indicate a barrier of impeccable reserve. It would probably be best, she decided, to say "West" at first, with an air of vagueness and hesitation. Then, when pressed, she might go as far as to say "Nevada." But no farther.

QUESTIONS

1. What is the meaning of the title? To whom does it refer?
2. How do the heroine's feelings toward her husband change during the story?

3. Discuss the significance of the theatrical imagery in the story.

4. Analyze the structural and stylistic techniques (point of view, diction, description) that reveal the author's judgment of her character.

5. How does the heroine's disillusionment affect her?

part 3

LITERARY CRITICISM

George Henry Lewes

George Henry Lewes (1817–1878) was what the Victorians called a "man of letters." As a journalist, editor, scholar, philosopher, novelist, and critic, he had a profound and intimate knowledge of the literary society of his time. Lewes' essay, "The Lady Novelists," which was published in 1852 in a distinguished English journal, The Westminster Review, *is an excellent example of the way women writers were treated by liberal male critics during the nineteenth century. Although his tone is complimentary and urbane, Lewes cannot disguise his assumption that women are innately handicapped in literary competition with men.*

This essay is particularly interesting in the light of Lewes' subsequent liaison with Mary Ann Evans (whose pseudonym was George Eliot), the greatest and most learned of all English "lady novelists," as they were called at this time. He met her in 1854, and, since he was married and could not afford the costly and difficult procedures of divorce, they lived together until his death twenty-four years later. Their relationship, which caused her to be shunned by polite society and forced her to conceal the authorship of her books by writing under a pseudonym, gave him a sensitive appreciation of the problems women writers faced, especially if they dared to rebel against middle-class morality. Lewes never dared to write about women writers after his 1852 essay, however, since he believed the public would have interpreted his comments as resulting from the influence of his illicit private life with George Eliot.

The Lady Novelists

The appearance of Woman in the field of literature is a significant fact. It is the correlate of her position in society. To some men the fact is doubtless as distasteful as the social freedom of women in Europe must be to an eastern mind: it must seem so unfeminine, so contrary to the real destination of woman; and it must seem so in both cases from the same cause. But although it is easy to be supercilious and sarcastic on Blue Stockings and Literary Ladies,—and although one may admit that such sarcasms have frequently their extenuation in the offensive pretensions of what are called "strong-minded women,"—it is certain that the philosophic eye sees in this fact of literature cultivated by women, a significance not lightly to be passed over. It touches both society and literature. The man who would deny to woman the cultivation of her intellect, ought, for consistency, to shut her up in a harem. If he recognise in the sex any quality which transcends the qualities demanded in a plaything or a handmaid—if he recognise in her the existence of an intellectual life not essentially dissimilar to his own, he must, by the plainest logic, admit that life to express itself in all its spontaneous forms of activity. It is very true that ink on the thumb is no ornament; but we have yet to learn that stains upon the blouse or the dissecting sleeves are ornamental; few incidents of work are. What then? Moreover we confess it is very awkward and uncomfortable to hear a woman venture on Greek, when you don't know Greek, or to quote from a philosophical treatise which would give you a headache; and something of this feeling doubtless lies at the core of much of the opposition to "learned women;" the men are "put out" by it. The enormity seems equivalent to the domestic partner of your joys assuming the privilege of a latch-key! "Where is our supremacy to find a throne if we admit women to share our imperious dominion—Intelligence?" So reasons the intellectual Jones. But one might quietly ask him whether he professed any immense delight in the society of the *man* who threw Greek and philosophy at his head? Pedantry is the ostentation of learning, the scholar's coxcombry; no one likes it, any more than he likes other forms of obtrusive self-assertion. . . .

One may admit that much folly is spoken and written on the subject of "woman's mission" and "emancipation:" folly *pro*, and folly *con*; one may admit that literary women are not *always* the most charming of their sex (are literary men of theirs?)—but let us leave all such side questions and definitely ask ourselves, What does the literature of women really mean? To aid us in arriving at something like distinctness, it will be well to settle a definition of literature itself.

Literature must be separated from philosophy and science; at least for our present purpose. Science is the expression of the forms and order of Nature; literature is the expression of the forms and order of human life.

All poetry, all fiction, all comedy, all *belles lettres*, even to the playful caprices of fancy, are but the expression of experiences and emotions; and these expressions are the avenues through which we reach the sacred adytum of Humanity, and learn better to understand our fellows and ourselves. In proportion as these expressions are the forms of universal truths, of facts common to all nations or appreciable by all intellects, the literature which sets them forth is permanently good and true. Hence the universality and immortality of Homer, Shakspeare, Cervantes, Molière. But in proportion as these expressions are the forms of individual, peculiar truths, such as fleeting fashions or idiosyncracies, the literature is ephemeral. Hence tragedy never grows old, for it arises from elemental experience; but comedy soon ages, for it arises from peculiarities. Nevertheless even idiosyncrasies are valuable as side glances; they are aberrations that bring the natural orbit into more prominent distinctness.

It follows from what has been said that literature, being essentially the expression of experience and emotion—of what we have seen, felt, and thought—that only *that* literature is effective, and to be prized accordingly, which has *reality for its basis* (needless to say that emotion is as real as the Three per Cents.), *and effective in proportion to the depth and breadth of that basis.*

It was M. de Bonald we believe who gave currency to the famous definition, so constantly accepted as accurate, "Literature is the expression of society." To make it acceptable, however, we must depart very widely from its direct meaning. The most cursory glance at literature on the one hand and at society on the other, will detect the glaring discrepancy. So far from literature being a mirror or expression of society, it is under most aspects palpably at variance with society. Idylls flourish on the eve of violent social outbreaks (as we see in Florian, Gesner, and George Sand); chivalry finds a voice as chivalry is passing from the world; wild adventurous novels agitated with hair-breadth 'scapes solace a money-making society "so eminently respectable;" love in a cottage makes the heart flutter that is about to sell itself for a splendid match.

. . .

Not only so, but our novels and plays, even when pretending to represent real life, represent it as no human being ever saw it.

If, however, instead of regarding literature as the expression of society, we regard it as the expression of the emotions, the whims, the caprices, the enthusiasms, the fluctuating idealisms which move each epoch, we shall not be far wrong; and inasmuch as women necessarily take part in these things, they ought to give them *their* expression. And this leads us to the heart of the question, What does the literature of women mean? It means this: while it is impossible for men to express life otherwise than as they know it—and they can only know it profoundly according to their own experience—the advent of female literature promises woman's view of life, woman's experience: in other words, a new element. Make what distinctions you please in the social world, it still remains true that men and women have different organisations, consequently different experiences. To know life you must have both sides depicted.

. . .

Let him paint what he knows. And if you limit woman's sphere to the domestic circle, you must still recognise the concurrent necessity of domestic life finding its homeliest and truest expression in the woman who lives it.

Keeping to the abstract heights we have chosen, too abstract and general to be affected by exceptions, we may further say that the Masculine mind is characterised by the predominance of the intellect, and the Feminine by the predominance of the emotions. According to this rough division the regions of philosophy would be assigned to men, those of literature to women. We need scarcely warn the reader against too rigorous an interpretation of this statement, which is purposely exaggerated the better to serve as a sign-post. It is quite true that no such absolute distinction exists in mankind, and therefore no such correlative distinction will be found in authorship. There is no man whose mind is shrivelled up into pure intellect; there is no woman whose intellect is completely absorbed by her emotions. But in most men the intellect does not move in such inseparable alliance with the emotions as in most women, and hence although often not so great as in women, yet the intellect is more commonly dominant. In poets, artists, and men of letters, *par excellence*, we observe this feminine trait, that their intellect habitually moves in alliance with their emotions; and one of the best descriptions of poetry was that given by Professor Wilson, as the "intellect coloured by the feelings."

Woman, by her greater affectionateness, her greater range and depth of emotional experience, is well fitted to give expression to the emotional facts of life, and demands a place in literature corresponding with that she occupies in society; and that literature must be greatly benefited thereby, follows from the definition we have given of literature.

But hitherto, in spite of splendid illustrations, the literature of women has fallen short of its function, owing to a very natural and very explicable weakness—it has been too much a literature of imitation. To write as men write, is the aim and besetting sin of women; to write as women, is the real office they have to perform. Our definition of literature includes this necessity. If writers are bound to express what they have really known, felt, and suffered, that very obligation imperiously declares they shall not quit their own point of view for the point of view of others. To imitate is to abdicate. We are in no need of more male writers; we are in need of genuine female experience. The prejudices, notions, passions, and conventionalisms of men are amply illustrated; let us have the same fulness with respect to women. Unhappily the literature of women may be compared with that of Rome; no amount of graceful talent can disguise the internal defect. Virgil, Ovid, and

Catullus were assuredly gifted with delicate and poetic sensibility; but their light is, after all, the light of moons reflected from the Grecian suns, and such as brings little life with its rays. To speak in Greek, to think in Greek, was the ambition of all cultivated Romans, who could not see that it would be a grander thing to utter their pure Roman natures in sincere originality. So of women. The throne of intellect has so long been occupied by men, that women naturally deem themselves bound to attend the Court. Greece domineered over Rome; its intellectual supremacy was recognised, and the only way of rivalling it seemed to be imitation. Yet not *so* did Rome vanquish Pyrrhus and his elephants; not by employing elephants to match his, but by Roman valour.

Of all departments of literature, Fiction is the one to which, by nature and by circumstance, women are best adapted. Exceptional women will of course be found competent to the highest success in other departments; but speaking generally, novels are their forte. The domestic experiences which form the bulk of woman's knowledge finds an appropriate form in novels; while the very nature of fiction calls for that predominance of Sentiment which we have already attributed to the feminine mind. Love is the staple of fiction, for it "forms the story of a woman's life." The joys and sorrows of affection, the incidents of domestic life, the aspirations and fluctuations of emotional life, assume typical forms in the novel. Hence we may be prepared to find women succeeding better in *finesse* of detail, in pathos and sentiment, while men generally succeed better in the construction of plots and the delineation of character. Such a novel as "Tom Jones" or "Vanity Fair," we shall not get from a woman; nor such an effort of imaginative history as "Ivanhoe" or "Old Mortality;" but Fielding, Thackeray, and Scott are equally excluded from such perfection in its kind as "Pride and Prejudice," "Indiana," or "Jane Eyre:" as an artist, Miss Austen surpasses all the male novelists that ever lived; and for eloquence and depth of feeling, no man approaches George Sand.

We are here led to another curious point in our subject, viz., the influence of Sorrow upon female literature. It may be said without exaggeration that almost all literature has some remote connexion with suffering. "Speculation," said Novalis, "is disease." It certainly springs from a vague disquiet. Poetry is analogous to the pearl which the oyster secretes in its malady.

> Most wretched men
> Are cradled into poetry by wrong,
> They learn in suffering what they teach in song.

What Shelley says of poets, applies with greater force to women. If they turn their thoughts to literature, it is—when not purely an imitative act—always to solace by some intellectual activity the sorrow that in silence wastes their lives, and by a withdrawal of the intellect from the contemplation of their pain, or by a transmutation of their secret anxieties into types, they escape from the pressure of that burden. If the accidents of her position make her solitary and inactive, or if her thwarted affections shut her somewhat from that sweet domestic and maternal sphere to which her whole being spontaneously moves, she turns to literature as to another sphere. We do not here simply refer to those notorious cases where literature has been taken up with the avowed and conscious purpose of withdrawing thoughts from painful subjects; but to the unconscious unavowed influence of domestic disquiet and unfulfilled expectations, in determining the sufferer to intellectual activity. The happy wife and busy mother are only forced into literature by some hereditary organic tendency, stronger even than the domestic; and hence it is that the cleverest women are not always those who have written books.

Having said thus much on the general subject of female novel writing, let us glance rapidly, and without pretence of exhaustive criticism, at some of the novelists; doing in careless prose what Leigh Hunt has done in genial verse in his "Blue Stocking Revels." We have been great readers and great admirers of female novels; and although it is difficult to give authors a *satisfactory* reason for not including their names among the most celebrated, we beg our fair novelists to put the most generous construction upon all our "omissions," and to believe that when we are ungallant and omissive, there is "a design under it" as profound as that under Swift's dulness. To include *all* would obviously be impossible in these limits; and we shall purposely exclude some names of undoubted worth and renown, in order not even to seem invidious.

First and foremost let Jane Austen be named, the greatest artist that has ever written, using the term to signify the most perfect mastery over the means to her end. There are heights and depths in human nature Miss Austen has never scaled nor fathomed, there are worlds of passionate existence into which she has never set foot; but although this is obvious to every reader, it is equally obvious that she has risked no failures by attempting to delineate that which she had not seen. Her circle may be restricted, but it is complete. Her world is a perfect orb, and vital. Life, as it presents itself to an English gentlewoman peacefully yet actively engaged in her quiet village, is mirrored in her works with a purity and fidelity that must endow them with interest for all time. To read one of her books is like an actual experience of life: you know the people as if you had lived with them, and you feel something of personal affection towards them. The marvellous reality and subtle distinctive traits noticeable in her portraits has led Macaulay to call her a prose Shakspeare. If the whole force of the distinction which lies in that epithet *prose* be fairly appreciated, no one, we think, will dispute the compliment; for out of Shakspeare it would be difficult to find characters so typical yet so nicely demarcated within the limits of their kind. We do not find such profound psychological insight as may be found in George Sand (not to mention male writers), but taking the type to which the characters belong, we see the most intimate and accurate knowledge in all Miss Austen's creations.

Only cultivated minds fairly appreciate the exquisite art of Miss Austen. Those who demand the stimulus of "effects;" those who can only see by strong lights and shadows, will find her tame and uninteresting. We may illustrate this by one detail. Lucy Steele's bad English, so delicately and truthfully indicated, would in the hands of another have been more obvious, more "effective" in its exaggeration, but the loss of this comic effect is more than replaced to the cultivated reader by his relish of the nice discrimination visible in its truthfulness. And so of the rest. *Strong* lights are unnecessary, *true* lights being at command. The incidents, the characters, the dialogue—all are of every day life, and so truthfully presented, that to appreciate the art we must try to imitate it, or carefully compare it with that of others.

We are but echoing an universal note of praise in speaking thus highly of her works, and it is from no desire of simply swelling that chorus of praise that we name her here, but to call attention to the peculiar excellence at once womanly and literary which has earned this reputation. Of all imaginative writers she is the most *real*. Never does she transcend her own actual experience, never does her pen trace a line that does not touch the experience of others. Herein we recognise the first quality of literature. We recognise the second and more special quality of womanliness in the tone and point of view: they are novels written by a woman, an Englishwoman, a gentlewoman; no signature could disguise that fact; and because she has so faithfully (although unconsciously) kept to her own womanly point of view, her works are durable. There is nothing of the *doctrinaire* in Jane Austen; not a trace of woman's "mission;" but as the most truthful, charming, humorous, pure-minded, quick-witted, and unexaggerated of writers, female literature has reason to be proud of her.

Of greater genius, and incomparably deeper experience, George Sand represents woman's literature more illustriously and more obviously. In her, quite apart from the magnificent gifts of Nature, we see the influence of Sorrow, as a determining impulse to write, and the abiding consciousness of the womanly point of view as the subject matter of her writings. In vain has she chosen the mask of a man, the features of a woman are everywhere visible. Since Goethe no one has been able to say with so much truth, "My writings are my confessions." Her biography lies there, presented, indeed, in a fragmentary shape, and under wayward disguises, but nevertheless giving to the motley groups the strange and unmistakable charm of reality. Her grandmother, by whom she was brought up, disgusted at her not being a boy, resolved to remedy the misfortune as far as possible by educating her like a boy.

We may say of this, as of all the other irregularities of her strange and exceptional life, that whatever unhappiness and error may be traceable thereto, its influence on her writings has been beneficial, by giving a greater range to her experience. It may be selfish to rejoice over the malady which secretes a pearl, but the possessor of the pearl may at least congratulate himself that at any rate the pearl has been produced; and so of the unhappiness of genius. Certainly few women have had such profound and varied experience as George Sand; none have turned it to more account. Her writings contain many passages that her warmest admirers would wish unwritten, but although severe criticism may detect the weak places, the severest criticism must conclude with the admission of her standing among the highest minds of literature. In the matter of eloquence, she surpasses everything France has yet produced. There has been no style at once so large, so harmonious, so expressive, and so unaffected: like a light shining through an alabaster vase, the ideas shine through her diction; while as regards rhythmic melody of phrase, it is a style such as Beethoven might have written had he uttered in words the melodious passion that was in him.

But deeper than all eloquence, grander than all grandeur of phrase, is that forlorn splendour of a life of passionate experience painted in her works. There is no man so wise but he may learn from them, for they are the utterances of a soul in pain, a soul that has been tried. No man could have written her books, for no man could have had her experience, even with a genius equal to her own. The philosopher may smile sometimes at her philosophy, for *that* is only a reflex of some man whose ideas she has adopted; the critic may smile sometimes at her failure in delineating men; but both philosopher and critic must perceive that those writings of hers are *original*, are genuine, are transcripts of experience, and as such fulfil the primary condition of all literature. It is not our present purpose to enter upon details, but we may add in passing that although *all* her works will be found to partake of the character of confessions, there is one wherein the biographical element takes a more definite and literal shape, viz., in "Lucrezia Floriani." Wide as the incidents of this story are from the truth, the characters of Lucrezia, Karol, and Vandoni, are more like portraits than is usual with her.

By a whimsical transition our thoughts wander to Lady Morgan, the "Wild Irish Girl," who delighted our fathers, and gave the "Quarterly" an opportunity of displaying its accustomed amenity and nice feeling for the sex. Lady Morgan has been a staunch upholder of the rights of woman, and in her own person vindicated the claims of the sex to be heard as authors. But Leigh Hunt shall touch her portrait for us:—

> And dear Lady Morgan! Look, look how she comes,
> With her pulses all beating for freedom, like drums—
> So Irish, so modish, so *mixtish*, so wild;

> So committing herself, as she talks, like a child,
> So trim yet so easy, polite yet high-hearted,
> That truth and she, try all she can, won't be parted.
> She'll put on your fashions, your latest new air,
> And then talk so frankly, she'll make you all stare.

From the same hand you shall have a sketch of Miss Edgeworth—a strange contrast to her countrywoman just named:—

> At the sight of Miss Edgeworth, he said, "Here comes one
> As sincere and as kind as lives under the sun,
> Not poetical, eh?—nor much given to insist
> On utilities not in utility's list.
> (Things, nevertheless, without which the large heart
> Of my world would but play a poor husk of a part.)
> But most truly within her own sphere sympathetic—
> And that's no mean help towards the practice poetic."
> Then, smiling, he said a most singular thing—
> He thanked her for making him "saving of string"!!
> But, for fear she should fancy he didn't approve her in
> Matters more weighty, praised much her "Manœuvring,"
> A book, which, if aught could pierce craniums so dense,
> Might supply cunning folks with a little good sense.
> And her Irish (he added) poor souls! so impressed him,
> He knew not if most they amus'd, or distress'd him!

Miss Edgeworth possesses in a remarkable degree the peculiarly feminine quality of *Observation*, though but little of that other quality *Sentiment*, which distinguishes female writers, and which, combined with observation, constitute the staple of novels. Indeed one might class novelists thus—1st, Those remarkable for Observation. 2nd, Those remarkable for Sentiment. 3rd, Those remarkable for the combination of the two. Observation without Sentiment usually leads to humour or satire; Sentiment without Observation to rhetoric and long-drawn lachrymosity. The extreme fault of the one is flippant superficiality; that of the other is what is called "sickly sentimentality."

Miss Burney, for example, had a quick Observation, notably of ridiculous details, and with a certain broad vulgar gauge of human nature, contrived to write one or two novels that admirably reflected the passing manners of her age; but when—as in the "Wanderer"—she attempted to interest by Sentiment, her failure was hopeless. L. E. L., on the other hand, was essentially deficient in that which made the reputation of Fanny Burney, but her quick emotive nature, trembling with sensibility, enabled her to write passages of exquisite beauty, which were not, however, more durable than mere emotion is. Mrs. Gore, again, who might perhaps, with more care bestowed upon her works, have been the Fanny

Burney of our age, exhibits in every chapter the marvellous finesse and quickness of Observation, winged with a certain airy gaiety of style which, if it be not wit, has half the charm of wit; and this faculty of Observation has allowed her to write heaps of fashionable novels, as fugitive as the fashions they reflect, yet as gay and pleasant. But who does not miss in them that element of serious Sentiment which gives to other novels their pathos, their poetry, their psychology?

We might run through the list of female writers thus contrasting them, noting the strong sarcastic observation of Mrs. Trollope and the wearisome sentimentality of Mrs. Marsh, (who has, nevertheless, written one most powerful tale "The Admiral's Daughter," and whose most popular work, "Emelia Wyndham," we are willing to take upon trust, not having read it,) but the excursion would carry us beyond our limits. Enough, if we have indicated the point of view.

Two celebrated women whose works have produced an extraordinary "sensation"—the authoress of "Jane Eyre," and the authoress of "Mary Barton," owe their success, we believe, to the union of rare yet indispensable qualities. They have both given imaginative expression to actual experience—they have not invented, but reproduced; they have preferred the truth, such as their own experience testified, to the vague, false, conventional notions current in circulating libraries. Whatever of weakness may be pointed out in their works, will, we are positive, be mostly in those parts where experience is deserted, and the supposed requirements of fiction have been listened to; whatever has really affected the public mind is, we are equally certain, the transcript of some actual incident, character, or emotion. Note, moreover, that beyond this basis of actuality these writers have the further advantage of deep feeling united to keen observation. The presence of observation is more apparent in "Mary Barton" than in "Jane Eyre," as it is possibly more predominant in the mind of the authoress; and this is why there never was even a momentary doubt as to the writer's sex—a woman's delicate hand being visible in the strongest pages; whereas "Jane Eyre" was not only attributed to a man, but one of the most keen witted and observing of female writers dogmatically pronounced upon internal evidence that none but a man could have written it. The force and even fierceness of the style certainly suggested doubts, but what man could have drawn Jane herself; above all, what man could *so* have drawn Rochester? The lyrical tendency—the psychological and emotional tendency which prevails in "Jane Eyre" may have blinded some to the rare powers of observation also exhibited in the book; a critical examination, however, will at once set this right, the more so when we know that the authoress has led a solitary life in a secluded part of Yorkshire, and has had but little opportunities of seeing the world. She has made the most of her material.

The deep impression produced on Europe by George Sand, has naturally caused many imitations—notably in Germany and France.

As to the Germans—*palmam qui meruit ferat!* let the most gifted bear away the palm—and the palm of bad novel writing certainly belongs to them. However, as the names of these Indianas and Lelias have scarcely crossed the German Ocean, we will leave them in untroubled emancipation.

· · ·

The name of Daniel Stern (pseudonyme for the Comtesse d'Agoult) has had more attention. Her first appearance was in "Nélida," a novel in which she idealised herself, and branded her truant lover, Franz Liszt. It had a certain "succès de scandale." The assumption of a man's name, and the abiding imitation of Madame Sand, lessened perhaps the admiration the novel would otherwise have excited, because it claimed a standard to which, in no sense, could it be compared. Since that, Daniel Stern has earned a more serious reputation as a political and historical writer. Her "History of the Revolution of 1848" is the best that has been written on that subject.

Apropos of "Nélida," and of Lady Bulwer Lytton's novels, it may be pertinent to distinguish between writing out your actual experience in fiction, and using fiction as a medium for obtruding your private history on the sympathies of the public. We hold that the author is bound to use actual experience as his material, or else to keep silent; but he is equally bound by all moral and social considerations not to use that experience in such forms that the public will recognise it, and become, as it were, initiated into the private affairs of his characters. If he avow himself as the Juvenal or Aristophanes of his age, and satirize his friends and foes, he has, at any rate, the excuse, that everyone is on guard against avowed satire. But if he have been mixed up in some deplorable history which has become notorious, and if he take advantage of that notoriety to tell *his* version of it under the transparent disguise of fiction, then we say he violates all principle of truth and of literature; because in fiction he has an immunity from falsehood. He does not profess to tell you the story, yet he gives you to understand what he wishes. He paints himself as an injured innocent; and if you object to his portrait of you, as that of an incarnate demon, his answer is ready —"*That* is a character in my novel; who said it was a portrait of you?"

It was notorious, for example, that Madame Sand had lived for some years with Chopin, and that Madame d'Agoult had children by Liszt, and that both women had finally separated from their lovers. Now, although we hold that if Madame Sand or Madame d'Agoult wished to write, they were bound to go back for material to their own personal experience, it is quite clear that, in so doing, they were bound by the very notoriety of their histories to work up that material into shapes so unlike the outward form of these histories, that no one should detect the origin. Instead of doing so, they both take the public into confidence, and manage to paint themselves as victims, and their lovers as insupportable. We are touching upon a delicate distinction, but the moral sense of every impartial reader easily distinguishes between the legitimate and illegitimate employment of experience.

As examples of the legitimate employment, let us name the works of Geraldine Jewsbury and Eliza Lynn, two writers in whom the influence of George Sand is traceable, and in whom, although we know that actual experience is taken as the material used, no one ever pretends to recognise private life. Recurring to our rough classification, we should cite Miss Jewsbury as one in whom Observation and Sentiment were about equal; but although she possesses, in an eminent degree, both qualities, she does not work them harmoniously together. Her keen womanly observation of life gives to her novels the piquancy of sarcasm, and her deep womanly feeling of life gives to them the warmth and interest of sentiment; but—there *is* a but!—the works seem rather the offspring of *two* minds than of one mind; there is a want of unity in them, arising perhaps from want of art. Curious it is to trace the development of her mind in the three novels she has published at wide intervals: "Zoe," in which the impetuous passionate style clearly betrays the influence of George Sand; "The Half Sisters," in which the style is toned down to a more truthful pitch; and "Marian Withers," in which there is scarcely any trace of the turbulence and fervor of "Zoe." If we look closely we shall find that age and experience have had their customary influence, and while subduing the exuberance of Sentiment, have brought into greater prominence the strong characteristics of Observation. Miss Jewsbury excels in subtle and sometimes deep observation of morals as of manners; and we look to her for still finer works than any she has yet written.

Miss Lynn occupies a strange and defiant position. In her first work, "Azeth," she astonished by the recondite reading exhibited in her Egyptian colouring, and by the daring voluptuousness of her eloquence. In her second romance, "Amymone," she quitted Egypt for Greece, showed an equal amount of laborious study and of exuberant rhetoric, but assumed a still more hostile position against received notions by a paradoxical defence of Aspasia. In "Realities," a novel of our day, the antagonism was avowed, incessant, impetuous; it was a passionate and exaggerated protest against conventions, which failed of its intended effect because it was too exaggerated, too manifestly unjust. Splendour of diction, and a sort of rhythmic passion, rising oftentimes into accents of startling power, have never been denied her; but one abiding defect of her novels we must allude to, and that is, the want of that Observation which we have insisted on as a requisite in fiction. In "Realities," this want was singularly apparent, and gave it the air of unreality so detrimental to such a work. The realm of imagination is better suited to her powers than that of fact; she feels deeply, paints vividly what she feels, but she sees dimly.

Miss Muloch has also a great gift of eloquence, and considerable power in the dramatic presentation of character. "The Ogilvies," "Olive," and the "Head of the Family," may be compared with Miss Jewsbury's three novels, as indicating the rapid progress in observation, and a more subdued employment of sentiment; although sentiment, after all, remains her forte. Not so the authoress of "Rose Douglas," and the "Two Families," in whom we recognise a wonderful truthfulness of touch in the portraiture of quiet village life, and quiet village character. The authoress of "Margaret Maitland" excels in delineation of character of greater range and depth; and her pictures of Scottish life are among the most memorable and agreeable we know. They place her beside the charming Madame Charles Reybaud, whose novels, we may parenthetically add, are among the few French fictions admissible into the libraries of young ladies.

But we must cease this rapid flight over the large field of female literature. We have done enough if in this bird's-eye view we have indicated the most characteristic details; and we have proved our case if we have proved the right of Woman to citizenship in the Republic of Letters.

QUESTIONS

1. What signs of Lewes' pedantry do you find in the essay?

2. Lewes writes, "Of all departments of literature, fiction is the one to which by nature and by circumstances, women are best adapted." What does he mean by "nature" and "circumstances"?

3. Discuss Lewes' theory that women write in order to compensate for an emotional loss.

4. Does Lewes' concept of women's talent deal with innate feminine qualities or with those that are socially conditioned? Do you agree with his allocation of literary qualities to women?

Virginia Woolf

Virginia Woolf (1882–1941) *spent her entire life amidst the intellectual aristocracy of her time and was herself one of the major innovators of the twentieth-century English novel. She was born in England to an aristocratic literary family, was married to a writer, and was a member of the literary, artistic, and political coterie known as the "Bloomsbury Group." Her lyrical novels, particularly* Mrs. Dalloway (1925) *and* To the Lighthouse (1927), *broke through the prosaic limits of documentary realism typical of some of her contemporaries to create a new form of fiction.*

Virginia Woolf's *feminism, expressed in many of her short essays as well as in* A Room of One's Own (1928), *has usually embarrassed her critics and has prompted them to apologize for her. Her friend and fellow novelist E. M. Forster, for example, thought that her attack on the masculine conspiracy to keep women from achieving top positions was exaggerated and anachronistic. "She did not appreciate," he wrote in 1941, "that the conspiracy is weakening yearly, and that before long women will be quite as powerful for good or evil as men."*

In comparison with Mary Wollstonecraft, however, or with recent women's liberationists, Virginia Woolf's feminism is subdued and her demands are moderate. A Room of One's Own, the fourth chapter of which is reprinted below, was originally a series of lectures delivered at the women's colleges of Oxford and Cambridge. In a sequence of dramatic anecdotes, the author illustrates her conviction that the failure of most women artists to achieve artistic greatness was the result of their social, economic, and legal disadvantages and was not a sign of their innate incapacity. According to the author, women had been denied economic independence and artistic autonomy (achievements that Woolf felt could be symbolized by women having rooms of their own) because they could not free themselves of society's bitter consciousness of sex, and they consequently wrote either to conciliate public opinion or to outrage it. In the chapter reprinted here, Virginia Woolf imagines herself in a library, reading about women writers of the past and asking whether any of them could have possessed the state of mind she defined as most favorable for creative work: one that is "incandescent" and free of grievance and spite, like the mind of Shakespeare.

from

A Room of One's Own

That one would find any woman in that state of mind in the sixteenth century was obviously impossible. One has only to think of the Elizabethan tombstones with all those children kneeling with clasped hands; and their early deaths; and to see their houses with their dark, cramped rooms, to realise that no woman could have written poetry then. What one would expect to find would be that rather later perhaps some great lady would take advantage of her comparative freedom and comfort to publish something with her name to it and risk being thought a monster. Men, of course, are not snobs, I continued, carefully eschewing "the arrant feminism" of Miss Rebecca West; but they appreciate with sympathy for the most part the efforts of a countess to write verse. One would expect to find a lady of title meeting with far greater encouragement than an unknown Miss Austen or a Miss Brontë at that time would have met with. But one would also expect to find that her mind was disturbed by alien emotions like fear and hatred and that her poems showed traces of that disturbance. Here is Lady Winchilsea, for example, I thought, taking down her poems. She was born in the year 1661; she was noble both by birth and by marriage; she was childless; she wrote poetry, and one has only to open her poetry to find her bursting out in indignation against the position of women:

> How are we fallen! fallen by mistaken rules,
> And Education's more than Nature's fools;
> Debarred from all improvements of the mind,
> And to be dull, expected and designed;
> And if some one would soar above the rest,
> With warmer fancy, and ambition pressed,
> So strong the opposing faction still appears,
> The hopes to thrive can ne'er outweigh the fears.

Clearly her mind has by no means "consumed all impediments and become incandescent." On the contrary, it is harassed and distracted with hates and grievances. The human race is split up for her into two parties. Men are the "opposing faction"; men are hated and feared, because they have the power to bar her way to what she wants to do— which is to write.

> Alas! a woman that attempts the pen,
> Such a presumptuous creature is esteemed,
> The fault can by no virtue be redeemed.
> They tell us we mistake our sex and way;
> Good breeding, fashion, dancing, dressing, play,
> Are the accomplishments we should desire;
> To write, or read, or think, or to enquire,
> Would cloud our beauty, and exhaust our time,
> And interrupt the conquests of our prime,
> Whilst the dull manage of a servile house
> Is held by some our utmost art and use.

Indeed she has to encourage herself to write by supposing that what she writes will never be published; to soothe herself with the sad chant:

> To some few friends, and to thy sorrows sing,
> For groves of laurel thou wert never meant;
> Be dark enough thy shades, and be thou there content.

Yet it is clear that could she have freed her mind from hate and fear and not heaped it with bitterness and resentment, the fire was hot within her. Now and again words issue of pure poetry:

> Nor will in fading silks compose,
> Faintly the inimitable rose.

—they are rightly praised by Mr. Murry, and Pope, it is thought, remembered and appropriated those others:

> Now the jonquille o'ercomes the feeble brain;
> We faint beneath the aromatic pain.

It was a thousand pities that the woman who could write like that, whose mind was turned to nature and reflection, should have been forced to anger and bitterness. But how could she have helped herself? I asked, imagining the sneers and the laughter, the adulation of the toadies, the scepticism of the professional poet. She must have shut herself up in a room in the country to write, and been torn asunder by bitterness and scruples perhaps, though her husband was of the kindest, and their married life perfection. She "must have," I say, because when one comes to seek out the facts about Lady Winchilsea, one finds, as usual, that almost nothing is known about her. She suffered terribly from melancholy, which we can explain at least to some extent when we find her telling us how in the grip of it she would imagine:

> My lines decried, and my employment thought,
> An useless folly or presumptuous fault:

The employment, which was thus censured was, as far as one can see, the harmless one of rambling about the fields and dreaming:

> My hand delights to trace unusual things,
> And deviates from the known and common way,
> Nor will in fading silks compose,
> Faintly the inimitable rose.

Naturally, if that was her habit and that was her delight, she could only expect to be laughed at; and, accordingly, Pope or Gay is said to have satirised her "as a blue-stocking with an itch for scribbling." Also it is thought that she offended Gay by laughing at him. She said that his *Trivia* showed that "he was more proper to walk before a chair than to ride in one." But this is all "dubious gossip" and, says Mr. Murry, "uninteresting." But there I do not agree with him, for I should have liked to have had more even of dubious gossip so that I might have found out or made up some image of this melancholy lady, who loved wandering in the fields and thinking about unusual things and scorned, so rashly, so unwisely, "the dull manage of a servile house." But she became diffuse, Mr. Murry says. Her gift is all grown about with weeds and bound with briars. It had no chance of showing itself for the fine distinguished gift it was. And so, putting her back on the shelf, I turned to the other great lady, the Duchess whom Lamb loved, hare-brained, fantastical Margaret of Newcastle, her elder, but her contemporary. They were very different, but alike in this that both were noble and both childless, and both were married to the best of husbands. In both burnt the same passion for poetry and both are disfigured and deformed by the same causes. Open the Duchess and one finds the same outburst of rage, "Women live like Bats or Owls, labour like Beasts, and die like Worms. . . ." Margaret too might have been a poet; in our day all that activity would have turned a wheel of some sort. As it was, what could bind, tame or civilise for human use that wild, generous, untutored intelligence? It poured itself out, higgledy-piggledy, in torrents of rhyme and prose, poetry and philosophy which stand congealed in quartos and folios that nobody ever reads. She should have had a microscope put in her hand. She should have been taught to look at the stars and reason scientifically. Her wits were turned with solitude and freedom. No one checked her. No one taught her. The professors fawned on her. At Court they jeered at her. Sir Egerton Brydges complained of her coarseness—"as flowing from a female of high rank brought up in the Courts." She shut herself up at Welbeck alone.

What a vision of loneliness and riot the thought of Margaret Cavendish brings to mind! As if some giant cucumber had spread itself over all the roses and carnations in the garden and choked them to death. What a waste that the woman who wrote "the best bred women are those whose minds are civilest" should have frittered her time away scribbling nonsense and plunging ever deeper into obscurity and folly till the people crowded round her coach when she issued out. Evidently the crazy Duchess became a bogey to frighten clever girls with. Here, I remembered, putting away the Duchess and opening Dorothy Osborne's letters, is Dorothy writing to Temple about the Duchess's new book. "Sure the poore woman is a little distracted, shee could never bee soe rediculous else as to venture at writeing book's and in verse too, if I should not sleep this fortnight I should not come to that."

And so, since no woman of sense and modesty could write books, Dorothy, who was sensitive and melancholy, the very opposite of the Duchess in temper, wrote nothing. Letters did not count. A woman might write letters while she was sitting by her father's sick-bed. She could write them by the fire whilst the men talked without disturbing them. The strange thing is, I thought, turning over the pages of Dorothy's letters, what a gift that untaught and solitary girl had for the framing of a sentence, for the fashioning of a scene. Listen to her running on:

> After dinner wee sitt and talk till Mr. B. com's in question and then I am gon. the heat of the day is spent in reading or working and about sixe or seven a Clock, I walke out into a Common that lyes hard by the house where a great many young wenches keep Sheep and Cow's and sitt in the shades singing of Ballads; I goe to them and compare their voyces and Beauty's to some Ancient Shepherdesses that I have read of and finde a vaste difference there, but trust mee I think these are as innocent as those could bee. I talke to them, and finde they want nothing to make them the happiest People in the world, but the knoledge that they are soe. most commonly when we are in the middest of our discourse one looks aboute her and spyes her Cow's goeing into the Corne and then away they all run, as if they had wing's at theire heels. I that am not soe nimble stay behinde, and when I see them driveing home theire Cattle I think tis time for mee to retyre too. when I have supped I goe into the Garden and soe to the syde of a small River that runs by it where I sitt downe and wish you with mee. . . .

One could have sworn that she had the makings of a writer in her. But "if I should not sleep this fortnight I should not come to that"— one can measure the opposition that was in the air to a woman writing when one finds that even a woman with a great turn for writing has brought herself to believe that to write a book was to be ridiculous, even to show oneself distracted. And so we come, I continued, replacing the single short volume of Dorothy Osborne's letters upon the shelf, to Mrs. Behn.

And with Mrs. Behn we turn a very important corner on the road. We leave behind, shut up in their parks among their folios, those solitary great ladies who wrote without audience or criticism, for their own delight alone. We come to town and rub shoulders with ordinary people in the streets. Mrs. Behn was a middle-class woman with all the plebeian virtues of humour, vitality and courage; a woman forced by the death of her husband and some unfortunate adventures of her own to make her living by her wits. She had to work on equal terms with men. She made, by working very hard, enough to live on. The importance of that fact outweighs anything that she actually wrote, even the splendid "A Thousand Martyrs I have made," or "Love in Fantastic Triumph sat," for here begins the freedom of the mind, or rather the possibility that in the course of time the mind will be free to write what it likes. For now that Aphra Behn had done it, girls could go to their parents and say, You need not give me an allowance; I can make money by my pen. Of course the answer for many years to come was, Yes, by living the life of Aphra Behn! Death would be better! and the door was slammed faster than ever. That profoundly interesting subject, the value that men set upon women's chastity and its effect upon their education, here suggests itself for discussion, and might provide an interesting book if any student at Girton or Newnham cared to go into the matter. Lady Dudley, sitting in diamonds among the midges of a Scottish moor, might serve for frontispiece. Lord Dudley, *The Times* said when Lady Dudley died the other day, "a man of cultivated taste and many accomplishments, was benevolent and bountiful, but whimsically despotic. He insisted upon his wife's wearing full dress, even at the remotest shooting-lodge in the Highlands; he loaded her with gorgeous jewels," and so on, "he gave her everything—always excepting any measure of responsibility." Then Lord Dudley had a stroke and she nursed him and ruled his estates with supreme competence for ever after. That whimsical despotism was in the nineteenth century too.

But to return. Aphra Behn proved that money could be made by writing at the sacrifice, perhaps, of certain agreeable qualities; and so by degrees writing became not merely a sign of folly and a distracted mind, but was of practical importance. A husband might die, or some disaster overtake the family. Hundreds of women began as the eighteenth century drew on to add to their pin money, or to come to the rescue of their families by making translations or writing the innumerable bad novels which have ceased to be recorded even in text-books, but are to be picked up in the fourpenny boxes in the Charing Cross Road. The extreme activity of mind which showed itself in the later eighteenth century among women—the talking, and the meeting, the writing of essays on Shakespeare, the translating of the classics—was founded on the solid fact that women could make money by writing. Money dignifies what is frivolous if unpaid for. It might still be well to sneer at "blue stockings with an itch for scribbling," but it could not be denied that they could put money in their purses. Thus, towards the end of the eighteenth century a change came about which, if I were re-writing history, I should describe more fully and think of greater importance than the Crusades or the Wars of the Roses. The middle-class woman began to write. For if *Pride and Prejudice* matters, and *Middlemarch* and *Villette* and *Wuthering Heights* matter, then it matters far more than I can prove in an hour's discourse that women generally, and not merely the lonely aristocrat shut up in her country house among her folios and her flatterers, took to writing. Without those forerunners, Jane Austen and the Brontës and George Eliot could no more have written than Shakespeare could have written without Marlowe, or Marlowe without Chaucer, or Chaucer without those forgotten poets who paved the ways and tamed the natural savagery of the tongue. For masterpieces are not single and solitary births; they are the outcome of many years of thinking in common, of thinking by the body of the people, so that the experience of the mass is behind the single voice. Jane Austen should have laid a wreath upon the grave of Fanny Burney, and George Eliot done homage to the robust shade of Eliza Carter—the valiant old woman who tied a bell to her bedstead in order that she might wake early and learn Greek. All women together ought to let flowers fall upon the tomb of Aphra Behn which is, most scandalously but rather appropriately, in Westminster Abbey, for it was she who earned them the right to speak their minds. It is she—shady and amorous as she was—who makes it not quite fantastic for me to say to you tonight: Earn five hundred a year by your wits.

Here, then, one had reached the early nineteenth century. And here, for the first time, I found several shelves given up entirely to the works of women. But why, I could not help asking, as I ran my eyes over them, were they, with very few exceptions, all novels? The original impulse was to poetry. The "supreme head of song" was a poetess. Both in France and in England the women poets precede the women novelists. Moreover, I thought, looking at the four famous names, what had George Eliot in common with Emily Brontë? Did not Charlotte Brontë fail entirely to understand Jane Austen? Save for the possibly relevant fact that not one of them had a child, four more incongruous characters could not have met together in a room—so much so that it is tempting to invent a meeting and a dialogue between them. Yet by some strange force they were all compelled, when they wrote, to write novels. Had it something to do with being born of the middle class, I asked; and with the fact, which Miss Emily Davies a little later was so strikingly to demonstrate, that the middle-class family in the early nineteenth century was possessed only of a single sitting-room between them? If a woman wrote, she would have to write in the common sitting-room. And, as Miss Nightingale was so vehemently to complain, —"women never have an half hour . . . that they can call their own" —she was always interrupted. Still it would be easier to write prose and fiction there than to write poetry or a play. Less concentration is required. Jane Austen wrote like that to the end of her days. "How she was able to effect all this," her nephew writes in his Memoir, "is surprising, for she had no separate study to repair to, and most of the work must have been done in the general sitting-room, subject to all kinds of casual interruptions. She was careful that her occupation should not be suspected by servants or visitors or any persons beyond her own family party." [1] Jane Austen hid her manuscripts or covered them with a piece of blotting-paper. Then, again, all the literary train- ing that a woman had in the early nineteenth century was training in the observation of character, in the analysis of emotion. Her sensibility had been educated for centuries by the influences of the common sitting-room. People's feelings were impressed on her; personal relations were always before her eyes. Therefore, when the middle-class woman took to writing, she naturally wrote novels, even though, as seems evi- dent enough, two of the four famous women here named were not by nature novelists. Emily Brontë should have written poetic plays; the overflow of George Eliot's capacious mind should have spread itself when the creative impulse was spent upon history or biography. They wrote novels, however; one may even go further, I said, taking *Pride and Prejudice* from the shelf, and say that they wrote good novels. Without boasting or giving pain to the opposite sex, one may say that *Pride and Prejudice* is a good book. At any rate, one would not have been ashamed to have been caught in the act of writing *Pride and Prejudice*. Yet Jane Austen was glad that a hinge creaked, so that she might hide her manuscript before any one came in. To Jane Austen there was something discreditable in writing *Pride and Prejudice*. And, I wondered, would *Pride and Prejudice* have been a better novel if Jane Austen had not thought it necessary to hide her manuscript from visitors? I read a page or two to see; but I could not find any signs that her circumstances had harmed her work in the slightest. That, perhaps, was the chief miracle about it. Here was a woman about the year 1800 writing without hate, without bitterness, without fear, with-

---

[1] *Memoir of Jane Austen,* by her nephew, James Edward Austen-Leigh.

out protest, without preaching. That was how Shakespeare wrote, I thought, looking at *Antony and Cleopatra*; and when people compare Shakespeare and Jane Austen, they may mean that the minds of both had consumed all impediments; and for that reason we do not know Jane Austen and we do not know Shakespeare, and for that reason Jane Austen pervades every word that she wrote, and so does Shakespeare. If Jane Austen suffered in any way from her circumstances it was in the narrowness of life that was imposed upon her. It was impossible for a woman to go about alone. She never travelled; she never drove through London in an omnibus or had luncheon in a shop by herself. But perhaps it was the nature of Jane Austen not to want what she had not. Her gift and her circumstances matched each other completely. But I doubt whether that was true of Charlotte Brontë, I said, opening *Jane Eyre* and laying it beside *Pride and Prejudice*.

I opened it at chapter twelve and my eye was caught by the phrase, "Anybody may blame me who likes." What were they blaming Charlotte Brontë for, I wondered? And I read how Jane Eyre used to go up on to the roof when Mrs. Fairfax was making jellies and looked over the fields at the distant view. And then she longed—and it was for this that they blamed her—that "then I longed for a power of vision which might overpass that limit; which might reach the busy world, towns, regions full of life I had heard of but never seen: that then I desired more of practical experience than I possessed; more of intercourse with my kind, of acquaintance with variety of character than was here within my reach. I valued what was good in Mrs. Fairfax, and what was good in Adèle; but I believed in the existence of other and more vivid kinds of goodness, and what I believed in I wished to behold.

"Who blames me? Many, no doubt, and I shall be called discontented. I could not help it: the restlessness was in my nature; it agitated me to pain sometimes. . . .

"It is vain to say human beings ought to be satisfied with tranquillity: they must have action; and they will make it if they cannot find it. Millions are condemned to a stiller doom than mine, and millions are in silent revolt against their lot. Nobody knows how many rebellions ferment in the masses of life which people earth. Women are supposed to be very calm generally: but women feel just as men feel; they need exercise for their faculties and a field for their efforts as much as their brothers do; they suffer from too rigid a restraint, too absolute a stagnation, precisely as men would suffer; and it is narrow-minded in their more privileged fellow-creatures to say that they ought to confine themselves to making puddings and knitting stockings, to playing on the piano and embroidering bags. It is thoughtless to condemn them, or laugh at them, if they seek to do more or learn more than custom has pronounced necessary for their sex.

"When thus alone I not unfrequently heard Grace Poole's laugh. . . ."

That is an awkward break, I thought. It is upsetting to come upon Grace Poole all of a sudden. The continuity is disturbed. One might say, I continued, laying the book down beside *Pride and Prejudice*, that the woman who wrote those pages had more genius in her than Jane Austen; but if one reads them over and marks that jerk in them, that indignation, one sees that she will never get her genius expressed whole and entire. Her books will be deformed and twisted. She will write in a rage where she should write calmly. She will write foolishly where she should write wisely. She will write of herself where she should write of her characters. She is at war with her lot. How could she help but die young, cramped and thwarted?

One could not but play for a moment with the thought of what might have happened if Charlotte Brontë had possessed say three hundred a year—but the foolish woman sold the copyright of her novels outright for fifteen hundred pounds; had somehow possessed more knowledge of the busy world, and towns and regions full of life; more practical experience, and intercourse with her kind and acquaintance with a variety of character. In those words she puts her finger exactly not only upon her own defects as a novelist but upon those of her sex at that time. She knew, no one better, how enormously her genius would have profited if it had not spent itself in solitary visions over distant fields; if experience and intercourse and travel had been granted her. But they were not granted; they were withheld; and we must accept the fact that all those good novels, *Villette, Emma, Wuthering Heights, Middlemarch*, were written by women without more experience of life than could enter the house of a respectable clergyman; written too in the common sitting-room of that respectable house and by women so poor that they could not afford to buy more than a few quires of paper at a time upon which to write *Wuthering Heights* or *Jane Eyre*. One of them, it is true, George Eliot, escaped after much tribulation, but only to a secluded villa in St. John's Wood. And there she settled down in the shadow of the world's disapproval. "I wish it to be understood," she wrote, "that I should never invite any one to come and see me who did not ask for the invitation"; for was she not living in sin with a married man and might not the sight of her damage the chastity of Mrs. Smith or whoever it might be that chanced to call? One must submit to the social convention, and be "cut off from what is called the world." At the same time, on the other side of Europe, there was a young man living freely with this gipsy or with that great lady; going to the wars; picking up unhindered and uncensored all that varied experience of human life which served him so splendidly later when he came to write his books. Had Tolstoi lived at the Priory in seclusion with a married lady "cut off from what is called the world," however edifying the moral lesson, he could scarcely, I thought, have written *War and Peace*.

But one could perhaps go a little deeper into the question of novel-writing and the effect of sex upon the novelist. If one shuts one's eyes and thinks of the novel as a whole, it would seem to be a creation own- ing a certain looking-glass likeness to life, though of course with sim- plifications and distortions innumerable. At any rate, it is a structure leaving a shape on the mind's eye, built now in squares, now pagoda shaped, now throwing out wings and arcades, now solidly compact and domed like the Cathedral of Saint Sofia at Constantinople. This shape, I thought, thinking back over certain famous novels, starts in one the kind of emotion that is appropriate to it. But that emotion at once blends itself with others, for the "shape" is not made by the relation of stone to stone, but by the relation of human being to human being. Thus a novel starts in us all sorts of antagonistic and opposed emotions. Life conflicts with something that is not life. Hence the difficulty of coming to any agreement about novels, and the immense sway that our private prejudices have upon us. On the one hand, we feel You— John the hero—must live, or I shall be in the depths of despair. On the other, we feel, Alas, John, you must die, because the shape of the book requires it. Life conflicts with something that is not life. Then since life it is in part, we judge it as life. James is the sort of man I most detest, one says. Or, This is a farrago of absurdity. I could never feel anything of the sort myself. The whole structure, it is obvious, thinking back on any famous novel, is one of infinite complexity, be- cause it is thus made up of so many different judgments, of so many different kinds of emotion. The wonder is that any book so composed holds together for more than a year or two, or can possibly mean to the English reader what it means for the Russian or the Chinese. But they do hold together occasionally very remarkably. And what holds them together in these rare instances of survival (I was thinking of *War and Peace*) is something that one calls integrity, though it has nothing to do with paying one's bills or behaving honourably in an emergency. What one means by integrity, in the case of the novelist, is the convic- tion that he gives one that this is the truth. Yes, one feels, I should never have thought that this could be so; I have never known people behaving like that. But you have convinced me that so it is, so it hap- pens. One holds every phrase, every scene to the light as one reads— for Nature seems, very oddly, to have provided us with an inner light by which to judge of the novelist's integrity or disintegrity. Or perhaps it is rather that Nature, in her most irrational mood, has traced in invisible ink on the walls of the mind a premonition which these great artists confirm; a sketch which only needs to be held to the fire of genius to become visible. When one so exposes it and sees it come to life one exclaims in rapture, But this is what I have always felt and known and desired! And one boils over with excitement, and, shutting the book even with a kind of reverence as if it were something very precious, a stand-by to return to as long as one lives, one puts it back on the shelf, I said, taking *War and Peace* and putting it back in its place. If, on the other hand, these poor sentences that one takes and tests rouse first a quick and eager response with their bright colouring and their dashing gestures but there they stop: something seems to check them in their development: or if they bring to light only a faint scribble in that corner and a blot over there, and nothing appears whole and entire, then one heaves a sigh of disappointment and says, Another failure. This novel has come to grief somewhere.

And for the most part, of course, novels do come to grief somewhere. The imagination falters under the enormous strain. The insight is confused; it can no longer distinguish between the true and the false; it has no longer the strength to go on with the vast labour that calls at every moment for the use of so many different faculties. But how would all this be affected by the sex of the novelist, I wondered, looking at *Jane Eyre* and the others. Would the fact of her sex in any way interfere with the integrity of a woman novelist—that integrity which I take to be the backbone of the writer? Now, in the passages I have quoted from *Jane Eyre*, it is clear that anger was tampering with the integrity of Charlotte Brontë the novelist. She left her story, to which her entire devotion was due, to attend to some personal grievance. She remembered that she had been starved of her proper due of experience —she had been made to stagnate in a parsonage mending stockings when she wanted to wander free over the world. Her imagination swerved from indignation and we feel it swerve. But there were many more influences than anger tugging at her imagination and deflecting it from its path. Ignorance, for instance. The portrait of Rochester is drawn in the dark. We feel the influence of fear in it; just as we constantly feel an acidity which is the result of oppression, a buried suffering smouldering beneath her passion, a rancour which contracts those books, splendid as they are, with a spasm of pain.

And since a novel has this correspondence to real life, its values are to some extent those of real life. But it is obvious that the values of women differ very often from the values which have been made by the other sex; naturally, this is so. Yet it is the masculine values that prevail. Speaking crudely, football and sport are "important"; the worship of fashion, the buying of clothes "trivial." And these values are inevitably transferred from life to fiction. This is an important book, the critic assumes, because it deals with war. This is an insignificant book because it deals with the feelings of women in a drawing-room. A scene in a battlefield is more important than a scene in a shop—everywhere and much more subtly the difference of value persists. The whole structure, therefore, of the early nineteenth-century novel was raised, if one was a woman, by a mind which was slightly pulled from the straight, and made to alter its clear vision in deference to external authority. One has only to skim those old forgotten novels and listen to the tone of voice in which they are written to divine that the writer was meeting criticism; she was saying this by way of aggression, or that by way of conciliation. She was admitting that she was "only a woman," or protesting that she was "as good as a man." She met that criticism as her temperament dictated, with docility and diffidence, or with anger and emphasis. It does not matter which it was; she was thinking of something other than the thing itself. Down comes her book upon our heads. There was a flaw in the centre of it. And I thought of all the women's novels that lie scattered, like small pock-marked apples in an orchard, about the secondhand book shops of London. It was the flaw in the centre that had rotted them. She had altered her values in deference to the opinion of others.

But how impossible it must have been for them not to budge either to the right or to the left. What genius, what integrity it must have required in face of all that criticism, in the midst of that purely patri-archal society, to hold fast to the thing as they saw it without shrink-ing. Only Jane Austen did it and Emily Brontë. It is another feather, perhaps the finest, in their caps. They wrote as women write, not as men write. Of all the thousand women who wrote novels then, they alone entirely ignored the perpetual admonitions of the eternal peda-gogue—write this, think that. They alone were deaf to that persistent voice, now grumbling, now patronising, now domineering, now grieved, now shocked, now angry, now avuncular, that voice which cannot let women alone, but must be at them, like some too conscientious gov-erness, adjuring them, like Sir Egerton Brydges, to be refined; dragging even into the criticism of poetry criticism of sex;[2] admonishing them, if they would be good and win, as I suppose, some shiny prize, to keep within certain limits which the gentleman in question thinks suitable: ". . . female novelists should only aspire to excellence by courageously acknowledging the limitations of their sex." [3] That puts the matter in a nutshell, and when I tell you, rather to your surprise, that this sen-tence was written not in August 1828 but in August 1928, you will agree, I think, that however delightful it is to us now, it represents a vast body of opinion—I am not going to stir those old pools, I take only what chance has floated to my feet—that was far more vigorous and far more vocal a century ago. It would have needed a very stalwart young woman in 1828 to disregard all those snubs and chidings and promises of prizes. One must have been something of a firebrand to

---

[2] "[She] has a metaphysical purpose, and that is a dangerous obsession, especially with a woman, for women rarely possess men's healthy love of rhetoric. It is a strange lack in the sex which is in other things more primitive and more materialistic."— *New Criterion*, June 1928.

[3] "If, like the reporter, you believe that female novelists should only aspire to ex-cellence by courageously acknowledging the limitations of their sex (Jane Austen [has] demonstrated how gracefully this gesture can be accomplished). . . ." *Life and Letters*, August 1928.

say to oneself, Oh, but they can't buy literature too. Literature is open to everybody. I refuse to allow you, Beadle though you are, to turn me off the grass. Lock up your libraries if you like; but there is no gate, no lock, no bolt that you can set upon the freedom of my mind.

But whatever effect discouragement and criticism had upon their writing—and I believe that they had a very great effect—that was unimportant compared with the other difficulty which faced them (I was still considering those early nineteenth-century novelists) when they came to set their thoughts on paper—that is that they had no tradition behind them, or one so short and partial that it was of little help. For we think back through our mothers if we are women. It is useless to go to the great men writers for help, however much one may go to them for pleasure. Lamb, Browne, Thackeray, Newman, Sterne, Dickens, De Quincey—whoever it may be—never helped a woman yet, though she may have learnt a few tricks of them and adapted them to her use. The weight, the pace, the stride of a man's mind are too unlike her own for her to lift anything substantial from him successfully. The ape is too distant to be sedulous. Perhaps the first thing she would find, setting pen to paper, was that there was no common sentence ready for her use. All the great novelists like Thackeray and Dickens and Balzac have written a natural prose, swift but not slovenly, expressive but not precious, taking their own tint without ceasing to be common property. They have based it on the sentence that was current at the time. The sentence that was current at the beginning of the nineteenth century ran something like this perhaps: "The grandeur of their works was an argument with them, not to stop short, but to proceed. They could have no higher excitement or satisfaction than in the exercise of their art and endless generations of truth and beauty. Success prompts to exertion; and habit facilitates success." That is a man's sentence; behind it one can see Johnson, Gibbon and the rest. It was a sentence that was unsuited for a woman's use. Charlotte Brontë, with all her splendid gift for prose, stumbled and fell with that clumsy weapon in her hands. George Eliot committed atrocities with it that beggar description. Jane Austen looked at it and laughed at it and devised a perfectly natural, shapely sentence proper for her own use and never departed from it. Thus, with less genius for writing than Charlotte Brontë, she got infinitely more said. Indeed, since freedom and fullness of expression are of the essence of the art, such a lack of tradition, such a scarcity and inadequacy of tools, must have told enormously upon the writing of women. Moreover, a book is not made of sentences laid end to end, but of sentences built, if an image helps, into arcades or domes. And this shape too has been made by men out of their own needs for their own uses. There is no reason to think that the form of the epic or of the poetic play suits a woman any more than the sentence suits her. But all the older forms of literature were hardened and set by the time she became a writer. The novel alone was young enough to be soft in her hands—another reason, perhaps, why she wrote novels. Yet who shall say that even now "the novel" (I give it inverted commas to mark my sense of the words' inadequacy), who shall say that even this most pliable of all forms is rightly shaped for her use? No doubt we shall find her knocking that into shape for herself when she has the free use of her limbs; and providing some new vehicle, not necessarily in verse, for the poetry in her. For it is the poetry that is still denied outlet. And I went on to ponder how a woman nowadays would write a poetic tragedy in five acts—would she use verse—would she not use prose rather?

But these are difficult questions which lie in the twilight of the future. I must leave them, if only because they stimulate me to wander from my subject into trackless forests where I shall be lost and, very likely, devoured by wild beasts. I do not want, and I am sure that you do not want me, to broach that very dismal subject, the future of fiction, so that I will only pause here one moment to draw your attention to the great part which must be played in that future so far as women are concerned by physical conditions. The book has somehow to be adapted to the body, and at a venture one would say that women's books should be shorter, more concentrated, than those of men, and framed so that they do not need long hours of steady and uninterrupted work. For interruptions there will always be. Again, the nerves that feed the brain would seem to differ in men and women, and if you are going to make them work their best and hardest, you must find out what treatment suits them—whether these hours of lectures, for instance, which the monks devised, presumably, hundreds of years ago, suit them—what alternations of work and rest they need, interpreting rest not as doing nothing but as doing something but something that is different; and what should that difference be? All this should be discussed and discovered; all this is part of the question of women and fiction. And yet, I continued, approaching the bookcase again, where shall I find that elaborate study of the psychology of women by a woman? If through their incapacity to play football women are not going to be allowed to practise medicine—

Happily my thoughts were now given another turn.

QUESTIONS

1. It has been said that the literary feminism and the social feminism of Virginia Woolf conflict. Distinguish between these two kinds of feminism and discuss how each is represented in this chapter. Do you agree that there is any contradiction between literary and social feminism?

2. Compare the impediments imposed on seventeenth-, eight-

eenth-, and nineteenth-century women writers, as described by Woolf, with those that today's literary women encounter.

3. What does Virginia Woolf mean by the "integrity" of the artist? What prevented women from attaining that integrity?

4. What reasons does the author give for the relative success women have had writing novels?

Elizabeth Hardwick

Elizabeth Hardwick (b. 1916) is a novelist and the editor of The New York Review of Books. *Her book* A View of My Own (1962) *includes "The Subjection of Women," which examines the French existentialist Simone de Beauvoir's* The Second Sex (*see Bibliography*), *a book that sets out to comprehensively study woman in relation to biology, psychoanalysis, history, myth, literature, and sexuality, and that concludes by envisioning the liberated woman.*

The Subjection of Women

Vassal, slave, inferior, other, thing, victim, dependent, parasite, prisoner—oh, bitter, raped, child-swollen flesh doomed to immanence! Sisyphean goddess of the dust pile! Demeter, Xantippe, Ninon de Lenclos, Marie Bashkirtsev, and "a friend of mine. . . ." From cave to café, boudoir to microscope, from the knitting needles to the short story: they are all here in a potency of pages, a foreshortened and exaggerated, a mysterious and too clear relief, an eloquent lament and governessy scolding, a poem and a doctoral thesis. I suppose there is bound to be a little laughter in the wings at the mere thought of this madly sensible and brilliantly obscure tome on women by Simone de Beauvoir, *The Second Sex.*

Still the more one sinks into this very long book, turning page after page, the more clearly it seems to lack a subject with reasonable limitations and concreteness, a subject on which offered illustrations may wear some air of finality and conviction. The theme of the work is that women are not simply "women," but are, like men, in the fullest sense human beings. Yet one cannot easily write the history of people! This point may appear trivial; nevertheless, to take on this glorious and fantastic book is not like reading at all—from the first to the last sentence one has the sensation of playing some breathlessly exciting and finally exhausting game. You gasp and strain and remember; you point out and deny and agree, trying always to find some way of taking hold, of confining, defining, and understanding. What is so unbearably whirling is that the author too goes through this effort to include nearly every woman and attitude that has ever existed. There is no difference of opinion, unless it be based upon a fact of which she may be ignorant, she has not thought of also. She makes her own points and all one's objections too, often in the same sentence. The effort required for this work must have been killing. No discredit to the donkey-load undertaking is meant when one imagines Simone de Beauvoir at the end may have felt like George Eliot when she said she began *Romola* as a young woman and finished it an old one. (This touching remark did not refer to the time spent in composition, but to the wrinkling weight of the task.)

I quote a sentence about the *promises* the Soviet Union made to women: ". . . pregnancy leaves were to be paid for by the State, which would assume charge of the children, signifying not that they would be *taken away* from their parents, but that they would not be *abandoned* to them." There is majesty here and the consolations of philosophy, perhaps also, in this instance, a bit of willful obfuscation; but that kind of strangeness occurs endlessly, showing, for purposes of argument at least, an oversensitivity to difficulties. A devastating dialogue goes on at this author's desk. After she has written, "the State, which would assume charge of the children," there is a comma pause. In that briefest of grammatical rests, voices assault her intelligence saying, "But suppose people don't want their children taken away by the State?" If all these disputing voices are admitted, one on top of the other, you are soon lost in incoherence and fantasy. Another instance: "It is understandable, in this perspective, that women take exception to masculine logic. Not only is it inapplicable to her experience, but in his hands, as she knows, masculine reasoning becomes an underhanded form of force." A few pages on: "One can bank on her credulity. Woman takes an attitude of respect and faith toward the masculine universe. . . ."

I take up the bewildering inclusiveness of this book, because there is hardly a thing I would want to say contrary to her thesis that Simone de Beauvoir has not said herself, including the fact, mentioned in the preface, that problems peculiar to women are not particularly pressing at the moment and that, by and large, "we have won." These acknowledgments would seem of tremendous importance, but they are a mere batting of the eye in this eternity of "oppression."

In spite of all positions being taken simultaneously, there is an unmistakable *drift* to the book. Like woman's life, *The Second Sex* is extremely repetitious and some things are repeated more often than others, although nearly every idea is repeated more than once. One is justified, then, in assuming what is repeated most often is most profoundly felt. The diction alone is startling and stabs the heart with its vigor in finding phrases of abjection and debasement. It is as though one had lived forever in that intense, shady, wretched world of *Wozzeck*, where the humor draws tears, the gaiety is fearful and children skip rope neither knowing nor caring their mother has been murdered. "Conjugal slavery, annihilation, servant, devaluation, tyranny, passive, forbidden, doomed, abused, trapped, prey, domineer, helpless, imprisoned," and so on. This immediately suggests a masochistic view of life, reinforced by the fact that for the male quite an opposite vocabulary has dug into this mind like a tick: "free, busy, active, proud, arrogant, master, existent, liberty, adventure, daring, strength, courage. . . ."

Things being as they are, it is only fair to say that Simone de Beauvoir, in spite of her absorbing turn of phrase, miraculously does *not* give to me, at least, the impression of being a masochist, a Lesbian, a termagant, or a man-hater, and that this book is not "the self-pitying cry of one who resents being born a woman," as one American housewife-reviewer said. There is a nervous, fluent, rare aliveness on every page and the writer's more "earnest" qualities, her discipline, learning and doggedness, amount not only to themselves, that is, qualities which certainly help one to write long books, but to a kind of "charm" that ought to impress the most contented woman. This book is an accomplishment; on the other hand, if one is expecting something truly splendid and unique like *The Origins of Totalitarianism* by Hannah Arendt, to mention another woman, he will be disappointed.

The Second Sex begins with biological material showing that in nature there are not always two sexes and reproduction may take place asexually. I have noticed in the past that many books strongly presenting feminine claims begin in this manner, as if under a compulsion to veil the whole idea of sexual differentiation with a buzzing, watery mist of insect habits and unicellular forms of life. This is dramaturgy, meant to put one, after a heavy meal, in a receptive frame of mind. It is the dissonant, ambiguous music as the curtain rises on the all too familiar scene of the man at the hunt and the woman at the steaming pot; the scene looks clear enough, but the music suggests things may not be as they appear. That woman may not have to carry those screaming brats in her womb, after all, but will, if you don't watch out, simply "divide"! And the man: it is possible in the atomic age that a pin prick may fertilize the egg and then where will he be? This material is followed by curiosities from anthropology: some primitive societies thought the woman did it all alone and the man was no more important than a dish of herbs or a draft of beet juice.

These biological and anthropological matters are of enormous fascination, but often, and a bit in this present work too, a false and dramatic use is made of them: they carry a weight of mystification and intensity quite unjustified when the subject is the modern woman. They would seem to want to throw doubt upon what is not yet doubtful: the bisexual nature of human reproduction. We are relieved when the dividing amoebas and budding sponges swim out of view.

The claim of *The Second Sex* is that what we call the feminine character is an illusion and so is feminine "psychology," both in its loose meaning and in the psychoanalytical view. None of these female traits is "given"—the qualities and incapacities women have shown rather consistently in human history are simply the result of their "situation." This situation is largely the work of men, the male sex which has sought its own convenience with undeviating purpose throughout history. The female situation does not derive, at least not sufficiently to explain it, from women's natural physical and psychological difference, but has much of its origin in economics. When man developed the idea of private property, woman's destiny was "sealed." At this time women were cut off from the more adventurous activities of war, forays, explorations, to stay at home to *protect* and *maintain* what men had achieved by their far-reaching pursuits. The woman was reduced to a state of *immanence:* stagnation, the doing of repetitive tasks, concerned with the given, with maintaining, keeping, mere functioning. Man, however, is a free being, an *existent* who makes choices, decisions, has projects which are not confined to securing the present but point to the unknown future; he dares, fails, wanders, grabs, insists. By means of his activities he *transcends* his mere animal nature. What a man gives, the woman accepts; she decides nothing, changes nothing; she polishes, mends, cleans what he has invented and shaped. The man risks life, the woman merely produces it as an unavoidable function. "That is why superiority has been accorded in humanity not to the sex that brings forth but that which kills." The man imagines, discovers religions; the women worship. He has changed the earth; she arises each morning to an expectation of stove, nursing, scrubbing which has remained nearly as fixed as the course of our planets. Women continue in immanence not out of desire, but from "complicity." Having been robbed of economic independence, experience, substance, she clings unhappily because she has not been "allowed" to prepare for a different life.

Naturally, it is clear many women do not fit this theory and those who may be said to do so would not describe it in the words of Simone de Beauvoir. These persons' claims are admitted quite fully throughout the book, but always with the suggestion that the women who seem to be "existents" really aren't and those who insist they find fulfillment in the inferior role are guilty of "bad faith."

That is as it may be, but what, one asks at the beginning, about the man who, almost without exception in this work, is a creature of the greatest imagination, love of liberty, devotion to projects; ambitious, potent and disciplined, he scorns a life of mere "love," refuses to imprison himself in another's being, but looks toward the world, seeks to transcend himself, change the course of history. This is an exaggeration of course. For every Ophelia one remembers not only Cleopatra but poor Swann, unable, for all his taste and enthusiasm, to write his book on Vermeer, drowning his talent in the pursuit of pure pleasure which can only be given by the "other," Odette; for every excited Medea who gave up herself, her place, to follow the fickle man you remember not only Joan of Arc but that being of perfect, blowsy immanence, the Duke of Windsor, who abandoned the glories of a complex project for the sweet, repetitive, futureless domesticity of ocean liners and resorts. And Sartre has written a whole book on Baudelaire, a fascinating and immensely belligerent one, that claims Baudelaire, resented responsibility for his own destiny, refused his possibilities of transcendence, would not make decisions, define himself, but flowed along on a tepid river of dependence, futility, refusal—like women, fond of scents and costumes, nostalgic, procrastinating, wishful.

It would seem then that men, even some "heroic" ones, often allow themselves to be what women are forced to be. But, of course, with the greatest will in the world a man cannot allow himself to be that most extremely doomed and chained being—the mother who must bear and raise children and whose figure naturally hangs over such a work as *The Second Sex* like Spanish moss. Simone de Beauvoir's opinion of the division of labor established in the Garden of Eden, if not as some believe earlier, is very striking:

> . . . giving birth and suckling are not *activities*, they are natural functions; no projects are involved; and that is why woman found in them no reason for a lofty affirmation of her existence—she submitted passively to her biologic fate. The domestic cares of maternity imprisoned her in repetition and immanence; they were repeated from day to day in an identical form, which was perpetuated almost without change from century to century; they produced nothing new.

But what difference does it make that childbearing is not an activity, nor perhaps an instinct; it is a necessity.

The Second Sex is so briskly Utopian it fills one with a kind of shame and sadness, like coming upon old manifestoes and committee programs in the attic. It is bursting with an almost melancholy desire for women to take their possibilities *seriously*, to reject the given, the easy, the traditional. I do not, as most reviewers seem to, think the picture offered here of a woman's life is entirely false—a lifetime of chores is bad luck. But housework, child rearing, cleaning, keeping, nourishing, looking after—these must be done by someone, or worse by millions of someones day in and day out. In the home at least it would seem "custom" has not been so much capricious as observant in finding that women are fairly well adapted to this necessary routine. And they must keep at it whether they like it or not.

George Orwell says somewhere that reformers hate to admit nobody will do the tedious, dirty work of the world except under "some form of coercion." Mopping, ironing, peeling, feeding—it is not absurd to call this unvarying routine *slavery*, Simone de Beauvoir's word. But its necessity does not vanish by listing the tropical proliferation of open and concealed forms of coercion that may be necessary to make women do it. Bachelors are notoriously finicky, we have all observed. The dust pile is revoltingly real.

Most men, also, are doomed to work of brutalizing monotony. Hardly any intellectuals are willing to undertake a bit of this dreadful work their fellow beings must do, no matter what salary, what working conditions, what degree of "socialist dignity" might be attached to it. If artists could save a man from a lifetime of digging coal by digging it themselves one hour a week, most would refuse. Some would commit suicide. "It's not the time, it's the anticipation! It ruins the whole week! I can't even read, much less write!"

Childbearing and housekeeping may be repetitive and even intellectually stunting. Yet nothing so fills one with despair as those products of misplaced transcendent hope, those millions of stupid books, lunatic pamphlets, absurd editorials, dead canvases and popular songs which have clogged up the sewers and ashcans of the modern world, representing more wretched labor, dreaming, madness, vanity and waste of effort than one can bear to think of. There is an annihilating nothingness in these undertakings by comparison with which the production of one stupid, lazy, lying child is an event of some importance. Activity, transcendence, project—this is an optimistic, exhilarating vocabulary. Yet Sartre had to disown the horde of "existents" who fell to like farm hands at the table, but were not themselves able to produce so much as a carrot.

Are women "the equal" of men? This is an embarrassing subject.

Women are certainly physically inferior to men and if this were not the case the whole history of the world would be different. No comradely socialist legislation on woman's behalf could accomplish a millionth of what a bit more muscle tissue, gratuitously offered by nature, might do for this "second" being.

> On the average she is shorter than the male and lighter, her skeleton is more delicate . . . muscular strength is much less in women . . . she has less respiratory capacity, the lungs and trachea being smaller. . . . The specific gravity of the blood is lower . . . and there is less hemoglobin; women are therefore less robust and more disposed to anemia than are males. Their pulse is more rapid, the vascular system less stable. . . . Instability is strikingly characteristic of woman's organization in general. . . . In comparison with her the male seems infinitely favored.

There is a kind of poetry in this description which might move a flighty person to tears. But it goes on:

> These biological considerations are extremely important. . . . But I deny that they establish for her a fixed and inevitable destiny. They are insufficient for setting up a hierarchy of the sexes . . . they do not condemn her to remain in a subordinate role forever.

Why doesn't this "condemn her to remain in a subordinate role forever"? In my view this poor endowment would seem to be all the answer one needs to why women don't sail the seven seas, build bridges, conquer foreign lands, lay international cables and trudge up Mount Everest. But forgetting these daring activities, a woman's physical inferiority to a man is a limiting reality every moment of her life. Because of it women are "doomed" to situations that promise reasonable safety against the more hazardous possibilities of nature which they are too weak and easily fatigued to endure and against the stronger man. Any woman who has ever had her wrist twisted by a man recognizes a fact of nature as humbling as a cyclone to a frail tree branch. How can *anything* be more important than this? The prodigious ramifications could occupy one for an eternity. For instance:

> At eighteen T. E. Lawrence took a long bicycle tour through France by himself; no young girl would be allowed to engage in any escapade, still less to adventure on foot in a half-desert and dangerous country, as Lawrence did a year later.

Simone de Beauvoir's use of "allow" is inaccurate; she stresses "permission" where so often it is really "capacity" that is involved. For a woman a solitary bicycle tour of France would be dangerous, but not impossible; Lawrence's adventure in Arabia would be suicidal and so a woman is nearly unimaginable as the author of *The Seven Pillars of Wisdom*. First of all the Arabs would rape this unfortunate female soldier or, if they had some religious or practical reason for resisting temptation, they would certainly have to leave her behind on the march, like yesterday's garbage, as the inevitable fatigue arrived. To say that physical weakness doesn't, in a tremendous number of activities, "condemn her to a subordinate role" is a mere assertion, not very convincing to the unmuscled, light breathing, nervously unstable, blushing feminine reality.

Arabian warfare is indeed an extreme situation. But what about solitary walks through the town after midnight? It is true that a woman's freedom to enjoy this simple pleasure would be greatly increased if men had no aggressive sexual feelings toward her. Like a stray dog, also weaker than men, she might roam the world at will, arousing no more notice than a few pats on the head or an irritable kick now and then.

Whether such a change is possible in the interest of the weaker sex is very doubtful.

There is the notion in *The Second Sex,* and in other radical books on the subject, that if it were not for the tyranny of custom, women's sexual life would be characterized by the same aggressiveness, greed and command as that of the male. This is by no means certain: so much seems to lead right back where we've always been. Society must, it seems, inhibit to some extent the sexuality of all human beings. It has succeeded in restraining men much less than women. Brothels, which have existed from the earliest times, are to say the least a rarity for the use of women. And yet women will patronize opium dens and are frequently alcoholic, activities wildly destructive to their home life, beauty, manners and status and far more painful and time-consuming than having children. Apparently a lot of women are dying for dope and cocktails; nearly all are somewhat thrifty, cautious and a little lazy about hunting sex. Is it necessarily an error that many people think licentious women are incapable of experiencing the slightest degree of sexual pleasure and are driven to their behavior by an encyclopedic curiosity to know if such a thing exists? A wreck of a man, tracking down girls in his Chevrolet, at least can do *that!* Prostitutes are famously cold; pimps, who must also suffer professional boredom, are not automatically felt to be impotent. Homosexual women, who have rebelled against their "conditioning" in the most crucial way, do not appear to "cruise" with that truly astonishing, ageless zest of male homosexuals. A pair seems to find each other sufficient. Drunken women who pick up a strange man look less interested in a sexual partner than in a companion for a drink the next morning. There is a staggering amount of evidence that points to the idea that women set a price of one kind or another on sexual intercourse; they are so often not in the mood.

This is not to say women aren't interested in sex *at all.* They clearly want a lot of it, but in the end the men of the world seem to want still more. It is only the quantity, the capacity in that sense, in which the sexes appear to differ. Women, in the language of sociology books, "fight very hard" to get the amount of sexual satisfaction they want—and even harder to keep men from forcing a superabundance their way. It is difficult to see how anyone can be sure that it is only man's voracious appetite for conquest which has created, as its contrary, this reluctant, passive being who has to be wooed, raped, bribed, begged, threatened, married, supported. Perhaps she really has to be. After she has been conquered she has to "pay" the man to restrain his appetite, which he is so likely to reveal at cocktail parties, and in his pitifully longing glance at the secretary—she pays with ironed shirts, free meals, the pleasant living room, a son.

And what about the arts—those womanish activities which are, in our day, mostly "done at home." For those who desire this form of transcendence, the other liberating activities of mankind, the office, the factory, the world of commerce, public affairs, are horrible pits where the extraordinary man is basely and casually slain.

Women have excelled in the performance arts: acting, dancing and singing—for some reason Simone de Beauvoir treats these accomplishments as if they were usually an extension of prostitution. Women have contributed very little to the art of painting and they are clearly weak in the gift for musical composition. (Still whole nations seem without this latter gift, which may be inherited. Perhaps even nations inherit it, the male members at least. Like baldness, women may transmit the gift of musical composition but they seldom ever suffer from it.)

Literature is the art in which women have had the greatest success. But a woman needs only to think of this activity to feel her bones rattling with violent distress. Who is to say that *Remembrance of Things Past* is "better" than the marvelous *Emma*? *War and Peace* better than *Middlemarch*? *Moby Dick* superior to *La Princesse de Clèves*? But everybody says so! It is only the whimsical, cantankerous, the eccentric critic, or those who refuse the occasion for such distinctions, who would say that any literary work by a woman, marvelous as these may be, is on a level with the very greatest accomplishments of men. Of course the *best* literature by women is superior to *most* of the work done by men and anyone who values literature at all will approach all excellence with equal enthusiasm.

The Second Sex is not whimsical about women's writing, but here again perhaps too much is made of the position in which women have been "trapped" and not enough of how "natural" and inevitable their literary limitations are. Nevertheless, the remarks on artistic women are among the most brilliant in this book. Narcissism and feelings of inferiority are, according to Simone de Beauvoir, the demons of literary women. Women want to please, "but the writer of originality, unless dead, is always shocking, scandalous; novelty disturbs and repels." Flattered to be in the world of art at all, the woman is "on her best behavior; she is afraid to disarrange, to investigate, to explode. . . ." Women are timid and fall back on "ancient houses, sheepfolds, kitchen gardens, picturesque old folks, roguish children . . ." and even the best are conservative. "There are women who are mad and there are women of sound method; none has that madness in her method that we call genius."

If women's writing seems somewhat limited, I don't think it is only due to these psychological failings. Women have much less experience of life than a man, as everyone knows. But in the end are they suited to the kind of experiences men have? *Ulysses* is not just a work of genius, it is Dublin pubs, gross depravity, obscenity, brawls. Stendhal as a soldier in Napoleon's army, Tolstoy on his Cossack campaigns, Dostoevsky before the firing squad, Proust's obviously first-hand knowledge of vice, Conrad and Melville as sailors, Michelangelo's tortures on the scaffolding in the Sistine chapel, Ben Jonson's drinking bouts, dueling, his ear burnt by the authorities because of a political indiscretion in a play—these horrors and the capacity to endure them are *experience*. Experience is something more than going to law school or having the nerve to say honestly what you think in a drawing room filled with men; it is the privilege as well to endure brutality, physical torture, unimaginable sordidness, and even the privilege *to want*, like Boswell, to grab a miserable tart under Westminster Bridge. Syphilis and epilepsy—even these seem to be tragic afflictions a male writer can endure more easily than a woman. I should imagine a woman would be more depleted by epilepsy than Dostoevsky seems to have been, more ravaged by syphilis than Flaubert, more weakened by deprivation than Villon. Women live longer, safer lives than men and a man may, if he wishes, choose that life; it is hard to believe a woman could choose, like Rimbaud, to sleep in the streets of Paris at seventeen.

If you remove the physical and sexual experiences many men have made literature out of, you have carved away a great hunk of masterpieces. There is a lot left: James, Balzac, Dickens; the material in these books, perhaps not always in Balzac, is a part of women's lives too or might be "worked up"—legal practices and prison conditions in Dickens, commerce in Balzac, etc.

But the special *vigor* of James, Balzac, Dickens or Racine, the queer, remaining strength to produce masterpiece after masterpiece—that is belittling! The careers of women of prodigious productivity, like George Sand, are marked by a great amount of failure and waste, indicating that though time was spent at the desk perhaps the supreme effort was not regularly made. Who can help but feel that *some* of James's vigor is sturdily rooted in his masculine flesh and that this repeatedly successful creativity is less likely with the "weaker sex" even in the socialist millennium. It is not suggested that muscles write books, but there is a certain sense in which, talent and experience being equal, they may be considered a bit of an advantage. In the end, it is in the matter of experience that women's disadvantage is catastrophic. It is very difficult to know how this may be extraordinarily altered.

Coquettes, mothers, prostitutes and "minor" writers—one sees these faces, defiant or resigned, still standing at the Last Judgment. They are all a little sad, like the Chinese lyric:

> Why do I heave deep sighs?
> It is natural, a matter of course, all
> creatures have their laws.

QUESTIONS

1. How does the first paragraph set the tone for the review and establish the main parts of Elizabeth Hardwick's critique?

2. What are the author's objections to Simone de Beauvoir's book?

3. How valid is Elizabeth Hardwick's contention that women's inferior strength must keep them in a subordinate role?

4. What sorts of experience does the author think are essential for writers in order for them to produce great literature? According to the author, are any of these experiences possible for women? What is your opinion?

Mary Ellmann

Mary Ellmann is a literary critic and scholar who was educated at the University of Massachusetts and at Yale University. "Phallic Criticism," reprinted below, is the second chapter of her book, Thinking About Women *(1968), a witty and devastating analysis of sexual rhetoric in literature.*

Phallic Criticism

Through practice, begun when they begin to read, women learn to read about women calmly. Perhaps there have been some, but I have not heard of women who killed themselves simply and entirely because they were women.[1] They are evidently sustained by the conviction that I can never be They, by the fact that the self always, at least to itself, eludes identification with others. And, in turn, this radical separateness is fortified in some of us by phlegm, in others by vanity or most of all by ignorance (the uneducated are humiliated by class rather than by sex) —by all the usual defenses against self-loathing. Moreover, both men and women are now particularly accustomed, not so much to the resolution of issues, as to the proliferation of irreconcilable opinions upon them. In this intellectual suspension, it is possible for women, most of the time, to be more interested in what *is* said about them than in what

---

FROM *Thinking About Women*. Copyright © 1968, by Mary Ellmann. Reprinted by permission of Harcourt Brave Jovanovich, Inc.
[1] Men, however, have been known to kill themselves for this reason. Otto Weininger, the German author of *Sex and Character*, killed himself because of the femininity which he ascribed to the Jews, of whom he was one.

presumably and finally *should* be said about them. In fact, none of them knows what should be said.

Their detachment is perhaps especially useful in reading literary criticism. Here, the opinions of men about men and of women about women are at least possibly esthetic, but elsewhere they are, almost inescapably, sexual as well. Like eruptions of physical desire, this intellectual distraction is no less frequent for being gratuitous as well. With a kind of inverted fidelity, the discussion of women's books by men will arrive punctually at the point of preoccupation, which is the fact of femininity. Books by women are treated as though they themselves were women, and criticism embarks, at its happiest, upon an intellectual measuring of busts and hips. Of course, this preoccupation has its engaging and compensatory sides.[2] Like such minor physical disorders as shingles and mumps, it often seems (whether or not it *feels* to the critic) comical as well as distressing. Then too, whatever intellectual risks this criticism runs, one of them is not abstraction. Any sexual reference, even in the most dryasdust context, shares the power which any reference to food has, of provoking fresh and immediate interest. As lunch can be mentioned every day without boring those who are hungry, the critic can always return to heterosexual (and, increasingly, to homosexual) relations and opinions with certainty of being read.

Admittedly, everyone is amused by the skillful wrapping of a book, like a negligee, about an author. Stanley Kauffmann opened a review of Françoise Sagan's *La Chamade* with this simile:

> Poor old Françoise Sagan. Just one more old-fashioned old-timer, bypassed in the rush for the latest literary vogue and for youth. Superficially, her career in America resembles the lifespan of those medieval beauties who flowered at 14, were deflowered at 15, were old at 30 and crones at 40.[3]

A superior instance of the mode—the play, for example, between *flowered* and *deflowered* is neat. And quite probably, of course, women

---

[2] It has an unnerving side as well, though this appears less often in criticism, I think, than in fiction or poetry. For example, James Dickey's poem "Falling" expresses an extraordinary concern with the underwear of a woman who has fallen out of an airplane. While this woman, a stewardess, was in the airplane, her girdle obscured, to the observation of even the most alert passenger, her mesial groove. The effect was, as the poem recalls, "monobuttocked." As the woman falls, however, she undresses and "passes her palms" over her legs, her breasts, and "deeply between her thighs." Beneath her, "widowed farmers" are soon to wake with futile (and irrelevant?) erections. She lands on her back in a field, naked, and dies. The sensation of the poem is necrophilic: it mourns a vagina rather than a person crashing to the ground.

[3] Stanley Kauffmann, "Toujours Tristesse," *New Republic*, October 29, 1966; p. 2.

might enjoy discussing men's books in similar terms. Some such emulative project would be diverting for a book season or two, if it were possible to persuade conventional journals to print its equivalent remarks. From a review of a new novel by the popular French novelist, François Sagan:

> Poor old François Sagan. . . . Superficially, his career in America resembles the life-span of those medieval troubadours who masturbated at 14, copulated at 15, were impotent at 30 and prostate cases at 40.

Somehow or other, No. It is not that male sexual histories, in themselves, are not potentially funny—even though they seem to be thought perceptibly less so than female sexual histories. It is rather that the literal fact of masculinity, unlike femininity, does not impose an erogenic form upon all aspects of the person's career.

I do not mean to suggest, however, that this imposition necessarily results in injustice. (Stanley Kauffmann went on to be more than just, *merciful* to Françoise Sagan.) In fact, it sometimes issues in fulsome praise. Excess occurs when the critic, like Dr. Johnson congratulating the dog who walked like a man, is impressed that the woman has—not so much written well, as written at all. But unfortunately, benign as this upright-pooch predisposition can be in the estimate of indifferent work, it can also infect the praise of work which deserves (what has to be called) asexual approval. In this case, enthusiasm issues in an explanation of the ways in which the work is free of what the critic ordinarily dislikes in the work of a woman. He had despaired of ever seeing a birdhouse built by a woman; now *here* is a birdhouse built by a woman. Pleasure may mount even to an admission of male envy of the work examined: an exceptionally sturdy birdhouse at that! In *Commentary*, Warren Coffey has expressed his belief that "a man would give his right arm to have written Flannery O'Connor's 'Good Country People.' " [4] And here, not only the sentiment but the confidence with which the cliché is wielded, is distinctly phallic. It is as though, merely by thinking about Flannery O'Connor or Mrs. Gaskell or Harriet Beecher Stowe, the critic experienced acute sensations of his own liberty. The more he considers a feeble, cautious and timid existence, the more devil-may-care he seems to himself. This exhilaration then issues, rather tamely, in a daring to be commonplace.

And curiously, it often issues in expressions of contempt for delicate men as well. In this piece, for example, Flannery O'Connor is praised not only as a woman writer who writes as well as a man might wish to write, but also as a woman writer who succeeds in being less feminine

---

[4] Warren Coffey, *Commentary*, November 1965, p. 98.

than some men. She is less "girlish" than Truman Capote or Tennessee Williams.[5] In effect, once the critic's attention is trained, like Sweeney's, upon the Female Temperament, he invariably sideswipes at effeminacy in the male as well. The basic distinction becomes nonliterary: it is less between the book under review and other books, than between the critic and other persons who seem to him, regrettably, less masculine than he is. The assumption of the piece is that no higher praise of a woman's work exists than that such a critic should like it or think that other men will like it. The same ploy can also be executed in reverse. Norman Mailer, for example, is pleased to think that Joseph Heller's *Catch-22* is a man's book to read, a book which merely "puzzles" women. Women cannot comprehend male books, men cannot tolerate female books. The working rule is simple, basic: there must always be two literatures like two public toilets, one for Men and one for Women.

Sometimes it seems that no achievement can override this division. When Marianne Moore received the Poetry Society of America's Gold Medal for Poetry, she received as well Robert Lowell's encomium, "She is the best woman poet in English." The late Langston Hughes added, "I consider her the most famous Negro woman poet in America," and others would have enjoyed "the best blue-eyed woman poet." [6] Lowell has also praised Sylvia Plath's last book of poems, *Ariel*. His foreward begins:

> In these poems, written in the last months of her life and often rushed out at the rate of two or three a day, Sylvia Plath becomes herself, becomes something imaginary, newly, wildly and subtly created—hardly a person at all, or a woman, certainly not another "poetess," but one of those super-real, hypnotic, great classical heroines. The character is feminine, rather than female, though almost everything we customarily think of as feminine is turned on its head. The voice is now coolly amused, witty, now sour, now fanciful, girlish, charming, now sinking to the strident rasp of the

---

[5] Though Tennessee Williams is cited here to enhance Flannery O'Connor's virtues, he is just as easily cited to prove other women's defects. For example, Dr. Karl Stern has resorted to Williams and Edward Albee as witnesses to the modern prevalence of the Castrating Woman. (*Barat Review*, January 1967, p. 46.) Naturally, in this context, both playwrights assume a status of unqualified virility.

[6] Miss Moore's femininity leaves her vulnerable even to the imagination of John Berryman:

Fancy a lark with Sappho,
a tumble in the bushes with Miss Moore,
a spoon with Emily, while Charlotte glare.
Miss Bishop's too noble-O.

("Four Dream Songs," *Atlantic*, February 1968, p. 68.)

vampire—a Dido, Phaedra, or Medea, who can laugh at herself as "cow-heavy and floral in my Victorian nightgown."

A little cloudburst, a short heavy rain of sexual references. The word *poetess,* whose gender killed it long ago, is exhumed—to be denied. Equivalently, a critic of W. H. Auden would be at pains, first of all, to deny that Auden is a poetaster. But *poetess* is only part of the general pelting away at the single fact that Sylvia Plath belonged to a sex (that inescapable membership) and that her sex was not male—*woman, heroines, feminine, female, girlish, fanciful, charming, Dido, Phaedra, Medea. Vampire,* too. And it would of course be this line, "Cow-heavy and floral in my Victorian nightgown," which seizes attention first and evokes the surprised pleasure of realizing that Sylvia Plath "can laugh at herself." Self-mockery, particularly sexual self-mockery, is not expected in a woman, and it is irresistible in the criticism of women to describe what was expected: the actual seems to exist only in relation to the preconceived.

Lowell's distinction between *feminine* and *female* is difficult, though less difficult than a distinction between *masculine* and *male* would be— say, in an introduction to Blake's *Songs of Innocence.* What helps us with the first is our all knowing, for some time now, that femaleness is a congenital fault, rather like eczema or Original Sin. An indicative denunciation, made in 1889: "They are no ladies. The only word good enough for them is the word of opprobrium—females." But fortunately, some women can be saved. By good manners, they are translated from females into ladies; and by talent, into feminine creatures (or even into "classical heroines"). And we are entirely accustomed to this generic mobility on their part: the individual is assumed into the sex and loses all but typical meaning within it. The emphasis is finally macabre, as though women wrote with breasts instead of pens—in which event it would be remarkable, as Lowell feels that it is, if one of them achieved ironic detachment.

When the subject of the work by a woman is also women (as it often has to be, since everyone has to eat what's in the cupboard), its critical treatment is still more aberrant. Like less specialized men, critics seem to fluctuate between attraction and surfeit. An obsessive concern with femininity shifts, at any moment, into a sense of being confined or suffocated by it. In the second condition, a distaste for books *before they are read* is not uncommon, as in Norman Mailer's unsolicited confession of not having been able to read Virginia Woolf, or in Anthony Burgess's inhibitory "impression of high-waisted dresses and genteel parsonage flirtation" [7] in Jane Austen's novels. More luckily, the work may be patronized by mild minds already persuaded that the human temperament

---

[7] *New York Times Book Review,* December 4, 1966, p. 1.

combines traits of both sexes and that even masculine natures may respond, through their subterranean femininity, to the thoroughly feminine book.

A similar indulgence is fostered by any association, however tenuous, which the critic forms between the woman writer and some previous student of his own. Now that almost everyone who writes teaches too, the incidence of this association is fairly high. Robert Lowell remembers that Sylvia Plath once audited a class of his at Boston University:

> She was never a student of mine, but for a couple of months seven years ago, she used to drop in on my poetry seminar at Boston University. I see her dim against the bright sky of a high window, viewless unless one cared to look down on the city outskirts' defeated yellow brick and square concrete pillbox filling stations. She was willowy, long-waisted, sharp-elbowed, nervous, giggly, gracious —a brilliant tense presence embarrassed by restraint. Her humility and willingness to accept what was admired seemed at times to give her an air of maddening docility that hid her unfashionable patience and boldness.[8]

It is not easy, of course, to write about a person whom one knew only slightly in the past. The strain is felt here, for example, in the gratuitous street scene from the classroom window. And in general, there is a sense of a physical recollection emended by a much later intellectual and poetic impression. The "brilliant tense presence" of the final poetry is affixed, generously enough, to the original figure of a young girl. The "maddening docility" too must have been a sexual enlargement, now reduced to an "air" of docility, since again the poems demonstrate the artistic (rather than "feminine") union of "patience and boldness." (Elsewhere they are, according to Lowell, "modest" poems too, they are uniquely "modest" *and* "bold.") But then the poet Anne Sexton's recollections, which originate in the same poetry seminar, makes no reference to elbows or giggles or docility. Miss Sexton seems to have seen even at that time a woman entirely congruous with her later work. After class, the two used to drink together—at the Ritz bar, some distance away from those "concrete pillbox filling stations"—and conduct workmanlike discussions of suicidal techniques:

> But suicides have a special language.
> Like carpenters they want to know *which tools*.
> They never ask *why build*.
>
> ("Wanting to Die")[9]

---

[8] Foreword to Sylvia Plath's *Ariel*, p. xi.
[9] Anne Sexton, "The barfly ought to sing," *Tri-Quarterly*, Fall 1966, p. 90.

Lowell seems honestly caught between two ways of comprehending what exists outside the self. And certainly there is nothing of the stag posture about his remarks, no pretense of writing only for other men about women. All critics are of course secretly aware that no literary audience, except perhaps in Yemen, is any longer restricted to men. The man's-man tone is a deliberate archaism, coy and even flirtatious, like wearing spats. No one doubts that some silent misogyny may be dark and deep, but written misogyny is now generally a kind of chaffing, and not frightfully clever, gambit. For the critic in this style, the writer whose work is most easily related to established stereotypes of femininity is, oddly, the most welcome. What-to-say then flows effortlessly from the stereotypes themselves. The word *feminine* alone, like a grimace, expresses a displeasure which is not less certain for its being undefined. In a review of Fawn Brodie's biography of Sir Richard Burton, *The Devil Drives*, Josh Greenfeld remarked on the "feminine biographer's attachment to subject," and suggested that this quality (*or else* a "scholarly objectivity") prevented Mrs. Brodie's conceding Burton's homosexuality.[10] So her book is either too subjective or too objective: we will never know which.

But the same word can be turned upon men too. John Weightman has remarked that Genet's criminals cannot play male and female effectively because "a convicted criminal, however potent, has been classified as an object, and therefore feminized, by society." [11] An admirably simple social equation: a man in prison amounts to a woman. Similarly, *feminine* functions as an eight-letter word in the notorious Woodrow Wilson biography by Freud and William Bullitt. At one heated point, Clemenceau calls Wilson feminine, Wilson calls Clemenceau feminine, then both Freud and Bullitt call Wilson feminine again. The word means that all four men thoroughly dislike each other. It is also sufficient for Norman Mailer to say that Herbert Gold reminds him "of nothing so much as a woman writer," [12] and for Richard Gilman to consign Philip Roth to the "ladies' magazine" level.[13] In fact, chapters of *When She Was Good* were first published, and seemed to settle in snugly, at the *haut bourgeois* level of *Harper's* and the *Atlantic*. But, except perhaps in the *Daily Worker*, the consciousness of

---

[10] *Book Week*, May 28, 1967, p. 2. Mrs. Brodie had still more trouble in the *Times Literary Supplement* (January 11, 1968, p. 32), where her nationality as well as her sex was at fault: "So immense is this gulf, so inalienably remote are the societies that produced biographer and subject, *so difficult is it, even now, for a woman to get beneath a man's skin*, that only some imaginative genius could really have succeeded in the task Mrs. Brodie so boldly undertook." [My italics.]

[11] *New York Review of Books*, August 24, 1967, p. 8.

[12] *Advertisements for Myself*, p. 435.

[13] Richard Gilman, "Let's Lynch Lucy," *New Republic*, June 24, 1967, p. 19.

class is less insistent than that of sex: the phrase "ladies' magazine" is one of those which refuses not to be written once a month.[14]

But at heart most of these "the-ladies-bless-them" comments are as cheerful and offhand as they are predictable. When contempt, like anything else, has an assigned route to follow, and when it is accustomed to its course, it can proceed happily. This is evident, for example, in Norman Mailer's lively, even jocular, essay on the deplorable faults of Mary McCarthy's *The Group*. What accounts for these high spirits, except the fact that Mailer rejoices in what he spanks so loudly? The pleasure lies in Mary McCarthy's having capitulated, as it seems to Mailer, having at last written what he can securely and triumphantly call a female novel.[15] Not that Mailer's treatment of *The Group*, even in these familiar terms, is not still remarkable—even frightening, and that is a rare treat in criticism. One does not expect a disdain for feminine concerns, which is entirely commonplace, to mount to cloacal loathing. Mary McCarthy has soiled an abstraction, a genre, the novel-yet-to-be: "Yes, Mary deposited a load on the premise, and it has to be washed all over again, this little long-lived existential premise." [16]

But few rise to that kind of washing-up with Mailer's alacrity. In most critics, revulsion is an under-developed area. What rouses a much more interesting hostility in many is the work which does not conform to sexual preconception. That is, if feminine concerns can be found, they are conventionally rebuked; but their absence is shocking. While all women's writing should presumably strive for a suprafeminine condition, it is profoundly distrusted for achieving it. So for all Anthony Burgess's resistance to Jane Austen, he is still less pleased by George Eliot ("The male impersonation is wholly successful") or by Ivy Compton-Burnett ("A big sexless nemesic force"). Similarly, he cannot leave alone what strikes him as the contradiction between Brigid

---

[14] The phrase is at least sociologically interesting: it suggests the impossibility of remarking that some bad novel is fit for the "men's magazine." For fiction, there is none. At the same level of intelligence and cultivation, women evidently prefer stories (*McCall's, Redbook, The Ladies' Home Journal*, etc.) and men prefer facts (or quasi-facts) and photographs (*Time, Life, Look, Dude, Gent*, etc.). *Playboy* is exceptional in presupposing an eclectic male audience (does it exist?) for both photographs *and* fiction.

[15] A female novel, Mailer indicates, is one which deals with the superficial details of women's lives instead of their lower depths. Such a book is at once tedious and cowardly. On the other hand, Joseph Heller's *Catch-22* is a book for men (rather than a male novel) which deals with the superficial details of men's lives. It speaks, according to Mailer, to the man who "prefers to become interested in quick proportions and contradictions; in the practical surface of things." Both novels, then, are tedious but the first is a disgrace while the second has "a vast appeal." Obviously, it all depends on which practical surface of things the commentator himself is glued to.

[16] *Cannibals and Christians*, p. 138.

Brophy's appearance and her writing.[17] His review of her book of essays, *Don't Never Forget*, opens in this sprightly manner:

> An American professor friend of mine, formerly an admirer of Miss Brophy's work, could no longer think of her as an author once he'd seen her in the flesh. "That girl was made for love," he would growl. Various writers who have smarted from her critical attentions might find it hard to agree.[18]

It is as though Elizabeth Hardwick, asked to review William Manchester's *Death of a President*, was obliged to refuse, growling, "That man was made for love." The same notion of an irreconcilable difference between the nature of woman and the mind of man prompts the hermaphroditic fallacy according to which one half the person, separating from the other half, produces a book by binary fission. So Mary McCarthy has been complimented, though not by Norman Mailer, on her "masculine mind" while, through the ages, poor Virgil has never been complimented on his "effeminacy." (Western criticism begins with this same tedious distinction—between manly Homer and womanish Virgil.) At the same time, while sentiment is a disadvantage, the alternative of feminine coolness is found still more disagreeable. Mary McCarthy used to be too *formidable*, Jean Stafford has sometimes been *clinical*, and others (going down, down) are *perverse, petulant, catty, waspish*.

The point is that comment upon Violette Leduc, who is not directly assertive, will be slurring; but the slur hardens into resentment of those writers who seem to endorse the same standards of restraint and reason which the critic presumably endorses. If for nothing else, for her tolerance of Sade, Simone de Beauvoir must be referred to (scathingly!) as "the lady," and then even her qualifications of tolerance must be described as a reluctance "to give herself unreservedly" to Sade.[19]

---

[17] Burgess has also furnished this country, in a "Letter from London" (*Hudson Review*, Spring 1967), the following couplet:

People who read Brigid Brophy
Should contend for the Krafft-Ebing Trophy.

In fact, he seems unfailingly exhilarated by Miss Brophy's faults, thrilled by them as Norman Mailer is by Mary McCarthy's. Burgess's most recent agitation was a review of *Fifty Works of English Literature We Could Do Without* (by Miss Brophy, Michael Levey and Charles Osborne): "The authors are now rubbing themselves in an ecstacy of the kind granted only to Exclusive Brethren." (*Encounter*, August 1967, p. 71.)

[18] *Manchester Guardian Weekly*, November 24, 1966, p. 11. There is, incidentally, An American Professor who exists only in the minds of English journalists. The *Times Literary Supplement* would be halved without him.

[19] Leslie Schaeffer, *New Republic*, August 19, 1967, p. 28.

Similarly, it is possible that much of the voluble male distaste for Jane Austen is based, not upon her military limitations (her infamous failure to discuss the Napoleonic Wars), but upon her antipathetic detachment. So a determined counteremphasis was first placed by her relatives, and has been continued since by most of her critics, upon her allegiance to domestic ideals—when, in fact, she is read only for her mockery of them.

What seems to be wanted, insisted upon, is the critic's conception of women expressed in his conception of feminine terms—that is, a confirmation of the one sex's opinions by the imagination of the other, a difficult request which can seldom be gratified. It is perhaps this request which explains Louis Auchincloss's erratic view of Mary McCarthy in his *Pioneers and Caretakers.* Suddenly she is sister to Ellen Glasgow and Sarah Orne Jewett, as one of our feminine "caretakers of the culture," a guise in which few other readers can easily recognize her. But if one's thesis is sexual, the attachment of women to the past and the incapacity of women for "the clean sweep," then Mary McCarthy only seems to hate a few present things and actually loves many past things. One might as well argue that it was Swift's finding babies so sweet that made him think of eating them for dinner.

QUESTIONS

1. Define "phallic criticism." What criteria does it apply to literature?

2. Explain what Mary Ellmann means by the "upright-pooch predisposition." How does it affect the criticism of women writers?

3. According to the author, how has literature been divided into "masculine" and "feminine" genres? Can you suggest other ways this division has been effected?

4. What is a "female" book and what is a "male" book?

Hortense Calisher

Hortense Calisher (b. 1911) is a distinguished American novelist and short story writer whose work has been enthusiastically reviewed in England and the United States. The article reprinted below was written in 1970 for a special issue of Mademoiselle *on women's liberation.*

No Important Woman Writer

The world does breed—and isn't altogether to be talked out of it. At present. As food and good rivers grow scarcer, sexual difference, already on its way to optional, may sink the whole frame of reference we now know, in a purée of pills. Right now, we still think we know who and what a "heterosexual" is. I know what a true heterosexual writer is, of course—it's a man. At least in America. Where, in spite of the sexual revolution, a writer who is a woman is a "woman writer," and therefore not really as heterosexual as the male.

The "woman writer" still must earn her way across to the male side of art's living room, much as in American provincial society. So be it. It can be done. I'm much more interested in how all writers in America, and the "heterosexuals" as much as any, suffer from their connection with a society which in the most rigidly gross way has arrogated what shall be considered male or female in people.

What these binding divisions of sexual characteristic have done to American writers goes deeper than what is in their books—because it apprehends it. Deeper even than the dreary round of fictional orgasm

FROM *Mademoiselle*, February 1970. Reprinted by permission of Robert Lantz-Candida Donadio Literary Agency, Inc. Copyright © 1970, by Hortense Calisher.

or bedsheet romanticism, or the use of sex as the sole revelation. No artist ever draws strength from keeping to concerns defined for him (by somebody else) as proper to what he or she is. Yet, by and large, American writers have kept to being men, women, or homosexuals as the case may be, very much in terms of what the times have told them that they are. In fact, doing what one is told, in this area, seems to me the primary *secondary* sexual characteristic of all Americans.

We already know how doing what society expects of the male, or overdoing, has sucked many a male writer into the virility calisthenic. There are some still extant, doomed to hunt deer even in Brooklyn, or to fish for pussy in the Caribbean, or to make the cock itself their Chanticleer—all with the penis envy of men infinitely grateful because they have got one. We think of these writers now as those who too early got hung up on Hemingway's jockstrap.

What we forget is that, prior to this, something in the society hung up him. Behind him, at home, was the conviction that artists were sissy (and drink and the shotgun were dashing), ahead of him a Europe in which Freud was prying into the neurosis of art, and Mann had perpetrated his own guilty notion that art was neurosis—wasn't any artist deserting his life by not "living" it? Was art life? A *man's* life?

"Women writers" in America have acted expectedly also. In the 19th century, if they weren't hidden poets like Emily Dickinson, or album ones like Felicia Hemans and Jean Ingelow, they were either journalists to the philosophical passions of the hour, like Margaret Fuller, or to the political ones, like Harriet Beecher Stowe. All the rest were ladies, in a three-named tradition that was to survive well past the age of Adela Rogers St. Johns, and never quite die.

None here were novelists with either the breadth or daring of the European "George's," Eliot and Sand, or even the formidable pomp of Mrs. Humphry Ward. As women here passed through the period of the expansion of women's rights, they might be expected to take the right to be an artist as one of these; many did, and have, and do. But the freedom to be an artist isn't granted like a vote—it is made. And American women continue to make it, most of them, in terms of the sexual image allowed.

In the early 1900s, before literary sexual taboos began to be broken—by men writers, but please remember at first *not* by Americans—the gap between what male and female writers could *say* of experience was narrower, quite aside from the experience. When so much of life had to be left out of art anyway, there was naturally less surprise or threat in the idea that the powers of women might be up to it. For a while, the image allowed them was actually less separate, more equal, than it has ever been since.

Cast back. To Edith Wharton, Ellen Glasgow, and Willa Cather. The first two, as women of means and position, were part of a society which, with its confined sexual mores, was the world of William Dean

Howells and Henry James, as well. Lucky or not for them, the difference between male and female writers in terms of sexual subject and language wasn't as severe as it had been for women of an earlier day, and far less violent than in days to come, when the major division would be that women didn't go to war, to sea, or into any of the virile professions which would so affect the "realistic" portrayal of life. Neither the experience expected of a writer, nor the language, had then yet so exploded over here. James Branch Cabell could still say of a book by Glasgow that it was so much like Henry James it could have been written by Mrs. Wharton.

Cather was saved by "the land." It allowed her to speak from a major vision, and for that, even from a woman, to be acceptable—more acceptable than it is now. As that vision recedes for us, a writer of less authority begins to appear. But as a woman of her time, her consciousness of being able to speak for her country and its cosmos gave her the confidence to write "like a man." To the country itself, she would be no more unfeminine in that respect than some of their pioneer grandmothers. Meanwhile, her male colleagues, whether from the city, the town, or Stephen Crane's open boat, still were allowed a dignity sufficient to them, as "men of letters." Their society hadn't yet placed them in their present bind, where they must defend *their* part of life or of literature as the important whole of it.

Nowadays, art takes more responsibility for what is said of it popularly, and has more influence there. If, once past the basic physical facts, society is what makes children (and artists) "manly" or "womanly," then artists are still reporting back to the society in terms of what it may have made of them. Academy culture is merely popular culture early aware of itself; the roads between are very quick. America at present is provincially cowed by the artist in general and the successful one in particular—this meaning one who makes either money or news. Society will now accept what it has made of him (occasionally even of *her*)—and looks to them to tell it what art *is*.

A male heterosexual writer no longer has to apologize to America for being unmanly. But he still may have to overcompensate for it to himself. His women rivals are getting equaler all the time. As women. Teachers, mothers, dominant purchaser, and stockholders; there's no end to it. The Freudians have told them and told them they've nothing to waggle in front of them, but they seem to have got used to it. He doesn't want to hate them—that would be homosexual. So he approaches the subject of women as artists very cannily—on the highest plane possible. And the most objective. Let them remember they can never make major art.

So his report to the society still goes somewhat like this: "Major Art is about the activities of men." That's why so much of it is about women. But not by them. "Major Art includes where women can't go, or shouldn't, or never have." Childbed is not a place or an event; it is merely what women do. "Major Art is never about the activities of women." Except when it's by men. "Women are household artists. Jane Austen's art is a travelogue between houses; Emily Brontë's, too. Emily Dickinson hid in one all her life. Colette had to be locked into one before she could write. George Eliot had to be cut dead by some of the best London houses, before she could write a study of marriage like *Middlemarch*—and she had to change her name. Let's face it, dear ladies —a house is not a cosmic home."

Note, too: "Women who do write scarcely ever have guts enough for the full real life of a woman." According to some men's conception of it. "Of all the writers so far mentioned, plus a more recent American generation of Katherine Anne Porter, Eudora Welty, Carson McCullers, Flannery O'Connor, only Colette had a child. And she was AC/DC— talented women usually are. That extra chromosome coming out in 'em, the wrong way. Art is really wrong for women." How otherwise could it be so right for men? "And Marianne Moore? She never went to war."

To which those critics who model themselves on the male writers of the day (and perhaps once wanted to be one) add: "And look at women writers' *style!*" Critics of this type always know what major art is—and wish to discuss only major artists. That's how they know they're major critics. A Major Artist writes only in a "masculine" style. "Which uses short words." Like Faulkner. "Whose sentences don't inch forward on little iambs but are rough and clumsy." Like Hemingway's. "What a masculine and major art must never be is jeweled—beg pardon, lapidary. A jeweled fancy is always feminine." Like Shakespeare's. And Melville's. And Sir Thomas Browne's.

Most symptomatic of all, when I, or any woman really, complains of male injustices—we must joke. The bind here is extraordinarily interesting—if only to women and anthropologists. For men will rarely acknowledge that the authority in the world *is* still generally male, and therefore the rules are. (For rules can change; some have been. And so can authority.)

Their answer to complaint will more likely go like this: "Women who complain of injustices done them are in reality not angry at the different or inequitous treatment, but at the difference between men and women—which, of course, is ineradicable." The subject of female injustice therefore becomes ridiculous. Women who act as a group on any subject also become so—even to women. "They are really only being *personal*. Whereas men never allege injustice on the grounds of *being men*." (They don't have to. They can pick something sensible—like being black, or Bahai, or poor.) "Men are impersonal." That's why they can afford to act sociologically. "Women can really only act sexually." That's why "all women are the same." And that's why they're funny in groups. And why men who think like this take any rise in women's status as a sexual threat.

Accordingly, in this ethic, a woman, an American woman writer for instance, never merely wants her work to be treated equally with her peers of any sex, and with due allowance for the sexual bias of all—thus allowing her to be a writer who is, or happens to be, a woman. No, she wants to be a *male* writer. In her body she has the mind of a man (whatever that is).

So the tangle, first sent up by the society, then implemented by the male artists themselves, gathers around the woman of good mind until she half believes it—or more. Women writers in America, by the evidence, are often made to believe it totally. Partly because of the real present differences between male and female in their attitudes toward the public world—of which so much literature is made.

Women can learn pomps, but from a long history of humility, they generally begin with less of it. In a democratic country, where women can never be queens and have never been Presidents or astronauts, how could this be otherwise? England, in spite of many other inequities to women there, has a female minister of culture, since culture there doesn't feel itself impugned. But if Americans were to create such a post, it would probably still be better for the "culture," for the post to be filled by a man.

Women artists are often made to feel that the "honesty" of their work, or its depth, is impugned by their affect as women. Particularly if it's a good one. Dare they have beauty, style, or even the vanities approved of as womanly? Or must they bloomerize? Historically, both men and women have dressed to show the fashion of their convictions: after which women usually get the credit for the fashion, and men for the convictions. Ringlets are affectation. Beards are sincere. So, just as men have worried whether art in a man isn't affection or worse, women wonder whether their affectations as women can coincide with art. Or whether their femininity can.

In reaction, some literary women become scholars, or Xanthippes of the lit'ry quarterlies, or salonistes—or columnistes. Or males. Or use their profession to fend off the female experience.

"Hortense, did you want yo' chi'drun?" Carson McCullers once said to me. "Ah diddun want any. Ah always felt they would innafere with my woik."

My answer is yes, I did want them, and they did interfere—but everything does. (Often the more important experience it is.) And everything contributes. Writers know this instinctively. My guess is that if a man or a woman refuses the natural experience of life, it is not the writer in them that is refusing.

But I can understand why a writer can become confused. As women, we lack the pomp to be sure that when *we* spread our breast to the world, a major eagle will come and peck at it. We've been taught that a man's role is to hunt experience, a woman's to let it come upon her. And that this makes all female experience less exciting document. Women, for instance, are likely to be constantly immersed in, and/or interested in, the minutiae of daily living. So are many great male writers: much of Dickens, Balzac, Tolstoi takes place in the "Dutch interiors" of life. But in writers who are women this is likely to be called domesticity—of subject, and is considered a limitation, or contrasted with "virile" subject. So they in turn often fail to see the real scope there. Or fail to use it, fearing the lady writer in themselves.

It's absurd, of course, to hold up any class of women, by the heels as it were, and shake them to see how much of their sex filters into their life and works. That's the trick the males are always playing. Testing literature in terms of any one topic is even sillier. Nor is any writer under obligation to "appear" in his own works. Yet the psychic history of some women artists, since the time of women's so-called civil-psychological emancipation, should have significance for us all. And when a whole generation of some of the most articulate of American women seem to have chosen not to appear in their own works in a particular way, then something may be said of it.

Cast back. To the second-to-third quarters of the century, and to some of the American short-story tellers who are a kind of renaissance in themselves. How many, straining perhaps toward a world sensibility, or one equivalent to the roaming consciences of the men, strove for what seemed to them the *neutral* voices of art? Or dispensed with whatever was clearly female in their sensibility or experience? Not as a male might—putting by for the moment the particularly male sensibility—but almost as if theirs was a hindrance to hide?

They had other powerful places to go, of course, or they couldn't have been what they are. To the American South, to Catholicism, to the past. But in an era when the male writer was exploring and exhausting his basic dowry, the role of his sexuality, it is curious how comparatively little some American women writers let theirs intrude.

Almost alone in that era, Mary McCarthy wrote of sex apart from love, as a Frenchwoman might or American males tried to—copying not the manner but the privilege. Katherine Anne Porter wrote of "love," with fairy-tale cool. In Flannery O'Connor, a sexuality not necessarily religious or even Catholic extruded allegorically, from the snake-dark of the Southern Baptist basilica. It was never Eudora Welty's subject—though family, nativity, and locality were. McCullers, more lyrically endowed than any, and with an asexual mobility which wavered between adult and child, wrote of "love" as undifferentiated sex, and bothered so little with the customary alignments of the day that the day could do nothing but call her an original. In most of these and other writers, the female and the feminine appear, of course. But so little of the basic female experience, from puberty on through childbed! And so greedy is art for such material usually, that one can well ask if it was the artist making the choice here, or the woman—and according to an image given her, not made.

One advantage to any writer as an alien—to the disinherited, dis-franchised, or dispossessed—is that whether or not they themselves are great, they can write from passionate aspiration, often with the furious energy of the repressed. (Which is often what makes a renaissance.) Satire, too—the worm's eye turning—comes to such writers naturally, as it does to those without full passport privileges, or to the kind of neutral perspective that attaches to small borderland nations. Or they are led into marvelous allegories, grotesqueries, where the whole human race is on a level with them.

So far, women artists in general have done less out of outrage at being Sex Two, than might have been expected. Maybe wisely. Outrage over what one is, or is made to be, can be a dead end, in female writers lead-ing to that hen-huffing of the feathers, suffragette in the worst sense—a desire to write "like a man." (I recall a woman's novel in which the mind of a male character said "crud" to itself every ten paces, creating a page on which the word stood out like button-tufts on a French pouf.) Sometimes the journalists do flex their biceps, or hare off to storm the Oak Room of the Plaza. But no important woman writer, I think, has really wanted to write "like a man." They had too much taste.

Only, sometimes, their taste has been too much for them. The sexual state of things in America had perhaps taught them, as women, that whole areas of their sensibility are best ignored. They were not going to be trapped into speaking for women only, and in this—like any artist who refuses category—they were right. But often this has meant that as artists they would be keeping their cool long after the men had given cool up.

Once a woman artist of any kind flees from the image society projects on her (thereby believing in it), she will be reluctant to tout or even value equally in the human scale her own preferential experience as a female. She knows her own capacity for the universal, and will not have it contaminated with the particular—if the particularity is feminine. Looking abroad, it can be seen what happens to women who do ride their femininity in the literary races: Doris Lessing, tied to psychiatry, suffragettism, and the vaginal reflex; Simone de Beauvoir, tied in the inimitable French way to the coattails of a man. But the American artist has sometimes avoided that, by getting her mental hysterectomy early. She will often not speak for female experience even when the men do; she will be the angel-artist, with celestially muted lower parts. Sometimes, in any of the arts, where women's work remains beautifully mandarin or minor, it may be not because of their womanhood, but from their lack of it.

There's a lesson in it for all. A woman (or a man) who wishes to write only as men do has confused it with the inborn freedom to write about anything (including the female experience). Other people may similarly confuse living "the same as a man" or "only as a man" with getting their fair share of life. Or probing their own.

I find ugly, or sad, or ridiculous the feminism which comes only from the head, or from hatred of men. Or from anger at what men have done and do to us. Humor is a better answer to that. And anger should be directed at the rules.

For myself: the feminism that comes straight from the belly, from the bed, and from childbed. A sensibility trusting itself for what it is, as the *other* half of basic life. And able to look at the world from there.

QUESTIONS

1. According to Hortense Calisher, what effects have the rigid definitions of masculinity and femininity in our society had on American literature?

2. In what ways, in the author's opinion, have American women writers been able to avoid dealing with female experience in their writing?

3. Is there any conflict between women's biological and artistic creativity?

4. Do you think that feminine experience is less interesting to read about than male experience?

part 4
WOMEN
AND
PSYCHOLOGY

Marynia F. Farnham
Ferdinand Lundberg

"Some Aspects of Woman's Psyche," reprinted below, is a chapter from Modern Woman: The Lost Sex (1947), *a remarkable book written by a psychiatrist, Dr. Marynia F. Farnham (b. 1899), and a sociologist, Ferdinand Lundberg (b. 1905). The thesis of the book, in the authors' words, was that "contemporary women in very large numbers are psychologically disordered and . . . their disorder is having terrible social and personal effects involving men in all departments of their lives as well as women." Farnham and Lundberg used Freud's theory of female psychology to show that career ambitions were a sign of feminine neurosis. Ten appendices, totaling a fourth of the book, contain most of the publication's evidence. The authors claimed that the falling birth rate, increases in homicide, juvenile delinquency, and alcoholism all could be attributed to the "masculinization" of women through feminist strivings. In Appendix IX, Farnham and Lundberg quoted "Views of Feminists," classifying excerpts from feminist writings under such headings as "Penis-Envy," "Masculinity Complex," "Vaginal Superiority," and "Passive-Feminine Males," among whom they included John Stuart Mill.*

One of the most elaborate discussions in the book is an analysis of Mary Wollstonecraft, who the authors call "an extreme neurotic of a compulsive type." They describe her as being "afflicted with a severe case of penis-envy" and as a "masochist" who sought "to deprive the male of his power, to castrate him." According to the authors, her defiance of convention was an expression of hostility towards her parents, "as it has been since of feminists, radicals, and bohemians in general."

Despite its exaggerations, Modern Woman: The Lost Sex *had enormous influence on the postwar generation and contributed to the counterrevolution that halted the progress of women's liberation until the mid-sixties.*

Some Aspects of Woman's Psyche

Woman's psychic development is complex and there is still no unanimity of opinion about it. We present here the view most generally agreed upon in psychiatry today, in its essence derived from Freud, but with modifications.

Usually, as we have already said, the first critical event peculiar to the life of the girl is the discovery, under social and cultural conditions already portrayed, of the anatomical differences between herself and her brother or whatever boy in her life serves this purpose. Parenthetically it should be said that it is very nearly universal to our culture for a girl to have this experience, irrespective of the pattern of her own family or the supervision with which she is provided. At this point she begins to face the dominant circumstance of her life as a female. The way she solves it will be decisive, crucial, in her later life as a woman. When she discovers that her brother differs from her by possessing an organ she lacks, she comes to the conclusion, for reasons we have indicated, that his entire structure and sphere of activity is superior.

The feeling is accentuated because the girl is unable to discover in herself any compensatory anatomical possession. Her reproductive structure is wholly within her body and for many years she may believe she is completely defective and undesirable because of this supposed anatomical deficiency. She cannot be expected to discover her own secret and hidden reproductive organs and their great powers, and many times it is years before she learns the facts. It is not uncommon in psychiatric practice to encounter adults who are grossly ignorant of female anatomy and cherish various false beliefs. For example, some women believe the urinary and reproductive apparatus have a common orifice. This is an error easily come by, since in the male—constant yardstick—this happens to be a fact.

Thus it is that the girl is faced with an entirely uncompensated sense of loss in a social setting depreciatory of women. She regards her brother's organ with considerable awe and envy because it supplies him with sources of real and imagined satisfaction she feels are denied to her. The feeling of loss and inferiority may be further exaggerated by her mother's preference for her brother, or her lament that she is a girl in a "man's world." When this happens, the little girl will be likely to ascribe it to her lack of the penis.

She has, to be sure, an analogous organ: the clitoris. This does not wholly compensate her, however. Her brother's organ is larger, it provides him with a seemingly superior method of urination and is believed to be a greater source of pleasure or mastery. At this point she cannot understand the fact that her self-projective satisfactions are to be obtained later in the form of babies and that these must compensate her for the feelings of envy which her brother's organ arouses in her. Babies themselves, as she often hears or understands, are themselves a calamity, and the idea makes her doubly doubtful of herself. For her, it is enough that she is denied and must go without, and this cannot fail to arouse initial resentment and envy. It is the long Odyssey of every girl child that she must travel from these feelings of deprivations to the discovery of her own rewards, far distant and culturally dubious. Every little girl, necessarily, suffers a kind of humiliation in this discovery. It may inflict serious and permanent damage upon her character. That it does not always do so is because there are circumstances available to the girl for resolving these feelings. These circumstances lie in her relationship to her parents.

As soon as she discovers she is a girl, which she does before her twenty-fourth month, she also discovers that she resembles her mother and must expect to develop into a woman *like* her mother. She is soon aware of the fact that women, including herself and her mother, have babies and that men do not. This, at first, is to her the whole of the relationship between her father and mother. Later, she comes to some understanding of its pleasure-giving capacity. Whatever the girl's knowledge of the sexual relation, is it unquestionably true that she understands that there *is* a relation of some sort, that it is exclusive and intimate, that it has to do with the production of babies and that it also concerns the parts of the body she soon comes to regard as important, secret and fearsomely surrounded by taboos.

The tabooed or forbidden aspect of sexuality is impressed upon her through all her education. Parents are, of necessity, governed by their own attitudes and transmit them to children. The feelings of the culture as a whole are thus transmitted. The young child therefore acquires all the cultural attitudes toward sexuality, in varying emphasis. With European-Americans these are: sexual privileges and pleasures belong exclusively to adults, are not permitted to children; they are extremely secret; investigation and talk about them is strongly taboo and often

(special puritanic, ascetic, or morbid emphasis) carries with it implications of wickedness and uncleanness; the sexual function is surrounded by strict regulations and controls that must be obeyed in order
to avoid serious consequences. These attitudes are shared by everyone
in the culture to a certain extent, accounting for much morbid emphasis
on sex. Even those who regard themselves as liberated from all the
shibboleths of society are more bound by than free of them, and show
it by extravagant flauntings of their "liberation."

Sexual training of children may be more or less severe, more or less
open and accepting of sexuality; more or less secretive and dirty seeming; more or less punitive and dangerous, more or less permissive. However it is given, the result varies in degree, not in kind. For there is important and substantial agreement on all basic considerations, sexual and
nonsexual, leading to the formation of a basic, generally shared personality. The result is that the child gets only part of his understanding
of sex from direct instruction and observation, the rest by implication
and subtle influence.

What is primary is that the little girl finds that all her mother's satisfactions, pre-eminently having babies, are forbidden to her. She is required to wait. This she does not wish to do and consequently develops
feelings of envy and rivalry toward her mother. In other words, she
wishes to enjoy immediately the satisfactions that she observes her
mother to have.

This circumstance leads her directly into the final critical sphere of
infantile development, known in psychoanalytic phraseology as the
Oedipus complex, which occurs from ages four to six. (There has been
some tendency to designate this in girls as the Electra complex.) This
complex consists, in the girl, of the development toward her mother of
rivalrous attitudes governed by certain fixed desires. She develops strong
partiality for her father and a wish to enjoy the satisfaction he gives her
mother. In other words, she wishes to displace her mother and take possession herself of her mother's attributes and privileges. Secondary to
this wish is the destructive and hostile attitude toward her mother, who
must of necessity be somehow removed from the scene if the little girl
is to take her place. The little girl knows and has always realized her own
immense helplessness in comparison with her mother's seeming omnip-
otence. This is everyday knowledge, repeatedly tested. She therefore
realizes the hopelessness of a struggle between them. She further believes that her mother will in turn inflict upon *her* the selfsame destructiveness which in spontaneous, primordial fantasy she has wished
for her mother. This is the law of talion—"an eye for an eye—a tooth for
a tooth." The belief in turn arouses intense anxiety. The anxiety forces
her to attempt to give up her envious and resentful attitude and over-
power her untenable wishes.

In order to do so successfully, the little girl needs primarily the un-
questioned devotion and love of her mother. It is as if she needs to feel

that her mother says, "I know and recognize your hostility, but I bear no hostility to you and love you in spite of it." Continued devotion is the bridge she needs in order to cross successfully into childhood from infancy. If her mother is to provide her with this very necessary support, it is imperative that the mother, herself, have fully integrated attitudes toward her own femininity. There must, for example, never be any question about the devotion existing between father and mother. The mother, in short, must have, with the wisdom of the serpent, selected an adequate man as father of her child.

The child needs this firm assurance of her own hopeless position, as it were, in order to be successful in overpowering her wishes and strivings toward her father. If she is able to observe that the relations between her parents are faulty or that there is lack of sympathy between them, then she will be doubly threatened. In one direction, she may see a greater opportunity for satisfaction of her own wishes and in another, she will feel greater anxiety as a result of it. Everything about her life must state to her firmly and without any doubt that the relations between her father and mother are intact, that they are bound together by their love for each other, that their love for her is parental only, and, especially in the case of the mother, that her love is unimpaired and unaffected by the little girl's hostility. Then she can safely leave behind, repress, her old wishes and successfully go forward to the next period of development. So things will go if there is a normal home life and healthy parental attitudes upon which the little girl may rely.

Unfortunately, this happens all too infrequently. There are all sorts of difficulties and hazards in the way of this smooth development. Many of them are becoming more and more frequent in the home of the present.

In the first place, if the little girl is rejected by her mother she immediately suffers a vital loss of security necessary to her development. If the parents are in any way alienated from each other, one or the other will look to the children for compensation. The father who feels he does not have the love of his wife will tend to form a greater attachment to his daughter and more strenuously attempt to make her his own. He may thus, unwittingly, consolidate and fix her in an attitude that should be only transitory. The little girl, having fallen in love with her father, may find an answering and excessive love in him which will forever prevent her from recovering from this infantile state. This is the "father-fixation" so popular and little understood in present-day speech.

The girl in struggling to become an adult woman must rely upon some pattern or model from which she can derive a design for femininity. She is provided with one in her mother and she will have to believe for a long time that her mother's nature, temperament and attitudes are ideals toward which she must strive as a woman. Not until much later in her life will she be free to discover other ideals and models. Thus it is her mother's grasp on femininity on which the little girl chiefly depends.

Here is the real crux of the situation, because the mother's feelings for herself as a woman and acceptance of her feminine role dictate her attitudes toward children and husband. If the girl has the good fortune to have a mother who finds complete satisfaction, without conflict or anxiety, in living out her role as wife and mother, it is unlikely that she will experience serious difficulties. If, however, the mother is beset by distaste for her role, strives for accomplishment outside her home and can only grudgingly give attention to her children, has regrets for whatever reason at being a woman, then, no matter how much or little of it she betrays, the child cannot escape the confused impression that the mother is without love, is not a satisfactory model.

Such a woman is not only an unsatisfactory model for her daughter, but gives her no sure grasp on the solid satisfactions inherent in feminine development. She may produce a still more dangerous impression on the small girl, in that she will inject into her attitudes her own covert strivings toward masculinity.

Such mothers, for example, are frequently unimpressed and unconcerned with the appearance of their daughters. It is natural to girls, part of their developing narcissism, to feel physical beauty as an attribute especially theirs and especially valued. The value the mother places upon it permanently fixes the attitude the little girl develops. Lack of appreciation, lack of concern, ultimately lack of love for her physical self on the part of the mother can only make the child feel that she is displeasing and, finally, has no very conspicuous feminine value. Such a mother, however, places enormous value on the little girl's achievements.

Dependent upon her parents for life itself, the child must seek every possible means of insuring personal safety. The best and most certain way is to assure herself of her parents' love. Their demands must be met. All of this has little or no basic value to the girl in her strivings for femininity. Achievement is overvalued, beyond the child's intrinsic self. Self as self, apart from achievement, must be valued by the parent if the child is to grow up with inner maturity.

We come now to the fact that the mother, under conditions of modern social change, is very often deeply disturbed. Although not a feminist or a courtesan type, necessarily, she is herself afflicted very often at a deep level with penis-envy, which plays itself out in various ways with respect to her children. She is disturbed, discontented, complaining, unreasonably demanding, aggressive and shows it directly or indirectly. The damage she does, to boys as well as girls, is great.

Dr. Wilhelm Reich makes the development of penis-envy revolve entirely around the father. He says:

> A father who exerts little frustration will contribute more to the formation of a feminine character than will a stern or brutal father. The typical reaction of the girl to a brutal father is the formation of a masculine, hard character. Penis envy is activated

and leads, characterologically, to a masculinity complex. [This happened, as we have seen, in the case of Mary Wollstonecraft.]

. . . The hard, masculine-aggressive armoring serves as a defense against the infantile-feminine attitude toward the father which had to be repressed because of his hardness and lovelessness. If the father is mild and loving, the girl can retain and develop her object-love; she does not need to identify herself with her father. True, she also is likely to have acquired penis envy; but, as there were no serious frustrations of heterosexual tendencies, it remained harmless as far as character formation is concerned. We see, then, that to say that this or that woman has penis envy does not mean anything. What matters is its influence on character or symptom formation. The decisive factor in this type is that a mother identification in the ego took place; it expresses itself in those character traits which are called "feminine."

Whether or not this character structure can be maintained depends on whether, in puberty, vaginal eroticism comes to form a lasting basis of femininity. Disappointments in the father or in father images at this age may give rise to a masculine identification which failed to materialize in childhood and may activate dormant penis envy and initiate the change from the feminine to the masculine character. This is often seen in girls who repress their heterosexual desires for moralistic reasons (identification with the authoritarian moralistic mother) and who provoke disillusioning experiences with men. In most cases, such female types tend to develop hysterical characteristics. One then finds an ever-repeated approach to genitality (coquetry) and shrinking back when the situation threatens to become serious (hysterical genital anxiety). The hysterical character in the woman serves the function of a protection against her own genital desires and against the male aggression of the object.

All of which, though true, we feel must be put in a social setting. Have all or a significant number of women in whom penis-envy is found had brutal fathers? A number have, but many have not. However, their fathers have appeared to them as *represented to them by their mothers*. This is what is, in our opinion, truly significant. Psychoanalysis in its early days, as has been pointed out, took the European-American family situation as classic. This family situation was the typical middle-class, monogamous family, with the father filling the supposed standard "patriarchal" role and the mother the traditional submissive role. The family as psychoanalysis found it, however, no longer existed in its Western traditional form. The father's direct influence in it, so far as the children could discern, was almost nil. Father was absent about ten hours a day at work and asleep about eight hours at home. Nor was he, usually, available and in view six hours of the day, for he sometimes tarried elsewhere. On Sundays he was remote. In many cases, because he was a traveling salesman, an engineer, a trainman, an itinerant worker, he was gone for long periods.

Father, to the children, was *what mother represented him to be*. If mother was discontented with her "lot," as she was by the millions, it was, somehow, father's fault. He was a brute, cold, heartless and unfeeling. Or a person who did not try to understand a woman's difficulties. He had all the fun, controlled the purse strings, etc. Of course, if the mother was able to fill a feminine role, despite the lack of ego rewards in her life, and if she was pleased with her husband, the children obtained an altogether different view of the father. Then he appeared benign, reliable, a model of all men.

Psychoanalysis, we may say, has rarely encountered the traditional patriarchal family situation. It has, of necessity, been confined to the family of the Industrial Revolution, the family in upheaval. Observation of neurotics almost invariably shows a deeply disturbed mother, disturbed by reason of her own childhood conditioning, by conditions encountered in adulthood, or by both. Less often, but frequently nevertheless, the case points to a disturbed father, overvaluing material success to the extent that any setback in job or career is reflected in unpleasant attitudes toward his family.

The man, on losing a job, has had to face the open or silent accusations of a wife unconsciously waiting in ambush for him, waiting to punish him for the privilege of being a man. The wife, on the other hand, has had to face the open or silent accusations of a husband who has indicated that she and the children are a burden to him in his strivings for "success."

The man, like a gambler, has staked his entire feeling of well-being on the whirling wheel of success. If he has succeeded to his own satisfaction he has, very often, aroused the envy of his wife—a disturbing circumstance. If he has failed he has visited his dejection or hostility on his family, or has aroused the open or silent recriminations of his wife. Whether he has succeeded or failed, the wife has had to cope with her own sense of ego insufficiency. If truly feminine she has, of course, escaped this. If she has been truly feminine the entire family has escaped, as many have escaped. But many, on the other hand, have not.

Further complicating elements arise when the mother also absents herself at work or career. Such absences, particularly if not compensated for by true love for the children, can only blur their image of femininity. Early twisted attitudes persist into adult life, to block and thwart the drive toward self-consummation. But whatever the distortions or inhibitions, nothing can wholly destroy the final biologic drive for womanhood. Conflicts, however, often deeply underlie the achievement of desired satisfactions, and they are disregarded or by-passed at great peril to the individual and those related to her. In the light of these fundamentals we can judge how well the "liberated" woman is able to provide herself with deep and lasting satisfactions.

We may dispose of the legal and political aspects of woman's new position as being not significantly important in and of themselves.

In these areas women gained a rightful privilege and ego-support, not dangerous to her fundamental peace of mind. It is rather in the aggressive and misdirected use to which these privileges are put that we see arising the difficulties into which many women have plunged themselves. The economic, educational, social and sexual facts of the woman's life, intertwined and interdependent as they are, are those which implement all others.

The woman arriving at maturity today does so with certain fixed attitudes derived from her background and training. Her home life, very often, has been distorted. She has enjoyed an education identical with that of her brother. She expects to be allowed to select any kind of work for which she has inclination and training. She also, generally, expects to marry. At any rate, she usually intends to have "a go" at it. Some women expect to stop working when they marry; many others do not. She expects to find sexual gratification and believes in her inalienable right so to do. She is legally free to live and move as she chooses. She may seek divorce if her marriage fails to gratify her. She has access to contraceptive information so that, theoretically, she may control the size and spacing of her family. In very many instances, she owns and disposes of her own property. She has, it appears, her destiny entirely in her own hands.

All of this serves less to clarify and simplify her life than to complicate it with conflict piled on conflict. These conflicts are between her basic needs as a woman and the destiny she has carved out for herself—conflicts between the head and the heart, if you will.

Her necessity is to find some kind of consummation for her specific femininity and for herself as a human being. The circumstances with which she is now surrounded, as well as those of her upbringing, tend to prevent these two consummations—instinct and ego—from being fused together. Conflict and compromise are almost inevitable. Her basic needs for satisfaction as a woman would inevitably lead her in the direction of marriage and children inside the home. However, the woman who chooses this course runs into two serious obstacles: she does not obtain under present conditions satisfaction of her need for self-esteem nor does she obtain a sense of social importance. In attempting to gain these, she is led in the direction of economic independence, which carries her outside her home, away from children and childbearing. It was, of course, the failure of society after the Industrial Revolution to provide her with needed sources of self-esteem that forced her into the battle for her economic "rights" which, as we have shown, she has at least formally won. In winning them she was forced, too, into dubious battle for all the other rights auxiliary to them.

Thus she finds herself squarely in the middle of the most serious kind of divided purpose. If she is to undertake occupation outside her home with any kind of success, it is almost certain in the present day to be time-consuming and energy-demanding. So it is also with the problems she faces in her home. Certainly the tasks of a woman in bearing and educating children as well as maintaining, as best she may, the inner integrity of her home are capable of demanding all her time and best attention. However, she cannot obtain from them, so attenuated are these tasks now, the same sort of community approval and ego-satisfaction that she can from seemingly more challenging occupations which take her outside the home. Inevitably the dilemma has led to one compromise after another which we see exemplified on every hand in the modern woman's adaptation—an uneasy patchwork.

Unable to relinquish either satisfaction, she necessarily attempts to obtain both. In making the attempt, she must divide her attention and one of her occupations must be sacrificed in some measure to the other. Many women at first adopt the attitude that work will be undertaken only as a preliminary to marriage, then only as long as necessary for the economic support of the home. Later it will be abandoned when there are children and the home needs are more demanding. These women often also emphasize that they wish to have some occupation on which they can reasonably rely in case of an emergency. They are altogether too well aware of the insecurities and uncertainties of modern economic life to fail to take into account that at any time they may have to work, quite apart from inclination.

The present-day feeling regarding the impoverishment of the home is shown too in the frequent statement that women must fortify themselves with interests and occupations to which they can turn when their children no longer require their attention. Many no doubt carry out their aim and manage to obtain satisfactions inside their homes during the period of their children's dependency or even longer. For others, however, the work experience provides such satisfaction that they almost inevitably find it impossible to relinquish it. This is probably traceable to the fact that the underlying drives of these women, instilled in their childhood homes, are in the direction of such satisfactions. In present-day society, these basically masculine drives find an atmosphere which encourages rather than disapproves and depreciates their development.

It is becoming unquestionably more and more common for the woman to attempt to combine both home and child care and an outside activity, which is either work or career. Increasing numbers train for professional careers. When these two spheres are combined it is inevitable that one or the other will become of secondary concern and, this being the case, it is certain that the home will take that position. This is true, if only for the practical reason that no one can find and hold remunerative employment where the job itself doesn't take precedence over all other concerns. All sorts of agencies and instrumentalities have therefore been established to make possible the playing of this dual role. These are all in the direction of substitutes for the attention of the mother in the home and they vary from ordinary, untrained domestic service through the more highly trained grades of such service, to the public and private agencies now designed for the care, supervision and emotional untanglement of the children. The day nursery and its more elegant counterpart, the nursery school, are outstanding as the major agencies which make it possible for women to relinquish the care of children still in their infancy.

All these services and facilities produce what appears on the surface to be a smoothly functioning arrangement and one that provides children with obviously highly trained, expert and efficient care as well as with superior training in early skills and techniques and in adaptation to social relations. This surface, however, covers a situation that is by no means so smoothly functioning nor so satisfying either to the child or the woman. She must of necessity be deeply in conflict and only partially satisfied in either direction. Her work develops aggressiveness, which is essentially a denial of her femininity, an enhancement of her girlhood-induced masculine tendencies. It is not that work is essentially masculine or feminine, but that the pursuit of a career (which is work plus prestige goal) is essentially masculine because exploitative. The statement may cause enormous protest but it remains a fact.

Work that entices women out of their homes and provides them with prestige only at the price of feminine relinquishment, involves a response to masculine strivings. The more importance outside work assumes, the more are the masculine components of the woman's nature enhanced and encouraged. In her home and in her relationship to her children, it is imperative that these strivings be at a minimum and that her femininity be available both for her own satisfaction and for the satisfaction of her children and husband. She is, therefore, in the dangerous position of having to live one part of her life on the masculine level, another on the feminine. It is hardly astonishing that few can do so with success. One of these tendencies must of necessity achieve dominance over the other. The plain fact is that increasingly we are observing the masculinization of women and with it enormously dangerous consequences to the home, the children (if any) dependent on it, and to the ability of the woman, as well as her husband, to obtain sexual gratification.

The effect of this "masculinization" on women is becoming more apparent daily. Their new exertions are making demands on them for qualities wholly opposed to the experience of feminine satisfaction. As the rivals of men, women must, and insensibly do, develop the characteristics of aggression, dominance, independence and power. These are qualities which insure success as co-equals in the world of business, industry and the professions. The distortion of character under pressure of modern attitudes and upbringing is driving women steadily deeper into personal conflict soluble only by psychotherapy. For their need to achieve and accomplish doesn't lessen, in any way, their deeper need to find satisfactions profoundly feminine. Much as they consciously seek those gratifications of love, sensual release and even motherhood, they are becoming progressively less able unconsciously to accept or achieve them.*

First of their demands is for sexual gratification. . . . This is the core of the goal—sexual, orgastic equality with men. These women have intellectualized and rationalized their sexual lives, determining that they will have for themselves the experiences and, therefore, the satisfactions that men have. So far as the experiences are concerned, they can carry out their intentions, but where the gratifications are concerned they meet with abysmal, tragic failure. Sexual gratification is not an experience to be obtained through the simple performance of the sexual act. To a very great extent the unconscious exertions of these women to obtain absolute parity with men have resulted in crippling them precisely for this much desired objective. Dr. Helene Deutsch, among many other psychiatrists, affirms this when she states, "In the light of psychoanalysis, the sexual act assumes an immense, dramatic, and profoundly cathartic significance for the woman—but this only under the condition that it is experienced in a feminine, dynamic way and is not transformed into an act of erotic play or sexual 'equality.'" It

---

* In outward expression of the rivalry increasingly felt, women attacked and revised traditional symbols of male-female relations. As soon as it was said, erroneously, that the wedding ring symbolized the original enslavement of the female by the male the double-ring marriage ceremony was devised to make the "enslavement" mutual. As soon as it was said that women took the names of their husbands because women had originally been the property of men (another factually false assertion), married women were encouraged to retain their maiden names. In so doing women merely assumed their father's names, and if they took their mother's, as some did, then their maternal grandfather's. But even though they could not escape taking some man's name they could challenge the man nearest them by declining to take his name. In some cases a woman took her husband's name but insisted that it be coupled with her own—that is, with her father's. The men who put up with this pathological nonsense invariably got just about what they were entitled to in a woman. Attack was also made on the word "obey" in the marriage ceremony, more and more women finding this difficult to swallow. The modern male is perhaps a poor commander for anyone to follow and perhaps this particular defiance has been earned only by an incompetent male. The marital relationship consists of only two persons, however, and majority votes on issues are not always possible. In the event of divided opinion sovereignty, as it were, must be vested in someone. If it is not vested in the male, then not only is his power questioned but his responsibility is undermined. At any rate, women, in making a point of the traditional word were only saying, "I can't conceive of any situation arising wherein your judgment would be preferable to mine." In so saying, a woman was serving notice that she was a castrater, although it took some males a long, confused time to discover this and others never discovered it because they had already been castrated by their mothers, would have found it strange to be suddenly endowed with full male attributes. The "Battle of the Sexes" is a reality, and one of its results has been rather extensive psychological castration of the male.

is precisely in development of femininity that capacity for female sexual gratification lies. The greater the denial of the feminine, in childhood and later, the surer and more extensive is the loss of capacity for satisfaction in both tenderness and sensuality: love.

The dominant direction of feminine training and development today is directly opposed to the truth of such a dictum as Dr. Deutsch's. It discourages just those traits necessary to the attainment of sexual pleasure: receptivity and passiveness, a willingness to accept dependence without fear or resentment, with a deep inwardness and readiness for the final goal of sexual life—impregnation. It doesn't admit of wishes to control or master, to rival or dominate. The woman who is to find true gratification must love and accept her own womanhood as she loves and accepts her husband's manhood. Women's rivalry with men today, and the need to "equal" their accomplishments, engenders all too often anger and resentfulness toward men. Men, challenged, frequently respond in kind. So it is that women envy and feel hostile to men for just the attributes which women themselves require for "success" in the world. The woman's unconscious wish herself to possess the organ upon which she must thus depend militates greatly against her ability to accept its vast power to satisfy her when proffered to her in love.

Many women can find no solution to their dilemma and are defeated in attempts at adaptation. These constitute the array of the sick, unhappy, neurotic, wholly or partly incapable of dealing with life. In a veritable army of women, the tensions and anxieties make their way to the surface in physical guise. They have always been known and dimly recognized for what they are—the miserable, the half-satisfied, the frustrated, the angered. Unable to cope with the disappointments that they have met in their emotional lives, they become ill. Their illnesses take varied forms, attack any part of the body and are often disabling. Where formerly the connection was only suspected and assumed between these multifarious physical disorders and disturbing feeling states, we are now coming to the point of really understanding their sources in the child-based emotional disorders that give rise to them. Whether it be "sick headaches," pains of indeterminate nature in the back and limbs, gastric disorders, constipation, hypertension, or the enormous collections of disorders of the reproductive system, it is all one and all arises from an inability to master unconscious feelings constantly aroused by disappointment and frustration.

Such women are constant visitors to doctors or patrons of patent medicines. They are never cured and never comfortable. They suffer as authentically as those whose complaints rest upon physically determined pathology. They are just as sick and most emphatically their illnesses are not "imaginary." They can be helped permanently only by understanding obtained through psychological insight, therefore, through psychiatry. Many of them today are beginning to find their way to such help but many, many more are not. These remain the complaining army who keep their families, friends and physicians constantly at their beck and call by their sufferings.

Other women, more obviously in need of psychiatry for a solution of their troubles, do not show their difficulties in physical symptoms but present them more directly in the form of disturbances recognizably emotional. These are the "nervous," the sleepless, the depressed, the anxious, the driven, the sexually maladjusted, those who complain directly of misery and discontent.

These women are the overtly neurotic. They may have recurrent depressions which are either mild enough to be of only limited and passing concern or so severe as to require hospitalization. Whichever form they take, they are disabling for their duration and a constant threat when not actually present. A very large group of these women describe themselves as "nervous." They are often sleepless, hyper-irritable and extremely demanding of husbands and children, whom they unconsciously seek to punish for their own disabilities. There are many others with more obvious and easily categorized neurotic disorders some of whom complain of intense anxiety which renders them more or less helpless. The anxiety is often related to fear of some impending catastrophe for which they have no immediate evidence. Nevertheless, they constantly feel they are about to suffer from some physical disorder such as cancer or heart disease for which no relief will be found.

The relatively large number of women who complain of immediate sexual and marital difficulties stands out among the neurotic. Their complaints usually revolve about the sexual act and its insufficiency or unsatisfactory nature. Often, however, the general marital relationship is under attack, the woman not being able directly to place her problem as sexual. The husband is criticized for a thousand reasons as inconsiderate, selfish, harsh or thoughtless, which he may not in fact be. These women range all the way from the frankly and completely frigid to those who complain of neglect and indifference on the part of their husbands and the feelings of loneliness and uselessness that arise from it. Many of them have the prospect of divorce prominently in mind, in hope either of finding satisfaction through removal of the irritating circumstance or, more remotely, of discovering gratification through another marriage.

A certain number of these women of inner masculine tendency are making a reasonable and satisfying adjustment. They have found, through an uneasy balance between work and home, a way of compromise that offers sufficient satisfaction in both spheres to provide happiness and completion. No doubt careful examination might discover defects in this adaptation, but it must be remembered that all adaptations are products of compromise and that where there is real satisfaction there is little reason to be captious. The difficulty lies not in the small group of women who have managed the difficult compromise, but in the much larger group who have not and who suffer from resulting frustrations.

It is not only the masculine woman who has met with an unhappy fate in the present situation. There are still many women who succeed in achieving adult life with largely unimpaired feminine strivings, for which home, a husband's love and children are to them the entirely adequate answers. It is their misfortune that they must enter a society in which such attitudes are little appreciated and are attended by many concrete, external penalties. Such women cannot fail to be affected by finding that their traditional activities are held in low esteem and that the woman who voluntarily undertakes them is often deprecated by her more aggressive contemporaries. She may come to believe that her situation is difficult, entailing serious deprivations, as against the more glamorous and exciting life other women seemingly enjoy. She may be set away from the main stream of life, very much in a backwater and fearful lest she lose her ability and talents through disuse and lack of stimulation. She may become sorry for herself and somewhat angered by her situation, gradually developing feelings of discontent and pressure. As her children grow older and require less of her immediate attention, the feelings of loss increase.

Unless she busies herself extensively with the poorly organized and generally unrewarding voluntary civic or cultural activities, she may find herself with much idle time and much frustration on her hands. Her home alone, unless it is a rural one, cannot occupy her whole time and attention because so much in it is now completely prefabricated and automatic. For amusement she is forced to resort either to the radio "soap opera," or to some other equally unrewarding use of leisure such as game playing, movie-going or aimless shopping. She is deprived of her husband's companionship during the long hours of the day when he is away from home and often the evening finds him preoccupied and disinterested in the affairs that concern her. Consequently she must construct her life out of artificial undertakings with no organic functional connection with the realities of her relationships or her interests. In this way she may easily and quickly develop attitudes of discontent and anger injurious to her life adjustment. She may begin to malfunction sexually, her libidinal depths shaken by her ego frustrations.

So it is that society today makes it difficult for a woman to avoid the path leading to discontent and frustration and resultant hostility and destructiveness. Such destructiveness is, unfortunately, not confined in its effects to the woman alone. It reaches into all her relationships and all her functions. As a wife she is not only often ungratified but ungratifying and has, as we have noted, a profoundly disturbing effect upon her husband. Not only does he find himself without the satisfactions of a home directed and cared for by a woman happy in providing affection and devotion, but he is often confronted by circumstances of even more serious import for his own emotional integrity. His wife may be his covert rival, striving to match him in every aspect of their joint undertaking. Instead of supporting and encouraging his manliness and wishes for domination and power, she may thus impose upon him feelings of insufficiency and weakness. Still worse is the effect upon his sexual satisfactions. Where the woman is unable to admit and accept dependence upon her husband as the source of gratification and must carry her rivalry even into the act of love, she will seriously damage his sexual capacity. To be unable to gratify in the sexual act is for a man an intensely humiliating experience; here it is that mastery and domination, the central capacity of the man's sexual nature, must meet acceptance or fail. So it is that by their own character disturbances these women succeed ultimately in depriving themselves of the devotion and power of their husbands and become the instruments of bringing about their own psychic catastrophe.

But no matter how great a woman's masculine strivings, her basic needs make themselves felt and she finds herself facing her fundamental role as wife and mother with a divided mind. Deprived of a rich and creative home in which to find self-expression, she tries desperately to find a compromise. On the one hand she must retain her sources of real instinctual gratification and on the other, find ways of satisfying her need for prestige and esteem. Thus she stands, Janus-faced, drawn in two directions at once, often incapable of ultimate choice and inevitably penalized whatever direction she chooses.

QUESTIONS

1. What reasoning leads the authors to the conclusion that the mother who "strives for accomplishment outside the home" will damage her children psychologically?

2. What do the authors mean by the "truly feminine" woman?

3. What can be inferred regarding the authors' view of the "truly masculine" man?

4. What traits do the authors see as essential to woman's sexual fulfillment? How has her changing role affected her chances for this fulfillment?

5. What are the implications of the authors' theory for women's education?

6. How do you think the authors would regard an unmarried woman?

Betty Friedan

Betty Friedan is a clinical psychologist who in 1966 founded the National Organization for Women (NOW), a civil rights organization working for sexual equality. In 1963 her forceful analysis of the plight of American women, The Feminine Mystique, *set off a new wave of feminism in the United States and has continued to be one of the major texts of the women's liberation movement. As she defines it, the feminine mystique is an ethic that*

> . . . *says that the highest value and the only commitment for women is the fulfillment of their femininity. It says that the great mistake of Western culture, through most of its history, has been the undervaluation of this femininity. . . . The root of women's troubles in the past is that women envied men, women tried to be like men, instead of accepting their own nature, which can find fulfillment only in sexual passivity, male domination, and nurturing maternal love.*

Mrs. Friedan diagnosed the nameless discontent of millions of housewives as frustration stemming from this systematic repression of their ambitions and needs as individuals. In the chapter reprinted below, she attacks the Freudian sources of the feminine mystique.

The Sexual Solipsism of Sigmund Freud

It would be half-wrong to say it started with Sigmund Freud. It did not really start, in America, until the 1940's. And then again, it was less a start than the prevention of an end. The old prejudices—women are animals, less than human, unable to think like men, born merely to breed and serve men—were not so easily dispelled by the crusading feminists, by science and education, and by the democratic spirit after all. They merely reappeared in the forties, in Freudian disguise. The feminine mystique derived its power from Freudian thought; for it was an idea born of Freud, which led women, and those who studied them, to misinterpret their mothers' frustrations, and their fathers' and brothers' and husbands' resentments and inadequacies, and their own emotions and possible choices in life. It is a Freudian idea, hardened into apparent fact, that has trapped so many American women today.

The new mystique is much more difficult for the modern woman to question than the old prejudices, partly because the mystique is broadcast by the very agents of education and social science that are supposed to be the chief enemies of prejudice, partly because the very nature of Freudian thought makes it virtually invulnerable to question. How can an educated American woman, who is not herself an analyst, presume to question a Freudian truth? She knows that Freud's discovery of the unconscious workings of the mind was one of the great breakthroughs in man's pursuit of knowledge. She knows that the science built on that discovery has helped many suffering men and women. She has been taught that only after years of analytic training is one capable of understanding the meaning of Freudian truth. She may even know how the human mind unconsciously resists that truth. How can she presume to tread the sacred ground where only analysts are allowed?

No one can question the basic genius of Freud's discoveries, nor the

FROM *The Feminine Mystique*, by Betty Friedan. Reprinted by permission of W. W. Norton & Company, Inc. Copyright © 1963, by Betty Friedan.

contribution he has made to our culture. Nor do I question the effectiveness of psychoanalysis as it is practiced today by Freudian or anti-Freudian. But I do question, from my own experience as a woman, and my reporter's knowledge of other women, the application of the Freudian theory of femininity to women today. I question its use, not in therapy, but as it has filtered into the lives of American women through the popular magazines and the opinions and interpretations of so-called experts. I think much of the Freudian theory about women is obsolescent, an obstacle to truth for women in America today, and a major cause of the pervasive problem that has no name.

There are many paradoxes here. Freud's concept of the superego helped to free man of the tyranny of the "shoulds," the tyranny of the past, which prevents the child from becoming an adult. Yet Freudian thought helped create a new superego that paralyzes educated modern American women—a new tyranny of the "shoulds," which chains women to an old image, prohibits choice and growth, and denies them individual identity.

Freudian psychology, with its emphasis on freedom from a repressive morality to achieve sexual fulfillment, was part of the ideology of women's emancipation. The lasting American image of the "emancipated woman" is the flapper of the twenties: burdensome hair shingled off, knees bared, flaunting her new freedom to live in a studio in Greenwich Village or Chicago's near North Side, and drive a car, and drink, and smoke and enjoy sexual adventures—or talk about them. And yet today, for reasons far removed from the life of Freud himself, Freudian thought has become the ideological bulwark of the sexual counter-revolution in America. Without Freud's definition of the sexual nature of woman to give the conventional image of femininity new authority, I do not think several generations of educated, spirited American women would have been so easily diverted from the dawning realization of who they were and what they could be.

The concept "penis envy," which Freud coined to describe a phenomenon he observed in women—that is, in the middle-class women who were his patients in Vienna in the Victorian era—was seized in this country in the 1940's as the literal explanation of all that was wrong with American women. Many who preached the doctrine of endangered femininity, reversing the movement of American women toward independence and identity, never knew its Freudian origin. Many who seized on it—not the few psychoanalysts, but the many popularizers, sociologists, educators, ad-agency manipulators, magazine writers, child experts, marriage counselors, ministers, cocktail-party authorities—could not have known what Freud himself meant by penis envy. One needs only to know what Freud *was* describing, in those Victorian women, to see the fallacy in literally applying his theory of femininity to women today. And one needs only to know *why* he described it in that way to understand that much of it is obsolescent, contradicted by knowledge that is part of every social scientist's thinking today, but was not yet known in Freud's time.

Freud, it is generally agreed, was a most perceptive and accurate observer of important problems of the human personality. But in describing and interpreting those problems, he was a prisoner of his own culture. As he was creating a new framework for our culture, he could not escape the framework of his own. Even his genius could not give him, then, the knowledge of cultural processes which men who are not geniuses grow up with today.

The physicist's relativity, which in recent years has changed our whole approach to scientific knowledge, is harder, and therefore easier to understand than the social scientist's relativity. It is not a slogan, but a fundamental statement about truth to say that no social scientist can completely free himself from the prison of his own culture; he can only interpret what he observes in the scientific framework of his own time. This is true even of the great innovators. They cannot help but translate their revolutionary observations into language and rubrics that have been determined by the progress of science up until their time. Even those discoveries that create new rubrics are relative to the vantage point of their creator.

The knowledge of other cultures, the understanding of cultural relativity, which is part of the framework of social scientists in our own time, was unknown to Freud. Much of what Freud believed to be biological, instinctual, and changeless has been shown by modern research to be a result of specific cultural causes.[1] Much of what Freud described as characteristic of universal human nature was merely characteristic of certain middle-class European men and women at the end of the nineteenth century.

For instance, Freud's theory of the sexual origin of neurosis stems from the fact that many of the patients he first observed suffered from

---

[1] Clara Thompson, *Psychoanalysis: Evolution and Development*, New York, 1950, pp. 131 ff.:

Freud not only emphasized the biological more than the cultural, but he also developed a cultural theory of his own based on his biological theory. There were two obstacles in the way of understanding the importance of the cultural phenomena he saw and recorded. He was too deeply involved in developing his biological theories to give much thought to other aspects of the data he collected. Thus he was interested chiefly in applying to human society his theory of instincts. Starting with the assumption of a death instinct, for example, he then developed an explanation of the cultural phenomena he observed in terms of the death instinct. Since he did not have the perspective to be gained from knowledge of comparative cultures, he could not evaluate cultural processes as such. . . . Much which Freud believed to be biological has been shown by modern research to be a reaction to a certain type of culture and not characteristic of universal human nature.

hysteria—and in those cases, he found sexual repression to be the cause. Orthodox Freudians still profess to believe in the sexual origin of all neurosis, and since they look for unconscious sexual memories in their patients, and translate what they hear into sexual symbols, they still manage to find what they are looking for.

But the fact is, cases of hysteria as observed by Freud are much more rare today. In Freud's time, evidently, cultural hypocrisy forced the repression of sex. (Some social theorists even suspect that the very absence of other concerns, in that dying Austrian empire, caused the sexual preoccupation of Freud's patients.[2]) Certainly the fact that his culture denied sex focused Freud's interest on it. He then developed his theory by describing all the stages of growth as sexual, fitting all the phenomena he observed into sexual rubrics.

His attempt to translate all psychological phenomena into sexual terms, and to see all problems of adult personality as the effect of childhood sexual fixations also stemmed, in part, from his own background in medicine, and from the approach to causation implicit in the scientific thought of his time. He had the same diffidence about dealing with psychological phenomena in their own terms which often plagues scientists of human behavior. Something that could be described in physiological terms, linked to an organ of anatomy, seemed more comfortable, solid, real, scientific, as he moved into the unexplored country of the unconscious mind. As his biographer, Ernest Jones, put it, he made a "desperate effort to cling to the safety of cerebral anatomy."[3] Actually, he had the ability to see and describe psychological phenomena so vividly that whether his concepts were given names borrowed from physiology, philosophy or literature—penis envy, ego, Oedipus complex—they seemed to have a concrete physical reality. Psychological facts, as Jones said, were "as real and concrete to him as metals are to a metallurgist."[4] This ability became a source of great confusion as his concepts were passed down by lesser thinkers.

The whole superstructure of Freudian theory rests on the strict determinism that characterized the scientific thinking of the Victorian era. Determinism has been replaced today by a more complex view of cause and effect, in terms of physical processes and phenomena as well as psychological. In the new view, behavioral scientists do not need to borrow language from physiology to explain psychological events, or give them pseudo-reality. Sexual phenomena are no more nor less real than, for instance, the phenomenon of Shakespeare's writing *Hamlet*, which cannot exactly be "explained" by reducing it to sexual terms.

---

[2] Richard La Piere, *The Freudian Ethic*, New York, 1959, p. 62.

[3] Ernest Jones, *The Life and Work of Sigmund Freud*, New York, 1953, Vol. I, p. 384.

[4] *Ibid.*, Vol. II (1955), p. 432.

Even Freud himself cannot be explained by his own deterministic, physiological blueprint, though his biographer traces his genius, his "divine passion for knowledge" to an insatiable sexual curiosity, before the age of three, as to what went on between his mother and father in the bedroom.[5]

Today biologists, social scientists, and increasing numbers of psychoanalysts see the need or impulse to human growth as a primary human need, as basic as sex. The "oral" and "anal" stages which Freud described in terms of sexual development—the child gets his sexual pleasure first by mouth, from mother's breast, then from his bowel movements—are now seen as stages of human growth, influenced by cultural circumstances and parental attitudes as well as by sex. When the teeth grow, the mouth can bite as well as suck. Muscle and brain also grow; the child becomes capable of control, mastery, understanding; and his need to grow and learn, at five, twenty-five, or fifty, can be satisfied, denied, repressed, atrophied, evoked or discouraged by his culture as can his sexual needs.

Child specialists today confirm Freud's observation that problems between mother and child in the earliest stages are often played out in terms of eating; later in toilet training. And yet in America in recent years there has been a noticeable decline in children's "eating problems." Has the child's instinctual development changed? Impossible, if by definition, the oral stage is instinctual. Or has the culture removed eating as a focus for early childhood problems—by the American emphasis on permissiveness in child care, or simply by the fact that in our affluent society food has become less a cause for anxiety in mothers? Because of Freud's own influence on our culture, educated parents are usually careful not to put conflict-producing pressures on toilet training. Such conflicts are more likely to occur today as the child learns to talk or read.[6]

In the 1940's, American social scientists and psychoanalysts had already begun to reinterpret Freudian concepts in the light of their growing cultural awareness. But, curiously, this did not prevent their literal application of Freud's theory of femininity to American women.

The fact is that to Freud, even more than to the magazine editor on Madison Avenue today, women were a strange, inferior, less-than-human species. He saw them as childlike dolls, who existed in terms only of man's love, to love man and serve his needs. It was the same kind of unconscious solipsism that made man for many centuries see the sun only as a bright object that revolved around the earth. Freud grew up with this attitude built in by his culture—not only the culture

[5] *Ibid.*, Vol. I, pp. 7–14, 294; Vol. II, p. 483.

[6] Bruno Bettelheim, *Love Is Not Enough: The Treatment of Emotionally Disturbed Children*, Glencoe, Ill., 1950, pp. 7 ff.

of Victorian Europe, but that Jewish culture in which men said the daily prayer: "I thank Thee, Lord, that Thou hast not created me a woman," and women prayed in submission: "I thank Thee, Lord, that Thou has created me according to Thy will."

Freud's mother was the pretty, docile bride of a man twice her age; his father ruled the family with an autocratic authority traditional in Jewish families during those centuries of persecution when the fathers were seldom able to establish authority in the outside world. His mother adored the young Sigmund, her first son, and thought him mystically destined for greatness; she seemed to exist only to gratify his every wish. His own memories of the sexual jealousy he felt for his father, whose wishes she also gratified, were the basis of this theory of the Oedipus complex. With his wife, as with his mother and sisters, his needs, his desires, his wishes, were the sun around which the household revolved. When the noise of his sisters' practicing the piano interrupted his studies, "the piano disappeared," Anna Freud recalled years later, "and with it all opportunities for his sisters to become musicians."

Freud did not see this attitude as a problem, or cause for any problem, in women. It was woman's nature to be ruled by man, and her sickness to envy him. Freud's letters to Martha, his future wife, written during the four years of their engagement (1882–1886) have the fond, patronizing sound of Torvald in A Doll's House, scolding Nora for her pretenses at being human. Freud was beginning to probe the secrets of the human brain in the laboratory at Vienna; Martha was to wait, his "sweet child," in her mother's custody for four years, until he could come and fetch her. From these letters one can see that to him her identity was defined as child-housewife, even when she was no longer a child and not yet a housewife.

> Tables and chairs, beds, mirrors, a clock to remind the happy couple of the passage of time, an armchair for an hour's pleasant daydreaming, carpets to help the housewife keep the floors clean, linen tied with pretty ribbons in the cupboard and dresses of the latest fashion and hats with artificial flowers, pictures on the wall, glasses for everyday and others for wine and festive occasions, plates and dishes . . . and the sewing table and the cozy lamp, and everything must be kept in good order or else the housewife who has divided her heart into little bits, one for each piece of furniture, will begin to fret. And this object must bear witness to the serious work that holds the household together, and that object, to a feeling for beauty, to dear friends one likes to remember, to cities one has visited, to hours one wants to recall. . . . Are we to hang our hearts on such little things? Yes, and without hesitation. . . .
>
> I know, after all, how sweet you are, how you can turn a house into a paradise, how you will share in my interests, how gay yet painstaking you will be. I will let you rule the house as much as you wish, and you will reward me with your sweet love and by rising above all those weaknesses for which women are so often despised.

As far as my activities allow, we shall read together what we want to learn, and I will initiate you into things which could not interest a girl as long as she is unfamiliar with her future companion and his occupation . . .[7]

On July 5, 1885, he scolds her for continuing to visit Elise, a friend who evidently is less than demure in her regard for men:

What is the good of your feeling that you are now so mature that this relationship can't do you any harm? . . . You are far too soft, and this is something I have got to correct, for what one of us does will also be charged to the other's account. You are my precious little woman and even if you make a mistake, you are none the less so. . . . But you know all this, my sweet child . . .[8]

The Victorian mixture of chivalry and condescension which is found in Freud's scientific theories about women is explicit in a letter he wrote on November 5, 1883, deriding John Stuart Mill's views on "female emancipation and the woman's question altogether."

In his whole presentation, it never emerges that women are different beings—we will not say lesser, rather the opposite—from men. He finds the suppression of women an analogy to that of Negroes. Any girl, even without a suffrage or legal competence, whose hand a man kisses and for whose love he is prepared to dare all, could have set him right. It is really a stillborn thought to send women into the struggle for existence exactly as man. If, for instance, I imagined my gentle sweet girl as a competitor, it would only end in my telling her, as I did seventeen months ago, that I am fond of her and that I implore her to withdraw from the strife into the calm, uncompetitive activity of my home. It is possible that changes in upbringing may suppress all a woman's tender attributes, needful of protection and yet so victorious, and that she can then earn a livelihood like men. It is also possible that in such an event one would not be justified in mourning the passing away of the most delightful thing the world can offer us—our ideal of womanhood. I believe that all reforming action in law and education would break down in front of the fact that, long before the age at which a man can earn a position in society, Nature has determined woman's destiny through beauty, charm, and sweetness. Law and custom have much to give women that has been withheld from them, but the position of women will surely be what it is: in youth an adored darling and in mature years a loved wife.[9]

---

[7] Ernest L. Freud, *Letters of Sigmund Freud*, New York, 1960, Letter 10, p. 27; Letter 26, p. 71; Letter 65, p. 145.

[8] *Ibid.*, Letter 74, p. 60; Letter 76, pp. 161 ff.

[9] Jones, *op. cit.*, Vol. I, pp. 176 f.

Since all of Freud's theories rested, admittedly, on his own penetrating, unending psychoanalysis of himself, and since sexuality was the focus of all his theories, certain paradoxes about his own sexuality seem pertinent. His writings, as many scholars have noted, give much more attention to infantile sexuality than to its mature expression: His chief biographer, Jones, pointed out that he was, even for those times, exceptionally chaste, puritanical and moralistic. In his own life, he was relatively uninterested in sex. There were only the adoring mother of his youth, at sixteen a romance that existed purely in fantasy with a girl named Gisele, and his engagement to Martha at twenty-six. The nine months when they both lived in Vienna were not too happy because she was, evidently, uneasy and afraid of him; but separated by a comfortable distance for four years, there was a "grande passion" of 900 love letters. After their marriage, the passion seems to have quickly disappeared, though his biographers note that he was too rigid a moralist to seek sexual satisfaction outside of marriage. The only woman on whom, as an adult, he ever focused the violent passions of love and hate of which he was capable was Martha, during the early years of their engagement. After that, such emotions were focused on men. As Jones, his respectful biographer, said: "Freud's deviation from the average in this respect, as well as his pronounced mental bisexuality, may well have influenced his theoretical views to some extent." [10]

Less reverent biographers, and even Jones himself, point out that when one considers Freud's theories in terms of his own life, one is reminded of the puritanical old maid who sees sex everywhere.[11] It is interesting to note that his main complaint about his docile hausfrau was that she was not "docile" enough—and yet, in interesting ambivalence, that she was not "at her ease" with him, that she was not able to be a "comrade-in-arms."

> But, as Freud was painfully to discover, she was not at heart docile and she had a firmness of character that did not readily lend itself to being molded. Her personality was fully developed and well integrated: it would well deserve the psychoanalyst's highest compliment of being "normal." [12]

---

[10] *Ibid.*, Vol. II, p. 422.

[11] *Ibid.*, Vol. I, p. 271:

His descriptions of sexual activities are so matter-of-fact that many readers have found them almost dry and totally lacking in warmth. From all I know of him, I should say that he displayed less than the average personal interest in what is often an absorbing topic. There was never any gusto or even savor in mentioning a sexual topic. . . . He always gave the impression of being an unusually chaste person—the word "puritanical" would not be out of place—and all we know of his early development confirms this conception.

[12] *Ibid.*, Vol. I, p. 102.

One gets a glimpse of Freud's "intention, never to be fulfilled, to mold her to his perfect image," when he wrote her that she must "become quite young, a sweetheart, only a week old, who will quickly lose every trace of tartness." But he then reproaches himself:

> The loved one is not to become a toy doll, but a good comrade who still has a sensible word left when the strict master has come to the end of his wisdom. And I have been trying to smash her frankness so that she should reserve opinion until she is sure of mine.[13]

As Jones pointed out, Freud was pained when she did not meet his chief test—"complete identification with himself, his opinions, his feelings, and his intentions. She was not really his unless he could perceive his 'stamp' on her." Freud "even admitted that it was boring if one could find nothing in the other person to put right." And he stresses again that Freud's love "could be set free and displayed only under very favorable conditions. . . . Martha was probably afraid of her masterful lover and she would commonly take refuge in silence." [14]

So, he eventually wrote her, "I renounce what I demanded. I do not need a comrade-in-arms, such as I hoped to make you into. I am strong enough to fight alone. . . . You remain for me a precious sweet, loved one." [15] Thus evidently ended "the only time in his life when such emotions [love and hate] centered on a woman." [16]

The marriage was conventional, but without that passion. As Jones described it:

> There can have been few more successful marriages. Martha certainly made an excellent wife and mother. She was an admirable manager—the rare kind of woman who could keep servants indefinitely—but she was never the kind of Hausfrau who put things before people. Her husband's comfort and convenience always ranked first. . . . It was not to be expected that she should follow the roaming flights of his imagination any more than most of the world could.[17]

She was as devoted to his physical needs as the most doting Jewish mother, organizing each meal on a rigid schedule to fit the convenience of "der Papa." But she never dreamed of sharing his life as an equal. Nor did Freud consider her a fit guardian for their children, especially

---

[13] *Ibid.*, Vol. I, pp. 110 ff.
[14] *Ibid.*, Vol. I, p. 124.
[15] *Ibid.*, Vol. I, p. 127.
[16] *Ibid.*, Vol. I, p. 138.
[17] *Ibid.*, Vol. I, p. 151.

of their education, in case of his death. He himself recalls a dream in which he forgets to call for her at the theater. His associations "imply that forgetting may be permissible in unimportant matters." [18]

That limitless subservience of woman taken for granted by Freud's culture, the very lack of opportunity for independent action or personal identity, seems often to have generated that uneasiness and inhibition in the wife, and that irritation in the husband, which characterized Freud's marriage. As Jones summed it up, Freud's attitude toward women "could probably be called rather old-fashioned, and it would be easy to ascribe this to his social environment and the period in which he grew up rather than to any personal factors."

> Whatever his intellectual opinions may have been in the matter, there are many indications in his writing and correspondence of his emotional attitude. It would certainly be going too far to say that he regarded the male sex as the lords of creation, for there was no tinge of arrogance or superiority in his nature, but it might perhaps be fair to describe his view of the female sex as having as their main function to be ministering angels to the needs and comforts of men. His letters and his love choice make it plain that he had only one type of sexual object in his mind, a gentle feminine one. . . .
>
> There is little doubt that Freud found the psychology of women more enigmatic than that of men. He said once to Marie Bonaparte: "The great question that has never been answered and which I have not yet been able to answer, despite my thirty years of research into the feminine soul, is, what does a woman want?" [19]

Jones also remarked:

> Freud was also interested in another type of woman, of a more intellectual and perhaps masculine cast. Such women several times played a part in his life, accessory to his men friends though of a finer caliber, but they had no erotic attraction for him.[20]

---

[18] Helen Walker Puner, *Freud, His Life and His Mind,* New York, 1947, p. 152.

[19] Jones, *op. cit.,* Vol. II, p. 121.

[20] *Ibid.,* Vol. I, pp. 301 ff. During the years Freud was germinating his sexual theory, before his own heroic self-analysis freed him from a passionate dependence on a series of men, his emotions were focused on a flamboyant nose-and-throat doctor named Fliess. This is one coincidence of history that was quite fateful for women. For Fliess had proposed, and obtained Freud's lifelong allegiance to, a fantastic "scientific theory" which reduced all phenomena of life and death to "bisexuality," expressed in mathematical terms through a periodic table based on the number 28, the female menstrual cycle. Freud looked forward to meetings with Fliess "as for the satisfying of hunger and thirst." He wrote him: "No one can replace the intercourse with a friend that a particular, perhaps feminine side of me, demands." Even after his own self-analysis, Freud still expected to die on the day predicted by Fliess' periodic table, in which everything could be figured out in terms of the fe-

These women included his sister-in-law, Minna Bernays, much more intelligent and independent than Martha, and later women analysts or adherents of the psychoanalytic movement: Marie Bonaparte, Joan Riviere, Lou Andreas-Salomé. There is no suspicion, however, from either idolators or hostile biographers that he ever sought sexual satisfaction outside his marriage. Thus it would seem that sex was completely divorced from his human passions, which he expressed throughout the productive later years of his long life in his thought and, to a lesser extent, in friendships with men and those women he considered his equals, and thus "masculine." He once said: "I always find it uncanny when I can't understand someone in terms of myself." [21]

Despite the importance of sex in Freud's theory, one gets from his words the impression that the sex act appeared degrading to him; if women themselves were so degraded, in the eyes of man, how could sex appear in any other light? That was not his theory, of course. To Freud, it was the idea of incest with mother or sister that makes man "regard the sex act as something degrading, which soils and contaminates not only the body." [22] In any event, the degradation of women was taken for granted by Freud—and is the key to his theory of femininity. The motive force of woman's personality, in Freud's theory, was her envy of the penis, which causes her to feel as much depreciated in her own eyes "as in the eyes of the boy, and later perhaps of the man," and leads, in normal femininity, to the wish for the penis of her husband, a wish that is never really fulfilled until she possesses a penis through giving birth to a son. In short, she is merely an "homme manqué," a man with something missing. As the eminent psychoanalyst Clara Thompson put it:

> Freud never became free from the Victorian attitude toward women. He accepted as an inevitable part of the fate of being a woman the limitation of outlook and life of the Victorian era. . . . The castration complex and penis envy concepts, two of the most basic ideas in his whole thinking, are postulated on the assumption that women are biologically inferior to men. [23]

What did Freud mean by the concept of penis envy? For even those who realize that Freud could not escape his culture do not question that he reported truly what he observed within it. Freud found the phenomenon he called penis envy so unanimous, in middle-class women

---

male number 28, or the male 23, which was derived from the end of one female menstrual period to the beginning of the next.

[21] *Ibid.*, Vol. I, p. 320.

[22] Sigmund Freud, "Degradation in Erotic Life," in *The Collected Papers of Sigmund Freud*, Vol. IV.

[23] Thompson, *op. cit.*, p. 133.

in Vienna, in that Victorian time, that he based his whole theory of femininity on it. He said, in a lecture on "The Psychology of Women":

> In the boy the castration-complex is formed after he has learned from the sight of the female genitals that the sexual organ which he prizes so highly is not a necessary part of every woman's body . . . and thenceforward he comes under the influence of castration-anxiety, which supplies the strongest motive force for his further development. The castration-complex in the girl, as well, is started by the sight of the genital organs of the other sex. She immediately notices the difference and, it must be admitted, its significance. She feels herself at a great disadvantage, and often declares that she would like to have something like that too and falls a victim to penis envy, which leaves ineradicable traces on her development and character-formation, and even in the most favorable instances, is not overcome without a great expenditure of mental energy. That the girl recognizes the fact that she lacks a penis does not mean that she accepts its absence lightly. On the contrary, she clings for a long time to the desire to get something like it, and believes in that possibility for an extraordinary number of years; and even at a time when her knowledge of reality has long since led her to abandon the fulfillment of this desire as being quite unattainable, analysis proves that it still persists in the unconscious, and retains a considerable charge of energy. The desire after all to obtain the penis for which she so much longs may even contribute to the motives that impel a grown-up woman to come to analysis, and what she quite reasonably expects to get from analysis, such as the capacity to pursue an intellectual career, can often be recognized as a sublimated modification of this repressed wish.[24]

"The discovery of her castration is a turning-point in the life of the girl," Freud went on to say. "She is wounded in her self-love by the unfavorable comparison with the boy, who is so much better equipped." Her mother, and all women, are depreciated in her own eyes, as they are depreciated for the same reason in the eyes of man. This either leads to complete sexual inhibition and neurosis, or to a "masculinity complex" in which she refuses to give up "phallic" activity (that is, "activity such as is usually characteristic of the male") or to "normal femininity," in which the girl's own impulses to activity are repressed, and she turns to her father in her wish for the penis. "The feminine situation is, however, only established when the wish for the penis is replaced by the wish for a child—the child taking the place of the penis." When she played with dolls, this "was not really an expression of her femininity," since this was activity, not passivity. The "strongest feminine wish," the desire for a penis, finds real fulfillment only

---

[24] Sigmund Freud, "The Psychology of Women," in *New Introductory Lectures on Psychoanalysis*, tr. by W. J. H. Sprott, New York, 1933, pp. 170 f.

if the child is a little boy, who brings the longed-for penis with him.
. . . The mother can transfer to her son all the ambition she has
had to suppress in herself, and she can hope to get from him the
satisfaction of all that has remained to her of her masculinity complex.[25]

But her inherent deficiency, and the resultant penis envy, is so hard
to overcome that the woman's superego—her conscience, ideals—are
never as completely formed as a man's: "women have but little sense of
justice, and this is no doubt connected with the preponderance of envy
in their mental life." For the same reason, women's interests in society
are weaker than those of men, and "their capacity for the sublimation
of their instincts is less." Finally, Freud can not refrain from mentioning "an impression which one receives over and over again in analytical
work"—that not even psychoanalysis can do much for women, because
of the inherent deficiency of femininity.

A man of about thirty seems a youthful, and, in a sense, an in-
completely developed individual, of whom we expect that he will be
able to make good use of the possibilities of development, which
analysis lays open to him. But a woman of about the same age,
frequently staggers us by her psychological rigidity and unchange-
ability. . . . There are no paths open to her for further development; it is as though the whole process had been gone through
and remained unaccessible to influence for the future; as though, in
fact, the difficult development which leads to femininity had exhausted all the possibilities of the individual . . . even when we
are successful in removing the sufferings by solving her neurotic
conflict.[26]

What was he really reporting? If one interprets "penis envy" as other
Freudian concepts have been reinterpreted, in the light of our new
knowledge that what Freud believed to be biological was often a
cultural reaction, one sees simply that Victorian culture gave women
many reasons to envy men: the same conditions, in fact, that the feminists fought against. If a woman who was denied the freedom, the
status and the pleasures that men enjoyed wished secretly that she
could have these things, in the shorthand of the dream, she might
wish herself a man and see herself with that one thing which made men
unequivocally different—the penis. She would, of course, have to learn
to keep her envy, her anger, hidden: to play the child, the doll, the toy,
for her destiny depended on charming man. But underneath, it might
still fester, sickening her for love. If she secretly despised herself, and

---

[25] *Ibid.*, p. 182.
[26] *Ibid.*, p. 184.

envied man for all she was not, she might go through the motions of love, or even feel a slavish adoration, but would she be capable of free and joyous love? You cannot explain away woman's envy of man, or her contempt for herself, as mere refusal to accept her sexual deformity, unless you think that a woman, by nature, is a being inferior to man. Then, of course, her wish to be equal is neurotic.

It is recognized now that Freud never gave proper attention, even in man, to growth of the ego or self: "the impulse to master, control or come to self-fulfilling terms with the environment." [27] Analysts who have freed themselves from Freud's bias and joined other behavioral scientists in studying the human need to grow, are beginning to believe that this is the basic human need, and that interference with it, in any dimension, is the source of psychic trouble. The sexual is only one dimension of the human potential. Freud, it must be remembered, thought all neuroses were sexual in origin; he saw women only in terms of their sexual relationship with men. But in all those women in whom he saw sexual problems, there must have been very severe problems of blocked growth, growth short of full human identity—an immature, incomplete self. Society as it was then, by explicit denial of education and independence, prevented women from realizing their full potential, or from attaining those interests and ideals that might have stimulated their growth. Freud reported these deficiencies, but could only explain them as the toll of "penis envy." He saw women's envy of man *only* as sexual sickness. He saw that women who secretly hungered to be man's equal would not enjoy being his object; and in this, he seemed to be describing a fact. But when he dismissed woman's yearning for equality as "penis envy," was he not merely stating his own view that women could never really be man's equal, anymore than she could wear his penis?

Freud was not concerned with changing society, but in helping man, and woman, adjust to it. Thus he tells of a case of a middle-aged spinster whom he succeeded in freeing from a symptom-complex that prevented her from taking any part in life for fifteen years. Freed of these symptoms she "plunged into a whirl of activity in order to develop her talents, which were by no means small, and derive a little appreciation, enjoyment, and success from life before it was too late." But all her

---

[27] Thompson, *op. cit.*, pp. 12 f:
The war of 1914–18 further focused attention on ego drives. . . . Another idea came into analysis around this period . . . and that was that aggression as well as sex might be an important repressed impulse. . . . The puzzling problem was how to include it in the theory of instincts. . . . Eventually Freud solved this by his second instinct theory. Aggression found its place as part of the death instinct. It is interesting that normal self-assertion, i.e., the impulse to master, control or come to self-fulfilling terms with the environment, was not especially emphasized by Freud.

attempts ended when she saw that there was no place for her. Since she could no longer relapse into her neurotic symptoms, she began to have accidents; she sprained her ankle, her foot, her hand. When this also was analyzed, "instead of accidents, she contracted on the same occasions slight illnesses, such as catarrh, sore throat, influenzal conditions or rheumatic swellings, until at last, when she made up her mind to resign herself to inactivity, the whole business came to an end." [28]

Even if Freud and his contemporaries considered women inferior by God-given, irrevocable nature, science does not justify such a view today. That inferiority, we now know, was caused by their lack of education, their confinement to the home. Today, when women's equal intelligence has been proved by science, when their equal capacity in every sphere except sheer muscular strength has been demonstrated, a theory explicitly based on woman's natural inferiority would seem as ridiculous as it is hypocritical. But that remains the basis of Freud's theory of women, despite the mask of timeless sexual truth which disguises its elaborations today.

Because Freud's followers could only see woman in the image defined by Freud—inferior, childish, helpless, with no possibility of happiness unless she adjusted to being man's passive object—they wanted to help women get rid of their suppressed envy, their neurotic desire to be equal. They wanted to help women find sexual fulfillment as women, by affirming their natural inferiority.

But society, which defined that inferiority, had changed drastically by the time Freud's followers transposed bodily to twentieth-century America the causes as well as the cures of the condition Freud called penis envy. In the light of our new knowledge of cultural processes and of human growth, one would assume that women who grew up with the rights and freedom and education that Victorian women were denied would be different from the women Freud tried to cure. One would assume that they would have much less reason to envy man. But Freud was interpreted to American woman in such curiously literal terms that the concept of penis envy acquired a mystical life of its own, as if it existed quite independent of the women in whom it had been observed. It was as if Freud's Victorian image of woman became more real than the twentieth-century women to whom it was applied. Freud's theory of femininity was seized in America with such literalness that women today were considered no different than Victorian women. The real injustices life held for women a century ago, compared to men, were dismissed as mere rationalizations of penis envy. And the real opportunities life offered to women now, compared to women then, were forbidden in the name of penis envy.

---

[28] Sigmund Freud, "Anxiety and Instinctual Life," in *New Introductory Lectures on Psychoanalysis*, p. 149.

The literal application of Freudian theory can be seen in these passages from *Modern Woman: The Lost Sex*, by the psychoanalyst Marynia Farnham and the sociologist Ferdinand Lundberg, which was paraphrased ad nauseam in the magazines and in marriage courses, until most of its statements became a part of the conventional, accepted truth of our time. Equating feminism with penis envy, they stated categorically:

> Feminism, despite the external validity of its political program and most (not all) of its social program, was at its core a deep illness. . . . The dominant direction of feminine training and development today . . . discourages just those traits necessary to the attainment of sexual pleasure: receptivity and passiveness, a willingness to accept dependence without fear or resentment, with a deep inwardness and readiness for the final goal of sexual life—impregnation. . . .
>
> It is not in the capacity of the female organism to attain feelings of well-being by the route of male achievement. . . . It was the error of the feminists that they attempted to put women on the essentially male road of exploit, off the female road of nurture. . . .
>
> The psychosocial rule that begins to take form, then, is this: the more educated the woman is, the greater chance there is of sexual disorder, more or less severe. The greater the disordered sexuality in a given group of women, the fewer children do they have. . . . Fate has granted them the boon importuned by Lady Macbeth; they have been unsexed, not only in the matter of giving birth, but in their feelings of pleasure.[29]

Thus Freud's popularizers embedded his core of unrecognized traditional prejudice against women ever deeper in pseudoscientific cement. Freud was well aware of his own tendency to build an enormous body of deductions from a single fact—a fertile and creative method, but a two-edged sword, if the significance of that single fact was misinterpreted. Freud wrote Jung in 1909:

> Your surmise that after my departure my errors might be adored as holy relics amused me enormously, but I don't believe it. On the contrary, I think that my followers will hasten to demolish as swiftly as possible everything that is not safe and sound in what I leave behind.[30]

But on the subject of women, Freud's followers not only compounded his errors, but in their tortuous attempt to fit their observations of real

---

[29] Marynia Farnham and Ferdinand Lundberg, *Modern Woman: The Lost Sex*, New York and London, 1947, pp. 142 ff.

[30] Ernest Jones, *op. cit.*, Vol. II, p. 446.

women into his theoretical framework, closed questions that he himself had left open. Thus, for instance, Helene Deutsch, whose definitive two-volume *The Psychology of Woman—A Psychoanalytical Interpretation* appeared in 1944, is not able to trace all women's troubles to penis envy as such. So she does what even Freud found unwise, and equates "femininity" with "passivity," and "masculinity" with "activity," not only in the sexual sphere, but in all spheres of life.

> While fully recognizing that woman's position is subjected to external influence, I venture to say that the fundamental identities "feminine-passive" and "masculine-active" assert themselves in all known cultures and races, in various forms and various quantitative proportions.
> Very often a woman resists this characteristic given her by nature and in spite of certain advantages she derives from it, displays many modes of behavior that suggest that she is not entirely content with her own constitution . . . the expression of this dissatisfaction, combined with attempts to remedy it, result in woman's "masculinity complex." [31]

The "masculinity complex," as Dr. Deutsch refines it, stems directly from the "female castration complex." Thus, anatomy is still destiny, woman is still an "homme manqué." Of course, Dr. Deutsch mentions in passing that "With regard to the girl, however, the environment exerts an inhibiting influence as regards both her aggressions and her activity." So, penis envy, deficient female anatomy, and society "all seem to work together to produce femininity." [32]

"Normal" femininity is achieved, however, only insofar as the woman finally renounces all active goals of her own, all her own "originality," to identify and fulfill herself through the activities and goals of husband, or son. This process can be sublimated in nonsexual ways—as, for instance, the woman who does the basic research for her male superior's discoveries. The daughter who devotes her life to her father is also making a satisfactory feminine "sublimation." Only activity of her own or originality, on a basis of equality, deserves the opprobrium of "masculinity complex." This brilliant feminine follower of Freud states categorically that the women who by 1944 in America had achieved eminence by activity of their own in various fields had done so at the expense of their feminine fulfillment. She will mention no names, but they all suffer from the "masculinity complex."

How could a girl or woman who was not a psychoanalyst discount such ominous pronouncements, which, in the forties, suddenly began to pour out from all the oracles of sophisticated thought?

---

[31] Helene Deutsch, *The Psychology of Women—A Psychoanalytical Interpretation*, New York, 1944, Vol. I, pp. 224 ff.

[32] *Ibid.*, Vol. I, pp. 251 ff.

It would be ridiculous to suggest that the way Freudian theories were used to brainwash two generations of educated American women was part of a psychoanalytic conspiracy. It was done by well-meaning popularizers and inadvertent distorters; by orthodox converts and bandwagon faddists; by those who suffered and those who cured and those who turned suffering to profit; and, above all, by a congruence of forces and needs peculiar to the American people at that particular time. In fact, the literal acceptance in the American culture of Freud's theory of feminine fulfillment was in tragicomic contrast to the personal struggle of many American psychoanalysts to reconcile what they saw in their women patients with Freudian theory. The theory said women should be able to fulfill themselves as wives and mothers if only they could be analyzed out of their "masculine strivings," their "penis envy." But it wasn't as easy as that. "I don't know why American women are so dissatisfied," a Westchester analyst insisted. "Penis envy seems so difficult to eradicate in American women, somehow."

A New York analyst, one of the last trained at Freud's own Psychoanalytic Institute in Vienna, told me:

> For twenty years now in analyzing American women, I have found myself again and again in the position of having to superimpose Freud's theory of femininity on the psychic life of my patients in a way that I was not willing to do. I have come to the conclusion that penis envy simply does not exist. I have seen women who are completely expressive, sexually, vaginally, and yet who are not mature, integrated, fulfilled. I had a woman patient on the couch for nearly two years before I could face her real problem—that it was not enough for her to be just a housewife and mother. One day she had a dream that she was teaching a class. I could not dismiss the powerful yearning of this housewife's dream as penis envy. It was the expression of her own need for mature self-fulfillment. I told her: "I can't analyze this dream away. You must do something about it."

This same man teaches the young analysts in his postgraduate clinicum at a leading Eastern university: "If the patient doesn't fit the book, throw away the book, and listen to the patient."

But many analysts threw the book *at* their patients and Freudian theories became accepted fact even among women who never lay down on an analyst's couch, but only knew what they read or heard. To this day, it has not penetrated to the popular culture that the pervasive growing frustration of American women may not be a matter of feminine sexuality. Some analysts, it is true, modified the theories drastically to fit their patients, or even discarded them altogether—but these facts never permeated the public awareness. Freud was accepted so quickly and completely at the end of the forties that for over a decade no one even questioned the race of the educated American woman back to the home. When questions finally had to be asked because something was obviously going wrong, they were asked so completely within the Freudian framework that only one answer was possible: education, freedom, rights are wrong for women.

The uncritical acceptance of Freudian doctrine in America was caused, at least in part, by the very relief it provided from uncomfortable questions about objective realities. After the depression, after the war, Freudian psychology became much more than a science of human behavior, a therapy for the suffering. It became an all-embracing American ideology, a new religion. It filled the vacuum of thought and purpose that existed for many for whom God, or flag, or bank account were no longer sufficient—and yet who were tired of feeling responsible for lynchings and concentration camps and the starving children of India and Africa. It provided a convenient escape from the atom bomb, McCarthy, all the disconcerting problems that might spoil the taste of steaks, and cars and color television and backyard swimming pools. It gave us permission to suppress the troubling questions of the larger world and pursue our own personal pleasures. And if the new psychological religion—which made a virtue of sex, removed all sin from private vice, and cast suspicion on high aspirations of the mind and spirit—had a more devastating personal effect on women than men, nobody planned it that way.

Psychology, long preoccupied with its own scientific inferiority complex, long obsessed with neat little laboratory experiments that gave the illusion of reducing human complexity to the simple measurable behavior of rats in a maze, was transformed into a life-giving crusade that swept across the barren fields of American thought. Freud was the spiritual leader, his theories were the bible. And how exciting and real and important it all was. Its mysterious complexity was part of its charm to bored Americans. And if some of it remained impenetrably mystifying, who would admit that he could not understand it? America became the center of the psychoanalytic movement, as Freudian, Jungian and Adlerian analysts fled from Vienna and Berlin and new schools flourished on the multiplying neuroses, and dollars, of Americans.

But the practice of psychoanalysis as a therapy was not primarily responsible for the feminine mystique. It was the creation of writers and editors in the mass media, ad-agency motivation researchers, and behind them the popularizers and translators of Freudian thought in the colleges and universities. Freudian and pseudo-Freudian theories settled everywhere, like fine volcanic ash. Sociology, anthropology, education, even the study of history and literature became permeated and transfigured by Freudian thought. The most zealous missionaries of the feminine mystique were the functionalists, who seized hasty gulps of predigested Freud to start their new departments of "Marriage and Family Life Education." The functional courses in marriage taught American college girls how to "play the role" of woman—the old role became a new science. Related movements outside the colleges—parent education, child-study groups, prenatal maternity study groups and mental-health education—spread the new psychological superego throughout the land, replacing bridge and canasta as an entertainment for educated young wives. And this Freudian superego worked for growing numbers of young and impressionable American women as Freud said the superego works—to perpetuate the past.

> Mankind never lives completely in the present; the ideologies of the superego perpetuate the past, the traditions of the race and the people, which yield but slowly to the influence of the present and to new developments, and, so long as they work through the superego, play an important part in man's life, quite independently of economic conditions.[33]

The feminine mystique, elevated by Freudian theory into a scientific religion, sounded a single, overprotective, life-restricting, future-denying note for women. Girls who grew up playing baseball, baby-sitting, mastering geometry—almost independent enough, almost resourceful enough, to meet the problems of the fission-fusion era—were told by the most advanced thinkers of our time to go back and live their lives as if they were Noras, restricted to the doll's house by Victorian prejudice. And their own respect and awe for the authority of science—anthropology, sociology, psychology share that authority now—kept them from questioning the feminine mystique.

QUESTIONS

1. What does Betty Friedan mean by the phrase "sexual solipsism"?

2. In what sense does Freudian psychology carry a built-in defense against attack on its theories?

3. How does Friedan account for Victorian women's envy of men?

4. Why, according to the author, did Freudian psychology become so widespread in the United States? Can you suggest other possible reasons for this phenomenon?

5. What evidence does Friedan give that Freud's theories on female psychology led women to repudiate their own experience? Do you think the author's evidence successfully supports her belief? Do women today tend toward this repudiation or do you perceive a change in their behavior?

---

[33] Sigmund Freud, "The Anatomy of the Mental Personality," in *New York Introductory Lectures on Psychoanalysis*, p. 96.

Naomi Weisstein

Naomi Weisstein, an assistant professor of psychology at Loyola University in Chicago, is a member of the women's liberation movement. Her essay reprinted below is an example of the new feminist scholarship produced since Betty Friedan's angry analysis of the Freudian psychology cult. In her selection she goes beyond Friedan to challenge the conclusions that a whole generation of clinical and academic psychologists made regarding the female psyche.

Psychology Constructs the Female, or the Fantasy Life of the Male Psychologist

It is an implicit assumption that the area of psychology which concerns itself with personality has the onerous but necessary task of describing the limits of human possibility. Thus when we are about to consider the liberation of women, we naturally look to psychology to tell us what "true" liberation would mean: what would give women the freedom to fulfill their own intrinsic natures. Psychologists have set

---

This is a revised and expanded version of "Kinder, Kuche, Kirche as Scientific Law: Psychology Constructs the Female," New England Free Press, Boston, Mass., 1968. Reprinted by permission of Naomi Weisstein.

NOTE: Sources mentioned in the text are alphabetically listed in full at the end of this selection.

about describing the true natures of women with a certainty and a sense of their own infallibility rarely found in the secular world. Bruno Bettelheim, of the University of Chicago, tells us (1965) that "We must start with the realization that, as much as women want to be good scientists or engineers, they want first and foremost to be womanly companions of men and to be mothers." Erik Erikson of Harvard University (1964), upon noting that young women often ask whether they can "have an identity before they know whom they will marry, and for whom they will make a home," explains somewhat elegiacally that "Much of a young woman's identity is already defined in her kind of attractiveness and in the selectivity of her search for the man (or men) by whom she wishes to be sought. . . ." Mature womanly fulfillment, for Erikson, rests on the fact that a woman's ". . . somatic design harbors an 'inner space' destined to bear the offspring of chosen men, and with it, a biological, psychological, and ethical commitment to take care of human infancy." Some psychiatrists even see the acceptance of woman's role by women as a solution to societal problems. "Woman is nurturance . . . ," writes Joseph Rheingold (1964), a psychiatrist at Harvard Medical School,

> . . . anatomy decrees the life of a woman . . . when women grow up without dread of their biological functions and without subversion by feminist doctrine, and therefore enter upon motherhood with a sense of fulfillment and altruistic sentiment, we shall attain the goal of a good life and a secure world in which to live it. (p. 714)

These views from men who are assumed to be experts reflect, in a surprisingly transparent way, the cultural consensus. They not only assert that a woman is defined by her ability to attract men, they see no alternative definitions. They think that the definition of a woman in terms of a man is the way it should be; and they back it up with psychosexual incantation and biological ritual curses. A woman has an identity if she is attractive enough to obtain a man, and thus, a home; for this will allow her to set about her life's task of "joyful altruism and nurturance."

Business certainly does not disagree. If views such as Bettelheim's and Erikson's do indeed have something to do with real liberation for women, then seldom in human history has so much money and effort been spent on helping a group of people realize their true potential. Clothing, cosmetics, home furnishings, are multi-million dollar businesses: if you don't like investing in firms that make weaponry and flaming gasoline, then there's a lot of cash in "inner space." Sheet and pillowcase manufacturers are concerned to fill this inner space:

> Mother, for a while this morning, I thought I wasn't cut out for married life. Hank was late for work and forgot his apricot juice and

walked out without kissing me, and when I was all alone I started crying. But then the postman came with the sheets and towels you sent, that look like big bandana handkerchiefs, and you know what I thought? That those big red and blue handkerchiefs, are for girls like me to dry their tears on so they can get busy and do what a housewife has to do. Throw open the windows and start getting the house ready, and the dinner, maybe clean the silver and put new geraniums in the box. *Everything to be ready for him when he walks through that door.* (Fieldcrest 1966; emphasis added.)

Of course, it is not only the sheet and pillowcase manufacturers, the cosmetics industry, the home furnishing salesmen who profit from and make use of the cultural definitions of man and woman. The example above is blatantly and overtly pitched to a particular kind of sexist stereotype: the child nymph. But almost all aspects of the media are normative, that is, they have to do with the ways in which beautiful people, or just folks, or ordinary Americans, or extraordinary Americans should live their lives. They define the possible; and the possibilities are usually in terms of what is male and what is female. Men and women alike are waiting for Hank, the Silva Thins man, to walk back through that door.

It is interesting but limited exercise to show that psychologists and psychiatrists embrace these sexist norms of our culture, that they do not see beyond the most superficial and stultifying media conceptions of female nature, and that their ideas of female nature serve industry and commerce so well. Just because it's good for business doesn't mean it's wrong. What I will show is that it *is wrong*; that there isn't the tiniest shred of evidence that these fantasies of servitude and childish dependence have anything to do with women's true potential; that the idea of the nature of human possibility which rests on the accidents of individual development of genitalia, on what is possible today because of what happened yesterday, on the fundamentalist myth of sex organ causality, has strangled and deflected psychology so that it is relatively useless in describing, explaining or predicting humans and their behavior. It then goes without saying that present psychology is less than worthless in contributing to a vision which could truly liberate—men as well as women.

The central argument of my paper, then, is this. Psychology has nothing to say about what women are really like, what they need and what they want, essentially because psychology does not know. I want to stress that this failure is not limited to women; rather, the kind of psychology which has addressed itself to how people act and who they are has failed to understand, in the first place, why people act the way they do, and certainly failed to understand what might make them act differently.

The kind of psychology which has addressed itself to these questions divides into two professional areas: academic personality research, and clinical psychology and psychiatry. The basic reason for failure is the same in both these areas: the central assumption for most psychologists of human personality has been that human behavior rests on an individual and inner dynamic, perhaps fixed in infancy, perhaps fixed by genitalia, perhaps simply arranged in a rather immovable cognitive network. But this assumption is rapidly losing ground as personality psychologists fail again and again to get consistency in the assumed personalities of their subjects (Block, 1968). Meanwhile, the evidence is collecting that what a person does and who he believes himself to be, will in general be a function of what people around him expect him to be, and what the overall situation in which he is acting implies that he is. Compared to the influence of the social context within which a person lives, his or her history and "traits," as well as biological makeup, may simply be random variations, "noise" superimposed on the true signal which can predict behavior.

Some academic personality psychologists are at least looking at the counter evidence and questioning their theories; no such corrective is occurring in clinical psychology and psychiatry. Freudians and neo-Freudians, Adlerians and neo-Adlerians, classicists and swingers, clinicians and psychiatrists, simply refuse to look at the evidence against their theory and practice. And they support their theory and their practice with stuff so transparently biased as to have absolutely no standing as empirical evidence.

To summarize: the first reason for psychology's failure to understand what people are and how they act is that psychology has looked for inner traits when it should have been looking for social context; the second reason for psychology's failure is that the theoreticians of personality have generally been clinicians and psychiatrists, and they have never considered it necessary to have evidence in support of their theories.

Theory Without Evidence

Let us turn to this latter cause of failure first: the acceptance by psychiatrists and clinical psychologists of theory without evidence. If we inspect the literature of personality, it is immediately obvious that the bulk of it is written by clinicians and psychiatrists, and that the major support for their theories is "years of intensive clinical experience." This is a tradition started by Freud. His "insights" occurred during the course of his work with his patients. Now there is nothing wrong with such an approach to theory *formulation*; a person is free to make up theories with any inspiration which works: divine revelation, intensive clinical practice, a random numbers table. But he is not free to claim any validity for his theory until it has been tested and confirmed. But theories are treated in no such tentative way in ordinary clinical practice. Consider

Freud. What he thought constituted evidence violated the most minimal conditions of scientific rigor. In *The Sexual Enlightenment of Children* (1963), the classic document which is supposed to demonstrate empirically the existence of a castration complex and its connection to a phobia, Freud based his analysis on the reports of the father of the little boy, himself in therapy, and a devotee of Freudian theory. I really don't have to comment further on the contamination in this kind of evidence. It is remarkable that only recently has Freud's classic theory on the sexuality of women—the notion of the double orgasm—been actually tested physiologically and found just plain wrong. Now those who claim that fifty years of psychoanalytic experience constitute evidence enough of the essential truths of Freud's theory should ponder the robust health of the double orgasm. Did women, until Masters and Johnson (1966), believe they were having two different kinds of orgasm? Did their psychiatrists cow them into reporting something that was not true? If so, were there other things they reported that were also not true? Did psychiatrists ever learn anything different than their theories had led them to believe? If clinical experience means anything at all, surely we should have been done with the double orgasm myth long before the Masters and Johnson studies.

But certainly, you may object, "years of intensive clinical experience" is the only reliable measure in a discipline which rests for its findings on insight, sensitivity, and intuition. The problem with insight, sensitivity, and intuition, is that they can confirm for all time the biases that one started out with. People used to be absolutely convinced of their ability to tell which of their number were engaging in witchcraft. All it required was some sensitivity to the workings of the devil.

Years of intensive clinical experience is not the same thing as empirical evidence. The first thing an experimenter learns in any kind of experiment which involves humans is the concept of the "double blind." The term is taken from medical experiments, where one group is given a drug which is presumably supposed to change behavior in a certain way, and a control group is given a placebo. If the observers or the subjects know which group took which drug, the result invariably comes out on the positive side for the new drug. Only when it is not known which subject took which pill, is validity remotely approximated. In addition, with judgments of human behavior, it is so difficult to precisely tie down just what behavior is going on, let alone what behavior should be expected, that one must test again and again the reliability of judgments. How many judges, blind, will agree in their observations? Can they replicate their own judgments at some later time? When, in actual practice, these judgment criteria are tested for clinical judgments, then we find that the judges cannot judge reliably, nor can they judge consistently: they do no better than chance in identifying which of a certain set of stories were written by men and which by women; which of a whole battery of clinical test results are the products of homosexuals and which are the products of heterosexuals (Hooker, 1957), and which, of a battery of clinical test results and interviews (where questions are asked such as "Do you have delusions?" Little and Schneidman, 1959) are products of psychotics, neurotics, psychosomatics, or normals. Lest this summary escape your notice, let me stress the implications of these findings. The ability of judges, chosen for their clinical expertise, to distinguish male heterosexuals from male homosexuals on the basis of three widely used clinical projective tests—the Rorschach, the TAT, and the MAP—was *no better than chance*. The reason this is such devastating news, of course, is that sexuality is supposed to be of fundamental importance in the deep dynamic of personality; if what is considered gross sexual deviance cannot be caught, then what are psychologists talking about when they, for example, claim that at the basis of paranoid psychosis is "latent homosexual panic"? They can't even identify what homosexual anything is, let alone "latent homosexual panic." [1] More frightening, expert clinicians cannot be consistent on what diagnostic category to assign to a person, again on the basis of both tests and interviews; a number of normals in the Little and Schneidman study were described as psychotic, in such categories as "schizophrenic with homosexual tendencies" or "schizoid character with depressive trends." But most disheartening, when the judges were asked to rejudge the test protocols some weeks later, their diagnoses of the same subjects on the basis of the same protocol differed markedly from their initial judgments. It is obvious that even simple descriptive conventions in clinical psychology cannot be consistently applied; that these descriptive conventions have any explanatory significance is therefore, of course, out of the question.

As a graduate student at Harvard some years ago, I was a member of a seminar which was asked to identify which of two piles of a clinical test, the TAT, had been written by males and which by females. Only four students out of twenty identified the piles correctly, and this was after one and a half months of intensively studying the differences between men and women. Since this result is below chance—that is, this result would occur by chance about four out of a thousand times—we may conclude that there is finally a consistency here; students are judging knowledgeably within the context of psychological teaching about the

---

[1] It should be noted that psychologists have been as quick to assert absolute truths about the nature of homosexuality as they have about the nature of women. The arguments presented in this paper apply equally to the nature of homosexuality; psychologists know nothing about it; there is no more evidence for the "naturalness" of heterosexuality than for the "naturalness" of homosexuality. Psychology has functioned as a pseudo-scientific buttress for our cultural sex-role notions, that is, as a buttress for patriarchal ideology and patriarchal social organization: women's liberation and gay liberation fight against a common victimization.

differences between men and women; the teachings themselves are simply erroneous.

You may argue that the theory may be scientifically "unsound" but at least it cures people. There is no evidence that it does. In 1952, Eysenck reported the results of what is called an "outcome of therapy" study of neurotics which showed that, of the patients who received psychoanalysis the improvement rate was 44%; of the patients who received psychotherapy the improvement rate was 64%; and of the patients who received no treatment at all the improvement rate was 72%. These findings have never been refuted; subsequently, later studies have confirmed the negative results of the Eysenck study. (Barron and Leary, 1955; Bergin, 1963; Cartwright and Vogel, 1960; Truax, 1963; Powers and Witmer, 1951). How can good clinicians and psychiatrists, then, in all good conscience, continue to practice? Largely by ignoring these results and being careful not to do outcome-of-therapy studies. The attitude is nicely summarized by Rotter (1960) (quoted in Astin, 1961): "Research studies in psychotherapy tend to be concerned with psychotherapeutic procedure and less with outcome . . . to some extent, it reflects an interest in the psychotherapy situation as a kind of personality laboratory." Some laboratory.

The Social Context

Thus, since clinical experience and tools can be shown to be worse than useless when tested for consistency, efficacy, agreement, and reliability, we can safely conclude that theories of a clinical nature advanced about women are also worse than useless. I want to turn now to the second major point in my paper, which is that, even when psychological theory is constructed so that it may be tested, and rigorous standards of evidence are used, it has become increasingly clear that in order to understand why people do what they do, and certainly in order to change what people do, psychologists must turn away from the theory of the causal nature of the inner dynamic and look to the social context within which individuals live.

Before examining the relevance of this approach for the question of women, let me first sketch the groundwork for this assertion.

In the first place, it is clear (Block, 1968) that personality tests never yield consistent predictions; a rigid authoritarian on one measure will be an unauthoritarian on the next. But the reason for this inconsistency is only now becoming clear, and it seems overwhelmingly to have much more to do with the social situation in which the subject finds himself than with the subject himself.

In a series of brilliant experiments, Rosenthal and his co-workers (Rosenthal and Jacobson, 1968; Rosenthal, 1966) have shown that if one group of experimenters has one hypothesis about what they expect to find, and another group of experimenters has the opposite hypothesis, both groups will obtain results in accord with their hypotheses. The results obtained are not due to mishandling of data by biased experimenters; rather, somehow, the bias of the experimenter creates a changed environment in which subjects actually act differently. For instance, in one experiment, subjects were to assign numbers to pictures of men's faces, with high numbers representing the subject's judgment that the man in the picture was a successful person, and low numbers representing the subject's judgment that the man in the picture was an unsuccessful person. The experimenters read the same set of instructions to two groups of subjects, and were required to say nothing else than what was in the instructions. One group of experimenters was told that the subjects tended to rate the faces high; another group of experimenters was told that the subjects tended to rate the faces low. Each group of experimenters was instructed to follow precisely the same procedure: they were required to read to subjects a set of instructions, and to *say nothing else*. For the 375 subjects run, the results showed clearly that those subjects who performed the task with experimenters who expected high ratings gave high ratings, and those subjects who performed the task with experimenters who expected low ratings gave low ratings. How did this happen? The experimenters all used the same words; it was something in their conduct which made one group of subjects do one thing, and another group of subjects do another thing.

The concreteness of the changed conditions produced by expectation is a fact, a reality: even with animal subjects, in two separate studies (Rosenthal and Fode, 1960; Rosenthal and Lawson, 1961), those experimenters who were told that rats learning mazes had been especially bred for brightness obtained better learning from their rats than did experimenters believing their rats to have been bred for dullness. In a very recent study, Rosenthal and Jacobson (1968) extended their analysis to the natural classroom situation. Here, they tested a group of students and reported to the teachers that some among the students tested "showed great promise." Actually, the students so named had been selected on a random basis. Some time later, the experimenters retested the group of students: those students whose teachers had been told that they were "promising" showed real and dramatic increments in their IQ's as compared to the rest of the students. Something in the conduct of the teachers towards who the teachers believed to be the "bright" students, made those students brighter.

Thus, even in carefully controlled experiments, and with no outward or conscious difference in behavior, the hypotheses we start with will influence enormously the behavior of another organism. These studies are extremely important when assessing the validity of psychological studies of women. Since it is beyond doubt that most of us start with notions as to the nature of men and women, the validity of a number of observations of sex differences is questionable, even when these observations have been made under carefully controlled conditions. Second, and more important, the Rosenthal experiments point quite clearly to the influence of social expectation. In some extremely important ways, people are what you expect them to be or at least they behave as you expect them to behave. Thus, if women, according to Bettelheim, want first and foremost to be good wives and mothers, it is extremely likely that this is what Bruno Bettelheim, and the rest of society, want them to be.

There is another series of brilliant social psychological experiments which point to the overwhelming effect of social context. These are the obedience experiments of Stanley Milgram (1965) in which subjects are asked to obey the orders of unknown experimenters, orders which carry with them the distinct possibility that the subject is killing somebody.

In Milgram's experiments, a subject is told that he is administering a learning experiment, and that he is to deal out shocks each time the other "subject" (in reality, a confederate of the experimenter) answers incorrectly. The equipment appears to provide graduated shocks ranging upwards from 15 volts through 450 volts; for each of four consecutive voltages there are verbal descriptions such as "mild shock," "danger, severe shock," and, finally, for the 435 and 450 volt switches, a red XXX marked over the switches. Each time the stooge answers incorrectly the subject is supposed to increase the voltage. As the voltage increases, the stooge begins to cry in pain; he demands that the experiment stop; finally, he refuses to answer at all. When he stops responding, the experimenter instructs the subject to continue increasing the voltage; for each shock administered the stooge shrieks in agony. Under these conditions, about 62.5% of the subjects administered shock that they believed to be possibly lethal.

No tested individual differences between subjects predicted how many would continue to obey, and which would break off the experiment. When forty psychiatrists predicted how many of a group of 100 subjects would go on to give the lethal shock, their predictions were orders of magnitude below the actual percentages; most expected only one-tenth of one per cent of the subjects to obey to the end.

But even though *psychiatrists* have no idea how people will behave in this situation, and even though individual differences do not predict which subjects will obey and which will not, it is easy to predict when subjects will be obedient and when they will be defiant. All the experimenter has to do is change the social situation. In a variant of Milgram's experiment, two stooges were present in addition to the "victim"; these worked along with the subject in administering electric shocks. When these two stooges refused to go on with the experiment, only ten per cent of the subjects continued to the maximum voltage. This is critical for personality theory. It says that behavior is predicted from the social situation, not from the individual history.

Finally, an ingenious experiment by Schachter and Singer (1962) showed that subjects injected with adrenalin, which produces a state of physiological arousal in all but minor respects identical to that which occurs when subjects are extremely afraid, became euphoric when they were in a room with a stooge who was acting euphoric, and became extremely angry when they were placed in a room with a stooge who was acting extremely angry.

To summarize: If subjects under quite innocuous and non-coercive social conditions can be made to kill other subjects and under other types of social conditions will positively refuse to do so; if subjects can react to a state of physiological fear by becoming euphoric because there is somebody else around who is euphoric or angry because there is somebody else around who is angry; if students become intelligent because teachers expect them to be intelligent, and rats run mazes better because experimenters are told the rats are bright, then it is obvious that a study of human behavior requires, first and foremost, a study of the social contexts within which people move, the expectations as to how they will behave, and the authority which tells them who they are and what they are supposed to do.

Biologically Based Theories

Two theories of the nature of women, which come not from psychiatric and clinical tradition, but from biology, can be disposed of now with little difficulty. The first biological theory of sex differences argues that since females and males differ in their sex hormones, and sex hormones enter the brain (Hamburg and Lunde in Maccoby, 1966), there must be innate differences in "nature." But the only thing this argument tells us is that there are differences in physiological state. The problem is whether these differences are at all relevant to behavior. Recall that Schachter and Singer (1962) have shown that a particular physiological state can itself lead to a multiplicity of felt emotional states, and outward behavior, depending on the social situation.

The second theory is a form of biological reductionism: sex-role behavior in some primate species is described, and it is concluded that this is the "natural" behavior for humans. Putting aside the not insignificant problem of observer bias (for instance, Harlow, 1962, of the University of Wisconsin, after observing differences between male and female rhesus monkeys, quotes Lawrence Sterne to the effect that women are silly and trivial, and concludes that "men and women have differed in the past and they will differ in the future"), there are a number of problems with this approach.

The most general and serious problem is that there are no grounds to assume that anything primates do is necessary, natural, or desirable in humans, for the simple reason that humans are not non-humans. For instance, it is found that male chimpanzees placed alone with infants

will not "mother" them. Jumping from hard data to ideological speculation researchers conclude from this information that *human* females
are necessary for the safe growth of human infants. It would be as
reasonable to conclude, following this logic, that it is quite useless to
teach human infants to speak, since it has been tried with chimpanzees
and it does not work.

One strategy that has been used is to extrapolate from primate behavior to "innate" human preference by noticing certain trends in primate behavior as one moves phylogenetically closer to humans. But
there are great difficulties with this approach. When behaviors from
lower primates are directly opposite to those of higher primates, or to
those one expects of humans, they can be dismissed on evolutionary
grounds—higher primate and/or humans grew out of that kid stuff. On
the other hand, if the behavior of higher primates is counter to the behavior considered natural for humans, while the behavior of some lower
primate is considered the natural one for humans, the higher primate
behavior can be dismissed also, on the grounds that it has diverged from
an older, prototypical pattern. So either way, one can select those behaviors one wants to prove as innate for humans. In addition, one does
not know whether the sex-role behavior exhibited is dependent on the
phylogenetic rank, or on the environmental conditions (both physical
and social) under which different species live.

Is there then any value at all in primate observations as they relate to
human females and males? There is a value but it is limited: its function can be no more than to show some extant examples of diverse sex-
role behavior. It must be stressed, however, that this is an extremely
limited function. The extant behavior does not begin to suggest all the
possibilities, either for non-human primates or for humans. Bearing
these caveats in mind, it is nonetheless interesting that if one inspects
the limited set of existing non-human primate sex-role behaviors, one
finds, in fact, a much larger range of sex-role behavior than is commonly
believed to exist. "Biology" appears to limit very little; the fact that a
female gives birth does not mean, even in non-humans, that she necessarily cares for the infant (in marmosets, for instance, the male carries
the infant at all times except when the infant is feeding [Mitchell,
1969]); "natural" female and male behavior varies all the way from females who are much more aggressive and competitive than males (e.g.,
Tamarins, see Mitchell, 1969) and male "mothers" (e.g., Titi monkeys,
night monkeys, and marmosets, see Mitchell, 1969)[2] to submissive and
passive females and male antagonists (e.g., rhesus monkeys).

But even for the limited function that primate arguments serve, the
evidence has been misused. Invariably, only those primates have been

---

[2] All these are lower-order primates, which makes their behavior with reference to
humans unnatural, or more natural; take your choice.

282 Women and Psychology

cited which exhibit exactly the kind of behavior that the proponents of the biological basis of human female behavior wish were true for humans. Thus, baboons and rhesus monkeys are generally cited: males in these groups exhibit some of the most irritable and aggressive behavior found in primates, and if one wishes to argue that females are naturally passive and submissive, these groups provide vivid examples. There are abundant counter examples, such as those mentioned above (Mitchell, 1969); in fact, in general, a counter example can be found for every sex-role behavior cited, including, as mentioned in the case of marmosets, male "mothers."

But the presence of counter examples has not stopped florid and over-arching theories of the natural or biological basis of male privilege from proliferating. For instance, there have been a number of theories dealing with the innate incapacity in human males for monogamy. Here, as in most of this type of theorizing, baboons are a favorite example, probably because of their fantasy value: the family unit of the hamadryas baboon, for instance, consists of a highly constant pattern of one male and a number of females and their young. And again, the counter examples, such as the invariably monogamous gibbon, are ignored.

An extreme example of this maiming and selective truncation of the evidence in the service of a plea for the maintenance of male privilege is a recent book, *Men in Groups* (1969) by a man who calls himself Tiger.[3] The central claim of this book is that females are incapable of honorable collective action because they are incapable of "bonding" as in "male bonding." What is "male bonding"? Its surface definition is simple: ". . . a particular relationship between two or more males such that they react differently to members of their bonding units as compared to individuals outside of it" (pp. 19–20). If one deletes the word male, the definition, on its face, would seem to include all organisms that have any kind of social organization. But this is not what Tiger means. For instance, Tiger asserts that females are incapable of bonding; and this alleged incapacity indicates to Tiger that females should be restricted from public life. Why is bonding an exclusively male behavior? Because, says Tiger, it is seen in male primates. All male primates? No, very few male primates. Tiger cites two examples where male bonding is seen: rhesus monkeys and baboons. Surprise, surprise. But not even all baboons: as mentioned above, the hamadryas social organization consists of one-male units; so does that of the Gelada baboon (Mitchell, 1969). And the great apes do not go in for male bonding much either. The "male bond" is hardly a serious contribution to scholarship; one reviewer for *Science* has observed that the book ". . . shows basically more resemblance to a partisan political tract than to a work of

---

[3] Schwarz-Belkin (1914) claims that the name was originally *Mouse*, but this may be a reference to an earlier L. Tiger (putative).

objective social science," with male bonding being ". . . some kind of behavioral phlogiston" (Fried, 1969, p. 884).

In short, primate arguments have generally misused the evidence; primate studies themselves have, in any case, only the very limited function of describing some possible sex-role behavior; and at present, primate observations have been sufficiently limited so that even the range of possible sex-role behavior for non-human primates is not known. This range is not known since there is only minimal observation of what happens to behavior if the physical or social environment is changed. In one study (Itani, 1963), different troops of Japanese macaques were observed. Here, there appeared to be cultural difference; males in 3 out of the 18 troops observed differed in their amount of aggressiveness and infant-caring behavior. There could be no possibility of differential evolution here; the differences seemed largely transmitted by infant socialization. Thus, the very limited evidence points to some plasticity in the sex-role behavior of non-human primates; if we can figure out experiments which massively change the social organization of primate groups, it is possible that we might observe great changes in behavior. At present, however, we must conclude that, since non-human primates are too stupid to change their social conditions by themselves, the "innateness" and fixedness of their behavior is simply not known. Thus, even if there were some way, which there isn't, to settle on the behavior of a particular primate species as being the "natural" way for humans, we would not know whether or not this were simply some function of the present social organization of that species. And finally, once again it must be stressed that even if non-human primate behavior turned out to be relatively fixed, this would say little about our behavior. More immediate and relevant evidence, i.e. the evidence from social psychology, points to the enormous plasticity in human behavior, not only from one culture to the next, but from one experimental group to the next. One of the most salient features of human social organization is its variety; there are a number of cultures where there is at least a rough equality between men and women (Mead, 1949). In summary, primate arguments can tell us very little about our "innate" sex-role behavior; if they tell us anything at all, they tell us that there is no one biologically "natural" female or male behavior, and that sex-role behavior in non-human primates is much more varied than has previously been thought.

In brief, the uselessness of present psychology with regard to women is simply a special case of the general conclusion: one must understand social expectations about women if one is going to characterize the behavior of women.

How are women characterized in our culture, and in psychology? They are inconsistent, emotionally unstable, lacking in a strong conscience or superego, weaker, "nuturant" rather than productive, "intuitive" rather than intelligent, and, if they are at all "normal," suited to the home and the family. In short, the list adds up to a typical minority group stereotype of inferiority (Hacker, 1951): if they know their place, which is in the home, they are really quite lovable, happy, childlike, loving creatures. In a review of the intellectual differences between little boys and little girls, Eleanor Maccoby (1966) has shown that there are no intellectual differences until about high school, or, if there are, girls are slightly ahead of boys. At high school, girls began to do worse on a few intellectual tasks, such as arithmetic reasoning, and beyond high school, the achievement of women now measured in terms of productivity and accomplishment drops off even more rapidly. There are a number of other, non-intellectual tests which show sex differences; I chose the intellectual differences since it is seen clearly that women start becoming inferior. It is no use to talk about women being different but equal; all of the tests I can think of have a "good" outcome and a "bad" outcome. Women usually end up at the "bad" outcome. In light of social expectations about women, what is surprising is not that women end up where society expects they will; what is surprising is that little girls don't get the message that they are supposed to be stupid until high school; and what is even more remarkable is that some women resist this message even after high school, college, and graduate school.

My paper began with remarks on the task of the discovery of the limits of human potential. Psychologists must realize that it is they who are limiting discovery of human potential. They refuse to accept evidence, if they are clinical psychologists, or, if they are rigorous, they assume that people move in a context-free ether, with only their innate dispositions and their individual traits determining what they will do. Until psychologists begin to respect evidence, and until they begin looking at the social contexts within which people move psychology will have nothing of substance to offer in this task of discovery. I don't know what immutable differences exist between men and women apart from differences in their genitals; perhaps there are some other unchangeable differences; probably there are a number of irrelevant differences. But it is clear that until social expectations for men and women are equal, until we provide equal respect for both men and women, our answers to this question will simply reflect our prejudices.

REFERENCES

Astin, A. W., "The Functional Autonomy of Psychotherapy." *American Psychologist*, Vol. 16 (1961), 75–78.

Barron, F., and Leary, T., "Changes in Psychoneurotic Patients With and Without Psychotherapy." *Journal of Consulting and Clinical Psychology*, Vol. 19 (1955), 239–45.

Bergin, A. E., "The Effects of Psychotherapy: Negative Results Revisited." *Journal of Consulting and Clinical Psychology*, Vol. 10 (1963), 244–50.

Bettelheim, B., "The Commitment Required of a Woman Entering a Scientific Profession in Present Day American Society." *Woman and the Scientific Professions*. The MIT symposium on American Women in Science and Engineering, 1965.

Block, J., "Some Reasons for the Apparent Inconsistency of Personality." *Psychological Bulletin*, Vol. 70 (1968), 210–12.

Cartwright, R. D., and Vogel, J. L., "A Comparison of Changes in Psychoneurotic Patients During Matched Periods of Therapy and No-Therapy." *Journal of Consulting Psychology*, Vol. 24 (1960), 121–27.

Erikson, E., "Inner and Outer Space: Reflections on Womanhood." *Daedalus*, Vol. 93 (1964), 582–606.

Eysenck, H. J. "The Effects of Psychotherapy: An Evaluation." *Journal of Consulting and Clinical Psychology*, Vol. 16 (1952), 319–24.

Fieldcrest Mills, Inc. Advertisement in the *New Yorker*, 1965.

Freud, S., *The Sexual Enlightenment of Children*. New York: Collier Books, 1963.

Fried, M. H. "Mankind excluding Woman." *Science*, Vol. 165 (1969), 883–84. (Review of Tiger's *Men in Groups*.)

Goldstein, A. P., and Dean, S. J., *The Investigation of Psychotherapy: Commentaries and Readings*. New York: John Wiley, 1966.

Hacker, H. M., "Women As a Minority Group." *Social Forces*, Vol. 30 (1951), 60–69.

Hamburg, D. A., and Lunde, D. T., "Sex Hormones in the Development of Sex Differences in Human Behavior," *The Development of Sex Differences*. E. E. Maccoby, ed. Stanford, Calif.: Stanford University Press, 1966.

Harlow, H. F., "The Heterosexual Affectional System in Monkeys." *The American Psychologist*, Vol. 17 (1962), 1–9.

Hooker, E., "Male Homosexuality in the Rorschach." *Journal of Projective Techniques*, Vol. 21 (1957), 18–31.

Itani, J., "Paternal Care in the Wild Japanese Monkeys, *Macaca fuscata*," *Primate Social Behavior*. C. H. Southwick, ed. Princeton: Van Nostrand, 1963.

Little, K. B., and Schneidman, E. S., "Congruences Among Interpretations of Psychological and Anamestic Data." *Psychological Monographs*, Vol. 73 (1959), 1–42.

Maccoby, E. E., "Sex Differences in Intellectual Functioning." *The Development of Sex Differences*, E. E. Maccoby, ed. Stanford, Calif.: Stanford University Press, 1966, 25–55.

Masters, W. H., and Johnson, V. E., *Human Sexual Response*. Boston: Little, Brown, 1966.

Mead, M., *Male and Female: A Study of the Sexes in a Changing World*. New York: William Morrow, 1949.

Milgram, S., "Some Conditions of Obedience and Disobedience to Authority." *Human Relations*, Vol. 18 (1965a), 57–76.

Milgram, S., "Liberating Effects of Group Pressure." *Journal of Personality and Social Psychology*, Vol. 1 (1965b), 127–34.

Mitchell, G. D., "Paternalistic Behavior in Primates." *Psychological Bulletin*, Vol. 71 (1969), 399–417.

Powers, E., and Witmer, H., *An Experiment in the Prevention of Delinquency*. New York: Columbia University Press, 1951.

Rheingold, J., *The Fear of Being a Woman*. New York: Grune & Stratton, 1964.

Rosenthal, R., "On the Social Psychology of the Psychological Experiment: The Experimenter's Hypothesis As Unintended Determinant of Experimental Results." *American Scientist*, Vol. 51 (1963), 268–83.

———, *Experimenter Effects in Behavioral Research*. New York: Appleton-Century-Crofts, 1966.

Rosenthal, R., and Fode, K. L., *The Effect of Experimenter Bias on the Performance of the Albino Rat*. Unpublished manuscript, Harvard University, 1960.

Rosenthal, R., and Jacobson, L., *Pygmalion in the Classroom: Teacher Expectation and Pupil's Intellectual Development*. New York: Holt, Rinehart and Winston, 1968.

Rosenthal, R., and Lawson, R., *A Longitudinal Study of the Effects of Experimenter Bias on the Operant Learning of Laboratory Rats*. Unpublished manuscript, Harvard University, 1961.

Rotter, J. B., "Psychotherapy." *Annual Review of Psychology*, Vol. 11 (1960), 381–414.

Schachter, S., and Singer, J. E., "Cognitive, Social and Physiological Determinants of Emotional State." *Psychological Review*, Vol. 69 (1962), 379–99.

Schwarz-Belkin, M., "Les Fleurs de Mal." *Festschrift for Gordon Piltdown*. New York: Ponzi Press, 1914.

Tiger, L., *Men in Groups*. New York: Random House, 1969.

Truax, C. B., "Effective Ingredients in Psychotherapy: An Approach to Unraveling the Patient-Therapist Interaction." *Journal of Counseling Psychology*, Vol. 10 (1963), 256–63.

QUESTIONS

1. What does Naomi Weisstein mean by the "sexist norms of our culture"?

2. As Weisstein points out, Masters and Johnson disproved Freud's theory that women had two distinct kinds of orgasm. What other evidence does she give of the unreliability of psychological theory?

3. Do you think the social sciences can be successfully reformed by any means short of social revolution?

part 5
CONTEMPORARY VIEWS

Kate Millett

Kate Millett (b. 1934) is the main theoretician of the new feminist move-
ment. Sexual Politics (1970), from which a chapter is reprinted below, was
written as her doctoral dissertation for Columbia University and is a learned
analysis of the political relationship between men and women—a relation-
ship, she argues, based on male dominance and female submission. Miss
Millett traces sexual politics through history, psychology, anthropology, re-
ligion, and literature. She finds our society basically an oppressive one, in
which all human beings are socialized to strict and limiting sex roles, re-
gardless of their individual potential. Like John Stuart Mill, she regards the
family as the model for all political relationships in which one group domi-
nates another by birthright. Ultimately the politics of sex leads, in her view,
to the denigration of traits regarded as feminine, and to the glorification of
aggression and violence, which are considered virile traits.

Kate Millett's general theory of sexual politics and her criticism of male
chauvinism in Norman Mailer, D. H. Lawrence, and Henry Miller aroused
considerable controversy. Jonathan Yardley's review, from the liberal New
Republic, *and Ernest van den Haag's, from the conservative* National Review, *are reprinted here as a sampling of the critical reactions to Kate Mil-*
lett's book.

Theory of Sexual Politics

The following sketch, which might be described as "notes toward a theory of patriarchy," will attempt to prove that sex is a status

---

category with political implications. Something of a pioneering effort, it must perforce be both tentative and imperfect. Because the intention is to provide an overall description, statements must be generalized, exceptions neglected, and subheadings overlapping and, to some degree, arbitrary as well.

The word "politics" is enlisted here when speaking of the sexes primarily because such a word is eminently useful in outlining the real nature of their relative status, historically and at the present. It is opportune, perhaps today even mandatory, that we develop a more relevant psychology and philosophy of power relationships beyond the simple conceptual framework provided by our traditional formal politics. Indeed, it may be imperative that we give some attention to defining a theory of politics which treats of power relationships on grounds less conventional than those to which we are accustomed.[1] I have therefore found it pertinent to define them on grounds of personal contact and interaction between members of well-defined and coherent groups: races, castes, classes, and sexes. For it is precisely because certain groups have no representation in a number of recognized political structures that their position tends to be so stable, their oppression so continuous.

In America, recent events have forced us to acknowledge at last that the relationship between the races is indeed a political one which involves the general control of one collectivity, defined by birth, over another collectivity, also defined by birth. Groups who rule by birthright are fast disappearing, yet there remains one ancient and universal scheme for the domination of one birth group by another—the scheme that prevails in the area of sex. The study of racism has convinced us that a truly political state of affairs operates between the races to perpetuate a series of oppressive circumstances. The subordinated group has inadequate redress through existing political institutions, and is deterred thereby from organizing into conventional political struggle and opposition.

Quite in the same manner, a disinterested examination of our system of sexual relationship must point out that the situation between the sexes now, and throughout history, is a case of that phenomenon Max Weber defined as *herrschaft*, a relationship of dominance and subordinance.[2] What goes largely unexamined, often even unacknowledged

---

[1] I am indebted here to Ronald V. Samson's *The Psychology of Power* (New York: Random House, 1968) for his intelligent investigation of the connection between formal power structures and the family and for his analysis of how power corrupts basic human relationships.

[2] "Domination in the quite general sense of power, i.e. the possibility of imposing one's will upon the behavior of other persons, can emerge in the most diverse forms." In this central passage of *Wirtschaft und Gesellschaft* Weber is particularly interested in two such forms: control through social authority ("patriarchal, magisterial, or princely") and control through economic force. In patriarchy as in other forms of

(yet is institutionalized nonetheless) in our social order, is the birthright priority whereby males rule females. Through this system a most ingenious form of "interior colonization" has been achieved. It is one which tends moreover to be sturdier than any form of segregation, and more rigorous than class stratification, more uniform, certainly more enduring. However muted its present appearance may be, sexual dominion obtains nevertheless as perhaps the most pervasive ideology of our culture and provides its most fundamental concept of power.

This is so because our society, like all other historical civilizations, is a patriarchy.[3] The fact is evident at once if one recalls that the military, industry, technology, universities, science, political office, and finance— in short, every avenue of power within the society, including the coercive force of the police, is entirely in male hands. As the essence of politics is power, such realization cannot fail to carry impact. What lingers of supernatural authority, the Deity, "His" ministry, together with the ethics and values, the philosophy and art of our culture—its very civilization—as T. S. Eliot once observed, is of male manufacture.

If one takes patriarchal government to be the institution whereby that half of the populace which is female is controlled by that half which is male, the principles of patriarchy appear to be two fold: male shall dominate female, elder male shall dominate younger. However, just as with any human institution, there is frequently a distance between the real and the ideal; contradictions and exceptions do exist within the system. While patriarchy as an institution is a social constant so deeply entrenched as to run through all other political, social, or economic forms, whether of caste or class, feudality or bureaucracy, just as it pervades all major religions, it also exhibits great variety in history and locale. In democracies,[4] for example, females have often held no office or do so (as now) in such minuscule numbers as to be below even token representation. Aristocracy, on the other hand, with its emphasis upon the magic and dynastic properties of blood, may at times permit women to hold power. The principle of rule by elder males is violated even more frequently. Bearing in mind the variation and degree in patriarchy—as

---

denomination "that control over economic goods, i.e. economic power, is a frequent, often purposively willed, consequence of domination as well as one of its most important instruments." Quoted from Max Rheinstein's and Edward Shil's translation of portions of *Wirtschaft und Gesellschaft* entitled *Max Weber on Law in Economy and Society* (New York: Simon and Schuster, 1967), pp. 323–24.

[3] No matriarchal societies are known to exist at present. Matrilineality, which may be, as some anthropologists have held, a residue or a transitional stage of matriarchy, does not constitute an exception to patriarchal rule, it simply channels the power held by males through female descent—,e.g. the Avunculate.

[4] Radical democracy would, of course, preclude patriarchy. One might find evidence of a general satisfaction with a less than perfect democracy in the fact that women have so rarely held power within modern "democracies."

say between Saudi Arabia and Sweden, Indonesia and Red China—we also recognize our own form in the U.S. and Europe to be much altered and attenuated by the reforms described in the next chapter.

I Ideological

Hannah Arendt[5] has observed that government is upheld by power supported either through consent or imposed through violence. Conditioning to an ideology amounts to the former. Sexual politics obtains consent through the "socialization" of both sexes to basic patriarchal polities with regard to temperament, role, and status. As to status, a pervasive assent to the prejudice of male superiority guarantees superior status in the male, inferior in the female. The first item, temperament, involves the formation of human personality along stereotyped lines of sex category ("masculine" and "feminine"), based on the needs and values of the dominant group and dictated by what its members cherish in themselves and find convenient in subordinates: aggression, intelligence, force, and efficacy in the male; passivity, ignorance, docility, "virtue," and ineffectuality in the female. This is complemented by a second factor, sex role, which decrees a consonant and highly elaborate code of conduct, gesture and attitude for each sex. In terms of activity, sex role assigns domestic service and attendance upon infants to the female, the rest of human achievement, interest, and ambition to the male. The limited role allotted the female tends to arrest her at the level of biological experience. Therefore, nearly all that can be described as distinctly human rather than animal activity (in their own way animals also give birth and care for their young) is largely reserved for the male. Of course, status again follows from such an assignment. Were one to analyze the three categories one might designate status as the political component, role as the sociological, and temperament as the psychological —yet their interdependence is unquestionable and they form a chain. Those awarded higher status tend to adopt roles of mastery, largely because they are first encouraged to develop temperaments of dominance. That this is true of caste and class as well is self-evident.

II Biological

Patriarchal religion, popular attitude, and to some degree, science as well [6] assumes these psycho-social distinctions to rest upon biological dif-

---

[5] Hannah Arendt, "Speculations on Violence," *The New York Review of Books,* Vol. XII, No. 4 (February 27, 1969), p. 24.

[6] The social, rather than the physical sciences are referred to here. Traditionally, medical science had often subscribed to such beliefs. This is no longer the case today,

ferencês between the sexes, so that where culture is acknowledged as shaping behavior, it is said to do no more than cooperate with nature. Yet the temperamental distinctions created in patriarchy ("masculine" and "feminine" personality traits) do not appear to originate in human nature, those of role and status still less.

The heavier musculature of the male, a secondary sexual characteristic and common among mammals, is biological in origin but is also culturally encouraged through breeding, diet and exercise. Yet it is hardly an adequate category on which to base political relations *within civilization*.[7] Male supremacy, like other political creeds, does not finally reside in physical strength but in the acceptance of a value system which is not biological. Superior physical strength is not a factor in political relations —vide those of race and class. Civilization has always been able to substitute other methods (technic, weaponry, knowledge) for those of physical strength, and contemporary civilization has no further need of it. At present, as in the past, physical exertion is very generally a class factor, those at the bottom performing the most strenuous tasks, whether they be strong or not.

It is often assumed that patriarchy is endemic in human social life, explicable or even inevitable on the grounds of human physiology. Such a theory grants patriarchy logical as well as historical origin. Yet if as some anthropologists believe, patriarchy is not of primeval origin, but was preceded by some other social form we shall call pre-patriarchal, then the argument of physical strength as a theory of patriarchal *origins* would hardly constitute a sufficient explanation—unless the male's superior physical strength was released in accompaniment with some change in orientation through new values or new knowledge. Conjecture about origins is always frustrated by lack of certain evidence. Speculation about prehistory, which of necessity is what this must be, remains nothing but

---

when the best medical research points to the conclusion that sexual stereotypes have no bases in biology.

[7] The historians of Roman laws, having very justly remarked their neither birth nor affection was the foundation of the Roman family, have concluded that this foundation must be found in the power of the father or husband. They make a sort of primordial institution of this power; but they do not explain how this power was established, unless it was by the superiority of strength of the husband over the wife, and of the father over the children. Now, we deceive ourselves sadly when we thus place force as the origin of law. We shall see farther on that the authority of the father or husband, far from having been the first cause, was itself an effect; it was derived from religion, and was established by religion. Superior strength, therefore, was not the principle that established the family.
—Numa Denis Fustel de Coulanges, *The Ancient City* (1864).

English translation by Willard Small (1873), Doubleday Anchor Reprint, pp. 41–42. Unfortunately Fustel de Coulanges neglects to mention how religion came to uphold patriarchal authority, since patriarchal religion is also an effect, rather than an original cause.

speculation. Were one to indulge in it, one might argue the likelihood of a hypothetical period preceding patriarchy.[8] What would be crucial to such a premise would be a state of mind in which the primary principle would be regarded as fertility or vitalist processes. In a primitive condition, before it developed civilization or any but the crudest technic, humanity would perhaps find the most impressive evidence of creative force in the visible birth of children, something of a miraculous event and linked analogically with the growth of the earth's vegetation.

It is possible that the circumstance which might drastically redirect such attitudes would be the discovery of paternity. There is some evidence that fertility cults in ancient society at some point took a turn toward patriarchy, displacing and downgrading female function in procreation and attributing the power of life to the phallus alone. Patriarchal religion could consolidate this position by the creation of a male God or gods, demoting, discrediting, or eliminating goddesses and constructing a theology whose basic postulates are male supremacist, and one of whose central functions is to uphold and validate the patriarchal structure.[9]

So much for the evanescent delights afforded by the game of origins. The question of the historical origins of patriarchy—whether patriarchy originated primordially in the male's superior strength, or upon a later mobilization of such strength under certain circumstances—appears at the moment to be unanswerable. It is also probably irrelevant to contemporary patriarchy, where we are left with the realities of sexual politics, still grounded, we are often assured, on nature. Unfortunately, as the psycho-social distinctions made between the two sex groups which are said to justify their present political relationship are not the clear, specific, measurable and neutral ones of the physical sciences, but are instead of an entirely different character—vague, amorphous, often even quasi-religious in phrasing—it must be admitted that many of the generally understood distinctions between the sexes in the more significant areas of role and temperament, not to mention status, have in fact, essentially cultural, rather than biological, bases. Attempts to prove that

---

[8] One might also include the caveat that such a social order need not imply the domination of one sex which the term "matriarchy" would, by its semantic analogue to patriarchy, infer. Given the simpler scale of life and the fact that female-centered fertility religion might be offset by male physical strength, pre-patriarchy might have been fairly equalitarian.

[9] Something like this appears to have taken place as the culture of Neolithic agricultural villages gave way to the culture of civilization and to patriarchy with the rise of cities. See Louis Mumford, *The City in History* (New York: Harcourt Brace Jovanovich, 1961), Chapter One. A discovery such as paternity, a major acquisition of "scientific" knowledge might, hypothetically, have led to an expansion of population, surplus labor and strong-class stratification. There is good reason to suppose that the transformation of hunting into war also played a part.

temperamental dominance is inherent in the male (which for its advocates, would be tantamount to validating, logically as well as historically, the patriarchal situation regarding role and status) have been notably unsuccessful. Sources in the field are in hopeless disagreement about the nature of sexual differences, but the most reasonable among them have despaired of the ambition of any definite equation between temperament and biological nature. It appears that we are not soon to be enlightened as to the existence of any significant inherent differences between male and female beyond the bio-genital ones we already know. Endocrinology and genetics afford no definite evidence of determining mental-emotional differences.[10]

Not only is there insufficient evidence for the thesis that the present social distinctions of patriarchy (status, role, temperament) are physical in origin, but we are hardly in a position to assess the existing differentiations, since distinctions which we know to be culturally induced at present so outweigh them. Whatever the "real" differences between the sexes may be, we are not likely to know them until the sexes are treated differently, that is alike. And this is very far from being the case at present. Important new research not only suggests that the possibilities of innate temperamental differences seem more remote than ever, but even raises questions as to the validity and permanence of psycho-sexual identity. In doing so it gives fairly concrete positive evidence of the overwhelmingly *cultural* character of gender, i.e. personality structure in terms of sexual category.

What Stoller and other experts define as "core gender identity" is now thought to be established in the young by the age of eighteen months. This is how Stoller differentiates between sex and gender:

> Dictionaries stress that the major connotation of *sex* is a biological one, as for example, in the phrases *sexual relations* or *the male sex*. In agreement with this, the word *sex*, in this work will refer to the male or female sex and the component biological parts that determine whether one is a male or a female; the word *sexual* will have connotations of anatomy and physiology. This obviously leaves tremendous areas of behavior, feelings, thoughts and fantasies that are related to the sexes and yet do not have primarily biological connotations. It is for some of these psychological phenomena that the term gender will be used: one can speak of the male sex or the female sex, but one can also talk about masculinity and feminity and not necessarily be implying anything about anatomy or phys-

---

[10] No convincing evidence has so far been advanced in this area. Experimentation regarding the connection between hormones and animal behavior not only yields highly ambivalent results but brings with it the hazards of reasoning by analogy to human behavior. For a summary of the argument see David C. Glass, ed., *Biology and Behavior* (New York: Rockefeller University and the Russell Sage Foundation, 1968).

iology. Thus, while *sex* and *gender* seem to common sense inextricably bound together, one purpose this study will be to confirm the fact that the two realms (sex and gender) are not inevitably bound in anything like a one-to-one relationship, but each may go into quite independent ways.[11]

In cases of genital malformation and consequent erroneous gender assignment at birth, studied at the California Gender Identity Center, the discovery was made that it is easier to change the sex of an adolescent male, whose biological identity turns out to be contrary to his gender assignment and conditioning—through surgery—than to undo the educational consequences of years, which have succeeded in making the subject temperamentally feminine in gesture, sense of self, personality and interests. Studies done in California under Stoller's direction offer proof that gender identity (I am a girl, I am a boy) is the primary identity any human being holds—the first as well as the most permanent and far-reaching. Stoller later makes emphatic the distinction that sex is biological, gender psychological, and therefore cultural: "*Gender* is a term that has psychological or cultural rather than biological connotations. If the proper terms for sex are "male" and "female," the corresponding terms for gender are "masculine" and "feminine"; these latter may be quite independent of (biological) sex." [12] Indeed, so arbitrary is gender, that it may even be contrary to physiology:

> . . . although the external genitalia (penis, testes, scrotum) contribute to the sense of maleness, no one of them is essential for it, not even all of them together. In the absence of complete evidence, I agree in general with Money, and the Hampsons who show in their large series of intersexed patients that gender role is determined by postnatal forces, regardless of the anatomy and physiology of the external genitalia.[13]

It is now believed [14] that the human fetus is originally physically female until the operation of androgen at a certain stage of gestation causes those with *y* chromosomes to develop into males. Psychosexually (e.g., in terms of masculine and feminine, and in contradistinction to

---

[11] Robert J. Stoller, *Sex and Gender* (New York: Science House, 1968), from the Preface, pp. viii–ix.

[12] *Ibid.*, p. 9.

[13] *Ibid.*, p. 48.

[14] See Mary Jane Sherfey, "The Evolution and Nature of Female Sexuality in Relation to Psychoanalytic Theory," *Journal of the American Psychoanalytic Association*, Vol. 14, No. 1 (January 1966) (New York: International Universities Press Inc.), and John Money, "Psychosexual Differentiation," *Sex Research, New Developments* (New York: Holt, Rinehart and Winston, 1965).

male and female) there is no differentiation between the sexes at birth. Psychosexual personality is therefore postnatal and learned.

> . . . the condition existing at birth and for several months there- after is one of psychosexual undifferentiation. Just as in the em- bryo, morphologic sexual differentiation passes from a plastic stage to one of fixed immutability, so also does psychosexual differentia- tion become fixed and immutable—so much so, that mankind has traditionally assumed that so strong and fixed a feeling as personal sexual identity must stem from something innate, instinctive, and not subject to postnatal experience and learning. The error of this traditional assumption is that the power and permanence of some- thing learned has been underestimated. The experiments of animal ethologists on imprinting have now corrected this misconception.[15]

John Money who is quoted above, believes that "the acquisition of a native language is a human counterpart to imprinting," and gender first established "with the establishment of a native language." [16] This would place the time of establishment at about eighteen months. Jerome Kagin's[17] studies in how children of pre-speech age are handled and touched, tickled and spoken to in terms of their sexual identity ("Is it a boy or a girl?" "Hello, little fellow," "Isn't she pretty," etc.) put the most considerable emphasis on purely tactile learning which would have much to do with the child's sense of self, even before speech is attained.

Because of our social circumstances, male and female are really two cultures and their life experiences are utterly different—and this is crucial. Implicit in all the gender identity development which takes place through childhood is the sum total of the parents', the peers', and the culture's notions of what is appropriate to each gender by way of temperament, character, interests, status, worth, gesture, and expres- sion. Every moment of the child's life is a clue to how he or she must think and behave to attain or satisfy the demands which gender places upon one. In adolescence, the merciless task of conformity grows to crisis proportions, generally cooling and settling in maturity.

Since patriarchy's biological foundations appear to be so very inse- cure, one has some cause to admire the strength of a "socialization" which can continue a universal condition "on faith alone," as it were, or through an acquired value system exclusively. What does seem de- cisive in assuring the maintenance of the temperamental differences

---

[15] Money, *op. cit.*, p. 12.
[16] *Ibid.*, p. 13.
[17] Jerome Kagin, "The Acquisition and Significance of Sex-Typing," *Review of Child Development Research*, M. Hoffman, ed. (New York: Russell Sage Founda- tion, 1964).

between the sexes is the conditioning of early childhood. Conditioning runs in a circle of self-perpetuation and self-fulfilling prophecy. To take a simple example: expectations the culture cherishes about his gender identity encourage the young male to develop aggressive impulses, and the female to thwart her own or turn them inward. The result is that the male tends to have aggression reinforced in his behavior, often with significant antisocial possibilities. Thereupon the culture consents to believe the possession of the male indicator, the testes, penis, and scrotum, in itself characterizes the aggressive impulse, and even vulgarly celebrates it in such encomiums as "that guy has balls." The same process of reinforcement is evident in producing the chief "feminine" virtue of passivity.

In contemporary terminology, the basic division of temperamental trait is marshaled along the line of "aggression is male" and "passivity is female." All other temperamental traits are somehow—often the most dexterous ingenuity—aligned to correspond. If aggressiveness is the trait of the master class, docility must be the corresponding trait of a subject group. The usual hope of such line of reasoning is that "nature," by some impossible outside chance, might still be depended upon to rationalize the patriarchal system. An important consideration to be remembered here is that in patriarchy, the function of norm is unthinkingly delegated to the male—were it not, one might as plausibly speak of "feminine" behavior as active, and "masculine" behavior as hyperactive or hyperaggressive.

Here it might be added, by way of a coda, that data from physical sciences has recently been enlisted again to support sociological arguments, such as those of Lionel Tiger[18] who seeks a genetic justification of patriarchy by proposing a "bonding instinct" in males which assures their political and social control of human society. One sees the implication of such a theory by applying its premise to any ruling group. Tiger's thesis appears to be a misrepresentation of the work of Lorenz and other students of animal behavior. Since his evidence of inherent trait is patriarchal history and organization, his pretensions to physical evidence are both specious and circular. One can only advance genetic evidence when one has genetic (rather than historical) evidence to advance. As many authorities dismiss the possibility of instincts (complex inherent behavioral patterns) in humans altogether, admitting only reflexes and drives (far simpler neural responses),[19] the prospects of a "bonding instinct" appear particularly forlorn.

Should one regard sex in humans as a drive, it is still necessary to

---

[18] Lionel Tiger, *Men in Groups* (New York: Random House, 1968).

[19] Through instinct subhuman species might undertake the activity of building a complex nest or hive; through reflex or drive a human being might simply blink, feel hunger, etc.

point out that the enormous area of our lives, both in early "socializa-tion" and in adult experience, labeled "sexual behavior," is almost en-tirely the product of learning. So much is this the case that even the act of coitus itself is the product of a long series of learned responses—responses to the patterns and attitudes, even as to the object of sexual choice, which are set up for us by our social environment.

The arbitrary character of patriarchal ascriptions of temperament and role has little effect upon their power over us. Nor do the mutually exclusive, contradictory, and polar qualities of the categories "mascu-line" and "feminine" imposed upon human personality give rise to sufficiently serious question among us. Under their aegis each personal-ity becomes little more, and often less than half, of its human potential. Politically, the fact that each group exhibits a circumscribed but com-plementary personality and range of activity is of secondary importance to the fact that each represents a status of power division. In the matter of conformity patriarchy is a governing ideology without peer; it is probable that no other system has ever exercised such a complete con-trol over its subjects.

III Sociological

Patriarchy's chief institution is the family. It is both a mirror of and a connection with the larger society; a patriarchal unit within a patriarchal whole. Mediating between the individual and the social structure, the family effects control and conformity where political and other author-ities are insufficient.[20] As the fundamental instrument and the founda-tion unit of patriarchal society the family and its roles are prototypical. Serving as an agent of the larger society, the family not only encourages its own members to adjust and conform, but acts as a unit in the government of the patriarchal state which rules its citizens through its family heads. Even in patriarchal societies where they are granted legal citizenship, women tend to be ruled through the family alone and have little or no formal relation to the state.[21]

As co-operation between the family and the larger society is essential, else both would fall apart, the fate of three patriarchal institutions, the

---

[20] In some of my remarks on the family I am indebted to Goode's short and con-cise analysis. See William J. Goode, *The Family* (Englewood Cliffs, N.J.: Prentice-Hall, 1964).

[21] Family, society, and state are three separate but connected entities: women have a decreasing importance as one goes from the first to the third category. But as each of the three categories exists within or is influenced by the overall institution of patriarchy, I am concerned here less with differentiation than with pointing out a general similarity.

family, society, and the state are interrelated. In most forms of patriarchy this has generally led to the granting of religious support in statements such as the Catholic precept that "the father is head of the family," or Judaism's delegation of quasi-priestly authority to the male parent. Secular governments today also confirm this, as in census practices of designating the male as head of household, taxation, passports, etc. Female heads of household tend to be regarded as undesirable; the phenomenon is a trait of poverty or misfortune. The Confucian prescription that the relationship between ruler and subject is parallel to that of father and children points to the essentially feudal character of the patriarchal family (and conversely, the familial character of feudalism) even in modern democracies.[22]

Traditionally, patriarchy granted the father nearly total ownership over wife or wives and children, including the powers of physical abuse and often even those of murder and sale. Classically, as head of the family the father is both begetter and owner in a system in which kinship is property.[23] Yet in strict patriarchy, kinship is acknowledged only through association with the male line. Agnation excludes the descendants of the female line from property right and often even from recognition.[24] The first formulation of the patriarchal family was made by Sir Henry Maine, a nineteenth-century historian of ancient jurisprudence. Maine argues that the patriarchal basis of kinship is put in terms of dominion rather than blood; wives, though outsiders, are assimilated into the line, while sister's sons are excluded. Basing his definition of the family upon the *patrio potestes* of Rome, Maine defined it as follows: "The eldest male parent is absolutely supreme in his household. His dominion extends to life and death and is as unqualified over his children and their houses as over his slaves." [25] In the archaic patriarchal family "the group consists of animate and inanimate property, of wife, children, slaves, land and goods, all held together by subjection to the despotic authority of the eldest male." [26]

McLennon's rebuttal [27] to Maine argued that the Roman *patria potestes* was an extreme form of patriarchy and by no means, as Maine

---

[22] J. K. Folsom makes a convincing argument as to the anomalous character of patriarchal family systems within democratic society. See Joseph K. Folsom, *The Family and Democratic Society* (New York: John Wiley, 1934, 1943).

[23] Marital as well as consanguine relation to the head of the family made one his property.

[24] Strict patriarchal descent is traced and recognized only through male heirs rather than through sister's sons, etc. In a few generations descendants of female branches lose touch. Only those who "bear the name," who descend from male branches, may be recognized for kinship or inheritance.

[25] Sir Henry Maine, *Ancient Law* (London: Murray, 1861), p. 122.

[26] Sir Henry Maine, *The Early History of Institutions* (London), pp. 310–11.

[27] John McLennon, *The Patriarchal Theory* (London: Macmillan, 1885).

had imagined, universal. Evidence of matrilineal societies (preliterate societies in Africa and elsewhere) refute Maine's assumption of the universality of agnation. Certainly Maine's central argument, as to the primeval or state of nature character of patriarchy is but a rather naïf [28] rationalization of an institution Maine tended to exalt. The assumption of patriarchy's primeval character is contradicted by much evidence which points to the conclusion that full patriarchal authority, particularly that of the *patria potestes* is a late development and the total erosion of female status was likely to be gradual as has been its recovery.

In contemporary patriarchies the male's *de jure* priority has recently been modified through the granting of divorce[29] protection, citizenship, and property to women. Their chattel status continues in their loss of name, their obligation to adopt the husband's domicile, and the general legal assumption that marriage involves an exchange of the female's domestic service and (sexual) consortium in return for financial support.[30]

The chief contribution of the family in patriarchy is the socialization of the young (largely through the example and admonition of their parents) into patriarchal ideology's prescribed attitudes toward the categories of role, temperament, and status. Although slight differences of definition depend here upon the parents' grasp of cultural values, the general effect of uniformity is achieved, to be further reinforced through peers, schools, media, and other learning sources, formal and informal. While we may niggle over the balance of authority between the personalities of various households, one must remember that the entire culture supports masculine authority in all areas of life and—outside of the home—permits the female none at all.

To insure that its crucial functions of reproduction and socialization of the young take place only within its confines, the patriarchal family insists upon legitimacy. Bronislaw Malinowski describes this as "the

---

[28] Maine took the patriarchal family as the cell from which society evolved as gens, phratry, tribe, and nation grew, rather in the simplistic manner of Israel's twelve tribes descending from Jacob. Since Maine also dated the origin of patriarchy from the discovery of paternity, hardly a primeval condition, this too operates against the eternal character of patriarchal society.

[29] Many patriarchies granted divorce to males only. It has been accessible to women on any scale only during this century. Goode states that divorce rates were as high in Japan during the 1880s as they are in the U.S. today. Goode, *op. cit.*, p. 3.

[30] Divorce is granted to a male for his wife's failure in domestic service and consortium: it is not granted him for his wife's failure to render him financial support. Divorce is granted to a woman if her husband fails to support her, but not for his failure at domestic service or consortium. But see Karczewski versus Baltimore and Ohio Railroad, 274 F. Supp. 169.175 N.D. Illinois, 1967, where a precedent was set and the common law that decrees a wife might not sue for loss of consortium overturned.

principle of legitimacy" formulating it as an insistence that "no child should be brought into the world without a man—and one man at that —assuming the role of sociological father." [31] By this apparently consistent and universal prohibition (whose penalties vary by class and in accord with the expected operations of the double standard) patriarchy decrees that the status of both child and mother is primarily or ultimately dependent upon the male. And since it is not only his social status, but even his economic power upon which his dependents generally rely, the position of the masculine figure within the family—as without—is materially, as well as ideologically, extremely strong.

Although there is no biological reason why the two central functions of the family (socialization and reproduction) need be inseparable from or even take place within it, revolutionary or utopian efforts to remove these functions from the family have been so frustrated, so beset by difficulties, that most experiments so far have involved a gradual return to tradition. This is strong evidence of how basic a form patriarchy is within all societies, and of how pervasive its effects upon family members. It is perhaps also an admonition that change undertaken without a thorough understanding of the socio-political institution to be changed is hardly productive. And yet radical social change cannot take place without having an effect upon patriarchy. And not simply because it is the political form which subordinates such a large percentage of the population (women and youth) but because it serves as a citadel of property and traditional interests. Marriages are financial alliances, and each household operates as an economic entity much like a corporation. As one student of the family states it, "the family is the keystone of the stratification system, the social mechanism by which it is maintained." [32]

IV Class

It is in the area of class that the castelike status of the female within patriarchy is most liable to confusion, for sexual status often operates in a superficially confusing way within the variable of class. In a society where status is dependent upon the economic, social, and educational circumstances of class, it is possible for certain females to appear to stand higher than some males. Yet not when one looks more closely at

---

[31] Bronislaw Malinowski, *Sex, Culture and Myth* (New York: Harcourt Brace Jovanovich, 1962), p. 63. An earlier statement is even more sweeping: "In all human societies moral tradition and the law decree that the group consisting of a woman and her offspring is not a sociologically complete unit." *Sex and Repression in Savage Society* (London: Humanities, 1927), p. 213.

[32] Goode, *op. cit.*, p. 80.

the subject. This is perhaps easier to see by means of analogy: a black doctor or lawyer has higher social status than a poor white sharecropper. But race, itself a caste system which subsumes class, persuades the latter citizen that he belongs to a higher order of life, just as it oppresses the black professional in spirit, whatever his material success may be. In much the same manner, a truck driver or butcher has always his "manhood" to fall back upon. Should this final vanity be offended, he may contemplate more violent methods. The literature of the past thirty years provides a staggering number of incidents in which the caste of virility triumphs over the social status of wealthy or even educated women. In literary contexts one has to deal here with wish-fulfillment. Incidents from life (bullying, obscene, or hostile remarks) are probably another sort of psychological gesture of ascendancy. Both convey more hope than reality, for class divisions are generally quite impervious to the hostility of individuals. And yet while the existence of class division is not seriously threatened by such expressions of enmity, the existence of sexual hierarchy has been re-affirmed and mobilized to "punish" the female quite effectively.

The function of class or ethnic mores in patriarchy is largely a matter of how overtly displayed or how loudly enunciated the general ethic of masculine supremacy allows itself to become. Here one is confronted by what appears to be a paradox: while in the lower social strata, the male is more likely to claim authority on the strength of his sex rank alone, he is actually obliged more often to share power with the women of his class who are economically productive; whereas in the middle and upper classes, there is less tendency to assert a blunt patriarchal dominance, as men who enjoy such status have more power in any case.[33]

It is generally accepted that Western patriarchy has been much softened by the concepts of courtly and romantic love. While this is certainly true, such influence has also been vastly overestimated. In comparison with the candor of "machismo" or oriental behavior, one realizes how much of a concession traditional chivalrous behavior represents—a sporting kind of reparation to allow the subordinate female certain means of saving face. While a palliative to the injustice of woman's social position, chivalry is also a technique for disguising it. One must acknowledge that the chivalrous stance is a game the master group plays in elevating its subject to pedestal level. Historians of courtly love stress the fact that the raptures of the poets had no effect upon the legal or economic standing of women, and very little upon their social status.[34] As the sociologist Hugo Beigel has observed, both

---

[33] Goode, *op. cit.*, p. 74.

[34] This is the gist of Valency's summary of the situation before the troubadours, acknowledging that courtly love is an utter anomaly: "With regard to the social background, all that can be stated with confidence is that we know nothing of the

the courtly and the romantic versions of love are "grants" which the male concedes out of his total powers.[35] Both have had the effect of obscuring the patriarchal character of Western culture and in their general tendency to attribute impossible virtues to women, have ended by confining them in a narrow and often remarkably conscribing sphere of behavior. It was a Victorian habit, for example, to insist the female assume the function of serving as the male's conscience and living the life of goodness he found tedious but felt someone ought to do anyway.

The concept of romantic love affords a means of emotional manipulation which the male is free to exploit, since love is the only circumstance in which the female is (ideologically) pardoned for sexual activity. And convictions of romantic love are convenient to both parties since this is often the only condition in which the female can overcome the far more powerful conditioning she has received toward sexual inhibition. Romantic love also obscures the realities of female status and the burden of economic dependency. As to "chivalry," such gallant gesture as still resides in the middle classes has degenerated to a tired ritualism, which scarcely serves to mask the status situation of the present.

Within patriarchy one must often deal with contradictions which are simply a matter of class style. David Riesman has noted that as the working class has been assimilated into the middle class, so have its sexual mores and attitudes. The fairly blatant male chauvinism which was once a province of the lower class or immigrant male has been absorbed and taken on a certain glamour through a number of contemporary figures, who have made it, and a certain number of other working-class male attitudes, part of a new, and at the moment, fashionable life style. So influential is this working-class ideal of brute virility (or more accurately, a literary and therefore middle-class version of it) become in our time that it may replace more discreet and "gentlemanly" attitudes of the past.[36]

One of the chief effects of class within patriarchy is to set one woman against another, in the past creating a lively antagonism between whore and matron, and in the present between career woman and housewife.

---

objective relationships of men and women in the Middle Ages which might conceivably motivate the strain of love-poetry which the troubadours developed." Maurice Valency, *In Praise of Love* (Macmillan: New York, 1958), p. 5.

[35] Hugo Beigel, "Romantic Love," *The American Sociological Review*, Vol. 16 (1951), p. 331.

[36] Mailer and Miller occur to one in this connection, and Lawrence as well. One might trace Rojack's very existence as a fictional figure to the virility symbol of Jack London's Ernest Everhard and Tennessee William's Stanley Kowalski. That Rojack is also literate is nothing more than an elegant finish upon the furniture of his "manhood" solidly based in the hard oaken grain of his mastery over any and every "broad" he can better, bludgeon, or bugger.

One envies the other her "security" and prestige, while the envied yearns beyond the confines of respectability for what she takes to be the other's freedom, adventure, and contact with the great world. Through the multiple advantages of the double standard, the male participates in both worlds, empowered by his superior social and economic resources to play the estranged women against each other as rivals. One might also recognize subsidiary status categories among women: not only is virtue class, but beauty and age as well.

Perhaps, in the final analysis, it is possible to argue that women tend to transcend the usual class stratifications in patriarchy, for whatever the class of her birth and education, the female has fewer permanent class association than does the male. Economic dependency renders her affiliations with any class a tangential, vicarious, and temporary matter. Aristotle observed that the only slave to whom a commoner might lay claim was his woman, and the service of an unpaid domestic still provides working-class males with a "cushion" against the buffets of the class system which incidentally provides them with some of the psychic luxuries of the leisure class. Thrown upon their own resources, few women rise above working class in personal prestige and economic power, and women as a group do not enjoy many of the interests and benefits any class may offer its male members. Women have therefore less of an investment in the class system. But it is important to understand that as with any group whose existence is parasitic to its rulers, women are a dependency class who live on surplus. And their marginal life frequently renders them conservative, for like all persons in their situation (slaves are a classic example here) they identify their own survival with the prosperity of those who feed them. The hope of seeking liberating radical solutions of their own seems too remote for the majority to dare contemplate and remains so until consciousness on the subject is raised.

As race is emerging as one of the final variables in sexual politics, it is pertinent, especially in a discussion of modern literature, to devote a few words to it as well. Traditionally, the white male has been accustomed to concede the female of his own race, in her capacity as "his woman" a higher status than that ascribed to the black male.[37] Yet as

---

[37] It would appear that the "pure flower of white womanhood" has at least at times been something of a disappointment to her lord as a fellow-racist. The historic connection of the Abolitionist and the Woman's Movement is some evidence of this, as well as the incident of white female and black male marriages as compared with those of white male and black female. Figures on miscegenation are very difficult to obtain: Goode (*op. cit.*, p. 37) estimates the proportion of white women marrying black men to be between 3 to 10 times the proportion of white men marrying black women. Robert K. Merton "Intermarriage and the Social Structure," *Psychiatry*, Vol. 4 (August 1941), p. 374, states that "most intercaste sex relations—not marriages— are between white men and Negro women." It is hardly necessary to emphasize that

white racist ideology is exposed and begins to erode, racism's older protective attitudes toward (white) women also begin to give way. And the priorities of maintaining male supremacy might outweigh even those of white supremacy; sexism may be more endemic in our own society than racism. For example, one notes in authors whom we would now term overtly racist, such as D. H. Lawrence—whose contempt for what he so often designates as inferior breeds is unabashed—instances where the lower-caste male is brought on to master or humiliate the white man's own insubordinate mate. Needless to say, the female of the non-white races does not figure in such tales save as an exemplum of "true" womanhood's servility, worthy of imitation by other less carefully instructed females. Contemporary white sociology often operates under a similar patriarchal bias when its rhetoric inclines toward the assertion that the "matriarchal" (e.g. matrifocal) aspect of black society and the "castration" of the black male are the most deplorable symptoms of black oppression in white racist society, with the implication that racial inequity is capable of solution by a restoration of masculine authority. Whatever the facts of the matter may be, it can also be suggested that analysis of this kind presupposes patriarchal values without questioning them, and tends to obscure both the true character of and the responsibility for racist injustice toward black humanity of both sexes.

V   Economic and Educational

One of the most efficient branches of patriarchal government lies in the agency of its economic hold over its female subjects. In traditional patriarchy, women, as non-persons without legal standing, were permitted no actual economic existence as they could neither own nor earn in their own right. Since women have always worked in patriarchal societies, often at the most routine or strenuous tasks, what is at issue here is not labor but economic reward. In modern reformed patriarchal societies, women have certain economic rights, yet the "woman's work" in which some two thirds of the female population in most developed countries are engaged is work that is not paid for.[38] In a money economy where autonomy and prestige depend upon currency, this is a fact of great

---

the more extensive sexual contacts between white males and black females have not only been extramarital, but (on the part of the white male) crassly exploitative. Under slavery it was simply a case of rape.

[38] Sweden is an exception in considering housework a material service rendered and calculable in divorce suits, etc. Thirty-three to forty per cent of the female population have market employment in Western countries: this leaves up to two thirds out of the market labor force. In Sweden and the Soviet Union that figure is lower.

importance. In general, the position of women in patriarchy is a continuous function of their economic dependence. Just as their social position is vicarious and achieved (often on a temporary or marginal basis) through males, their relation to the economy is also typically vicarious or tangential.

Of that third of women who are employed, their average wages represent only half of the average income enjoyed by men. These are the U. S. Department of Labor statistics for average year-round income: white male, $6704, non-white male $4277, white female, $3991, and non-white female $2816.[39] The disparity is made somewhat more remarkable because the educational level of women is generally higher than that of men in comparable income brackets.[40] Further, the kinds of employment open to women in modern patriarchies are, with few exceptions, menial, ill paid and without status.[41]

In modern capitalist countries women also function as a reserve labor force, enlisted in times of war and expansion and discharged in times of peace and recession. In this role American women have replaced immigrant labor and now compete with the racial minorities. In socialist countries the female labor force is generally in the lower ranks as well, despite a high incidence of women in certain professions such as medicine. The status and rewards of such professions have declined as women enter them, and they are permitted to enter such areas under a rationale that society or the state (and socialist countries are also patriarchal) rather than woman is served by such activity.

Since woman's independence in economic life is viewed with distrust, prescriptive agencies of all kinds (religion, psychology, advertising, etc.) continuously admonish or even inveigh against the employment of middle-class women, particularly mothers. The toil of working-class

---

[39] U. S. Department of Labor Statistics for 1966 (latest available figures). The proportion of women earning more than $10,000 a year in 1966 was 7/10 of 1%. See Mary Dublin Keyserling "Realities of Women's Current Position in the Labor Force" *Sex Discrimination in Employment Practices*, a report from the conference (pamphlet), University extension, U.C.L.A. and the Women's Bureau, September 19, 1968.

[40] See *The 1965 Handbook on Women Workers*, United States Department of Labor, Women's Bureau: "In every major occupational group the median wage or salary income of women was less than that of men. This is true at all levels of educational attainment." A comparison of the income received by women and men with equal amounts of schooling revealed that women who had completed four years of college received incomes which were only 47% of those paid to men with the same educational training; high school graduates earned only 38%, and grade school graduates only 33%.

[41] For the distribution of women in lower income and lower status positions see *Background Facts on Working Women* (pamphlet), U. S. Department of Labor, Women's Bureau.

women is more readily accepted as "need," if not always by the working-class itself, at least by the middle-class. And to be sure, it serves the purpose of making available cheap labor in factory and lower-grade service and clerical positions. Its wages and tasks are so unremunerative that, unlike more prestigious employment for women, it fails to threaten patriarchy financially or psychologically. Women who are employed have two jobs since the burden of domestic service and child care is unrelieved either by day care or other social agencies, or by the co-operation of husbands. The invention of labor-saving devices has had no appreciable effect on the duration, even if it has affected the quality of their drudgery.[42] Discrimination in matters of hiring, maternity, wages and hours is very great.[43] In the U. S. a recent law forbidding discrimination in employment, the first and only federal legislative guarantee of rights granted to American women since the vote, is not enforced, has not been enforced since its passage, and was not enacted to be enforced.[44]

In terms of industry and production, the situation of women is in many ways comparable both to colonial and to pre-industrial peoples. Although they achieved their first economic autonomy in the industrial revolution and now constitute a large and underpaid factory population, women do not participate directly in technology or in production. What they customarily produce (domestic and personal service) has no market value and is, as it were, pre-capital. Nor, where they do participate in production of commodities through employment, do they own or control or even comprehend the process in which they participate. An example might make this clearer: the refrigerator is a machine all women use, some assemble it in factories, and a very few with scientific education understand its principles of operation. Yet the heavy industries which roll its steel and produce the dies for its parts are in male hands. The same is true of the typewriter, the auto, etc. Now, while knowledge is fragmented even among the male population, collectively they could reconstruct any technological device. But in the absence of males, women's distance from technology today is sufficiently great that it is doubtful that they could replace or repair such machines on

---

[42] "For a married woman without children the irreducible minimum of work probably takes between fifteen to twenty hours a week, for a woman with small children the minimum is probably 70–80 hours a week." Margaret Benston, "The Political Economy of Women's Liberation," *Monthly Review*, Vol. XXI (September 1969).

[43] See the publications of the Women's Bureau and particularly *Sex Discrimination in Employment Practices* (*op. cit.*) and Carolyn Bird, *Born Female* (New York: McKay, 1968).

[44] Title VII of the 1964 Civil Rights Act. The inclusion of "sex" in the law upholding the civil right of freedom from discrimination in employment was half a joke and half an attempt on the part of Southern congressmen to force Northern industrial states to abandon passage of the bill.

any significant scale. Woman's distance from higher technology is even greater: large-scale building construction; the development of computers; the moon shot, occur as further examples. If knowledge is power, power is also knowledge, and a large factor in their subordinate position is the fairly systematic ignorance patriarchy imposes upon women.

Since education and economy are so closely related in the advanced nations, it is significant that the general level and style of higher education for women, particularly in their many remaining segregated institutions, is closer to that of Renaissance humanism than to the skills of mid-twentieth-century scientific and technological society. Traditionally patriarchy permitted occasional minimal literacy to women while higher education was closed to them. While modern patriarchies have, fairly recently, opened all educational levels to women,[45] the kind and quality of education is not the same for each sex. This difference is of course apparent in early socialization, but it persists and enters into higher education as well. Universities, once places of scholarship and the training of a few professionals, now also produce the personnel of a technocracy. This is not the case with regard to women. Their own colleges typically produce neither scholars nor professionals nor technocrats. Nor are they funded by government and corporations as are male colleges and those co-educational colleges and universities whose primary function is the education of males.

As patriarchy enforces a temperamental imbalance of personality traits between the sexes, its educational institutions, segregated or co-educational, accept a cultural programing toward the generally operative division between "masculine" and "feminine" subject matter, assigning the humanities and certain social sciences (at least in their lower or marginal branches) to the female—and science and technology, the professions, business and engineering to the male. Of course the balance of employment, prestige and reward at present lie with the latter. Control of these fields is very eminently a matter of political power. One might also point out how the exclusive dominance of males in the more prestigious fields directly serves the interests of patriarchal power

[45] We often forget how recent an event is higher education for women. In the U.S. it is barely one hundred years old; in many Western countries barely fifty. Oxford did not grant degrees to women on the same terms as to men until 1920. In Japan and a number of other countries universities have been open to women only in the period after World War II. There are still areas where higher education for women scarcely exists. Women do not have the same access to education as do men. The Princeton Report stated that "although at the high school level more girls than boys receive grades of "A," roughly 50% more boys than girls go to college." *The Princeton Report to the Alumni on Co-Education* (pamphlet), Princeton, N.J., 1968, p. 10. Most other authorities give the national ratio of college students as two males to one female. In a great many countries it is far lower.

in industry, government, and the military. And since patriarchy encourages an imbalance in human temperament along sex lines, both divisions of learning (science and the humanities) reflect this imbalance. The humanities, because not exclusively male, suffer in prestige: the sciences, technology, and business, because they are nearly exclusively male reflect the deformation of the "masculine" personality, e.g., a certain predatory or aggressive character.

In keeping with the inferior sphere of culture to which women in patriarchy have always been restricted, the present encouragement of their "artistic" interests through study of the humanities is hardly more than an extension of the "accomplishments" they once cultivated in preparation for the marriage market. Achievement in the arts and humanities is reserved, now, as it has been historically, for males. Token representation, be it Susan Sontag's or Lady Murasaki's, does not vitiate this rule.

VI Force

We are not accustomed to associate patriarchy with force. So perfect is its system of socialization, so complete the general assent to its values, so long and so universally has it prevailed in human society, that it scarcely seems to require violent implementation. Customarily, we view its brutalities in the past as exotic or "primitive" custom. Those of the present are regarded as the product of individual deviance, confined to pathological or exceptional behavior, and without general import. And yet, just as under other total ideologies (racism and colonialism are somewhat analogous in this respect) control in patriarchal society would be imperfect, even inoperable, unless it had the rule of force to rely upon, both in emergencies and as an ever-present instrument of intimidation.

Historically, most patriarchies have institutionalized force through their legal systems. For example, strict patriarchies such as that of Islam, have implemented the prohibition against illegitimacy or sexual autonomy with a death sentence. In Afghanistan and Saudi Arabia the adulteress is still stoned to death with a mullah presiding at the execution. Execution by stoning was once common practice through the Near East. It is still condoned in Sicily. Needless to say there was and is no penalty imposed upon the male corespondent. Save in recent times or exceptional cases, adultery was not generally recognized in males except as an offense one male might commit against another's property interest. In Tokugawa Japan, for example, an elaborate set of legal distinctions were made according to class. A samurai was entitled, and in the face of public knowledge, even obliged, to execute an adulterous wife, whereas a chōnin (common citizen) or peasant might respond as he pleased. In cases of cross-class adultery, the lower-class male convicted of sexual intimacy with his employer's wife would, because he had violated taboos of class and property, be beheaded together with her. Upper-strata males had, of course, the same license to seduce lower-class women as we are familiar with in Western societies.

Indirectly, one form of "death penalty" still obtains even in America today. Patriarchal legal systems in depriving women of control over their own bodies drive them to illegal abortions; it is estimated that between two and five thousand women die each year from this cause.[46]

Excepting a social license to physical abuse among certain class and ethnic groups, force is diffuse and generalized in most contemporary patriarchies. Significantly, force itself is restricted to the male who alone is psychologically and technically equipped to perpetrate physical violence.[47] Where differences in physical strength have become immaterial through the use of arms, the female is rendered innocuous by her socialization. Before assault she is almost universally defenseless both by her physical and emotional training. Needless to say, this has the most far-reaching effects on the social and psychological behavior of both sexes.

Patriarchal force also relies on a form of violence particularly sexual in character and realized most completely in the act of rape. The figures of rapes reported represent only a fraction of those which occur,[48] as the "shame" of the event is sufficient to deter women from the notion of civil prosecution under the public circumstances of a trial. Traditionally rape has been viewed as an offense one male commits upon another—a matter of abusing "his woman." Vendetta, such as occurs in the American South, is carried out for masculine satisfaction, the exhilarations of race hatred, and the interests of property and vanity (honor). In rape, the emotions of aggression, hatred, contempt, and the desire to break or violate personality, take a form consummately appropriate to sexual politics. In the passages analyzed at the outset of this study, such emotions were present at a barely sublimated level and were a key factor in explaining the attitude behind the author's use of language and tone.[49]

---

[46] Since abortion is extralegal, figures are difficult to obtain. This figure is based on the estimates of abortionists and referral services. Suicides in pregnancy are not officially reported either.

[47] Vivid exceptions come to mind in the wars of liberation conducted by Vietnam, China, etc. But through most of history, women have been unarmed and forbidden to exhibit any defense of their own.

[48] They are still high. The number of rapes reported in the city of New York in 1967 was 2432. Figure supplied by Police Department.

[49] It is interesting that male victims of rape at the hands of other males often feel twice imposed upon, as they have not only been subjected to forcible and painful intercourse, but further abused in being reduced to the status of a female. Much of this is evident in Genet and in the contempt homosexual society reserves for its "passive" or "female" partners.

Patriarchal societies typically link feelings of cruelty with sexuality, the latter often equated both with evil and with power. This is apparent both in the sexual fantasy reported by psychoanalysis and that reported by pornography. The rule here associates sadism with the male ("the masculine role") and victimization with the female ("the feminine role").[50] Emotional response to violence against women in patriarchy is often curiously ambivalent; references to wife-beating, for example, invariably produce laughter and some embarrassment. Exemplary atrocity, such as the mass murders committed by Richard Speck, greeted at one level with a certain scandalized, possibly hypo-critical indignation, is capable of eliciting a mass response of titillation at another level. At such times one even hears from men occasional expressions of envy or amusement. In view of the sadistic character of such public fantasy as caters to male audiences in pornography or semi-pornographic media, one might expect that a certain element of identification is by no means absent from the general response. Probably a similar collective *frisson* sweeps through racist society when its more "logical" members have perpetrated a lynching. Unconsciously, both crimes may serve the larger group as a ritual act, cathartic in effect.

Hostility is expressed in a number of ways. One is laughter. Misogynist literature, the primary vehicle of masculine hostility, is both an hortatory and comic genre. Of all artistic forms in patriarchy it is the most frankly propagandistic. Its aim is to reinforce both sexual factions in their status. Ancient, Medieval, and Renaissance literature in the West has each had a large element of misogyny.[51] Nor is the East without a strong tradition here, notably in the Confucian strain which held sway in Japan as well as China. The Western tradition was indeed moderated somewhat by the introduction of courtly love. But the old diatribes and attacks were coterminous with the new idealization of woman. In the case of Petrarch, Boccaccio, and some others, one can find both attitudes fully expressed, presumably as evidence of different moods, a courtly pose adopted for the ephemeral needs of the vernacular, a grave animosity for sober and eternal Latin.[52] As courtly love was transformed to romantic love, literary misogyny grew somewhat out of

---

[50] Masculine masochism is regarded as exceptional and often explained as latently homosexual, or a matter of the subject playing "the female role"—e.g., victim.

[51] The literature of misogyny is so vast that no summary of sensible proportions could do it justice. The best reference on the subject is Katherine M. Rogers, *The Troublesome Helpmate, A History of Misogyny in Literature* (Seattle: University of Washington Press, 1966).

[52] As well as the exquisite sonnets of love, Petrarch composed satires on women as the "De Remediis utriusque Fortunae" and *Epistolae Seniles*. Boccaccio too could balance the chivalry of romances (Filostrato, Ameto, and Fiammetta) with the vituperance of Corbaccio, a splenetic attack on women more than medieval in violence.

fashion. In some places in the eighteenth century it declined into ridicule and exhortative satire. In the nineteenth century its more acrimonious forms almost disappeared in English. Its resurrection in twentieth-century attitudes and literature is the result of a resentment over patriarchal reform, aided by the growing permissiveness in expression which has taken place at an increasing rate in the last fifty years.

Since the abatement of censorship, masculine hostility (psychological or physical) in specifically *sexual* contexts has become far more apparent. Yet as masculine hostility has been fairly continuous, one deals here probably less with a matter of increase than with a new frankness in expressing hostility in specifically sexual contexts. It is a matter of release and freedom to express what was once forbidden expression outside of pornography or other "underground" productions, such as those of De Sade. As one recalls both the euphemism and the idealism of descriptions of coitus in the Romantic poets (Keats's *Eve of St. Agnes*), or the Victorian novelists (Hardy, for example) and contrasts it with Miller or William Burroughs, one has an idea of how contemporary literature has absorbed not only the truthful explicitness of pornography, but its anti-social character as well. Since this tendency to hurt or insult has been given free expression, it has become far easier to assess sexual antagonism in the male.

The history of patriarchy presents a variety of cruelties and barbarities: the suttee execution in India, the crippling deformity of foot-binding in China, the lifelong ignominy of the veil in Islam, or the widespread persecution of sequestration, the gynaceum, and purdah. Phenomenon such as clitoroidectomy, clitoral incision, the sale and enslavement of women under one guise or another, involuntary and child marriages, concubinage and prostitution, still take place—the first in Africa, the latter in the Near and Far East, the last generally. The rationale which accompanies that imposition of male authority euphemistically referred to as "the battle of the sexes" bears a certain resemblance to the formulas of nations at war, where any heinousness is justified on the grounds that the enemy is either an inferior species or really not human at all. The patriarchal mentality has concocted a whole series of rationales about women which accomplish this purpose tolerably well. And these traditional beliefs still invade our consciousness and affect our thinking to an extent few of us would be willing to admit.

VII Anthropological: Myth and Religion

Evidence from anthropology, religious and literary myth all attests to the politically expedient character of patriarchal convictions about women. One anthropologist refers to a consistent patriarchal strain of assumption that "woman's biological differences set her apart . . . she is essentially inferior," and since "human institutions grow from deep and primal anxieties and are shaped by irrational psychological mechanisms . . . socially organized attitudes toward women arise from basic tensions expressed by the male." [53] Under patriarchy the female did not herself develop the symbols by which she is described. As both the primitive and the civilized worlds are male worlds, the ideas which shaped culture in regard to the female were also of male design. The image of women as we know it is an image created by men and fashioned to suit their needs. These needs spring from a fear of the "otherness" of woman. Yet this notion itself presupposes that patriarchy has already been established and the male has already set himself as the human norm, the subject and referent to which the female is "other" or alien. Whatever its origin, the function of the male's sexual antipathy is to provide a means of control over a subordinate group and a rationale which justifies the inferior station of those in a lower order, "explaining" the oppression of their lives.

The feeling that woman's sexual functions are impure is both worldwide and persistent. One sees evidence of it everywhere in literature, in myth, in primitive and civilized life. It is striking how the notion persists today. The event of menstruation, for example, is a largely clandestine affair, and the psycho-social effect of the stigma attached must have great effect on the female ego. There is a large anthropological literature on menstrual taboo; the practice of isolating offenders in huts at the edge of the village occurs throughout the primitive world. Contemporary slang denominates menstruation as "the curse." There is considerable evidence that such discomfort as women suffer during their period is often likely to be psychosomatic, rather than physiological, cultural rather than biological, in origin. That this may also be true to some extent of labor and delivery is attested to by the recent experiment with "painless childbirth." Patriarchal circumstances and beliefs seem to have the effect of poisoning the female's own sense of physical self until it often truly becomes the burden it is said to be.

Primitive peoples explain the phenomenon of the female's genitals in terms of a wound, sometimes reasoning that she was visited by a bird or snake and mutilated into her present condition. Once she was wounded, now she bleeds. Contemporary slang for the vagina is "gash." The Freudian description of the female genitals is in terms of a "castrated" condition. The uneasiness and disgust female genitals arouse in patriarchal societies is attested to through religious, cultural, and literary proscription. In preliterate groups fear is also a factor, as in the

---

[53] H. R. Hays, *The Dangerous Sex, the Myth of Feminine Evil* (New York: Putnam, 1964). Much of my summary in this section is indebted to Hays's useful assessment of cultural notions about the female.

belief in a castrating *vagina dentata.* The penis, badge of the male's superior status in both preliterate and civilized patriarchies, is given the most crucial significance, the subject both of endless boasting and endless anxiety.

Nearly all patriarchies enforce taboos against women touching ritual objects (those of war or religion) or food. In ancient and preliterate societies women are generally not permitted to eat with men. Women eat apart today in a great number of cultures, chiefly those of the Near and Far East. Some of the inspiration of such custom appears to lie in fears of contamination, probably sexual in origin. In their function of domestic servants, females are forced to prepare food, yet at the same time may be liable to spread their contagion through it. A similar situation obtains with blacks in the United States. They are considered filthy and infectious, yet as domestics they are forced to prepare food for their queasy superiors. In both cases the dilemma is generally solved in a deplorably illogical fashion by segregating the act of eating itself, while cooking is carried on out of sight by the very group who would infect the table. With an admirable consistency, some Hindu males do not permit their wives to touch their food at all. In nearly every patriarchal group it is expected that the dominant male will eat first or eat better, and even where the sexes feed together, the male shall be served by the female.[54]

All patriarchies have hedged virginity and defloration in elaborate rites and interdictions. Among preliterates virginity presents an interesting problem in ambivalence. On the one hand, it is, as in every patriarchy, a mysterious good because a sign of property received intact. On the other hand, it represents an unknown evil associated with the mana of blood and terrifyingly "other." So auspicious is the event of defloration that in many tribes the owner-groom is willing to relinquish breaking the seal of his new possession to a stronger or older personality who can neutralize the attendant dangers.[55] Fears of defloration appear to originate in a fear of the alien sexuality of the female. Although any physical suffering endured in defloration must be on the part of the female (and most societies cause her—bodily and mentally—to suffer anguish), the social interest, institutionalized in patriarchal ritual and custom, is exclusively on the side of the male's property interest, prestige, or (among preliterates) hazard.

Patriarchal myth typically posits a golden age before the arrival of women, while its social practices permit males to be relieved of female

---

[54] The luxury conditions of the "better" restaurant affords a quaint exception. There not only the cuisine but even the table service is conducted by males, at an expense commensurate with such an occasion.

[55] See Sigmund Freud, *Totem and Taboo,* and Ernest Crawley, *The Mystic Rose* (London: Methuen, 1902, 1927).

company. Sexual segregation is so prevalent in patriarchy that one encounters evidence of it everywhere. Nearly every powerful circle in contemporary patriarchy is a men's group. But men form groups of their own on every level. Women's groups are typically auxiliary in character, imitative of male efforts and methods on a generally trivial or ephemeral plane. They rarely operate without recourse to male authority, church or religious groups appealing to the superior authority of a cleric, political groups to male legislators, etc.

In sexually segregated situations the distinctive quality of culturally enforced temperament becomes very vivid. This is particularly true of those exclusively masculine organizations which anthropology generally refers to as men's house institutions. The men's house is a fortress of patriarchal association and emotion. Men's houses in preliterate society strengthen masculine communal experience through dances, gossip, hospitality, recreation, and religious ceremony. They are also the arsenals of male weaponry.

David Riesman has pointed out that sports and some other activities provide males with a supportive solidarity which society does not trouble to provide for females.[56] While hunting, politics, religion, and commerce may play a role, sport and warfare are consistently the chief cement of men's house comradery. Scholars of men's house culture from Hutton Webster and Heinrich Schurtz to Lionel Tiger tend to be sexual patriots whose aim is to justify the apartheid the institution represents.[57] Schurtz believes an innate gregariousness and a drive toward fraternal pleasure among peers urges the male away from the inferior and constricting company of women. Notwithstanding his conviction that a mystical "bonding instinct" exists in males, Tiger exhorts the public, by organized effort, to preserve the men's house tradition from its decline. The institution's less genial function of power center within a state of sexual antagonism is an aspect of the phenomenon which often goes unnoticed.

The men's house of Melanesia fulfill a variety of purposes and are both armory and the site of masculine ritual initiation ceremony. Their atmosphere is not very remote from that of military institutions in the modern world: they reek of physical exertion, violence, the aura of the kill, and the throb of homosexual sentiment. They are the scenes of scarification, headhunting celebrations, and boasting sessions. Here young men are to be "hardened" into manhood. In the men's houses boys have such low status they are often called the "wives" of their initiators, the term "wife" implying both inferiority and the status of

---

[56] David Riesman, "Two Generations," *The Woman in America*, Robert Lifton, ed. (Boston: Beacon, 1967). See also James Coleman, *The Adolescent Society*.

[57] Heinrich Schurtz, *Altersklassen und Männerbünde* (Berlin, 1902) and Lionel Tiger, *op. cit.*

·sexual object. Untried youths become the erotic interest of their elders and betters, a relationship also encountered in the Samurai order, in oriental priesthood, and in the Greek gymnasium. Preliterate wisdom decrees that while inculcating the young with the masculine ethos, it is necessary first to intimidate them with the tutelary status of the female. An anthropologist's comment on Melanesian men's houses is applicable equally to Genet's underworld, or Mailer's U. S. Army:

> It would seem that the sexual brutalizing of the young boy and the effort to turn him into a woman both enhances the older warrior's desire of power, gratifies his sense of hostility toward the maturing male competitor, and eventually, when he takes him into the male group, strengthens the male solidarity in its symbolic attempt to do without women.[58]

The derogation of feminine status in lesser males is a consistent patriarchal trait. Like any hazing procedure, initiation once endured produces devotees who will ever after be ardent initiators, happily inflicting their own former sufferings on the newcomer.

The psychoanalytic term for the generalized adolescent tone of men's house culture is "phallic state." Citadels of virility, they reinforce the most saliently power-oriented characteristics of patriarchy. The Hungarian psychoanalytic anthropologist Géza Róheim stressed the patriarchal character of men's house organization in the preliterate tribes he studied, defining their communal and religious practices in terms of a "group of men united in the cult of an object that is a materialized penis and excluding the women from their society." [59] The tone and ethos of men's house culture is sadistic, power-oriented, and latently homosexual, frequently narcissistic in its energy and motives.[60] The men's house inference that the penis is a weapon, endlessly equated with other weapons, is also clear. The practice of castrating prisoners is itself a comment on the cultural confusion of anatomy and status with weaponry. Much of the glamorization of masculine comradery in warfare originates in what one might designate as "the men's house sensibility." Its sadistic and brutalizing aspects are disguised in military glory and a particularly cloying species of masculine sentimentality. A great deal of our culture partakes of this tradition, and one might locate its

---

[58] Hays, *The Dangerous Sex*, p. 56.

[59] Géza Róheim, "Psychoanalysis of Primitive Cultural Types," *International Journal of Psychoanalysis*, Vol. XIII, London (1932).

[60] All these traits apply in some degree to the bohemian circle which Miller's novels project, the Army which never leaves Mailer's consciousness, and the homosexual sub-culture on which Genet's observations are based. Since these three subjects of our study are closely associated with the separatist men's house culture, it is useful to give it special attention.

first statement in Western literature in the heroic intimacy of Patroclus and Achilles. Its development can be traced through the epic and the saga to the *chanson de geste*. The tradition still flourishes in war novel and movie, not to mention the comic book.

Considerable sexual activity does take place in the men's house, all of it, needless to say, homosexual. But the taboo against homosexual behavior (at least among equals) is almost universally of far stronger force than the impulse and tends to effect a rechanneling of the libido into violence. This association of sexuality and violence is a particularly militaristic habit of mind.[61] The negative and militaristic coloring of such men's house homosexuality as does exist, is of course by no means the whole character of homosexual sensibility. Indeed, the warrior caste of mind with its ultravirility, is more *incipiently* homosexual, in its exclusively male orientation, than it is *overtly* homosexual. (The Nazi experience is an extreme case in point here.) And the heterosexual role-playing indulged in, and still more persuasively, the contempt in which the younger, softer, or more "feminine" members are held, is proof that the actual ethos is misogynist, or perversely rather than positively heterosexual. The true inspiration of men's house association therefore comes from the patriarchal situation rather than from any circumstances inherent in the homo-amorous relationship.

If a positive attitude toward heterosexual love is not quite, in Seignebos' famous dictum, the invention of the twelfth century, it can still claim to be a novelty. Most patriarchies go to great length to exclude love as a basis of mate selection. Modern patriarchies tend to do so through class, ethnic, and religious factors. Western classical thought was prone to see in heterosexual love either a fatal stroke of ill luck bound to end in tragedy, or a contemptible and brutish consorting with inferiors. Medieval opinion was firm in its conviction that love was sinful if sexual, and sex sinful if loving.

Primitive society practices its misogyny in terms of taboo and mana which evolve into explanatory myth. In historical cultures, this is transformed into ethical, then literary, and in the modern period, scientific rationalizations for the sexual politic. Myth is, of course, a felicitous advance in the level of propaganda, since it so often bases its arguments on ethics or theories of origins. The two leading myths of Western culture are the classical tale of Pandora's box and the Biblical story of the Fall. In both cases earlier mana concepts of feminine evil have passed through a final literary phase to become highly influential ethical justifications of things as they are.

Pandora appears to be a discredited version of a Mediterranean fertility goddess, for in Hesiod's *Theogony* she wears a wreath of flowers and a sculptured diadem in which are carved all the creatures of land

---

[61] Genet demonstrates this in *The Screens*; Mailer reveals it everywhere.

and sea.[62] Hesiod ascribes to her the introduction of sexuality which puts an end to the golden age when "the races of men had been living on earth free from all evils, free from laborious work, and free from all wearing sickness." [63] Pandora was the origin of "the damnable race of women—a plague which men must live with." [64] The introduction of what are seen to be the evils of the male human condition came through the introduction of the female and what is said to be her unique product, sexuality. In *Works and Days* Hesiod elaborates on Pandora and what she represents—a perilous temptation with "the mind of a bitch and a thievish nature," full of "the cruelty of desire and longings that wear out the body," "lies and cunning words and a deceitful soul," a snare sent by Zeus to be "the ruin of men." [65]

Patriarchy has God on its side. One of its most effective agents of control is the powerfully expeditious character of its doctrines as to the nature and origin of the female and the attribution to her alone of the dangers and evils it imputes to sexuality. The Greek example is interesting here: when it wishes to exalt sexuality it celebrates fertility through the phallus; when it wishes to denigrate sexuality, it cites Pandora. Patriarchal religion and ethics tend to lump the female and sex together as if the whole burden of the onus and stigma it attaches to sex were the fault of the female alone. Thereby sex, which is known to be unclean, sinful, and debilitating, pertains to the female, and the male identity is preserved as a human, rather than a sexual one.

The Pandora myth is one of two important Western archetypes which condemn the female through her sexuality and explain her position as her well-deserved punishment for the primal sin under whose unfortunate consequences the race yet labors. Ethics have entered the scene, replacing the simplicities of ritual, taboo, and mana. The more sophisticated vehicle of myth also provides official explanations of sexual history. In Hesiod's tale, Zeus, a rancorous and arbitrary father figure, in sending Epimetheus evil in the form of female genitalia, is actually chastising him for adult heterosexual knowledge and activity. In opening the vessel she brings (the vulva or hymen, Pandora's "box") the male satisfies his curiosity but sustains the discovery only by punishing himself at the hands of the father god with death and the

---

[62] Wherever one stands in the long anthropologists' quarrel over patriarchal versus matriarchal theories of social origins, one can trace a demotion of fertility goddesses and their replacement by patriarchal deities at a certain period throughout ancient culture.

[63] Hesiod, *Works and Days*, translated by Richmond Lattimore (University of Michigan, 1959), p. 29.

[64] Hesiod, *Theogony*, translated by Norman O. Brown (Indianapolis: Liberal Arts Press, 1953), p. 70.

[65] Hesiod, *Works and Days*, phrases from lines 53–100. Some of the phrases are from Lattimore's translation, some from A. W. Mair's translation (Oxford, 1908).

assorted calamities of postlapsarian life. The patriarchal trait of male rivalry across age or status line, particularly those of powerful father and rival son, is present as well as the ubiquitous maligning of the female.

The myth of the Fall is a highly finished version of the same themes. As the central myth of the Judeo-Christian imagination and therefore of our immediate cultural heritage, it is well that we appraise and acknowledge the enormous power it still holds over us even in a rationalist era which has long ago given up literal belief in it while maintaining its emotional assent intact.[66] This mythic version of the female as the cause of human suffering, knowledge, and sin is still the foundation of sexual attitudes, for it represents the most crucial argument of the patriarchal tradition in the West.

The Israelites lived in a continual state of war with the fertility cults of their neighbors; these latter afforded sufficient attraction to be the source of constant defection, and the figure of Eve, like that of Pandora, has vestigial traces of a fertility goddess overthrown. There is some, probably unconscious, evidence of this in the Biblical account which announces, even before the narration of the fall has begun— "Adam called his wife's name Eve; because she was the mother of all living things." Due to the fact that the tale represents a compilation of different oral traditions, it provides two contradictory schemes for Eve's creation, one in which both sexes are created at the same time, and one in which Eve is fashioned later than Adam, an afterthought born from his rib, peremptory instance of the male's expropriation of the life force through a god who created the world without benefit of female assistance.

The tale of Adam and Eve is, among many other things, a narrative of how humanity invented sexual intercourse. Many such narratives exist in preliterate myth and folk tale. Most of them strike us now as delightfully funny stories of primal innocents who require a good deal of helpful instruction to figure it out. There are other major themes in the story: the loss of primeval simplicity, the arrival of death, and the first conscious experience of knowledge. All of them revolve about sex. Adam is forbidden to eat of the fruit of life or of the knowledge of good and evil, the warning states explicitly what should happen if he tastes of the latter: "in that day that thou eatest thereof thou shalt surely

---

[66] It is impossible to assess how deeply embedded in our consciousness is the Eden legend and how utterly its patterns are planted in our habits of thought. One comes across its tone and design in the most unlikely places, such as Antonioni's film *Blow-Up*, to name but one of many striking examples. The action of the film takes place in an idyllic garden, loaded with primal overtones largely sexual, where, prompted by a tempter with a phallic gun, the female again betrays the male to death. The photographer who witnesses the scene reacts as if he were being introduced both to the haggard knowledge of the primal scene and original sin at the same time.

die." He eats but fails to die (at least in the story), from which one might infer that the serpent told the truth.

But at the moment when the pair eat of the forbidden tree they awake to their nakedness and feel shame. Sexuality is clearly involved, though the fable insists it is only tangential to a higher prohibition against disobeying orders in the matter of another and less controversial appetite—one for food. Róheim points out that the Hebrew verb for "eat" can also mean coitus. Everywhere in the Bible "knowing" is synonymous with sexuality, and clearly a product of contact with the phallus, here in the fable objectified as a snake. To blame the evils and sorrows of life—loss of Eden and the rest—on sexuality, would all too logically implicate the male, and such implication is hardly the purpose of the story, designed as it is expressly in order to blame all this world's discomfort on the female. Therefore it is the female who is tempted first and "beguiled" by the penis, transformed into something else, a snake. Thus Adam has "beaten the rap" of sexual guilt, which appears to be why the sexual motive is so repressed in the Biblical account. Yet the very transparency of the serpent's universal phallic value shows how uneasy the mythic mind can be about its shifts. Accordingly, in her inferiority and vulnerability the woman takes and eats, simple carnal thing that she is, affected by flattery even in a reptile. Only after this does the male fall, and with him, humanity—for the fable has made him the racial type, whereas Eve is a mere sexual type and, according to tradition, either expendable or replaceable. And as the myth records the original sexual adventure, Adam was seduced by woman, who was seduced by a penis. "The woman whom thou gavest to be with me, she gave me of the fruit and I did eat" is the first man's defense. Seduced by the phallic snake, Eve is convicted for Adam's participation in sex.

Adam's curse is to toil in the "sweat of his brow," namely the labor the male associates with civilization. Eden was a fantasy world without either effort or activity, which the entrance of the female, and with her sexuality, has destroyed. Eve's sentence is far more political in nature and a brilliant "explanation" of her inferior status. "In sorrow thou shalt bring forth children. And thy desire shall be to thy husband. And he shall rule over thee." Again, as in the Pandora myth, a proprietary father figure is punishing his subjects for adult heterosexuality. It is easy to agree with Róheim's comment on the negative attitude the myth adopts toward sexuality: "Sexual maturity is regarded as a misfortune, something that has robbed mankind of happiness . . . the explanation of how death came into the world." [67]

---

[67] Géza Róheim, "Eden," *Psychoanalytic Review*, Vol. XXVII, New York (1940). See also Theodor Reik, *The Creation of Woman*, and the account given in Hays, *op. cit.*

What requires further emphasis is the responsibility of the female, a marginal creature, in bringing on this plague, and the justice of her suborned condition as dependent on her primary role in this original sin. The connection of woman, sex, and sin constitutes the fundamental pattern of western patriarchal thought thereafter.

VIII Psychological

The aspects of patriarchy already described have each an effect upon the psychology of both sexes. Their principal result is the interiorization of patriarchal ideology. Status, temperament, and role are all value systems with endless psychological ramifications for each sex. Patriarchal marriage and the family with its ranks and division of labor play a large part in enforcing them. The male's superior economic position, the female's inferior one have also grave implications. The large quantity of guilt attached to sexuality in patriarchy is overwhelmingly placed upon the female, who is, culturally speaking, held to be the culpable or the more culpable party in nearly any sexual liaison, whatever the extenuating circumstances. A tendency toward the reification of the female makes her more often a sexual object than a person. This is particularly so when she is denied human rights through chattel status. Even where this has been partly amended the cumulative effect of religion and custom is still very powerful and has enormous psychological consequences. Woman is still denied sexual freedom and the biological control over her body through the cult of virginity, the double standard, the prescription against abortion, and in many places because contraception is physically or psychically unavailable to her.

The continual surveillance in which she is held tends to perpetuate the infantilization of women even in situations such as those of higher education. The female is continually obliged to seek survival or advancement through the approval of males as those who hold power. She may do this either through appeasement or through the exchange of her sexuality for support and status. As the history of patriarchal culture and the representations of herself within all levels of its cultural media, past and present, have a devastating effect upon her self image, she is customarily deprived of any but the most trivial sources of dignity or self-respect. In many patriarchies, language, as well as cultural tradition, reserve the human condition for the male. With the Indo-European languages this is a nearly inescapable habit of mind, for despite all the customary pretense that "man" and "humanity" are terms which apply equally to both sexes, the fact is hardly obscured that in practice, general application favors the male far more often than the female as referent, or even sole referent, for such designations.[68]

---

[68] Languages outside the Indo-European group are instructive. Japanese, for ex-

When in any group of persons, the ego is subjected to such invidious versions of itself through social beliefs, ideology, and tradition, the effect is bound to be pernicious. This coupled with the persistent though frequently subtle denigration women encounter daily through personal contacts, the impressions gathered from the images and media about them, and the discrimination in matters of behavior, employment, and education which they endure, should make it no very special cause for surprise that women develop group characteristics common to those who suffer minority status and a marginal existence. A witty experiment by Philip Goldberg proves what everyone knows, that having internalized the disesteem in which they are held, women despise both themselves and each other.[69] This simple test consisted of asking women undergraduates to respond to the scholarship in an essay signed alternately by one John McKay and one Joan McKay. In making their assessments the students generally agreed that John was a remarkable thinker, Joan an unimpressive mind. Yet the articles were identical: the reaction was dependent on the sex of the supposed author.

As women in patriarchy are for the most part marginal citizens when they are citizens at all, their situation is like that of other minorities, here defined not as dependent upon numerical size of the group, but on its status. "A minority group is any group of people who because of their physical or cultural characteristics, are singled out from others in the society in which they live for differential and unequal treatment." [70] Only a handful of sociologists have ever addressed themselves in any meaningful way to the minority status of women.[71] And psychology has yet to produce relevant studies on the subject of ego damage to the female which might bear comparison to the excellent work done on the

---

ample, has one word for man (*otōko*), another for woman (*ōnna*) and a third for human being (*ningen*). It would be as unthinkable to use the first to cover the third as it would be to use the second.

[69] Philip Goldberg, "Are Women Prejudiced Against Women?" *Transaction* (April 1968).

[70] Louis Wirth, "Problems of Minority Groups," *The Science of Man in the World Crisis*, Ralph Linton, ed. (New York: Appleton-Century-Crofts, 1945), p. 347. Wirth also stipulates that the group see itself as discriminated against. It is interesting that many women do not recognize themselves as discriminated against; no better proof could be found of the totality of their conditioning.

[71] The productive handful in question include the following:

Helen Mayer Hacker, "Women as a Minority Group," *Social Forces*, Vol. XXX (October 1951).

Gunnar Myrdal, *An American Dilemma*, Appendix 5 is a parallel of black minority status with women's minority status.

Everett C. Hughes, "Social Change and Status Protest: An Essay on the Marginal Man," *Phylon*, Vol. X, First Quarter (1949).

Joseph K. Folsom, *The Family and Democratic Society*, 1943.

Godwin Watson, "Psychological Aspects of Sex Roles," *Social Psychology, Issues and Insights* (Philadelphia: Lippincott, 1966).

effects of racism on the minds of blacks and colonials. The remarkably small amount of modern research devoted to the psychological and social effects of masculine supremacy on the female and on the culture in general attests to the widespread ignorance or unconcern of a conservative social science which takes patriarchy to be both the status quo and the state of nature.

What little literature the social sciences afford us in this context confirms the presence in women of the expected traits of minority status: group self-hatred and self-rejection, a contempt both for herself and for her fellows—the result of that continual, however subtle, reiteration of her inferiority which she eventually accepts as a fact.[72] Another index of minority status is the fierceness with which all minority group members are judged. The double standard is applied not only in cases of sexual conduct but other contexts as well. In the relatively rare instances of female crime too: in many American states a woman convicted of crime is awarded a longer sentence.[73] Generally an accused woman acquires a notoriety out of proportion to her acts and due to sensational publicity she may be tried largely for her "sex life." But so effective is her conditioning toward passivity in patriarchy, woman is rarely extrovert enough in her maladjustment to enter upon criminality. Just as every minority member must either apologize for the excesses of a fellow or condemn him with a strident enthusiasm, women are characteristically harsh, ruthless and frightened in their censure of aberration among their numbers.

The gnawing suspicion which plagues any minority member, that the myths propagated about his inferiority might after all be true often reaches remarkable proportions in the personal insecurities of women. Some find their subordinate position so hard to bear that they repress and deny its existence. But a large number will recognize and admit their circumstances when they are properly phrased. Of two studies which asked women if they would have preferred to be born male, one found that one fourth of the sample admitted as much, and in another sample, one half.[74] When one inquires of children, who have not yet developed as serviceable techniques of evasion, what their choice might be, if they had one, the answers of female children in a large majority of cases clearly favor birth into the elite group, whereas boys overwhelmingly re-

---

[72] My remarks on the minority status of women are summarized from all the articles listed, and I am particularly indebted to an accomplished critique of them in an unpublished draft by Professor Marlene Dixon, formerly of the University of Chicago's Department of Sociology and the Committee on Human Development, presently of McGill University.

[73] See The Commonwealth v. Daniels, 37 L.W. 2064, Pennsylvania Supreme Court, 7/1/68 (reversing 36 L.W. 2004).

[74] See Helen Hacker, *op. cit.*, and Carolyn Bird, *op. cit.*

ject the option of being girls.[75] The phenomenon of parents' prenatal preference for male issue is too common to require much elaboration. In the light of the imminent possibility of parents actually choosing the sex of their child, such a tendency is becoming the cause of some concern in scientific circles.[76]

Comparisons such as Myrdal, Hacker, and Dixon draw between the ascribed attributes of blacks and women reveal that common opinion associates the same traits with both: inferior intelligence, an instinctual or sensual gratification, an emotional nature both primitive and childlike, an imagined prowess in or affinity for sexuality, a contentment with their own lot which is in accord with a proof of its appropriateness, a wily habit of deceit, and concealment of feeling. Both groups are forced to the same accommodational tactics: an ingratiating or supplicatory manner invented to please, a tendency to study those points at which the dominant group are subject to influence or corruption, and an assumed air of helplessness involving fraudulent appeals for direction through a show of ignorance.[77] It is ironic how misogynist literature has for centuries concentrated on just these traits, directing its fiercest enmity at feminine guile and corruption, and particularly that element of it which is sexual, or, as such sources would have it, "wanton."

As with other marginal groups a certain handful of women are accorded higher status that they may perform a species of cultural policing over the rest. Hughes speaks of marginality as a case of status dilemma experienced by women, blacks, or second-generation Americans who have "come up" in the world but are often refused the rewards of their efforts on the grounds of their origins.[78] This is particularly the case with "new" or educated women. Such exceptions are generally obliged to make ritual, and often comic, statements of deference to justify their elevation. These characteristically take the form of pledges of "femininity," namely a delight in docility and a large appetite for masculine dominance. Politically, the most useful persons for such a role are entertainers and public sex objects. It is a common trait of minority status that a small percentage of the fortunate are permitted to entertain their rulers. (That they may entertain their fellow subjects in the process is less to the point.) Women entertain, please, gratify, satisfy and flatter men with their sexuality. In most minority groups athletes or intellectuals are allowed to emerge as "stars," identification with whom should con-

---

[75] "One study of fourth graders showed ten times as many girls wishing they could have been boys, as boys who would have chosen to be girls," Watson, *op. cit.*, p. 477.

[76] Amitai Etzioni, "Sex Control, Science, and Society," *Science* (September 1968), pp. 1107–12.

[77] Myrdal, *op. cit.*, Hacker, *op. cit.*, Dixon, *op. cit.*

[78] Hughes, *op. cit.*

tent their less fortunate fellows. In the case of women both such eventualities are discouraged on the reasonable grounds that the most popular explanations of the female's inferior status ascribe it to her physical weakness or intellectual inferiority. Logically, exhibitions of physical courage or agility are indecorous, just as any display of serious intelligence tends to be out of place.

Perhaps patriarchy's greatest psychological weapon is simply its universality and longevity. A referent scarcely exists with which it might be contrasted or by which it might be confuted. While the same might be said of class, patriarchy has a still more tenacious or powerful hold through its successful habit of passing itself off as nature. Religion is also universal in human society and slavery was once nearly so; advocates of each were fond of arguing in terms of fatality, or irrevocable human "instinct"—even "biological origins." When a system of power is thoroughly in command, it has scarcely need to speak itself aloud; when its workings are exposed and questioned, it becomes not only subject to discussion, but even to change. . . .

How Now, Kate?

Ernest van den Haag

This book is better—the research thorough (except for Latin phrases), the thinking intelligible, the writing smooth—than the usual female liberation tome. It fails in its purpose—to establish an undue universal domination and exploitation of females by males—but it fails richly and entertainingly, even instructively.

Writers such as Henry Miller, Norman Mailer and D. H. Lawrence are discussed judiciously and perceptively. The selection is biased, of course (why no mention, say, of Eugene O'Neill or Robert Graves?): Miller and Mailer are sitting ducks for feminists; their only flight is from castration fear into pseudo-virility. Some writers have not gone beyond the phallic stage of development, and rationalize their failure in their writing. Why do their wishful fantasies show that society oppresses females? And wherein does D. H. Lawrence's silly preaching? Is there any

FROM The *National Review*, September 22, 1970, pp. 1004–05. Reprinted by permission of Ernest van den Haag.

reason to take it more seriously than Ezra Pound's ideas on usury? Lawrence, of course, is a great writer—though one wouldn't guess it from *Lady Chatterley's Lover*. The other two are mostly tiresome.

Millett's comments on Freud and Erikson are more to the point and often on target (Erikson usually, Freud occasionally). But the logic is peculiar. If much psychoanalysis or literature rationalizes male superiority wishes, does it follow that what is being rationalized is wrong, or that the argument advanced for it is faulty? Ideas, however convenient they are shown to be for males, and however much advocated for the "wrong" motives, are not thereby shown to be wrong. And if male-produced literature rationalizes putative male-female differences, or supports female roles convenient to males, it does not follow that there are no differences other than anatomical and physiological ones, or that there should be none, or even that the role differentiation elaborated by our culture is inequitable or undesirable.

Again, if an alternative explanation explains as well or better what penis envy is meant to explain, it still does not invalidate, by itself, Freud's explanation: several factors may each be sufficient to explain a particular effect; and they may all be present. I may declare that Miss Millett writes well, just because I like her picture. Does it follow that she does not actually write well? At any rate her logic is odd, one is tempted to say feminine—but the sexist temptation must be resisted.

Miss Millett complains that all major societies are patriarchal (the minor ones which are not, are usually discovered by Margaret Mead) and that explanations of patriarchy are self-serving. But she herself does not explain the phenomenon. She thinks that "functionalist description inevitably becomes prescriptive" (which confuses "possibly" with "inevitably")—wherefore she can not explain why patriarchy is so universal, even though she bewails and berates it for nearly four hundred pages. Nor, although she (rightly) discards some justifications, does Miss Millett thereby or otherwise show patriarchy to be unjust: perhaps God is not an egalitarian after all, or even a democrat. (According to Holy Writ, He is neither.)

She quotes (at length) Karl Marx' friend Friedrich Engels ("It is no accident," Marxists might say, that some of her phraseology is "inevitably" Marxian). But Engels' theory of the family is wholly discredited, as she half-heartedly concedes, by the facts which discredit all evolutionist theories, however "dialectical," and economic theories most unequivocally. Miss Millett might have more profitably taken a hint from Marx himself: in his polemic (*The Poverty of Philosophy*) against Proudhon, who described property as "theft," Marx correctly pointed out that "theft" is a moral or legal category, whereas the task was to establish how and why the institution of property came into being and was developed—what its function is.

Marx' analysis did not actually go beyond a (disguised) moral statement, his scientific pretensions notwithstanding. But at least he attempted (and here and there succeeded in) a "functionalist description." It did not "inevitably" become prescriptive of the status quo. The prescription (no more inevitable) was for revolution. Her rejection of "functionalist description" makes it impossible for Miss Millett to establish whether, why, wherein and how, women are politically dominated by men. It keeps her misconceiving the relationship as "domination."

Had Miss Millett analyzed her own concepts of the domination of females by males, of the need to liberate females, of males and females as political groups or powers, she might have found that they make as much sense as Hitler's concept of the domination of Germans by Jews ("Germany Awake!"), or C. Wright Mills' dominant "power elite," or my own theory—as easily demonstrated as Miss Millett's—of the domination of society by (short-sighted) men with glasses who occupy all avenues of power. These taxonomic (or biological) groupings— "dominating" or "dominated"—are not politically relevant social groups of any kind. Above all, not in Miss Millett's political-power sense. They do not dominate nor are they dominated as political groups. Males do not cohere, strive in common for power, or hold it in common. They do not act, display subjective political solidarity based on group membership, or have objective common interests outweighing what divides them. Nor do females. (Identification must not be confused with political position or solidarity.) Which is why history—replete with warfare between actual social and political groups—knows of no collective battle between men and women.

Hitler was right in saying that the Jews in the Weimer Republic were influential beyond their numbers; possibly they did individually "dominate." But Hitler was wrong in believing that they conspired, acted in common, or dominated as a political group, or that (non-Jewish) Germans were dominated by them otherwise. So is Miss Millett wrong about males. They dominate females as men with glasses dominate those without.

All cultures elaborate on the physical differences between the sexes, each in its own way, but nearly all in the patriarchal mode. "Patriarchal," however, covers a multitude of sins and virtues, from legal subjection of females to legal (and actual) equality with males—such as we have in the United States. The elaborations change over time; they respond to variable social factors as well as to constant biological ones. No doubt, role distribution (and definition) in wholly industrialized, urbanized societies must be very different from that of rural society. Females may assume many roles previously reserved to males and vice versa; the family will change. We are now going through rapid changes and it would be interesting and timely to explore the likely, the possible and the desirable directions.

The idea of *Sexual Politics*—of male and female power-groups struggling with each other—is irrelevant to the problem and likely to hinder serious exploration. It fascinates because it makes unhappiness—wherever it actually originates—meaningful, blames the other sex, and legitimizes hostility. *Sexual Politics* totally misconceives the problem; the more remarkable that Miss Millett has written a rewarding book about it.

Women's Lib Gets Rough

Jonathan Yardley

Sexual Politics is nitty-gritty Women's Lib. Men willing to meet the book on its own uncompromising terms will find the experience lacerating, and it is my guess that any sensitive housewife who has never given much thought to her status will be persuaded that she has been an exploited ninny. Though Millett is demonstrably not a manhater and does not appear to be a clitoral absolutist, her tone is so unflaggingly militant (and irreverent) that only the true-blue feminist will read the book without discomfort. But Millett's militancy, even when overstated or misdirected, is to good purpose, as is that of Women's Lib generally; it forces the reconsideration of entrenched and invidious, but widely evaded, sexual/social assumptions.

One senses that the book began as an examination of sexism in contemporary literature and ballooned into the "ambitious, often rather overwhelming, undertaking" that Millett self-applaudingly calls it. It opens with "instances of sexual politics" in the work of D. H. Lawrence, Henry Miller, Norman Mailer and Jean Genet; it ends with extensive chapters devoted (with some fine wit and perceptive criticism) to each of the four. . . .

In its middle sections, *Sexual Politics* is concerned with defining its title, revealing the guises in which sexism is masked, exposing its deleterious effects and sketching its history. The book is essentially about female subjugation in the United States, and is wisely assessed within that framework. All its meanderings finally arrive at the consideration of sex in this country as "a status category with political implications," politics being broadly defined as "power-structured relationships, arrangements whereby one group of persons is controlled by another," "a set of stratagems designed to maintain a system." It is, or comes very close to being, a conspiracy theory, a view of history in which a diabolical patriarchy systematically holds women in a state of submission and dependency. Conspiracy is as far-fetched in this case as it was at Chicago, but the evidence that women are treated as a subordinate class, or caste, is considerable:

> What goes largely unexamined, often even unacknowledged (yet is institutionalized nonetheless) in our social order, is the birthright priority whereby males rule females. Through this system a most ingenious form of "interior colonization" has been achieved. It is one which tends moreover to be sturdier than any form of segregation, and more rigorous than class stratification, more uniform, certainly more enduring.

To be sure, we have been depicted as a nation of Momists, we celebrate Mother's Day and fete debutantes, we congratulate ourselves upon the memory of Jane Addams and the presence of Margaret Chase Smith; but the true situation is another matter. We (white) men view women much as, Millett claims, we view blacks: "inferior intelligence, an instinctual or sensual gratification, an emotional nature both primitive and childlike, an imagined prowess in or affinity for sexuality, a contentment with their own lot which is in accord with a proof of its appropriateness, a wily habit of deceit and concealment of feeling." Isn't our societal "worship" of woman merely a stratagem to lull her into submission, an extraordinary piece of sexual politics "a game the master group plays in elevating its subject to pedestal level?" The claim is an example of the brand of partial truth in which Millett excels. Her talent for coating the implausible with a veneer of the plausible is impressive indeed: "Achievement in the arts and humanities is reserved, now, as it has been historically, for males"—a ludicrous statement containing just enough truth to lend it respectability.

Most of the time her aim is better. It is more true than not that "women are a dependency class"; that their "relation to the economy is . . . typically vicarious or tangential"; that "the military, industry, technology, universities, science, political office, and finance—in short, every avenue of power within the society, including the coercive force of the police, is entirely in male hands"; that "a recent law forbidding discrimination, the first and only federal legislative guarantee of rights granted to American women since the vote, is not enforced, has not been enforced since its passage, and was not enacted to be enforced." . . .

One would think the girls would have marched on City Hall ages ago, but Millett explains that paternalism stays in office by "passing itself off as nature"—that "masculine ascendancy" is justified by its exponents as being naturally, indeed divinely, ordained. Either we men are great salesmen or women are great suckers, but no matter, Millett presses on. "Masculine" and "feminine" are not the complex natural distinctions we had assumed them to be, but "elaborate behavioral constructs for each sex within society, obviously cultural and subject to endless cross-cultural variations." "Sex is biological, gender psychological, and therefore cultural." Ignore our penises and our vaginas and we should all be the same; in a perfect world, no one would know the difference between Joe Willie Namath and Raquel Welch.

As biologist and anthropologist Millett obviously has her shortcomings, but her point that history has not been kind to the female must be conceded. As historian, she points out that women were generally held in thrall until the early 19th century. In a long, interesting section on sexual revolution and counter-revolution, she argues that the rebellion against male dominion began around 1830 and was "officially inaugurated" with the formation of the Women's Movement at Seneca Falls, New York, in 1848. The revolution lasted a hundred years, she contends, and accomplished a great deal by way of legal and economic gains, but foundered because it failed "to challenge patriarchal ideology at a sufficiently deep and radical level to break the conditioning processes of status, temperament and role"; it was "reform rather than revolution." . . .

If Millett had been willing to be less ambitious and more flexible, *Sexual Politics* would be a better book. It is too much of a literary-anthropological-sociological-historical-psychological grabbag to be a clear success in part or in sum, and its regressions into Women's Lib rigidities diminish its many splendid inquiries into sexual attitudes. Like Women's Lib it is most useful when it explores the daily forms of sexual discrimination, least when it wanders into biological theorizing. It most deserves our attention when it asserts that "the great cultural change which the beginnings of a sexual revolution represent is at least as dramatic as the four or five other social upheavals in the modern period to which historiographical attention is zealously devoted." If the book is received properly the rewriting of history may begin; for we *have* ignored the history of women, and demeaned it, just as we ignore and demean its makers.

A final caveat: as a male who is trying to kick sexism but has no particular expectation of doing so, I welcome the taunts and challenges of Kate Millett, but I am not sure they bear the seed of a final answer. That a society without sex, or without gender, is a desirable goal, seems to me unlikely. A nation finally rid of the canard of the ethnic melting pot should not rush to create a sexual melting pot. Our discriminations and cruelties are bitter ones, but our differences are healthy; we need to eliminate discrimination, not difference. A woman who has the refreshing arrogance to claim, as Millett does, that "the female possesses, biologically and inherently, a far greater capacity for sexuality than the male, both as to frequency of coitus, and as to frequency of orgasm in coition," should be the last person to urge that such unique attributes be eliminated in a wave of "unisex." But then maybe Women's Lib is more complex than even the [most] radical feminist realizes.

QUESTIONS

1. Must the family be destroyed in order to bring about a social revolution in sex roles?

2. How pertinent is the power factor in defining sexual politics?

3. Can we discuss changes in women's roles without corresponding changes in men's roles?

4. What is the relationship between feminism and other political movements?

5. What, according to Millett, are the differences between "sex" and "gender"? Do you agree with her views?

6. Do Ernest van den Haag and Jonathan Yardley treat Kate Millett as an intellectual equal in their reviews, or do they condescend to her as a woman?

Topics for Writing and Research

I. Short Papers
   1. Write a description of Nora or Aurora Leigh, using as a basis Farnham and Lundberg's analysis of the female psyche.
   2. Describe an ideal marriage as it might logically be conceived by one of the following:
      a. Farnham and Lundberg
      b. Mary Wollstonecraft
      c. Mary McCarthy
      d. John Stuart Mill
   3. Compare the views of marriage in any two of the following:
      a. *A Doll's House*
      b. *Cruel and Barbarous Treatment*
      c. *Mr. Durant*
      d. "Some Aspects of Woman's Psyche"
      e. *Aurora Leigh*
   4. Discuss the varieties of male egoism portrayed in Torvald, Romney Leigh, and Mr. Durant.
   5. Write an essay defining one of the following terms:
      a. penis envy
      b. femininity
      c. woman's sphere
      d. female experience
      e. patriarchy
      f. chivalry
      g. male chauvinism
   6. Contrast George Henry Lewes and Elizabeth Barrett Browning's discussions of the motives impelling a woman writer.
   7. Discuss the kinds of investigations of sex differences that have been made by scientists, noting those that seem most valid and giving reasons for your answers.
   8. Is there any correlation between the satiric techniques used by Mary Ellmann, Naomi Weisstein, and Hortense Calisher and the views they express?

9. Apply Mary Ellmann's analysis of "phallic criticism" to George Henry Lewes' comments about individual women novelists.

10. What kinds of arguments does Elizabeth Hardwick use to dispute the feminist allegations of Simone de Beauvoir?

11. Contrast the literary styles of Mary Wollstonecraft and John Stuart Mill.

12. Compare Virginia Woolf's account of the repression of the woman writer with that of Hortense Calisher.

13. Which of the three selections on women and psychology do you think is the most persuasive? Why?

14. Discuss the theme of feminine rivalry in Anne Sexton's "For My Lover, Returning to His Wife" and in Sylvia Plath's "Lesbos."

15. Analyze the use made of the narrative voice in the short stories by Mary McCarthy and Dorothy Parker.

II. Long Papers

1. Write a defense of the patriarchal system, justifying the place of women within it and answering the criticisms of John Stuart Mill, Mary Wollstonecraft, and Kate Millett.

2. *The Subjection of Women* and *A Doll's House* were published ten years apart. How are John Stuart Mill's theories dramatized by Henrik Ibsen's play?

3. Using the selections by Mary Wollstonecraft, John Stuart Mill, Betty Friedan, Naomi Weisstein, and Kate Millett, describe the changes of outlook that have taken place in feminist theory since the eighteenth century.

4. Compare and interpret the portrayals of feminine self-hatred in the works by Mary McCarthy, Anne Sexton, and Sylvia Plath.

5. Do the characters of Mary Wollstonecraft, Virginia Woolf, or Mary Ellmann, as revealed in their writings, fit the image of the "masculinized woman" described by Farnham and Lundberg?

6. It has been said that the liberation of women will inevitably involve a relaxation of many sexual prohibitions such as homosexuality, extramarital intercourse, and abortion. How do the writers in this book regard these particular problems and how do they treat the general relationship between feminism and a sexual revolution?

7. Betty Friedan and Naomi Weisstein argue that Sigmund Freud's theory of female psychology reflected his culturally induced biases against women rather than any objective scientific truth. How many of Freud's ideas are in agreement with the stereotypes of femininity typical of the nineteenth cen-

tury and depicted or discussed in the selections by Elizabeth Barrett Browning, Henrik Ibsen, John Stuart Mill, and George Henry Lewes?

8. Basing your arguments on current advertising in newspapers, magazines, and television, support or refute Betty Friedan's thesis that the Freudian feminine mystique is exploited by industry.

9. Discuss the case for a feminine consciousness in literature, showing what social conditions would be necessary to produce it and what forms it might take.

10. Discuss Kate Millett's theory that men are socialized to a sex role that glorifies aggression, considering historical and contemporary examples of "men's house cultures." Is aggression evil, or does it have value? Would the liberation of women eliminate aggression or redistribute it?

11. If, as John Stuart Mill and Kate Millett maintain, patriarchy is inculcated in children through the institution of the nuclear family, would radical social change in the role of women necessitate the elimination of the family? What might replace it? What effects would different life styles have on children?

12. Evaluate the educational system in this country with regard to its socialization of children to sex roles. What are the effects for girls? What are the effects for boys? What kind of education is needed to produce an adult capable of functioning usefully in contemporary society?

13. Consider the arguments of Mary Wollstonecraft, Virginia Woolf, Kate Millett, and Elizabeth Hardwick; examine your own experience; and discuss the possibilities of women achieving a unified political movement. What obstacles would they have to overcome?

Bibliography

I. Literature by and About Women
  Chopin, Kate, *The Awakening*. New York: H. S. Stone, 1899.
  Hellman, Lillian, *An Unfinished Woman*. New York: Little, Brown, 1969.
  Lessing, Doris, *The Golden Notebook*. New York: Simon and Schuster, 1962.
  Lewis, Sinclair, *Main Street*. New York: Harcourt Brace Jovanovich, 1920.
  McCarthy, Mary, *Memories of a Catholic Girlhood*. New York: Harcourt Brace Jovanovich, 1957.
  —— *The Group*. New York: Harcourt Brace Jovanovich, 1963.
  Woolf, Virginia, *Mrs. Dalloway*. New York: Harcourt Brace Jovanovich, 1925.
  —— *To the Lighthouse*. New York: Harcourt Brace Jovanovich, 1927.
  —— *Orlando*. New York: Harcourt Brace Jovanovich, 1929.
II. Major Texts of Feminism
  de Beauvoir, Simone, *The Second Sex*, H. M. Parshley, ed. and trans. New York: Alfred A. Knopf, 1953.
  Engels, Friedrich, *The Origin of Family, Private Property, and the State*. New York: International Publishers, 1969.
  Notes from the Second Year: Major Writings of the Radical Feminists, Shulamith Firestone, ed. New York: New York Radical Feminists, 1970.
  Millett, Kate, *Sexual Politics*. New York: Doubleday, 1970.
III. History of the Women's Movement
  Flexner, Eleanor, *A Century of Struggle*. Cambridge: Harvard University Press, 1959.
  Kamm, Josephine, *Rapiers and Battleaxes: The Women's Movement and Its Aftermath*. London: G. Allen, 1966.
  Kraditor, Aileen S., *Ideas of the Woman Suffrage Movement, 1890 to 1920*. New York: Columbia University Press, 1965.
  Up from the Pedestal: Selected Documents from the History

of American Feminism, Aileen S. Kraditor, ed. Chicago: Quadrangle Books, 1968.

O'Neill, William L., *Everyone Was Brave: The Rise and Fall of Feminism in America.* Chicago: Quadrangle Books, 1969.

IV. Law, Science, and Sociology

Bird, Caroline, *Born Female: The High Cost of Keeping Women Down.* New York: David McKay, 1968.

Freud, Sigmund, "The Psychology of Women," in *New Introductory Lectures on Psychoanalysis,* W. J. H. Sprott, trans. New York: W. W. Norton, 1933.

Kanowitz, Leo, *Women and the Law: The Unfinished Revolution.* Albuquerque: University of New Mexico Press, 1969.

The Woman in America, Robert J. Lifton, ed. New York: Beacon Press, 1965.

The Development of Sex Differences, Eleanor Maccoby, ed. California: Stanford University Press, 1966.

V. Literary Criticism

Eliot, George, "Silly Novels by Lady Novelists." *Westminster Review,* LXVI (1856), 442–61.

McCarthy, Mary, *On the Contrary.* New York: Farrar, Straus & Giroux, 1961.

Olsen, Tillie, "Silences—When Writers Don't Write." *Harper's* (October 1965), 153–61.

Shaw, George Bernard, "The Womanly Woman," in *The Quintessence of Ibsenism.* New York: Brentano's, 1903.

Woolf, Virginia, "Professions for Women," in *Collected Essays,* Vol. II. London: Hogarth Press, 1966.